REPRODUCTIVE

RIGHTS AND WRONGS

Advance praise for *Reproductive Rights and Wrongs*

"This is a book of conscience. Shocking, eloquent, carefully researched, it should be read—and acted upon."

—Gena Corea, author, *The Hidden Malpractice*
and *The Mother Machine*

"Stands out amid the rising tide of books on the population question. Hartman's critique of global special interests in population and the environment are must reading for students and policy analysts."

— Judy Norsigian and Norma Swenson,
co-authors, *The New Our Bodies, Ourselves*

"If I had time to read just one book to gain an understanding of the population and development link, this one would be it."

— Dianne J. Forte, National Black Women's Health Project

"It is unusual to find such a clear explanation of the complex issues involved in population control in the modern world; Ms. Hartmann's clarity can have come only from enormous work and deep understanding. This is a modern analysis which gives us hope."

—Jonathan Mann, Director, FXB Center for Health
and Human Rights, Harvard School of Public Health

"At this juncture in history when victim blaming has become more blatant and oppressive, there is a need for voices of sanity. This book is such a voice. It reflects conviction, courage, sensitivity, and deep insight."

—Mira Shiva, International Health Activist

REPRODUCTIVE
RIGHTS AND WRONGS
The Global Politics of
Population Control

REVISED EDITION

By Betsy Hartmann
Foreword by Helen Rodriguez-Trias

South End Press
Boston, Massachusetts

To Jim, who gave support
To Jamie and Thomas who gave inspiration
To my grandfather, Henry Bothfeld,
who helped teach me the value of giving

Copyright © 1995 by Betsy Hartmann

First edition published in 1987 by Harper & Row, Publishers, Inc., New York, NY. Originally titled *Reproductive Rights and Wrongs: The Global Politics of Population Control and Contraceptive Choice.* Copyright © 1987 by Betsy Hartmann.

REVISED EDITION

Cover design by Birgitta McAlevey
Text design and production by South End Press collective
Printed in the U.S.A.

Library of Congress Cataloging-in-Publication Data
Hartmann, Betsy.
Reproductive rights and wrongs : the global politics of population control / Betsy Hartmann.
  p. cm.
Includes bibliographical references and index.
ISBN 0-89608-492-2 (cloth) : $40.00.—ISBN 0-89608-491-4 (paper) : $16.00
1. Birth control. 2. Population policy. 3. Contraceptives. I. Title.
HQ766.H38 1994
363.9—dc20   94-3626
                                                                          CIP

South End Press, 116 Saint Botolph Street, Boston, MA 02115
99 98 97 96 95   1 2 3 4 5 6 7 8 9

TABLE OF CONTENTS

ACKNOWLEDGMENTS

This book was not written in isolation. Throughout the writing of both editions I have benefited enormously from the encouragement, support, and advice of many people. They have helped deepen my analysis and broaden the scope of the book, as well as renew my faith in the possibility of cooperative effort. My greatest pleasure in writing this book has been the valuable friendships and contacts I have made in the process.

For the first edition, thanks must first go to Gretta Goldenman. The book was her idea originally, and her commitment, insight, and endless patience helped carry it through to completion. Marge Berer gave freely of her time to comment extensively on the first two drafts of the manuscript. Her contacts and experience in reproductive rights work were formative in the development of my own thinking. Norma Swenson of the Boston Women's Health Book Collective played a vital role as book midwife. She not only gave detailed comments on the manuscript, but provided much needed moral support and continually shared her valuable insights on the subject. Judy Norsigian of the Boston Women's Health Book Collective cast a critical eye on the contraceptive chapters, guided me through the collective's extensive resource collection, and helped keep me up to date. At the Population Council Judith Bruce gave me excellent comments on two drafts of the manuscript, and I benefited greatly from her expertise in international family planning and women's issues.

Other people who gave generously of their time to comment on the manuscript are Jim Boyce, Gena Corea, Lynn Duggan, Joan Dunlop, Deborah Eade, Adrienne Germain, Andrew Graham, Keith Griffin, Polly Griffith, Judith Helzner, Jocelyn Knowles, Frances Moore Lappé, Amanda Milligan, and Edward Passerini.

Others who contributed are Jenneke Arens, Kai Bird, Audrey Bronstein, Therese Budoumit, Rebecca Chalker, Elizabeth Coit, Joseph Collins, Judith Condor, Sonia Corrêa, Belita Cowan, Ireen

Dubel, Posey Gault, Forrest Greenslade, Teresa Hayter, James Hobbs, Barbara Holland, Tony Jackson, Bernard Kervyn, Loes Keysers, Rodger King, Barbara Klugman, Brian Landers, Stephen Minkin, Ivan Nutbrown, Vivian Orlowski, Richard Palmer-Jones, Paula Park, Cheryl Payer, Sunanda Ray, Paul Rice, Andrew Rutherford, Rashid Shaikh, Weena Silapa-archa, Peter Stalker, Hilary Standing, and Jomo Kwame Sundaram.

Judith Hoffman gave many months to the project as a research assistant. Christopher Glazek also helped do research. At the IPPF Library in London, Graham Peck provided valuable assistance. Hilary Sloin painstakingly word-processed the manuscript in its final stages. Jesse Markham's advice and support gave peace of mind at a difficult time. My editor at Harper/Collins, Janet Goldstein, shepherded the book along with enthusiasm and insight.

For the second edition I would like to thank Lynn Lu and Loie Hayes at South End Press, who have been incredibly patient and supportive editors. Their enthusiasm for a second edition has helped spur me on—South End is one of the few beacons of light in these dark times of the American publishing industry.

Norma Swenson, who helped me so much on the first edition, has also been a constant source of support and critical insight. She suggested changes for the second edition and encouraged me to do more than I originally intended, which hopefully makes for a better, more up-to-date book.

At Hampshire College Marlene Fried offered much encouragement; in the years I have had the pleasure of working with her, she has taught be a lot about the U.S. reproductive rights movement as well as about political integrity. Also at Hampshire, I am grateful to Clare Lewis for proofing the scanned manuscript, M. J. Maccardini for helping me with research, Mary Sera for logistical support, and Dan Schnurr, social science librarian. I would like to thank Ben Wisner for giving me valuable information, ideas, and friendship, and Kay Johnson for her excellent work on China. Visiting international reproductive rights activists Mere Kisekka, Sundari Ravindran, and Adetoun Ilumoka all had an impact on my thinking, as well as the other activists we have had the privilege to invite to Hampshire for shorter lengths of time. I am grateful to Hampshire College in general for providing a supportive environment in which to work.

There are many other friends and colleagues to whom I am indebted, and I cannot do justice to them all. Following is only a partial list, for it is impossible to list by name all the many people in the international women's health movement and development community who have given me information and helped shape my views in the years between the two editions of the book. I am grateful to Faye Schrater, not only for sharing her knowledge of contraceptive vaccines, but for her friendship; to Judy Norsigian for continuing to keep me up to date with contraceptive technology and policy; to members of the Committee on Women, Population and the Environment with whom I have actively worked in the past several years, especially Patricia Hynes, Jael Silliman, Nalini Visvanathan, Asoka Bandarage, and Gabriela Canepa; to the Women's Global Network on Reproductive Rights Coordinating Committee, which has helped keep the radical spirit of reproductive rights alive in these difficult years; and to the Boston Women's Health Book Collective for continuing to be there.

Other individuals I would like to thank for their direct or indirect influence on the book are Adrina, Thais Corral, Dianne Forte, Peter Gillespie, Malini Karkal, Loes Keysers, Vicki Legion, Trine Lynggard, Kalpana Mehta, Fatima Mello, Ranjana Padhi, Rita Parikh, Judith Richter, Helen Rodriguez-Trias, Anna Sax, Ulrike Schaz, Karen Seabrooke, Sarah Sexton, Mira Shiva, and Maria Zuniga. I would also like to thank all my friends in Amherst and environs who helped me keep a sense of humor and perspective, especially Kate Pfister, Neil Stillings, Sam Gladstone, Joyce Duncan, Sonia Kruks, and the members of my writing group.

Last but not least, I must express my gratitude to my family and first of all to my husband, Jim Boyce, who has seen me through all the ups and downs of both editions and continues to be a more than generous source of moral and practical support. Thanks to my children, Jamie and Thomas, who let me work even when they didn't want me to. Other members of my extended family have also given me much encouragement, particularly Thomas and Martha Hartmann and James and Alice Boyce.

While all these individuals have helped me complete two editions of this book, I alone bear responsibility for the opinions and errors contained herein.

FOREWORD

By Helen Rodriguez-Trias, MD., FAAP

This second, completely updated edition of Betsy Hartmann's analysis of population policies and their effect on women's lives offers profound insight, solid research, and vivid case studies from the field to advance our understanding of the origins, development, and actions of the organizations that have espoused population control since the earlier part of this century. Although most such organizations active in the last four decades have helped women to gain desperately needed access to birth control, they have often limited women's choices by promoting some methods over others. And in their zeal to reduce birth rates, some programs have shown blatant disregard for individual rights.

Whether undemocratic or respectful of individual choices, all population control programs begin with a basic premise, that is: In order to achieve improvement in people's lives, there is an urgent need to reduce the rate of growth of the world's population. Most aim at reducing the fertility of women, particularly of women in developing countries, as the means of slowing worldwide population growth toward "sustainable" and "stable" numbers. It is this very basic premise that Hartmann questions.

Hartmann argues and substantiates that rapid population growth is a symptom, rather than a cause, of problematic economic and social development, that improvements in the status of women lead to voluntary decreases in family size, and that effective birth control services can only thrive within a comprehensive system of health care delivery responding to people's needs. Her vision of what people-centered economic and social development may mean includes tackling poverty and inequalities.

Hartmann's analysis is particularly relevant to the discussions that have just taken place on the international stage as I write this foreword in September 1994. With greater participation of women than ever before in an international forum, representatives of over 170 nations and of thousands of non-governmental organizations met in Cairo at the United Nations Conference on Population and Development. Delegates discussed and reached consensus on an action plan to slow the growth of the world's population and to promote economic development.

In this book, Hartmann traces the origin of a push for "consensus" in Cairo back to the 1984 international population conference in Mexico City. In addition to her critique of the centrality of population stabilization to international development deliberations, Hartmann points out the marked discrepancy between the large resource allocation for population activities as compared to pitifully small resources for development. Equally importantly, Hartmann cautions that we not be lulled into obscuring issues of class, race, and inequalities between developed and developing countries. She notes that, "In many population publications, women are presented as an undifferentiated mass which needs to be empowered, with little recognition of the many differences between them—poor or rich, rural or urban, black or white—which in turn impact on their survival and reproductive strategies."

Along with several hundred women from the United States, and as part of the United States delegation, I attended the Cairo conference, representing the American Public Health Association as its immediate past president. I was one of seventeen private sector advisors to the U.S. delegation, many of whom worked for three years drafting documents and organizing preparatory meetings for the conference. Some advisors were long time feminists, some represented foundations involved in population activities, others were providers of family planning and other reproductive health services, all were advocates of choice. By emphasizing that any agenda for women's health must advance the political, social, and economic empowerment of women, and providing concrete examples where women have taken leadership, Hartmann's work helped us prepare for Cairo and beyond.

In this new edition, Hartmann reminds us that discussions on the effect of population growth and environmental degradation pose further pitfalls. Some U.S. environmental organizations are influenced by Malthusian thinking and a few even advocate severe reductions in human populations to restore the wilderness. In urging that women frame environmental issues within an agenda toward social justice, she points out "Women's Action Agenda 21," endorsed by 1,500 women in non-governmental groups in advance of the 1992 United Nations Conference on Environment and Development, or Earth Summit, held in Rio de Janeiro. This document contained a condemnation of "suggestions that women's fertility rates are to blame for environmental degradation" and identified structural adjustment, militarism, and wasteful and unjust production and consumption patterns as the key culprits in environmental degradation, not overpopulation.

This book contains examples of activities and programs women have undertaken to improve production, protect the environment, and provide health care in impoverished areas. Out of their experiences as leaders in the field, women are also emerging as leaders in international programs. One effect of their participation has been to broaden the international discussion beyond global population growth to the need to improve women's status and all people's quality of life.

At home, violence against the reproductive rights movement continues to escalate, as does the intensity of the Vatican-led movement to delegitimize the Cairo agreement on reproductive choice. In confronting the contradictions and dilemmas that we face in attempting to establish women's rights to choices, we do well to heed Hartmann: "What is needed," she tells us, "is a genuinely prowomen alternative, which challenges both the population control and antiabortion positions and which guides family planning, contraceptive reasearch and health policy."

This book, and my experiences in the reproductive rights movement, lead me to urge caution in how we respond to the current violent attacks. To forge genuine prochoice alternatives, we must guard against the tendency to form too quick alliances when we are confronted by violent opponents. The search for protection from the seemingly powerful forces against women's rights could lead us to ally with population control advocates who speak of women's rights only out of opportunism. We need to keep foremost that alliances of women from different nations, ethnic groups, indigenous peoples, races, and social classes must be based on mutual respect, adherence to key principles of democracy, and, most importantly, on a commitment toward eliminating gross inequities among groups and nations.

In the international arena, I believe that we must avoid what to a large extent has happened in the United States: neglect of a social agenda toward equity. Women's organizations have poured an inordinate amount of energy and resources into the defense of abortion rights and not enough into advancing a broader women's agenda toward social and economic gains. Greater emphasis on women's social and economic rights by the reproductive rights movement would bring new forces and vigor to the struggle.

This book provides us with an inspiration and a basis for working on a women's agenda that pursues the reduction of inequities among us as a requisite for promoting women's health at home as well as abroad. As Hartmann clearly shows, the contradictions and conflicts will not disappear with the issuance of a "consensus" document, no matter what process leads to its creation. True consensus must rest on genuine commitments—men with women, white with people of color, rich with poor, landowners with landless, industrialized countries with developing nations—to share power, wealth, and knowledge.

INTRODUCTION:
WHOSE CHOICE?

I arrived at the population issue from two different directions.

Coming of age in the late 1960s, I was a member of the "pill generation." While the media extolled the contraceptive revolution as the key to sexual liberation, the college health clinic prescribed the pill with great enthusiasm. Like so many other young women, I soon discovered that the pill made me feel heavy and depressed, and that "sexual liberation" was often a euphemism for being readily available to men. As feminism began to reshape my view of sexual politics, and politics in general, I abandoned the pill and returned to the safer barrier birth control methods of my mother's generation. I wondered why the clinic never encouraged their use. Elsewhere some of my friends had far worse experiences, ending up in the hospital with IUD complications and worrying that they would never be able to bear children.

Then in the mid-1970s my long-standing interest in South Asia and international development took me to a village in Bangladesh, one of the poorest and most densely populated countries in the world. Here in the West, Bangladesh is typically thought of as an international basket case, a country whose population growth has already outstripped its resources. In the village, however, I encountered a very different reality. I found fertile land, plentiful water, and a climate warm enough for crops to be grown throughout the year. I met families with six or seven children who ate well and families with only two children who were starving.

The vital difference between them was land ownership. Almost a quarter of the village people owned no land at all and had to work for rich peasants and landlords for pitiful wages. They not only lacked the land on which to grow food, they also did not have enough cash to buy adequate supplies in the market. The real problem was not food scarcity, but land and income distribution.

Up to a point, villagers viewed children as an irreplaceable asset. From an early age, children worked in the home and the fields; instead of draining the family rice bin, they helped fill it. They also provided their parents' only source of security and support in old age. Because of inadequate nutrition and health care, one out of every four Bangladeshi children dies before the age of five. Thus families had to produce many children in order to ensure that a few would survive. My neighbor's first five children had all died in infancy. She bore six more and the youngest daughter died too.

Yet once villagers had enough children to meet their needs, they often wanted to limit family size. They complained about lack of living space and the fact that through inheritance, land was being subdivided into smaller and smaller plots. Suffering the burden of repeated pregnancies, women especially were desperate for birth control and repeatedly asked me to help them get it.

This widespread desire for birth control came to me as a surprise. Up to that point, it had been my understanding that the main obstacles to the use of birth control in Bangladesh and elsewhere in the Third World were ignorance and tradition, not the availability of contraception. Now I discovered that many women wanted birth control, but could not get it, even though the U.S. government and other nations were financing multimillion dollar population control programs in Bangladesh.

Later I learned that in other areas of Bangladesh, population control programs were in full force, indiscriminately putting women on the pill, injecting Depo-Provera, or inserting IUDs, without offering adequate medical screening, supervision, or follow-up. Most of the programs only targeted women, ignoring male responsibility for birth control. Due to the poor quality of services, many women experienced negative side effects and became disillusioned with contraception. The government's response was not to reform the programs to meet the women's needs, but instead to further intensify its population control efforts by pushing sterilization, even though its irreversibility and risks make it an unsuitable method for many women.

In both instances, whether they lacked access to contraception or had it forced upon them, Bangladeshi women were being denied real control over their own reproduction.

As a woman, I could not help but feel angered and intrigued by the connection between their experience and the experience of many of my peers in the United States. The two directions had converged, and I found myself increasingly absorbed by the population issue. On my return to the United States in 1976, I learned that many people were making the same connection. The women's health movement was gaining strength, and the campaigns against Depo-Provera, the Dalkon Shield IUD, and sterilization abuse of women of color were bringing to public attention the misuses of contraceptive technology occurring both at home and abroad.

I began work on the first edition of this book in the summer of 1983. I naively envisioned a six-month project; instead it took me over three years. My research followed several different lines. At first, I concentrated on reading a wide spectrum of the available population literature. My previous research and writing on international development proved a useful background. Then as I developed a framework for the book, I focused more closely on specific countries and contraceptives. I corresponded with people actively involved in family planning, health, and women's issues, particularly in the Third World. (I use "Third World" in this book for lack of a better term, but realize it does not accurately reflect the diversity of nations and cultures, or the fact that in the current global economy "Third World" conditions exist in many Western countries as well.) In England, where I wrote most of the book, and in the United States I made contact both with people in the population field and with health and reproductive rights activists, who not only guided me to resources, but gave me crucial feedback and support.

For this new edition, I have substantially updated and revised many sections of the book, while preserving its basic organization. Since the first edition was published in 1987, I have become even more involved in population politics, as an activist, writer, and professor. At times this feels less like a personal choice than a political necessity, since population control remains such a powerful force in terms of distorting both development policies and public attitudes. Although the work is often difficult, the rewards are many. It is empowering to be part of a broad international network of women's health, development and environmental activists who are not only fighting *against* population control, but *for* reproductive freedom and social justice.

In the course of my work, particularly during the Reagan and Bush administrations in the U.S., I have sometimes been accused of playing into the hands of the antiabortion movement. Better to remain silent about population control abuses, some liberals say, than to provide any ammunition to antichoice groups which not only oppose abortion, but most forms of birth control.

While I am well aware of the dangers of the antiabortion movement and religious fundamentalism, I reject this logic. The population control and antiabortion philosophies, although diametrically opposed, share one thing in common: They are both antiwomen. Population control advocates impose contraception and sterilization on women; the so-called Right to Life movement denies women the basic right of access to abortion and birth control. Neither takes the interests and rights of the individual woman as their starting point. Both approaches attempt to control women, instead of letting women control their bodies themselves.

What is needed is a genuinely prowomen alternative, which challenges both the population control and antiabortion positions and which guides family planning, contraceptive research, and health policy. If instead prochoice supporters turn a blind eye to coercive population control practices, they allow the antiabortion movement to capture the issue and to posture as champions of individual reproductive freedom. Such an abdication of responsibility is not only ethically bankrupt, but politically disastrous.

In the course of writing this book, I have come to believe more firmly in the inviolability of individual reproductive rights. The state and local community can play an important role in expanding and protecting those rights, through education and the provision of health and family planning services. However, no matter how perilous the population problem is deemed to be—and I believe it is greatly over-exaggerated—the use of force or coercive incentives/disincentives to promote population control is an unjustifiable intrusion of government power into the lives of its citizenry, amounting in many cases to physical violence against women's bodies. Similarly, the use of government power to deny women access to abortion and birth control is also a violation of basic human rights.

I do not believe this stand is culturally specific, simply the product of Western civil libertarian philosophy, as many in the population establishment argue. The United Nations World Population Plan of Action clearly endorses the principle that population policies should be consistent with "internationally and nationally recognized human rights" of individual freedom and justice. While writing this book, I have met many people from different cultures who share this point of view. They are working throughout the world to ensure that women and men have access to safe, effective birth control methods, as part of, not substitutes for, more comprehensive health services. At the same time, they are not prepared to see human rights sacrificed on the altar of population control.

The philosophy of population control rests upon three basic assumptions:

1. Rapid population growth is a primary cause of the Third World's development problems, notably hunger, environmental destruction, economic stagnation, and political instability.

2. People must be persuaded—or forced, if necessary—to have fewer children without fundamentally improving the impoverished conditions in which they live.

3. Given the right combination of finance, personnel, technology, and Western management techniques, birth control services can be "delivered" to Third World women in a top-down fashion and in the absence of basic health care systems. In both the development and promotion of contraceptives, efficacy in preventing pregnancy should take precedence over health and safety concerns.

For over twenty-five years this philosophy has shaped the activities of most population organizations and many international aid agencies in Asia, Africa, and Latin America, as well as among ethnic minorities and poor communities in many parts of the industrialized world.

The organizations and agencies constituting the population establishment have undoubtedly helped in many instances to make birth control more accessible. However, as I will demonstrate in this book, when the overriding goal of family planning programs is to reduce population growth, rather than to expand the freedom of individuals to decide whether and when to have children, the results are often detrimental to women's health and well-being, and ineffective even in terms of the stated goal of lowering birth rates.

In contrast to the assumptions of the population control philosophy, this book will explain the following:

1. Rapid population growth is not the root cause of development problems in the Third World; rather it is a symptom of those problems.

2. Improvements in living standards and the position of women, via more equitable social and economic development, are the best way to motivate people to want fewer children.

3. Safe, effective, and voluntary birth control services cannot be "delivered" in a top-down, technocratic fashion, but instead require the development of a popularly based health care system. Health, safety, and the individual's control over the method should be the primary concerns in the development and promotion of contraceptive technology.

The book is organized into four parts. Part One begins by analyzing the causes and consequences of rapid population growth in order to put the population problem into perspective. This new edition examines more closely the widely held view that population growth poses one of the biggest threats to the global environment. It then describes the reasons why many women lack control over their own reproduction and investigates how population control has distorted Third World family planning programs. It concludes with case studies of Indonesia and Kenya.

Part Two traces the history of the population control movement and its evolution into a powerful political lobby. It considers how the population control philosophy has changed over time and its impact on various family planning reforms. A new chapter on the 1990s population control "consensus" analyzes how the U.S. government, mainstream population and environmental groups, and the media have appropriated the language of women's rights and ecology in a carefully orchestrated campaign to build renewed support for population control. Within the U.S., this new "consensus" has dangerous implications for poor women, especially women of color, as well as refugees and immigrants. Part Two ends with a case study of China, which currently has the most drastic population control policy in the world.

Part Three examines the forces behind the development of today's major contraceptive technologies. It details how population control programs have sacrificed women's health and safety in the indiscriminate promotion of hormonal contraception, the IUD, and sterilization, at the same time as they have neglected barrier methods and male contraceptives. The neglect of condoms has had particularly serious health consequences given the important role they play in preventing the spread of HIV and other sexually transmitted diseases. A number of new contraceptives under development, most notably contraceptive "vaccines", pose serious risks both in terms of women's health and the potential for abuse. Meanwhile, millions of women around the world are still denied access to safe, affordable abortion. The case of Bangladesh highlights the serious ethical problems with sterilization incentives and with making population control a higher priority than basic health care.

Finally, Part Four explores the forces behind the "demographic transition" from high to low birth rates and presents examples of societies that have reduced population growth through more equitable paths of social and economic development. It concludes with an analysis of the impact and future directions of the international women's health movement.

While working on the new edition, I have remained convinced that population control not only restricts reproductive choice, but dangerously obscures the real causes of the earth's afflictions, helping to perpetuate poverty and heighten racial and ethnic tensions. When the affluent few regard the impoverished majority as simply a dark, faceless crowd overpopulating the earth, they deny poor people their humanity and diminish their own. At a time when fundamentalism and neo-fascism are on the rise, when "free trade" and unfettered consumerism are eroding community and threatening the environment, and when economic austerity measures and diseases such as AIDS threaten the very survival of poor people, we cannot afford to erect such an unnecessary barrier between human beings. My hope is that this book, in some small way, will contribute to removing that barrier.

I have understood the population explosion intellectually for a long time. I came to understand it emotionally one stinking hot night in Delhi, a few years ago...The streets seemed alive with people. People eating, people washing, people sleeping. People visiting, arguing, and screaming. People thrusting their hands through the taxi window, begging. People defecating and urinating. People clinging to buses. People herding animals. People, people, people, people...since that night I've known the feel of overpopulation.

Paul Ehrlich, *The Population Bomb*

Once men begin to feel cramped in their geographical, social, and mental habitat, they are in danger of being tempted by the simple solution of denying one section of the species the right to exist.

Claude Lévi Strauss, *Tristes Tropiques*

Part One

THE REAL
POPULATION
PROBLEM

1

SECURITY
AND SURVIVAL

An art historian turns to me at a party: "You're writing a book on population control? My field is aesthetics, and I feel that over-population is destroying the beauty of great cities like Paris. Ugly immigrants' housing is springing up all over the place."

The babysitter turns off the TV. "I've been thinking about it," he says. "If they don't force people to be sterilized in India, how are they going to cope with the population explosion?"

An accounting professor explains how pharmaceutical companies could develop cures for many of the basic diseases that afflict poor people, but don't because the people who need them are too poor to pay. "Maybe it's not such a bad thing," he adds. "After all, if more poor people survive, it will only exacerbate the population problem."

An economist, known for his radical views on the United States economy, surprises me by saying that many Third World countries have no choice but to initiate harsh population control measures. "Their economic survival is at stake," he asserts.

I have grown to expect such responses from people, no matter how well-meaning or well educated they are. They are repeating a message they have read in the newspaper, heard in the classroom, and seen on television so many times that it has become conventional wisdom. It first captured the popular imagination in 1968, when Stanford University biologist Paul Ehrlich published his famous book *The Population Bomb*. He warned that mankind was breeding itself into oblivion and endorsed stringent population control measures, including compulsion if necessary. Probably most readers of *Reproductive Rights and Wrongs* have the same impression: that the population bomb is exploding out of control. It is the starting point of most discussions about population—and, unfortunately, the end point as well.

The myth of overpopulation is one of the most pervasive myths in Western society, so deeply ingrained in the culture that it profoundly shapes the culture's world view. The myth is compelling because of its simplicity. More people equal fewer resources and more hunger, poverty, environmental degradation, and political instability. This equation helps explain away the troubling human suffering in that "other" world beyond the neat borders of affluence. By procreating, the poor create their own poverty. We are absolved of responsibility and freed from complexity.

The population issue is complex. To put it into proper perspective requires exploring many realms of human experience and addressing difficult philosophical and ethical questions. It entails making connections between fields of thought that have become disconnected as the result of narrow academic specialization. It demands the sharpening of critical facilities and clearing the mind of received orthodoxies. And above all, it involves transcending the alienation embodied in the very terms "population bomb" and "population explosion." Such metaphors suggest destructive technological processes outside human control. But the population issue is about living people, not abstract statistics.

The myth of overpopulation is destructive because it prevents constructive thinking and action on reproductive issues. Instead of clarifying our understanding of these issues, it obfuscates our vision and limits our ability to see the real problems and find workable solutions. Worst of all, it breeds racism and turns women's bodies into a political battlefield. It is a philosophy based on fear, not understanding.

FAMILY MATTERS

On the surface, fears of a population explosion are borne out by basic demographic statistics. In the twentieth century the world has experienced an unprecedented increase in population. In 1900 global population was 1.7 billion, in 1950 it reached 2.5 billion, and today roughly 5.7 billion people inhabit the earth. Three quarters of them live in the so-called Third World. The United Nations predicts that world population will reach 6 billion by the end of the century and will eventually stabilize at about 11.6 billion between 2150 and 2200, though such long-term demographic projections are notoriously imprecise.

Initially, this rapid increase in population was due in part to some very positive factors: Advances in medicine, public health measures, and better nutrition meant that more people lived longer. However, in other cases, notably in Africa, it may have been a response to colonialism, as indigenous communities sought to reconstitute themselves after suffering high death rates from slavery, diseases introduced from Europe, and oppressive labor conditions. In many countries colonialism also disrupted traditional methods of birth spacing.[1]

In most industrialized countries, the decline in mortality rates was eventually offset by declines in birth rates, so that population growth began to stabilize in what is called the "demographic transition." Most industrialized countries have now reached the "replacement level"* of fertility, and in some the population is actually declining.

---

* **(Crude) birth rate** is the number of births per thousand people in a given year.
(Crude) mortality or **death rate** is the number of deaths per thousand people in a given year.
Replacement-level fertility is the level of fertility at which women on the average are having only enough daughters to "replace" themselves in a given population.
Population growth rate is the rate at which a population is growing or declining in a given year from natural increase and net migration, computed as a percentage of the base population.

Today birth rates are also falling in virtually every area of the Third World. In fact, the *rate* of world population growth has been slowing since the mid-1960s. Population growth rates are highest in sub-Saharan Africa—about 2.9 percent in 1994—but are considerably less than that in Asia (1.9 percent) and Latin America (2.0 percent). It is also important to remember that despite higher rates of growth, Africa contains a relatively small share of the world's population—India will have more births in 1994 than all fifty sub-Saharan nations combined.

The United Nations estimates that by 2045 most countries will have reached replacement-level fertility. The reason population growth still seems to be "exploding" is that a large proportion of the present population is composed of men and women of child-bearing age. Half of the world's people are under the age of twenty-five. Barring major catastrophes, an inevitable demographic momentum is built into our present numbers, but this should be a subject of rational planning, not public paranoia. The truth is that the population "explosion" is gradually fizzling out.

Nevertheless, there is still considerable discrepancy between birth rates in the industrialized world and birth rates in many Third World countries, particularly in sub-Saharan Africa. Conventional wisdom has it that Third World people continue to have so many children because they are ignorant and irrational—they exercise no control over their sexuality, "breeding like rabbits." This "superiority complex" of many Westerners as well as some Third World elites is one of the main obstacles in the way of meaningful discussion of the population problem. It assumes that everyone lives in the same basic social environment and faces the same set of reproductive choices. Nothing is further from the truth.

In many Third World societies, having a large family is an eminently rational strategy of survival. Children's labor is a vital part of the family economy in many peasant communities of Asia, Africa, and Latin America. Children help in the fields, tend animals, fetch water and wood, and care for their younger brothers and sisters, freeing their parents for other tasks. Quite early in life, children's labor makes them an asset rather than a drain on family income. In Bangladesh, for example, boys produce more than they consume by the age of ten to thirteen, and by the age of fifteen their total production has exceeded their cumulative lifetime consumption. Girls likewise perform a number of valuable economic tasks, which include helping their mothers with cooking and the post-harvest processing of crops.[2]

In urban settings children often earn income as servants, messenger boys, etc., or else stay home to care for younger children while their parents work. Among the Yoruba community in Nigeria, demographer John Caldwell found that even urban professional families benefit from many children through "sibling assistance chains." As one child completes education and takes a job, he or she helps younger brothers and sisters move up the educational and employment ladder, and the connections and the influence of the family spread.[3]

In recent years, however, urbanization has been associated with fertility decline in a number of countries for both positive and negative reasons. For those with ample resources, living in an urban area can mean greater access to education, health and family planning services, and the kind of information and media that promote a smaller family norm. Since the debt crisis and economic recession of the 1980s, however, the quality of life of the urban poor has deteriorated in many countries. High unemployment or work in insecure, low-wage occupations mean that poor people simply do not have enough financial resources to support a large family. Brazil has experienced such a distress-related fertility decline. The government's failure to institute agrarian reforms in rural areas forced people to flee the poverty of the countryside, only to face the harsh realities of urban slums.[4]

Security is another crucial reason to have many children. In many Third World societies, the vast majority of the population has no access to insurance schemes, pension plans, or government social security. It is children who care for their parents in their old age; without them one's future is endangered. The help of grown children can also be crucial in surviving the periodic crises—illness, drought, floods, food shortages, land disputes, political upheavals—which, unfortunately, punctuate village life in most parts of the world.[5]

By contrast, parents in industrialized countries and their affluent counterparts among Third World urban elites have much less need to rely on children either for labor or old-age security. The economics of family size changes as income goes up, until children become a financial burden instead of an asset. When children are in school, for example, they no longer serve as a source of labor. Instead parents must pay for their education, as well as for their other needs, which cost far more in a high-consumption society than in a peasant village. And there is often no guarantee that parents' investment will buy the future loyalty of a grown child. As economist Nancy Folbre notes, "The 'gift' of education, unlike a bequest, cannot be made contingent upon conformity to certain expectations. Once given, it can hardly be revoked."[6]

In industrialized societies personal savings, pension plans, and government programs replace children as the basic forms of social security. These social changes fundamentally alter the value of children, making it far more rational from an economic standpoint to limit family size. Folbre also argues that as the value of children decreases, male heads of households are more willing to allow their wives to work outside the home, since the contribution of their wages to the family economy now exceeds the value of their household work.[7] This further spurs fertility decline.

Son preference can be another important motive for having large families. The subordination of women means that economically and socially daughters are not valued as highly as sons in many cultures, particularly in South Asia, China, and parts of the Middle East. Not only does daughters' domestic work have less prestige, but daughters typically provide fewer years of productive labor to their parents, because in many societies, they marry and leave home to live with their in-laws shortly after puberty.

Son preference, combined with high infant and child mortality rates, means that parents must have many children just to ensure that one or two sons survive.* A computer simulation found that in the 1960s an Indian couple had to bear an average of 6.3 children to

---

* *Infant mortality rate* is the number of deaths of infants under one year of age per thousand live births in a given year.
  Child mortality rate is the number of deaths of children aged one to four per thousand children in this age group in a given year.

be confident of having one son who would survive to adulthood.[8] Son preference can also lead to skewed sex ratios, so that there are more males than females in a given population. Although at birth boys outnumber girls by a ratio of about 105 to 100, this discrepancy soon disappears, all else being equal, because biologically girls have better survival rates beginning in the first months after birth. In China, much of South Asia, and parts of North Africa, however, discrimination against girls means that there continues to be fewer girls than boys, and women than men, in the population. Discrimination takes many forms, from more typical forms of unbenign neglect, such as giving girls less food and health care, to female infanticide and sex-selective abortion. According to one estimate, more than 100 million women are "missing" throughout the world as the result of such discrimination. The situation is particularly serious in North India and China (see Chapters 9 and 13).[9]

High infant and child mortality rates are major underlying causes of high birth rates. Each year in developing countries more than 12 million children die before reaching their fifth birthday. The average infant mortality rate is more than 71 deaths per 1,000 live births in developing countries as a whole, and over 100 in sub-Saharan Africa. By comparison, it is only 14 in industrialized countries.[10] In recent decades there has been some progress in reducing infant and child mortality, but not nearly enough.

High infant mortality means that parents cannot be sure their children will survive to contribute to the family economy and to take care of them in their old age. The poor are thus caught in a death trap: They have to keep producing children in order that some will survive. Most countries that have achieved a low birth rate have done so only after infant and child mortality has declined.

High infant mortality is primarily caused by poor nutrition, both of the mother and of the child. In situations of chronic scarcity, women often eat last and least, with a profound impact on infant health. Inadequately nourished mothers typically give birth to underweight babies, and low birth weight has been identified as the "greatest single hazard for infants," increasing their vulnerability to developmental problems and their risk of death from common childhood illnesses.[11] Severely undernourished women also give lower-quality breast milk; for a woman to breast-feed successfully without damaging her health, she must increase her calorie and nutrient intake by up to 25 percent, an impossibility for many poor women.[12]

Breast-feeding, in fact, has relevance to the population issue on several different but interconnected levels. In many countries, increases in infant mortality have been linked to the switch from breast-feeding to bottle feeding. Infant formula lacks the antibodies in breast milk that help to protect babies from disease. Poor women, moreover, often cannot afford a steady supply of formula and dilute it with too much water.

Proper sterilization of bottles, nipples, and drinking water is also problematic in poor households. As a result, Third World infants breast-fed for less than six months are *five* times more likely to die in the second six months of life than those who have been breast-fed longer. Overall the mortality rate for bottle-fed infants in the Third World is roughly double that for breast-fed infants.[13]

Intensive sales campaigns by multinational corporations, such as the Swiss-based Nestlé Company and American Home Products, bear a large share of the responsibility for the shift from breast- to bottle-feeding. Advertisements with pictures of plump, smiling white babies and the penetration of local health establishments by company representatives have helped convince women that they will have healthier children if they switch to formula. An international campaign against these formula "pushers" finally led the World Health Organization (WHO) in 1980 to establish a voluntary code of conduct, setting standards for the advertising and marketing of formula. Every country signed on, except for the United States.

Although the code has brought improvements in terms of mass advertising, the companies still widely promote formula through health establishments. A study of breast-feeding in four Third World cities found that formula marketers had close commercial ties with physicians, pharmacists, and midwives, and that as a result, women who used Western-type health and maternity services tended to introduce formula earlier.[14] The WHO code is clearly not strong enough.

The decline in breast-feeding is also due to the fact that more women are now employed outside the home in occupations and workplaces that actively discourage the practice or do not offer support. Extended maternity leave with pay, on-site daycare, and flexible scheduling would greatly facilitate breast-feeding, but unfortunately, in most countries, these are not high social priorities despite their obvious benefits to women and children.

In addition to giving protection against infection, another key advantage of breast-feeding is that it happens to be one of the world's most effective natural contraceptives. It frequently causes lactational amenorrhea, the suppression of ovulation and menstruation by the release of the hormone prolactin. Each month of breast-feeding adds up to three weeks to the interval between births, and women who breast-feed often, whenever the baby wants, delay the return to fertility even longer.[15]

Hence, a decline in breast-feeding without a corresponding use of effective contraception means that pregnancies are more closely spaced, and the close spacing of births is itself a major cause of infant mortality. The relationship can also go the other way: A child's death means a woman stops breast-feeding and resumes fertility sooner, with a higher risk of the next child's death. This vicious biological circle may be one of the key reasons high infant mortality and high fertility go hand in hand.[16]

The last (but not least) cause of high birth rates is the subordination of women. Male dominance in the family, patriarchal social mores, the systematic exclusion of women from the development process, and the absence of decent birth control services combine to force many women into having more children than they want (see Chapter 3). The social environment, in effect, leaves them little or no reproductive choice.

Behind the demographic statistics, then, lies a reality unfamiliar to many middle-class people, who do not have to worry from day to day about who will help in the fields, who will take care of them when they are old and sick, or how many children they need to have in order to ensure that a few survive to adulthood. High birth rates are often a distress signal that people's survival is endangered. Yet the proponents of population control put the argument the other way around, insisting that people are endangering their own survival—and the survival of future generations—by having so many children. This is the basis of the Malthusian philosophy that has defined the dimensions of the population problem for so long.

THE IMPACT OF AIDS

It is difficult to predict with any certainty the long-term demographic impact of the HIV/AIDS pandemic, given the non-existence or inaccuracy of data. The U.S. Census Bureau's *World Population Profile: 1994* makes a number of sobering projections, however.[1] Presently 14 million people world-wide are believed to be infected with the HIV virus, and this number is likely to rise to between 30 and 40 million by the year 2000. AIDS will have a greater effect on death rates than on birth rates, since the long incubation period of HIV means that many women will have completed their childbearing before contracting full-blown AIDS.

AIDS could increase crude death rates significantly in a number of the worst affected countries, for example, by more than 300 percent in Zambia and Zimbabwe by the year 2010. Mother-to-child transmission also augurs considerable increases in infant and child mortality, reversing recent improvements in child survival. The Census Bureau estimates that AIDS will triple child mortality rates in Zambia and Zimbabwe, double them in Kenya and Uganda, and increase them five-fold in Thailand by the year 2010.

AIDS could halve the population growth rates of a majority of the worst-affected countries. In 2010 the Central African Republic, Congo, Kenya, and Zimbabwe could have growth rates of 1 percent or less. Thailand, however, is the only country projected to experience negative population growth as the result of AIDS. Although these projections may prove incorrect, they point to the severity of the HIV/AIDS pandemic and call into question the international community's current obsession with controlling high birth rates instead of high death rates, particularly in Africa.

2

THE MALTHUSIAN
ORTHODOXY

The impact of population growth is a source of endless debate. There is a vast literature on the subject, by demographers and economists, sociologists and development planners. The subject not only involves the impact of population growth per se, but problems of population distribution between urban and rural areas and imbalances in the age structure of populations. What emerges most strongly from the literature is the difficulty of generalizing on a global level; the impact of population growth differs from country to country and is influenced by a variety of factors.

Yet the complexities of demographic research and the wide variation in scientific opinion have largely been screened from public view. Instead, Malthusian alarmists, who range from environmentalists like Paul Ehrlich to senior international technocrats like former World Bank president Robert McNamara, command the widest public audience. While the population bomb briefly went out of fashion in the 1980s, it is very much back in vogue today.

There are several reasons why the alarmist message enjoys such credibility. It not only makes good shock headlines in the press, but also draws on deep undercurrents of parochialism, racism, elitism, and sexism, complementing the Social Darwinist "survival of the fittest" view. The most extreme Malthusians even advocate that famine relief be cut off to poor overpopulated countries: Let the unfit starve until their numbers are brought under control. In 1985, at the height of a major African drought, Colorado Governor Richard D. Lamm wrote in the *New York Times* that the United States should stop giving emergency relief to African countries that failed to reduce their population growth, since such aid would "merely multiply empty stomachs."[1]

The fact that such suggestions are taken seriously is a sad commentary on just how far Malthusianism has penetrated our value system. So pervasive are its assumptions that many of us have internalized them without even realizing it. Only by understanding the basic fallacies of the Malthusian approach can the way be cleared for a fresh look at the population problem.

The alarmists draw their ideological inspiration from Thomas Malthus, the British clergyman-turned-economist who wrote in the late 1700s and early 1800s. Malthus maintained that, unless restrained by "preventive checks," human populations would double every twenty-five years. The result would be geometric growth—1, 2, 4, 8, 16, 32, 64, 128, etc.—outstripping the earth's capacity for food production, which could at best be expected to increase in an arithmetic progression—1, 2, 3, 4, 5, 6, 7, etc. Humans were, according to Malthus, little different from animals or plants in this respect; their numbers would be held in check by the limited carrying capacity of the planet. "The race of plants and the race of animals shrink under this great restrictive law," he proclaimed, "and man cannot by any efforts of reason escape from it."[2] Only "misery"—the poverty, famine, and pestilence brought on by overpopulation, supplemented by the man-made deprivations of war and slaughter— would keep human numbers down.

Malthus was wrong on two basic counts. First, contrary to his predictions, it is possible for population growth to slow and ultimately to stabilize, not because our numbers are held in check by "natural" forces of famine and pestilence, but rather as a result of improvements in living standards and other social changes which alter the need for many children. Malthus' native land underwent such a demographic transition.

Malthus' second mistake was to underestimate greatly the capacity of the earth to feed and clothe a growing human population. It is perhaps not surprising that someone writing at the close of the eighteenth century failed to foresee the tremendous advances in human productive powers that would soon unfold in both industry and agriculture, outstripping population growth. In fact, at least one school of economic history maintains that the crucial force behind technological change—the "prime mover" of economic progress—was none other than *population growth*. In their influential study, *The Rise of the Western World: A New Economic History*, historians Douglas North and Robert Thomas conclude that population growth "spurred the institutional innovations which account for the rise of the Western world."[3] Far from blocking any long-term improvement in mass living standards, population growth is thus seen by some historians as the basic *explanation* for such improvements.

The modern-day proponents of population control have reinterpreted Malthusian logic, selectively applying it only to the poor majority in the Third World and, in some cases, to ethnic minorities in the West. It is not a giant step from this partitioning of Malthusian laws to a similar partitioning in the realm of human rights: Upper- and middle-class people have the right to voluntary choice as to whether and when to bear children, but the rights of poor people are subordinate to the overriding imperative of population control.

In support of this scientific and ethical double standard, the new Malthusians point to the correlation between high birth rates and low living standards in the Third World today. It is undoubtedly true that Third World countries generally have higher birth rates than industrialized ones, East and West, and that among Third World countries, those with higher population growth tend to have lower per capita incomes. Drawing sustenance from this simple correlation, the Malthusians then move on to blame a host of complex social ills on overpopulation, with varying degrees of intellectual sophistication and according to the fashions of the time.

FOOD FOR THOUGHT

In the 1960s and 1970s it was fashionable to attribute hunger and food scarcity to overpopulation. "World food production cannot keep pace with the galloping growth of population," warned the Washington-based Environmental Fund, in one of the less sophisticated applications of Malthusian logic.[4] "The battle to feed all humanity is over," claimed Ehrlich's 1968 book, *The Population*

Bomb. "In the 1970s the world will undergo famines—hundreds of millions of people will starve to death."[5] While computer projections, such as the Club of Rome's famous *Limits to Growth*, gave these dire predictions a pseudo-respectability, hard facts contradicted the projections. For the galloping horse of population had met its match in the steady march of new agricultural technologies: We were about to enter the era of food surplus.

Tremendous advances in agricultural productivity mean that today the world produces enough grain alone to provide every man, woman, and child on earth with 3,000 calories a day, well above the 2,200-2,500 calorie average considered a minimally acceptable dietary level.[6] At least on a global scale, there is no shortage of food.

Simple Malthusian arithmetic says that more mouths to feed means less food per person. This would be true if the supply of food was somehow fixed and unaffected by the size of a country's population. But food supplies are *not* fixed and can be influenced by population growth in positive ways. This is not only because population growth expands the labor force—each additional mouth brings with it an additional pair of hands—but because the pressure of population on resources can induce technological and institutional change so as to raise output per person. Economist Colin Clark, for example, sees population growth as the principal force behind the extensive clearing of land, drainage of swamps, and the introduction of better crops and manures, changes which "historians tend to describe as 'agricultural revolutions.'"[7]

There is, of course, no guarantee that population growth will automatically trigger corresponding increases in food production, but neither is there an iron law that ensures that it will not. Indeed, in the past twenty years the output of major food crops has increased dramatically in every region of the world, mostly due to increases in yields rather than expansion in cropland. Food production has kept up with population growth, except in parts of Africa. The claim of Malthusians, notably Lester Brown of the Worldwatch Institute, that since 1984 per capita cereal production has declined in all major regions of the world, largely due to population growth, is seriously flawed. A closer look at the data by Tim Dyson reveals that per capita cereal output has not declined in Western Europe and Asia, home to two-thirds of humanity. Moreover, declines in output elsewhere are largely due to unfavorable grain prices and the switch to other crops. As Dyson concludes, "Overall, global per capita food output during the last decade has increased at only a slightly lower rate than it did during the 1970s. World population growth does not appear to be outpacing food production."[8] Today most countries have enough food to meet the needs of their growing populations or the economic resources with which to import it. Yet even when food is plentiful, millions of people go hungry.

They go hungry because individual families do not have land on which to grow food, or the money with which to buy it. The main problem is not that there are too many people and too few resources, but rather that too few people monopolize too many resources. The problem is not one of absolute scarcity, but one of distribution.

The unequal distribution of land is especially critical in many parts of the Third World, where the majority of the population still lives in rural areas. The agricultural laborer in Asia, the small subsistence farmer in Latin America, and the African peasant who must migrate seasonally to work on plantations or in the mines often live at the margin of survival. When crops fail or jobs are scarce, they do not have the cash to buy food, even when it is plentiful in the market.

Even famines have more to do with poor people's inability to command access to food than to its actual scarcity. During the Sahelian famine of the late 1960s and early 1970s in Africa, for example, almost all Sahelian countries had enough food to feed their populations, had that been a government priority. In fact, agricultural exports from the area actually increased during the period.[9]

Famine is usually due to a breakdown in the economic and political institutions which ensure food security through the distribution of surplus to regions suffering shortages. Public knowledge and pressure are vital in getting governments to act: According to economist A. K. Sen, there has never been a large-scale famine in any country, rich or poor, that is a democracy with a relatively free press.[10] Recent famines in Ethiopia and Somalia were largely caused by the ravages of civil war, aided and abetted by the Cold War policies of the U.S. and the former Soviet Union—not by population growth or natural disasters.

But what about those countries in Africa where food production has not kept pace with population growth? The United Nations Food and Agriculture Organization (FAO) estimates that in 1989, thirty-five of forty-seven African countries dropped below the per capita food production levels they had achieved during 1979-81.[11] At the same time the continent has been experiencing the world's highest rates of population growth. If Malthus was wrong about most of the world, was he right about Africa?

Africa's food crisis has less to do with high population growth than with low productivity. Sixty to eighty percent of the African rural labor force works at extremely low levels of productivity; the most common agricultural implement is a hand-held hoe, little advanced since the Iron Age. Not surprisingly, African cereal yields have not risen nearly as fast as those in other parts of the Third World.

One of the main reasons food production has stagnated is that resources have been concentrated on growing cash crops for export. This export-oriented policy can be traced back to the colonial period when peasants were made, by the use of oppressive taxation or force if necessary, to grow export crops. Subsequent research and development programs centered on the needs of commercial farmers and plantation managers, ignoring basic food crops and their producers, who were usually women.[12]

This same trend continues today, with most African governments giving low priority to peasant food production and neglecting women's role in agriculture. Instead the focus is on plantations, state farms, and land settlement schemes which produce export crops, often in cooperation with foreign agribusiness corporations. Since cash crops are typically grown on the best land, their expansion squeezes subsistence food producers into marginal areas, and the result is often land degradation and declining yields. Through state marketing boards, "parastatals," which set low prices for agricultural products, and biased taxation policies, African agriculture has also been bled to finance the development of urban areas and the luxurious lifestyles of elites. Meanwhile, foreign aid programs have tended to favor expensive, imported technology over indigenous techniques and labor and have pushed grandiose commercial schemes over the painstaking provision of training, credit, and inputs to the small (female) farmer or herder.[13]

In recent years, the process of "structural adjustment" has further undermined African food production. In response to the international debt crisis of the 1980s, the World Bank and International Monetary Fund (IMF) have forced many Third World countries to make major "free market" adjustments to their economies in order to receive new loans with which to pay back their debts. Governments have had to slash social expenditures, remove price subsidies for essential products, de-value their currencies, down-size the public sector, open their doors to foreign investment and products, and, in the case of agriculture, concentrate on export crops in order to earn foreign exchange.

At the same time prices for most agricultural products have been falling dramatically on the world market; by 1989, prices were only 60 to 70 percent of their 1970 levels. Traditional African exports have been particularly hard-hit.[14] Countries have had to increase the volume of their agricultural exports in order to earn the same amount of foreign exchange—in other words, they have had to run just to stay in place.

In Ghana, where the World Bank claims adjustment is a success, the concentration of resources on export crops, especially cocoa, has weakened basic food production and promoted dependence on food imports. In many countries, the dismantling of state supports which benefitted small farmers, notably fertilizer subsidies and credit programs, has also contributed to declining food production.[15]

In some parts of Africa, a shortage of human labor ironically lies behind both low yields and high fertility rates. Colonial and post-colonial policies have not only favored export crops, but have forced many men to migrate seasonally to work on plantations, in mines, or in urban areas. Women, the main food producers, are left behind to manage the fields on their own. In Burkina Faso, for example, during certain times of the year when young men migrate to raise cash for taxes and consumer needs, there is not enough labor to clear bush for new farms or maintain wells, and food production suffers accordingly.[16]

Cash-cropping has also increased women's workload, since they are expected to do virtually all of the labor involved in food production, as well as the sowing and weeding of cash crops controlled by male family members. The size of food harvests is "often dependent not on what the land will produce but on how much work in the fields women can squeeze into their already busy days."[17] Having many children to help in the fields is clearly a rational response to this situation.

Contrary to conventional wisdom, low population densities in many parts of Africa have served as a brake on food production, while high densities have often raised land productivity. The semi-arid Machakos District in Kenya was considered an environmental disaster in the 1930s, requiring famine relief and food imports. The population of the district increased fivefold in the next sixty years, but in 1990 the environment was in much better shape than in the 1930s. Per capita agricultural production has increased with new technologies and farming systems, but soil erosion has been reversed or slowed with terracing and the protection of trees.[18]

Although a decline in Africa's birth rate might help to relieve pressure on land and food supplies, it will never solve the more fundamental problems at the heart of the continent's agrarian crisis. Instead, major agricultural reforms are necessary. After independence, Zimbabwe, for example, experienced impressive increases in peasant food production by breaking white farmers' monopoly over rural credit and transportation facilities and through fairer pricing policies for agricultural inputs and produce.[19] Unfortunately, however, the best land in Zimbabwe is still controlled by a small number of white farmers.

The weight of the evidence shows that today it is increasingly difficult for Malthusians to blame hunger on population growth. Instead, they now make the argument that the effort to feed our growing numbers is taking an unprecedented environmental toll: draining fossil fuel and water reserves, degrading and contaminating soils, destroying other species, forcing expansion into marginal lands and forested areas, and ultimately threatening the survival of future generations. "In the simplest terms, we are in a race to see if we can slow, and eventually halt, population growth before local life-support systems collapse," warns Lester Brown of the Worldwatch Institute.[20]

The Malthusians of course have a point. No one wants a world of standing-room only, where every bit of land, drop of water, and unit of energy is pressed into producing sustenance for an endlessly expanding human mass. But population growth rates are coming down—the species is not likely to expand itself into oblivion. Moreover, while many of the environmentally harmful processes the Malthusians describe are real and extremely serious, they have less to do with population growth than with specific consumption patterns, land uses, and agricultural technologies. There is a vast difference, for example, between the land degradation caused by corporate grain farming in the United States, much of which goes to feed livestock, and small-scale, labor-intensive rice cultivation in Asia, which feeds millions of people.

Given that world population will continue to grow into the next century, there is a pressing need for policy changes and new agricultural techniques which will increase yields of basic food crops while restoring, not destroying, environmental resources. Many small farmers and peasants already practice sustainable agriculture, but their expertise and capacity for innovation have been largely overlooked or actively undermined by corporate agriculture.[21] To guarantee food security, we should be spending time, energy, and money on both preserving traditional knowledge systems and developing new environmentally sensitive agricultural techniques—not on spreading unproductive alarm about birth rates.

Unfortunately, alarm is the rallying cry of the Malthusian wing of the environmental movement. World population is already overshooting the carrying capacity of the planet, their spokespeople warn us. But what exactly is their concept of population, and how do they measure "carrying capacity"?

SPECIOUS VIEWS OF THE SPECIES

Stanford biologist Paul Ehrlich has probably done more than any other single scientist to legitimize and popularize the belief that overpopulation is the main cause of the environmental crisis, from global warming to the depletion of the ozone layer. Like many biologists, he sees the human species through the same lens with which he views animal and plant populations which multiply beyond the carrying capacity of their environments and subsequently die off. Thus, his latest book (co-authored with Anne Ehrlich) *The Population Explosion,* compares the exponential growth of human populations to that of pond weed, and warns us that nature may end the population explosion "in very unpleasant ways," such as famine and AIDS, if people do not act immediately.[22]

The Ehrlichs believe that virtually every nation is already vastly overpopulated. By their definition, carrying capacity is "the capacity of the environment to sustain human activities," and "if the long-term carrying capacity of an area is clearly being degraded by its current human occupants, that area is overpopulated."[23] By this logic, the land degradation caused by a uranium mine on a Native American reservation is a sign that the area has too many people!

The Ehrlichs' narrow view of the human species not only ignores historical changes in demographic dynamics, but the great cultural and temporal differences in how human populations relate to their environments. The Ehrlichs would like us to believe that, from the time of the wooly mammoth, humans have degraded the ecosystem. In fact, many cultures have long lived in harmony with their natural surroundings. The current era of widespread environmental devastation is tied primarily to a unique and hopefully transitory period of rapacious capital accumulation and commodity fetishism spreading outward from the United States, Europe, and Japan.

The pond weed view of the species reinforces racism and sexism. The white middle-class elite, to which the Ehrlichs and many other population control advocates belong, is unlikely to view itself in these terms; instead the metaphor extends primarily to the dark-skinned poor. In *The Population Explosion* the Ehrlichs refer to babies born in Bangladesh and the Philippines as "mouths"—a common Malthusian slur.[24] Implicitly, it is women's fertility which is out of control; it is as if women have never consciously exercised control over reproduction, except in modern family planning programs.

Furthermore, only people who are profoundly alienated and insulated from the realities of human suffering can view famine or AIDS as "nature's way" of controlling population. As noted above, there is nothing "natural" about famine. The rapid spread of HIV in marginalized communities around the world is a direct result of their poverty and lack of power–surely a failure of resource distribution rather than the revenge of abstract nature on the over-breeding poor.

The Ehrlichs and many other Malthusian environmentalists use a simple equation to support their view of the world: The impact (I) of any human group on the environment equals population size (P) times the level of affluence (or average individual resource consumption) (A) times an index of the environmental disruptiveness of the technologies which provide the goods consumed (T), or I=PAT.[25]

Taking the equation at face value, people can and do argue about the relative weights that should be attached to P, A, and T. Even though the Ehrlichs recognize the environmental destruction caused by affluence and technology, they inevitably return to population as the main factor. Critics of course point out that affluence has far more to do with the depletion of natural resources than does population size.

Currently, the industrialized nations, with 22 percent of the world's population, consume 70 percent of the world's energy, 75 percent of its metals, 85 percent of its wood, and 60 percent of its food.[26] The much smaller populations of Northern industrialized nations generate almost three quarters of all carbon dioxide emissions, which in turn comprise nearly half of the "manmade" greenhouse gases in the atmosphere.[27] They are also responsible for most of the ozone depletion.

Other critics, notably environmentalist Barry Commoner, argue convincingly that the nature of technology is the decisive factor determining environmental quality. Commoner points to the critical shift from more environmentally benign technologies to more harmful ones–for example, from rail freight to truck freight, natural products to synthetics, reusable goods to throwaways–which occurred in the post-World War II period.[28] On a global level, then, it simply does not make sense to blame environmental degradation on population growth.

The main problem with the equation, however, is what it leaves out, namely the question of social, economic, and political power, and the systems by which current power relations are enforced. These underlie P, A, and T, and the interaction between them.

Take P, for example. The very word "population" lumps all people together, reducing them into a set of statistics, or "bloodless entities that can be managed as characterless classes that reproduce, pollute, produce, or consume, and for the common good, call for control."[29] In her critique of I=PAT, environmentalist H. Patricia Hynes notes how P is gender-, race-, and class-blind, all but ignoring different people's differing impacts on the environment. Moreover, it neglects the crucial factor of human agency by viewing all humans as *takers from,* rather than *enhancers of,* the natural environment. "This truncated, culture-bound view of humans in their environment originates from an industrial, urban, consumerist society."[30]

P also ignores the issue of population distribution, which arguably can have a greater impact on the environment than population size per se. Millions of people crowded into megacities, particularly when they are located in environmentally vulnerable areas like southern California (where they drive cars!), can do far more damage to the environment than if they were more evenly distributed in towns and smaller cities. Carefully planned urbanization, on the other hand, is often more environmentally sound than unplanned suburbanization which consumes farmland and forests.

And precisely what is A? Affluence is not simply a matter of per capita consumption. Profound systemic inequities underlie consumption patterns; debt repayment, structural adjustment, and the "free market" economics of the 1980s and 1990s have meant an even greater concentration of wealth in the hands of the rich. According to the United Nations' *Human Development Report 1993,* global income disparity has doubled during the last three decades. The richest 20 percent of the world's people now receive 150 times the income of the poorest 20 percent, who receive in total a measly 1.3 percent of global income.[31]

In terms of both quantity and quality of consumption, advanced capitalism carefully orchestrates needs through mass advertising, destroying non-commodity-based culture and values. Unregulated and unchecked, it seeks endlessly to expand production and open new markets. But unchecked growth comes at a cost. Not only are many poor people left by the wayside, unemployed or in marginal jobs, but for the privileged, consumerism does not live up to its promises. Psychologist Paul Wachtel presents survey evidence that shows that Americans are no happier today than they were twenty to thirty years ago, even though they now have a higher standard of living. He asks,

> Why is it that growth has yielded us so little in enduring satisfaction?.... To begin with, the entire dynamic of a growth oriented economy absolutely requires discontent. If people begin to be satisfied with what they have, if they cease to organize their lives around having still more, the economy is in danger of grinding to a halt. Progress is not our most important product; discontent is.[32]

Those who have well-paid jobs work harder and harder to afford more things—leisure itself becomes something to consume, not to enjoy, and there is less and less of it. Overwork takes its toll on those human relationships within the family and community which could bring more enduring satisfaction. To compensate, people buy even more unnecessary goods and services, trapping themselves in a vicious cycle of overconsumption and discontent, with many negative consequences for the environment. Wachtel argues for a new "ecology of satisfaction" which fundamentally challenges the logic of unfettered capitalist growth.[33]

This is not to argue against economic growth per se, but for harnessing the market and organizing the workplace to serve the public good, not just the profit motive. It is also important to distinguish between luxury and survival consumption.[34] The planet may not have enough resources for everyone to own two cars and three TVs, but surely alternative systems of production and consumption are possible wherein everyone's basic needs are met.

This brings us to the big T of technology. Many Malthusian environmentalists fear that the use of modern technology to raise Third World living standards will degrade the environment even further. I have been asked more than once, "What will happen to the ozone layer when all those Chinese get refrigerators?" But even if the West had the power to do so, would it really make sense to deny the Chinese refrigerators to protect the environment? A far better approach would be to promote alternative coolants to ozone-depleting chemicals such as CFCs, not only in China, but everywhere.

Technology is not intrinsically harmful. The real issue is why current technologies are often so inappropriate and destructive. Why, in so many societies, for example, have public transport systems been sacrificed to the private automobile? Throughout the world, industries are allowed to pollute without bearing the cost. Public funds for technological research and development flow to the military and scarcely trickle down to new environmentally sound initiatives in energy and agriculture. These technological "choices" all reflect an absence of basic democracy, of popular control over technological development.

Conspicuously absent from the I=PAT equation is the chief enforcer of the power status quo, the military. Militaries also happen to be the main environmental criminals on the planet today. The German Research Institute for Peace Policy estimates that one-fifth of all global environmental degradation is due to military and related activities. In her book *Earth Follies* geographer Joni Seager catalogues a long list of military environmental atrocities from land grabbing to defoliation to nuclear testing to resource guzzling. The U.S. military alone is the largest domestic oil consumer and generates more toxic waste than the five largest multinational chemical companies combined.[35] Clearly, no equation intended to express the relationship between people and the environment can even pretend to mirror reality when it fails to include the military.

While I=PAT obscures power relations at the global level, the precise dynamics of environmental degradation at the local, regional, and national levels are also hidden behind a Malthusian veil. In developing countries, deforestation in particular is commonly blamed on rapid population growth.

WHO IS DESTROYING THE FOREST?

In recent years the United Nations Fund for Population Activities (UNFPA) has expended large amounts of resources promoting the view that population growth is one of the major causes of the environmental crisis. Its *State of World Population 1992* boldly states that in developing countries, population growth "is responsible for around 79 percent of deforestation, 72 percent of arable land expansion, and 69 percent of growth in livestock numbers."[36] Furthermore, the UNFPA maintains that the "bottom billion," the very poorest people in developing countries, "often impose greater environmental injury than the other 3 billion of their fellow citizens put together."[37]

How these grand statistics were generated is anyone's guess; however, it is clear that little attention was paid to the serious literature on the subject—even that produced by other U.N. agencies. For example, in an extensive study of the social dynamics of deforestation, the United Nations Research Institute for Social Development (UNRISD) notes that while many observers blame deforestation on forest clearing by poor migrants, they ignore the larger forces attracting or pushing these migrants into forest areas, such as the expansion of large-scale commercial farming, ranching, logging, and mining. "To blame poor migrants for destroying the forest is like blaming poor conscripts for the ravages of war."[38] The study finds an absence of any close correspondence between deforestation rates and rates of either total or agricultural population growth.

Brazil is a case in point. Starting in the late sixties, highway construction initiated destruction of the Amazon rain forest and its indigenous inhabitants. Among the chief financiers of the roads were the U. S. Agency for International Development (AID), the World Bank, the Inter-American Development Bank, and U.S. military aid to the Brazilian Army Corps of Engineers. Between 1966 and 1975, 11.5 million hectares of forest were cleared—an estimated 60 percent by highway developers and cattle ranchers, and only 17.6 percent by peasants.[39] National and multinational corporations, including Goodyear, Volkswagen, Nestlé, and Mitsubushi, quickly got into the act, stripping forests for ranching and mining.[40]

To the extent that peasants did cut down the forest, it was not the result of population growth, but government policy. The government encouraged peasant colonization of the Amazon in lieu of much needed land reform in other regions. In Brazil large estates of over 1,000 acres represent less than 1 percent of farms, yet occupy almost half of the nation's farmland.

Ironically, in the last twenty years, Brazil has undergone a rapid demographic transition from high to low birth rates "while environmental destruction has been increasing in inverse proportion to that decline."[41]

In Latin America in general, the extension of commercial ranching is widely recognized to have been the primary impetus behind deforestation. And it is not population growth that is the main force behind the increase in herds. Beef production in the region has doubled in the last twenty years, less to meet domestic consumption needs than to serve foreign markets.

Costa Rica, Honduras, and Nicaragua, for example, export over half of their total beef production.[42] Due to good prices and favorable tariff treatment, most beef in Latin America is exported to the United States, much of it for use in fast-food chains or pet food. The average Central American eats less beef than the average U.S. housecat.[43] U.S. taxpayers and consumers thus have as much—or more—to do with the destruction of the rain forest as the poor peasants contracted by ranchers to cut down the trees.

In Southeast Asia commercial logging has been the main cause of deforestation, notwithstanding growing populations and mounting local needs for wood as fuel. In the Philippines, where the once plentiful tropical forest cover has been virtually eliminated, the UNFPA maintains that the population pressure of "multitudes of landless people" moving into the uplands is the main culprit.[44] However, a careful statistical analysis by geographer David Kummer reveals zero correlation between population growth rates and rates of deforestation in the country's provinces.[45]

In fact, Philippine deforestation peaked during the Ferdinand Marcos era, when the dictator gave illegal logging concessions worth over 1 billion dollars to relatives and political cronies, depleting the country's forest reserves from 34.6 million acres in 1965, when Marcos took power, to only 5.4 million acres today.[46] Marcos, in turn, was supported by the U.S. government and World Bank. One dictator alone probably wreaked more havoc on Philippine forests than the poorest quarter of the country's population, 16 million people. As in the case of beef production, most tropical wood is destined for foreign markets. Between 1950 and 1980 consumption of tropical hardwoods in the industrialized nations was over twice that of all the tropical producer nations combined—despite their growing populations.[47]

This is not to deny that the poor are involved in deforestation or land degradation, though on a global level they are clearly not the main culprits. Moreover, it is important to look at the underlying reasons why poor people degrade their environment when they do. In some cases the reason may be the scarcity of fuel wood and the lack of alternative energy forms, in others the need to farm marginal land because the best land is controlled by a powerful few. Population pressure can contribute to the problem, but it is rarely the root cause.

This is nowhere clearer than in the case of El Salvador. Today the country faces accelerated erosion of an estimated 77 percent of its land, and almost all of its original forests have been destroyed. Major water sources are contaminated with toxic chemicals and pesticides, and in many areas watersheds are drying up.[48] Conventional wisdom has it that overpopulation is at the root of the ecological crisis. "Almost 6 million people are crowded into a country roughly the size of Massachusetts," the *Los Angeles Times* expresses in horror, neglecting to mention that Massachusetts has an even larger population.[49]

To find the real roots of environmental degradation in El Salvador, one must dig far deeper than just population pressure. As in many other parts of Central America, a major factor was the displacement of the peasantry by a small landowning elite. El Salvador is generally steep and mountainous, with fertile lands located in the middle of volcanic slopes, river basins, and coastal plains. Until recently, these few productive areas were monopolized by large estates growing cotton, sugar, coffee, and cattle for export. Meanwhile, the peasants were pushed onto the higher slopes, where, in order to survive, they had to cut down vegetation and grow subsistence crops on land unsuitable for cultivation. Erosion was the inevitable result.[50]

Sociologist Daniel Faber argues that both the social and ecological impoverishment of the peasantry was a necessary part of export-oriented commercial agriculture, which required a cheap, seasonal labor force. If the peasants had access to the economic and natural resources to meet all their subsistence needs, they would not have been available to work on a seasonal basis for meager wages. On the other hand, if they had no land at all, they would need fuller employment to survive. "In effect, exploitation of labor and exploitation of the environment were two different sides of the same coin...and reflected the class privileges and power of Central America's ruling oligarchies and agrarian bourgeoisie."[51]

In El Salvador ruling elites have savagely repressed peasant demands for access to land and other resources. Over 70,000 people were killed in the civil war which began in the 1970s and which only recently came to an uneasy end. The war itself was a major cause of environmental degradation. The Salvadoran military, with U.S. assistance, waged a "scorched earth" policy, bombing and burning forests and fields in order to destroy the resource base of peasants suspected of collaborating with the guerillas. War refugees also contributed to environmental degradation by settling in forest areas and peri-urban settlements located on marginal lands.[52] Inequality and insecurity in turn encouraged high birth rates as a survival mechanism, blocking an effective demographic transition.

The case of El Salvador points to the need to redefine the concept of carrying capacity. For the Ehrlichs, carrying capacity is the environment's capacity to sustain human activities, and when it can no longer do so, it is overpopulated. But is the main problem in El Salvador really human *numbers* or is it undemocratic human *systems* of labor and resource exploitation, backed by military repression? It would make more sense to talk about *political* carrying capacity, defined as the limited capacity of the environment to sustain inequality and injustice. Viewed this way, the solution to environmental degradation lies in greater democratic control over resources, not in a narrow population control agenda.

PIE IN THE SKY

Not all Malthusians base their case against population growth on the environment. The World Bank, for example, argues that rapid population growth is a "serious brake on development," resulting in "lost opportunities for raising living standards, particularly among the large numbers of the world's poor."[53] The World Bank has slightly altered the previous Malthusian line of causality. While it now maintains that poverty, not the sheer weight of human numbers, is responsible for hunger and environmental depletion, it blames much of poverty on the economic consequences of population growth, thus continuing to hold the poor responsible for their own misery.

The economic case against rapid population growth rests on several key assumptions. The first, and crudest, is that rapid population growth slows down the rate of increase of per capita incomes in a number of Third World countries. According to the Population Crisis Committee (now re-named Population Action International), this is a matter of "simple arithmetic."[54] Per capita income is measured by dividing gross national product (GNP) by the number of people in a country. Thus the basic argument goes that the more people there are, the smaller each individual's share of GNP will be. But people not only consume wealth and resources, they also create them: The numerator, GNP, seldom stays fixed as the denominator, population, grows. If economic conditions are favorable, population growth may itself contribute to more rapid growth of GNP, so that per capita income rises significantly.

In fact, the impressive economic performance of middle-income countries in the 1960s and 1970s occurred *alongside* rapid population growth.[55] This does not mean, of course, that rapid population growth was the main factor behind their success, but it certainly did not prevent it. Sub-Saharan Africa's ten richest countries in terms of per capita income have similar (even slightly higher) population growth rates as the ten poorest, again suggesting that population is not the crucial explanatory variable.[56]

The next assumption concerns the impact of population growth on government investment. According to a 1993 strategy paper of AID, "Rapid population growth renders inadequate or obsolete any investment in schools, housing, food production capacity, and infrastructure. It challenges the ability of governments to provide even the most basic health and social services."[57]

This analysis fails to take into account the basic political fact of life that the amount of resources a country devotes to education and other social services has less to do with population than with government priorities. The United Nations' *1993 Human Development Report* estimates that developing countries spend only one tenth of their national budgets on human development priorities, such as health care and education. Their military expenditures meanwhile soared from 91 percent of combined health and education expenditures in 1977 to 169 percent in 1990.[58]

The international foreign-aid budget looks much the same—less than 7 percent of official development assistance goes to human development priorities. Geo-political strategic concerns far outweigh the needs of poor people. In 1991 half of U.S. bilateral foreign aid went to five strategically important countries: Israel, Egypt, Turkey, the Philippines, and El Salvador.[59] And it is important to remember that many World Bank- and IMF-imposed structural adjustment programs have actually pressured Third World countries to reduce their per capita social service expenditures. During the 1980s more than three quarters of the countries in Africa and Latin America experienced dramatic declines in health spending.[60]

Perhaps the most common economic woe laid at the door of rapid population growth is unemployment. Open unemployment is rare in the Third World for the simple reason that most people cannot afford to be idle; in the absence of unemployment benefits or social insurance, they must somehow try to earn enough to survive. The real problem is *underemployment* in low-paying, low-productivity occupations such as street vending, domestic service, and handicraft production, which constitute the bottom end of the so-called informal sector in Third World economies.

It is undeniably true that millions of people today lack the opportunity to earn a decent living through their own labor. But is this because there are too many potential workers—or too few jobs?

The problem of surplus labor in Third World countries dates from the colonial period, when European powers appropriated land and other productive resources in Asia, Africa, and Latin America, while destroying any local industries that might compete with their own manufactured goods. Thrown off the land and thrown out of enterprises, thousands joined the ranks of underemployed labor. Political independence did not automatically break this pattern, as industrial development largely continued to be dominated by multinational corporations and international financial institutions, who promoted capital-intensive rather than labor-intensive industries. In recent years, structural adjustment has geared many economies toward the manufacture of exports, rather than industrial production for the domestic market.

The repression of labor goes hand in hand with this kind of economic "development"—if Third World exports are to remain competitive on the world market, then the price of labor must be kept down through restrictive laws and state violence if necessary. Yet according to AID, population growth is once again to blame: "As expanding populations demand an even greater number of jobs, a climate is created where workers, especially women and minorities, are oppressed."[61]

Despite the popular Western image of the Third World as a bottomless begging bowl, it has historically given more to the industrialized world than it has taken. Inflows of official "aid" and private loans and investment have often been exceeded by outflows in the form of repatriated profits, interest payments, and private capital sent abroad by Third World elites.[62]

The debt crisis has accelerated this trend. From 1985 to 1992 the net transfer on long-term debt for developing countries was negative $150 billion, that is, the interest and service payments on past loans exceeded new borrowing by that amount. Even so, thanks to the magic of cumulative interest, the developing countries fell deeper into debt during this same period—their long-term indebtedness rose from $900 billion to $1.4 trillion. Sub-Saharan Africa was particularly hard-hit—its total debt is now equivalent to over 110 percent of the region's GNP.[63]

Not everyone suffers in the Third World, of course. These neo-colonial patterns have continued precisely because of the collaboration of ruling groups in Third World countries, many of whom prefer investing in foreign bank accounts to investing in local job-creating industries. Between 1978 and 1983, for example, the Bank of International Settlements estimates that more than $55 million was "spirited away overseas" by rich Latin Americans, almost a third of the region's increase in borrowing from foreign banks during the period.[64] Such capital flight provides a rather dramatic counterpoint to the specter of chronic underemployment. When people migrate in search of work, this too is often blamed on population pressures rather than on the structure of the global economy.[65]

Ironically, at the same time that rapid population growth is seen as a brake on development in the Third World, many economists worry that declining or near-zero rates of population growth in industrial countries will have serious negative consequences. The main concern is that there will be too few young people in the labor force to support the social security costs of a large aging population. A number of European countries in fact offer financial incentives to people to have larger families.

This is not to say that rapid population growth poses no problem at all in the Third World. When agriculture and industry fail to provide employment to the underemployed, then population growth can have negative effects. Indeed, if the number of jobs stays fixed and more and more people vie for them, wages and living standards will tend to fall even for those with jobs. When the numerator remains the same and the denominator swells, then the trend is for each individual share of the economic pie to get smaller—though lately the rich are cutting themselves even bigger slices.

This "matter of simple arithmetic," however, is not an immutable mathematical law. The question is: Why do all things remain equal? Why are the majority condemned to a life of chronic poverty and low productivity?

The Malthusians do not have the answer to this question because they do not bother to ask it. They do not ask who owns the land, who fells the forests, who draws up the government budget, who steals the international bank loans, who were the colonialists, and who were the colonized. By a wave of some magic wand, they deny the role of the rich and powerful in creating and perpetuating the poverty of the powerless. Their ideological fervor masks a profound fatalism: The poor are born to their lot, and the only way out for them is to stop being born.

And what happens when the poor start demanding their rights? The Malthusians call that "political instability," and blame it too on overpopulation. The Population Crisis Committee views population pressures as one of the biggest "threats to democracy"—oppressive governments violate human rights, not because they are authoritarian to begin with, but "in their efforts to control restive populations."[66] In general, growing numbers of underemployed young males are viewed as increasing "the availability of people for revolutionary activity."[67] In this way Malthusianism directly serves to legitimize the status quo: If poor people are rising up, it is only because their numbers are rising too fast.

The Reverend Mr. Malthus himself put it succinctly two centuries ago:

> That the principal and most permanent cause of poverty has little or no *direct* relation to forms of government, or the unequal division of property; and that, as the rich do not in reality possess the *power* of finding employment and maintenance for the poor, the poor cannot, in the nature of things possess the *right* to demand them; are important truths flowing from the principle of population.[68]

The essence of Malthusianism boils down to this simple political imperative.

THE CORNUCOPIANS

In recent years, Malthusian fatalism has met its match in the unrepentant optimism of certain influential New Right economists. In their book *The Resourceful Earth,* Julian Simon and Herman Kahn challenge the "limits to growth" philosophy and claim that "if present trends continue, the world in 2000 will be less crowded (though more populated), less polluted, more stable ecologically, and less vulnerable to resource-supply disruption than the world we live in now."[69]

These conservative Cornucopians believe that free enterprise and nuclear energy can do the trick, just as long as there isn't too much government interference through environmental regulation. According to Simon, temporary shortages of resources simply spur the development of new techniques to find them, so that in the end we are better off than if the shortage had never occurred. Meanwhile, population growth produces the "ultimate resource," "skilled, spirited and hopeful people," who, provided they live in an unfettered market economy, can come up with the new ideas to make the system work.[70]

The Cornucopians, who found a sympathetic ear in the Reagan White House, heavily influenced the drafting of the official U.S. Policy Statement for the 1984 U.N. International Conference on Population. In a major reversal of policy, the document described population growth as a "neutral phenomenon," which has become a problem only because of too much "governmental control of economies" and an "outbreak of anti-intellectualism, which attacked science, technology and the very concept of material progress" in the West.[71]

There are a number of obvious flaws with the Cornucopian approach. The unbridled faith in science, technology, and human inventiveness translates into a lack of concern for the very real constraints on the environment we face at the end of the twentieth century and begs the question of appropriate versus inappropriate technologies. Arguably, what is needed is more government environmental regulation, not less. Nor will higher rates of population growth necessarily yield more geniuses if the majority of the world's people remain trapped in poverty. Even the best of brains need food for sustenance and education for development. And the savage pursuit of "free market" economics has hardly ushered in a new dawn of development—on the contrary, in the "lost decade" of the 1980s and these less than hopeful first years of the 1990s, more and more people are becoming marginalized. In the end, the Cornucopians dodge the real issues of power and inequality just as the Malthusians do.

The Cornucopians performed a great service, however, by opening up the population debate. After more than two decades of hegemony, the Malthusian orthodoxy was forced to go on the defensive and cede some ground in order to save the church.

The relaxation of the Malthusian position was reflected in a 1986 U.S. National Academy of Sciences report, which retreated substantially from past alarmist assessments of population growth. While concluding that population growth was more likely to impede progress than promote it, the report found that it was not the unmitigated environmental and economic evil it had been portrayed to be. According to the report, there is no "necessary relation" between population growth and resource exhaustion, and the effect of population growth on the economy is mixed. Even when population growth has a negative impact, slower growth alone will not guarantee progress.[72] The report helped to establish a "middle ground" in the population debate, a middle ground, one might note, already occupied by many demographers and economists who have consistently held a more reasoned view of the issue.

Today, however, that middle ground is shrinking as Malthusians in mainstream development, environment, and national security circles go on the offensive once again. As a political consensus builds for population control, critics are branded as either right-wing Cornucopians or agents of the Vatican (see Chapter 8). The result is a serious stifling of independent research and democratic debate, and the continued distortion of social policy.

WRONGS AND RIGHTS

Because it makes the wrong diagnosis of the population problem, Malthusianism does not prescribe the right cure, and often makes the problem worse. This occurs on several different levels.

In terms of social policy, Malthusianism diverts attention and resources away from addressing the real causes of poverty, and hence of high birth rates. It provides a smoke screen behind which Third World governments and Western aid agencies can hide their failure to challenge the unequal distribution of wealth and power, which prevents broad-based economic development. Population control is substituted for social justice, and much needed reforms—such as land redistribution, employment creation, the provision of mass education and health care, and the emancipation of women—are conveniently ignored.

On the level of culture, Malthusianism reinforces Western ethnocentrism. "Our" nuclear family is supposed to be right for "them" too, even though the circumstances of a U.S. suburb and a Third World village are very different indeed. Modern Western culture also tends to isolate children from adult activities, viewing them as a social as well as an economic burden. By contrast, many Third World cultures are more appreciative of children, a fact that Malthusians find hard to grasp. Today, many Third World elites are embracing Malthusianism with as much, or even more, zeal than their Western counterparts. This not only reflects the penetration of Western values, but the great social barriers of class, caste, and gender in many countries, which are often stronger than bonds of nationality. In the most extreme cases, Malthusianism is wielded as a weapon of cultural genocide, through, for example, the forced sterilization of Native American women in the United States and ethnic minorities in South Asia (see Chapter 13).

On the individual level, Malthusianism has intimately and negatively affected the experience of millions of women with birth control. Married to population control, family planning has been divorced from the concern for women's health and well-being that inspired the first feminist crusaders for birth control. The goal of many Third World health and family planning programs is simply to achieve or exceed specified "contraceptive acceptance" targets; counseling, follow-up, the provision of a range of contraceptive options, and information on risks and benefits are secondary concerns, if they are concerns at all. This is not the fault of individual health and family planning workers—they are themselves caught in a system where sensitivity in meeting women's needs goes unrecorded, and merit is judged by how well they achieve population control targets. The approach typically backfires: Suffering from unexplained and untreated contraceptive side effects and disillusioned with the quality of service, a high percentage of women drop out of family planning programs. This is another way Malthusianism contributes to the persistence of high birth rates.

In the field of contraceptive technology, Malthusianism has put a madness into the methods. The goal of pregnancy prevention has taken precedence over safety in contraceptive research, leading to a lopsided emphasis on the "more effective," or high-tech, methods, such as the pill, the injectable Depo-Provera, the IUD, and now Norplant and the contraceptive vaccine. Whatever their virtues in preventing pregnancy, these methods entail substantial health risks, risks which are compounded by the lack of screening and follow-up in many clinical trials and population programs.

Meanwhile, safer methods such as the condom and diaphragm have been grossly neglected, both in terms of the allocation of research funds for their improvement and their promotion and distribution in population programs. In a number of ways, these barrier technologies are highly appropriate to Third World conditions—they help prevent the spread of sexually transmitted diseases, have no adverse impact on breastfeeding, and are very suitable for birth spacing, even if they are not 100 percent effective in preventing pregnancy. Yet population agencies do not consider them effective enough, because they are under the user's control. The thrust of contraceptive research in fact has been to remove control of contraception from women, in the same way that women are being increasingly alienated from the birth process itself (see Part Three).

The targeting of women has also led to a neglect of male contraceptive methods.

On the ethical plain, Malthusianism diminishes human rights. In order to ensure the rights of future generations to environmental and economic resources, the Malthusians believe it is acceptable to abrogate the reproductive rights of the present one. Where they differ is over means. The more liberal favor friendly persuasion in family planning programs; the more conservative openly support coercion.

The Malthusians are fundamentally wrong. The solution to the population problem lies not in the diminution of rights, but in their *expansion*. This is because the population problem is not really about a surplus of human numbers, but a lack of basic rights. Too many people have too little access to resources. Too many women have too little control over their own reproduction. Rapid population growth is not the cause of underdevelopment; it is a symptom of the slow pace of social reform.

Two basic sets of rights are at issue. First is the right of everyone on the earth today, not just in the future, to enjoy a decent standard of living through access to food, shelter, health care, education, employment, and social security. Despite present rates of population growth, most—if not all—societies have the means to guarantee this right to all their people, if wealth and power were shared more equitably, economic growth were harnessed for the greater public good, and resources were shared more fairly between the North and the South.

Once people's physical survival is ensured and children are no longer their only source of security, history shows that population growth rates fall voluntarily. Higher living standards across the board were the motor force behind the demographic transition in the industrialized world. Similarly, those Third World countries, whether capitalist, socialist, or mixed economy, which have made broad-based development a priority have also experienced significant reductions in population growth, often at relatively low levels of per capita income. These include Cuba, Sri Lanka, Korea, and Taiwan (see Chapter 15). Meanwhile, a country like India, where the benefits of substantial economic growth have flowed disproportionately to a small elite, still has high rates of population growth despite the massive amount of resources the government has devoted to population control.

The right to a decent standard of living is necessary but not sufficient. The other critical right is the fundamental right of women to control their own reproduction. This is not just a question of having access to quality family planning and health services. The question of reproductive rights ultimately goes far beyond the bounds of these programs, involving women's role in the family and in society at large. Control over reproduction is predicated on women having greater control over their economic and social lives, sharing power equally with men, and being free of poverty and violence. It requires that their children too have a much better chance of survival.

While reducing poverty reduces birth rates, so does reducing patriarchy. The sheer physical burden of many pregnancies in close succession means that women who are free to control their reproduction seldom opt for having all the children it is biologically possible for them to have. And when women have access to education and meaningful employment, they tend to want fewer children for the obvious reason that they have other options.

To say that guaranteeing these two basic sets of rights will help to reduce population growth is not to say that these rights should be pursued for this purpose. On the contrary, once social reforms, women's projects, and family planning programs are organized for the explicit goal of reducing population growth, they are subverted and ultimately fail. The individual no longer matters in the grand Malthusian scheme of things, which is by its very nature hostile to social change. Instead, these basic rights are worthy of pursuit in and of themselves; they have far more relevance to the general improvement of human welfare than reducing population growth alone ever will.

There are of course no simple prescriptions for ensuring these rights. Social change is a complex process, involving subtle cultural transformations as well as not-so-subtle political shifts and power struggles between countries, classes, and sexes. One thing is clear, however: Malthusianism stands in the way of progress. For how one poses the population problem profoundly affects how one supports—or chooses not to support—the concrete attempts of Third World peoples to improve their lives and the efforts of women around the world to exercise meaningful control over their reproduction.

3

A WOMB OF
ONE'S OWN

There isn't much understanding in some marriages. My sister has six, and another one has eight. And I said to one of them that she shouldn't have any more. And she said, "What can I do? When my husband comes home drunk, he forces me to sleep with him." And that is what happens to a lot of women. And if the women don't do it, the men hit them, or treat them badly. Or the men get jealous and think their wives must be with other men. And the women have to do whatever they say. I think it is changing a little, because the young women are more aware.

—RENÉ, *a twenty-nine-year-old Peruvian woman,*
unmarried mother of one son[1]

It took place in the room of a gentleman whose name I did not know...it was fairly dark and the only light for the operation was an electric torch. Only the desire to get rid of the child I was carrying gave me the courage to stay. It was unthinkable that I should be expelled from college, and I couldn't bear my parents to find out that I was pregnant.

He began the operation. I felt a sharp and intense pain, worse than I had ever felt before. I wanted to cry out and scream. I felt as though part of my flesh was being ripped out by his metal instruments.... Gradually the pain lessened. I lay stretched out on the wooden table, almost unconscious, but only for a few moments. Then the man wrote a prescription and gave it to me, and showed me out....

This operation traumatized me and made me think that I might not be able to have children.... So when I did become pregnant, I felt so happy and liberated, as though I was being reborn....

Several years after we were married, my husband and I discussed my abortions. It turned out that my husband had known of the existence of contraceptives, but hadn't wanted to talk to me about it because he thought I was too young, and because he thought it could have gone to my head and led me to go off with someone else.

—ALIMA, *a thirty-year-old Senegalese woman who works as a secretary with a private firm in Dakar*

I am Indrani from Sri Lanka. I was living and working in the tea estate area.... The only birth control method we know is sterilization....

All medical and social welfare staff, including foreign aid people, are forcing us to be sterilized.... The tea plantation community is given 500 rupees for a female sterilization, and in the rest of the country half of this amount is given. When there is a serious illness, the factory management are supposed to provide transport to the hospital. But even if someone is unconscious, they are not given transport. But when a woman decides to say yes for a sterilization, immediately the lorry is ready to go to the hospital.

During or soon after childbirth, women are asked if they want sterilization. When a woman does not agree, she can be refused work in the fields and she may be refused Thriposha [a protein-enriched flour, provided free by CARE]. During the work in the fields, the supervisors are also encouraging women to be sterilized. If you do not agree to a sterilization after your second child, you are not admitted to hospital for your next delivery.

After sterilization, women feel very weak, and after years many still have complaints. Some women did not know that the operation is permanent and stops fertility forever.

—INDRANI, *a member of the Tamil minority in Sri Lanka, who is now living as a refugee in India*

On 1st March 1982, Mrs. K. gave birth by caesarian section to a second daughter. In the days following delivery, a young woman doctor put a great deal of pressure on Mrs. K. and her husband to sign forms of consent for what it appears were injections for rubella vaccination and Depo-Provera contraceptive cover. It seems no attempt was made to explain why the injections might be beneficial or the future effects or side effects of Depo-Provera. They were repeatedly told that the injections were a "good thing" and, as Mr. K. put it, "push push, pushed" to have them. Mrs. K. was in fact readmitted to the Accident and Emergency ward twice and once for a longer stay to the hospital with massive bleeding in the two months that followed the birth. The Ks seemed to think that this had something to do with these injections.

Although the Ks are native Bengali speakers, Mr. K. speaks reasonable English and understands more. I certainly found it perfectly possible to explain to him that Depo-Provera is a contraceptive—a fact which came as an obvious surprise to him.

—Letter dated July 1982, from Bloomsbury Community
Health Council, Great Britain

Although René, Alima, Indrani, and "Mrs. K." come from different societies and different walks of life, their experiences reflect a common plight: lack of control over their own reproduction. Today what should be a woman's birthright—the right to decide if and when to have a child and to have access to safe, voluntary birth control and abortion—is denied millions of women around the world. Pitted against them are a number of obstacles: economic discrimination, subordination within the family, religious and cultural restrictions, the nature of health care systems, and the distortion of family planning programs to serve the end of population control.

WOMEN IN UNDERDEVELOPMENT

In many Third World countries the economic subordination of women is directly linked to high birth rates, since it both increases their need for children and impedes their ability to practice birth control. It is the result of a long history of exploitation which in many cases was intensified by colonialism.

In much of Africa, for example, although women played an important role in food production, male-dominated colonial bureaucracies geared credit and extension services for cash crops exclusively to men, and overturned communal land tenure systems, vesting private ownership in the male "head of household." While men entered the cash economy not only as farmers, but as migrant laborers in the mines, plantation fields, and industries of the colonialists, women remained in subsistence agriculture. When the men migrated, the women had to take over the men's share of domestic tasks, leading to overwork and the subsequent decline in food crop production. This pattern repeated itself in trade. Although in a number of countries women dominated or actively participated in traditional marketing, under colonialism trade became the province of men.[2]

At the same time the processes of migration and urbanization encouraged by colonialism disrupted traditional patterns of life, including social mechanisms to space births. In many areas of sub-Saharan Africa, for example, an interval of up to four years between births was achieved through a taboo on intercourse during lactation, reinforced by the practice of polygamy. "Long before the influx of Western ideas, the understanding of the importance of child spacing to maternal and infant health was widespread in these cultures," concludes a study of traditional birth control methods in Zaire.[3] Meanwhile, the "Western ideas" of the colonialists were strongly pronatalist, encouraging many births and discouraging birth control. Contraception and abortion were generally proscribed by law, and missionaries actively campaigned against abstinence and polygamy.[4]

Although women played a key role in many nationalist movements, political independence all too often brought little in the way of concrete improvements in their position. The new native male elites continued to follow many of the same policies as their colonial predecessors.

Today women's work is still consistently undervalued, not only in terms of financial reward, but social recognition as well. In most countries the nonmonetary yet productive activities of women are rarely included in labor force statistics or measurements of the GNP. Yet researchers now estimate that women produce almost half the food crops grown in the world. In Africa women contribute two thirds of all hours spent in traditional agriculture and three fifths of the time spent in marketing. In Asia, they constitute over half the agricultural labor force, in Latin America at least 40 percent.[5] In many Third World agricultural societies, women not only labor in the field, but are responsible for the arduous post-harvest processing of crops, the provision of water and cooking fuel, the care of small livestock, cooking, and looking after the children, to name a few of their responsibilities. Many women are in fact desperately overworked and need many children just to relieve their workload. This is especially true in sub-Saharan Africa, where women and children perform nearly all the agricultural labor.[6]

Rather than relieve a woman's workload or reward her adequately for her labors, modernization of agriculture along Western lines has usually worsened her predicament. Commercial farming still remains a male enclave in most parts of the Third World (though women are an important source of cheap labor for plantations), and it is men who receive access to credit, technology, and extension services. The few outside resources that trickle into subsistence food production generally end up in the hands of men, even if it is women's hands that are doing most of the work. With the exception of a few countries such as Thailand and the Philippines, agricultural training and extension work are limited to men.[7]

The increasing mechanization of agriculture has also worked to the detriment of women. Although technology has the potential of eliminating the importance of differences in physical strength between men and women, it has seldom been used to female advantage. Instead, because of their greater command over resources, men (and usually rich men) inevitably take control of new technologies. When women's traditional tasks of palm oil pressing in Nigeria and rice husking in Indonesia and Bangladesh have been mechanized, for example, it is men who own and work the machines, cutting women out from yet another economic process.[8]

In increasing numbers women are now entering the wage labor force. The United Nations estimates that over half of all women in developing countries participate in the labor force,[9] yet they experience discrimination here as well. Women tend to be concentrated in the "informal sector," working for low wages as servants or street vendors, with virtually no job security, or in the service sector, where they are also typically underpaid. In industry women are channeled into unskilled, labor-intensive jobs, and in the professions into the traditionally female ghettos of nursing, clerical work, retail sales, and teaching, which are low-pay, low-status occupations.

In the formal labor force, women are generally paid less for equal work, often on the basis that they are simply supplementing their husbands' income. In reality, however, a large percentage of families are headed by single women, and many young women work before they marry.

A job in either the formal or informal labor force seldom relieves a woman of her domestic duties, so that she effectively has to manage two jobs at once.[10] Of course, there are middle- and upper-class women, with high-paying professional jobs and low-paid servants, whose lifestyles approach or surpass those of their counterparts in the West. These privileged few are the exception, however, not the rule.

Today, as multinational corporations expand their control over the world economy, Third World women, especially in Southeast Asia and Latin America, are joining the "global assembly line" in growing numbers. Many are employed by electronic, textile, and food-processing industries in labor-intensive, low-skilled jobs, with little or no security or benefits, dangerous working conditions, and repressive labor policies. A typical practice is firing women once they marry and have children or suffer job-related infirmities, so the company will not have to pay benefits.[11] In Mexico, along the border with the United States, there are now over 1,000 export-processing plants (*maquiladoras*), which employ 10 percent of the Mexican labor force. Seventy percent of the workers are women, whose median age is between eighteen and twenty-five years. The maquiladoras are infamous for their poor working conditions.[12]

The marginalization of the peasant woman, the exploitation of the female urban worker—these are two sides of the same coin of modernization. Women's economic subordination, meanwhile, is reinforced by deeply ingrained patriarchal cultural and religious attitudes. The world's great religions all have the insidious practice of placing the ideal woman on a pedestal while knocking the real woman down. Together these forces limit women's power within the household, as well as in the fields and on the job.

SURVIVING PATRIARCHY

Today a new generation of feminist research has articulated what many women have known for centuries: The harmonious household is largely a myth. In situations where men command resources and make decisions, many women battle to survive, emotionally, physically, or both.[13]

Women whose lives are bound by the subsistence household, for example, often come to depend on men—who derive authority from working away from home, bringing in cash, and developing broader social and political connections—to mediate with the world outside. This dependence not only undermines a woman's ability to make independent decisions, but in poor families can have a direct bearing on her physical condition. Unable to exert much control over limited family resources, women are often the last to eat and the last to receive medical attention when they are sick.[14]

Despite the many deprivations they face, poor women often have more power within the family than more prosperous women because their labor power is recognized as vital to family survival. According to Indian political scientist Dr. Vina Mazumdar:

> Upward economic mobility, instead of solving the problem of the oppression of poverty, begins the oppression of prosperity, and the entry of some form of social seclusion, withdrawal from public economic activity, and relative loss of individual freedom and status within the family.[15]

Physical violence often serves to reinforce women's subordinate position within the family. Wife-beating is unfortunately common all over the world, among all classes. In Mexico, where the phenomenon of *machismo* is particularly strong, an estimated 80 percent of women who live with men suffer from direct physical violence.[16] According to FBI statistics, in the U.S. every fifteen seconds a woman is beaten by her husband or boyfriend; every six minutes a woman is raped.[17] In recent years, national and international campaigns to pressure the United Nations and other agencies to recognize women's rights as basic human rights have drawn increased attention to the extent of violence against women.

Deprivation, seclusion, violence—all these serve to keep women "in their place." And part of being in that place can be having children. For with no other option but the home or at best a low-paying job, many women turn to children as their primary source of power. In many cultures the birth of a first child, especially a son, brings a woman an automatic status that other domestic roles such as cooking and cleaning do not. A child pleases a woman's husband and her in-laws, the people who control her life. *In such situations children are a woman's constituency within the narrow political world of the family*; the more she has, the stronger her clout. If she is infertile, her status plummets, and she often falls victim to polygamy, desertion, or divorce.

Children are often the main sources of a woman's pride and self-respect. "Social systems whose positive images of women are all linked to the reproductive role leave women with only one way to achieve a sense of purpose and accomplishment," concludes Kathleen Newland in her comprehensive study of women.[18] Children may also be a woman's only hedge against an uncertain future. Faced with the very real possibility of widowhood, divorce, or abandonment, many women need children, especially sons, both for old-age support and to protect their rights to land and other property. In Kenya, for example, where roughly a quarter of rural households are headed by women, women do not generally inherit land but instead are given the right to use land owned by male family members, including sons.[19] Children are a husbandless woman's lifeline; without children, her prospect is often utter destitution.

When a team of demographers studied a Bangladesh village, they found that under the pressures of deepening poverty, male bonds of obligation to women were weakening, increasing women's vulnerability. At the same time, outside employment opportunities for women were severely limited, so that there was little chance of earning an independent livelihood. Widows were particularly at risk. The study cites the case of a once prosperous village woman reduced to beggary upon her husband's death. The study concludes:

> The risk and insecurity that patriarchy imposes on women represent a powerful systemic incentive for high fertility.... The best risk insurance for women...is to produce sons, as many and as soon as possible.[20]

Today in many areas of the Third World, the traditional family is breaking down, and there are a growing number of female-headed households. Although many of these women work outside the home, it is usually in low-paying occupations. Their short-term independence then counts for precious little in the way of long-term security. Many women must still rely on children as their basic form of risk insurance.

If women's powerlessness can increase their need for children, then steps toward their empowerment could presumably have the opposite effect. This appears to be true in the case of literacy. The educational level of women is the single most consistent predictor of fertility and contraceptive use, even more important than income level. Female literacy is also associated with lower rates of infant mortality.[21]

Not only do educated women generally marry later and have access to better jobs, which compete with motherhood, they also tend to have a broader world view. As a study of fertility in India explains:

> An educated woman is usually less closely confined, physically and psychologically, with her husband's family and its narrow familial concerns than is the woman who is brought into their home as an uneducated girl.... She is more likely to feel that she can do something about the conditions of her life, including the conditions of pregnancies in close succession or conceiving during her later reproductive years.[22]

Although female literacy rates have been rising, they still fall considerably short of men's. In 1990 in the developing world as a whole, the female adult literacy rate was 55 percent, as opposed to 75 percent for men. In the least developed countries the female rate was only 33 percent, compared to 56 percent for men.[23] The male-female gap continues in higher education. The quality of education girls receive also tends to be inferior to that of boys, with girls typically channeled away from math and sciences toward subjects such as home economics and literature.

Women's employment in the skilled labor force is also linked to fertility decline, not only because of competition with motherhood, but because the availability of such jobs serves as an incentive to families to educate girls.[24]

Although poverty and patriarchy serve as inducements to high fertility, it does not necessarily follow that women want to bear as many children as is biologically possible—eight, ten, even more. Many women would like to practice birth control, to space their pregnancies, or to end them altogether once their need for children is met. What then is standing in their way?

BARRIERS TO REPRODUCTIVE CONTROL

Population agencies have long been in the business of trying to measure precisely women's "unmet need" for contraception. At the beginning of the 1980s, the World Fertility Survey, conducted in twenty-seven developing countries, found that almost half the married women questioned wanted no more children, and that younger women especially tended to desire a smaller family size. In general, the number of women who wanted no more children exceeded the number of those using contraception, and this was interpreted as indicating a large unmet need for birth control.[25] More recently Stephen Sinding of the Rockefeller Foundation has claimed that "if all unmet need were satisfied tomorrow, the average number of children born in the developing world would drop from just under 4 to around 3."[26]

Although there are many problems with such statements and the way unmet need is both measured and defined (see Chapter 4), it is nevertheless true that many women who want contraception lack access to decent services. The large number of induced abortions that occur worldwide every year—40 to 50 million—underlines the desire of women to control births. Up to one quarter of all recognized pregnancies end in induced abortion.[27]

Why women want to space or limit births is not difficult to fathom. The physical hardship of repeated pregnancies, closely spaced, can exact a terrible toll on a woman's health, especially if she is undernourished. In developing countries an estimated 20 to 45 percent of women of child-bearing age do not consume the World Health Organization's (WHO) recommended 2,250 calories a day, much less the 285 extra they require if they are pregnant. Nearly two thirds of pregnant women suffer from anemia.[28]

Childbirth literally kills hundreds of thousands of poor women every year. Maternal mortality rates in excess of 500 per 100,000 live births are not uncommon in many Third World countries, compared to an average of 26 in the industrialized world.

Put another way, the complications of pregnancy account for between 10 and 30 percent of *all* deaths of women of reproductive age in areas of Asia, Africa, and Latin America, but less than 2 percent in the United States and Europe.[29] The risk is greater for women under twenty or over thirty-four, and for women who have borne three or more children and suffer from the nutritional maternal depletion syndrome.[30] Many women do not have access even to rudimentary medical care during childbirth, much less sophisticated emergency equipment, so that even minor problems can lead to death.

Unsafe, illegal abortion is another major cause of maternal death. An estimated 25 to 45 percent of the abortions performed each year are illegal. The medical complications of improperly performed illegal abortions are now reaching epidemic proportions in many parts of the Third World, and represent a leading cause of death among women of childbearing age. From one to two hundred thousand women die each year in developing countries due to unsafe abortion.[31]

In Latin America, where abortion is outlawed in most countries because of opposition from the Catholic Church, one fifth to one half of all maternal deaths are due to illegal abortion, and scarce hospital beds are filled with victims. In Bolivia, complications from illegal abortions account for over 60 percent of the country's obstetrical and gynecological expenses.[32]

Seeking to limit their pregnancies, women, then, are also risking their lives.

Even in countries with liberal abortion laws, poor women often resort to illegal abortions because they lack access to legal abortion facilities or cannot afford to pay for the legal operation. In 1978, six years after the enactment of India's relatively liberal abortion law, for example, there were only 1 million legal abortions in the country compared to an estimated 5 million illegal ones.[33]

Recourse to dangerous illegal abortion not only underlines the need for widespread, cheap, legal abortion facilities, but the need for access to safe contraceptive alternatives. The problem is not simply supply—in many Third World countries the per capita availability of contraceptives is quite high—but more fundamental social barriers blocking women from birth control.

Male dominance is one of the strongest obstacles. In many cultures wives must have their husband's consent before they can decide to limit their fertility. And many men are reluctant to agree: They fear the possibility of their wife's infidelity or the loss of their control over her. As a doctor in a rural Mexican clinic explained,

> When a wife wants to do something on her own, such as trying to limit the number of mouths to feed in the family, the husband will become angry and even beat her. He thinks it is unacceptable that she is making a decision on her own. She is challenging his authority, his power over her—and thus the very nature of his virility.[34]

Not surprisingly, in households where men and women share power more equally, acceptance of family planning is much higher.[35] Including men in discussions with family planning workers also seems to make a difference. But more often than not, family planning programs are geared exclusively toward women, ignoring the basic reality of male dominance or male responsibility for birth control.

The absence of basic health care in many poor communities also limits access to quality family planning. In many countries the scant resources devoted to health are usually concentrated in urban areas, on modern hospitals and technologies which serve a small elite.[36] When population agencies make contraceptives available in poor rural areas, the lack of health infrastructure often undermines their safe and ethical delivery (see Chapters 4 and 5).

Many Third World health systems prefer modern Western-style medicine, undervaluing traditional forms. For family planning, this means that birth control methods in use for generations, whether they be herbal pessaries, withdrawal, abstinence, or prolonged breast-feeding, are passed over in favor of modern contraceptives, which are often less culturally acceptable and more disruptive of traditional practices. A Nigerian doctor warns of the implications for Africa: "The impact of a carelessly designed family planning program that may interfere with local beliefs and constraints can only serve to increase fertility levels."[37]

In order for women to feel confident about contraception and to use it effectively, they need to understand how the reproductive system works. Basic health education, however, is seldom emphasized in most health care systems or family planning programs. Even in an industrialized country like the United States, sex education is a source of endless controversy, for keeping women in the dark about their bodies is another powerful way of keeping them "in their place." In many countries, adolescents in particular are discriminated against—adults may have the right to information and birth control, but not teenagers. Unmarried women too are often refused services.

In many countries organized religion also presents a barrier to women's use of contraception. This is most obvious in the case of the Catholic Church's condemnation of all "artificial" forms of birth control. In the Church's view using contraceptives or having an abortion is a sin.

In the case of Islam, according to Egyptian feminist Nawal El Saadawi, nothing in the *Koran* either explicitly supports or opposes contraception. Thus among Islamic religious authorities, some "maintain that Islam approves of family planning and even abortion; yet others hold firmly to the position that Islam not only opposes abortion, but even the utilization of contraception." In the Arab world, she maintains, it is not religion per se that is the issue, but the way religion is used "by those who rule to keep down those who are ruled."[38]

Some governments have also followed pronatalist policies in the belief that an expanding population is vital to national development, prestige, and security. To facilitate economic growth (and, some speculate, to increase the proportion of the Malay ethnic group in the population), the Malaysian government announced in the mid-1980s that it wanted to achieve a fivefold increase in the population over the next 115 years. The Prime Minister told families to "go for five" children.[39]

In Latin America the Catholic Church has prevented many governments from establishing national family planning programs. In Peru, for example, the Church helped to block the implementation of the government's 1977 Population Policy, which called for voluntary family planning services.[40] In the past left-wing movements in Latin America also tended to oppose family planning, failing to distinguish between population control interventions from abroad and women's real need for birth control. However, this opposition has faded under the influence of feminism.

Unfortunately, many governments that have implemented national family planning programs have done so not for reasons of women's health or reproductive freedom, but because of pressure from international donors to control population growth. Ironically, population control itself often blocks women's access to safe birth control. It also leads to situations where the fundamental right to have children is under attack.

It would be mistaken to view this lack of reproductive control as simply a Third World women's problem. In industrialized countries too economic powerlessness and low status combine to place restrictions on women's reproductive choices. In fact, the basic pattern of sex discrimination shares much in common with the Third World. Women in Western countries are paid only one half to three quarters of what men earn at the same jobs; in the formal labor force their traditional occupations—clerical work, teaching, nursing, and unskilled factory jobs—are scandalously low-paid, and their domestic work is undervalued and unrewarded, even though it is estimated to contribute as much as one fifth to one third of the GNP.[41]

Many women in the West also face difficulties gaining access to legal abortion and safe birth control. In several European countries, including Belgium and Ireland, abortions are still illegal, and even in countries with more liberal laws, such as Great Britain and the United States, many women cannot afford them or obtain them easily. In Ireland, until the mid-1980s even selling condoms on a nonprescription basis was illegal![42] Relatively liberal abortion laws in former Eastern bloc countries—notably Poland and East Germany—have now become far more restrictive.

In the United States, the absence of a national health system that serves everyone, regardless of ability to pay, means that family planning services which provide a wide range of contraceptive choices are something that only the well-off can afford. As political scientist and reproductive rights activist Rosalind Petchesky explains:

> The careful and sensitive counseling that would be necessary for poor and uneducated women to use nonpermanent birth control successfully is reserved for private offices and clinics that cater mainly to middle-class women; in truth, there is little such care in the hurried, overcrowded conditions of large hospital outpatient clinics, on which poor women rely.[43]

The practice of population control is also not limited to the Third World. In the United States poor black, Native American, and Hispanic women have been forcibly sterilized in federal programs; in England recent immigrants have been given Depo-Provera without their consent (see Part Three).

Before the end of the Cold War, the situation was not much better in a number of Eastern European countries and the former Soviet Union. Although female labor force participation was high in these countries, women were still locked, like their Western sisters, into low-pay, low-prestige occupations, were responsible for almost all domestic work without as many modern conveniences, and were restricted in terms of contraceptive choice. In the Soviet Union, for example, abortion was the primary means of birth control, not by choice but because other forms of contraception were virtually unavailable.[44]

These are just some of the barriers to women's reproductive control in the industrialized world. Just as in the Third World, then, the issue goes far beyond the simple question of contraception to involve power relationships at almost every social level, from the family on up to the national government. Recognizing this basic reality, many feminists today are defining reproductive rights much more broadly. Their demands include the following:

- The right to economic security through the opportunity to earn equal pay for equal work, so that women can adequately care for themselves and their families.
- The right to a safe workplace and environment for all, so that women are not exposed to hazards that threaten their ability to bear healthy children, or forced to choose between sterilization and jobs.
- The right to quality child care, so that women can enter the work force secure in the knowledge that their children will be looked after.
- The right to abortion, free and informed contraceptive choice, and other forms of reproductive health care.
- The right to sex education, so that women and men of all ages are better able to understand and control their own bodies.

- The right to decent medical care, necessary not only to ensure contraceptive safety, but a basic human right.
- The right to choose how to give birth, and to have control over the development and use of new reproductive technologies.
- The right of lesbian women and women with disabilities to be mothers.
- The participation of men as equal partners in childbearing, housework, and birth control, so women no longer have to shoulder the "double burden."
- The right to be free of all forms of violence.
- An end to discrimination so that all people—regardless of race, sex, or class—can lead productive lives, and exercise real control over their own reproduction.

Clearly, reproductive rights are predicated on achieving basic rights in almost every sphere of life. For while reproduction may be an intensely personal experience, it is also a fundamentally social one, at the center of a web of human relations. It is important never to lose sight of the whole while focusing on the center. Indeed, it is the failure to see the whole that lies behind the narrow conception and single-minded pursuit of population control.

4

THE PLAN BEHIND
FAMILY PLANNING

Women the world over want family planning.

This statement is probably not much of an exaggeration. The difficulty comes when trying to define precisely what family planning means. In the Third World context many people believe family planning and population control programs are one and the same. So if you oppose population control, they automatically assume you are against any form of family planning.

Family planning, however, is a generic term, encompassing all types of birth control programs, in the same way that "health care" can refer to many kinds of medical treatment. Family planning programs can thus vary widely from each other, depending on whose interests they serve. A family planning program designed to improve health and to expand women's control over reproduction looks very different indeed from one whose main concern is to reduce birth rates as fast as possible.

Family planning programs of the first type aim to offer the following:

- A wide choice of male and female contraceptive methods, including safe abortion, with full information on benefits and risks, and supportive counseling on how to use them.
- Good screening and medical follow-up.

- A full range of reproductive health services, including treatment for infertility, prenatal and postnatal care, prevention of sexually transmitted diseases, and support for breast-feeding.
- Counseling on male as well as female responsibility for contraception, and sex education.
- Respect for the local culture and local health providers, and the incorporation of traditional fertility control methods practiced by the community, if they are safe.
- Freedom from pressure and coercion.

On the other hand, in trying to meet ambitious, and often unrealistic demographic objectives, population control programs impose birth control on women from above. They often limit choice of contraceptive method; fail to give adequate information and counseling; neglect screening, follow-up, and the overall health of the woman; ignore the sexual politics of reproduction; and are insensitive to local culture. In some cases, they even undermine the delivery of basic health services. The result is a tragic waste of resources.

Women the world over want family planning. This is the story of what population agencies have done to them in its name.

RHETORIC AND REALITY

Most of the major international agencies that shape Third World population policy are perched high atop Western metropolitan centers. In offices with the latest in communications equipment, a host of administrators, researchers, and consultants consider the business of "delivering" birth control to the Third World. A few peasant women's faces peek from glossy covers of promotional brochures or an occasional photograph in the lobby, but otherwise Third World women are mainly numbers in computer printouts, unidentified "targets," "clients," or "acceptors" in the technical journals adorning the office shelves. Their fate figures only in demographic calculations of "births averted" and "couple-years of protection."

A plane trip away, in the capital cities of the Third World, the offices of government family planning ministries are seldom so well appointed. There are ceiling fans and open windows rather than automated thermostats, an army of clerks instead of word processors, dusty files rather than crisp reports. But the peasants are missing there as well. The villages where family planning will or will not succeed lie just beyond the bounds of the city, but to the urban civil servant they are often an alien world. Distances are not only measured in miles.

Between the peasant "target groups" and the population experts yawns a wide social gulf, which is rarely crossed. The family planners plan, the contraceptive deliverers deliver, the acceptors accept. What could be simpler? The people on top decide what is best for the people on the bottom. Thus family planning becomes a profoundly technocratic exercise. This is no accident, but rather the direct outcome of three decades in which the philosophy of population control has won intellectual and political ascendancy.

Since the 1960s Western policymakers, especially in the United States, have embraced "overpopulation" as a primary cause of poverty and instability in the Third World. It was this concern—not concern for women's well-being—that shaped the initial pattern of family planning interventions overseas. Although these interventions have varied from country to country, they have usually involved a combination of these steps:

- Support for fledgling local family planning organizations, often staffed by Western-trained nationals with population control values, by private population agencies such as the International Planned Parenthood Federation (IPPF).
- The larger involvement of institutions such as the Ford Foundation, the Rockefeller Foundation, and the Population Council in the establishment of population research institutions, the training of top Third World personnel in the United States, and the sending of advisory missions to encourage governments to embark on population control programs.
- A flow of funds and personnel from the U.S. government's Agency for International Development (AID) as an integral part of foreign aid.
- The entry of multilateral institutions, such as the U.N. Fund for Population Activities (UNFPA) or the World Bank. In the

1980s and 1990s population programs have become an important component of World Bank structural adjustment programs, particularly in Africa. In some cases, aid has been made conditional on their acceptance.[1]

Out of these interventions has grown a whole imported science of family planning in the Third World, based on several key assumptions.

The first assumption is that there is already a large demand for modern family planning services among recipient populations and that people are prepared to use them right away, regardless of social, economic, and cultural conditions. In the early days, many foreign agencies designed and promoted programs on this basis. They developed the KAP (Knowledge, Attitude, and Practice) Survey, in which outside interviewers asked women sensitive questions about reproduction and fertility. When a woman answered yes to the questions of whether she was interested in contraception or already had enough children, she was assumed to be an immediate candidate for a family planning program.

Harvard researcher Donald Warwick provides an important critique of the KAP approach in his book *Bitter Pills*, an evaluation of family planning programs, which was commissioned and then disavowed by the UNFPA for being too critical. He points out how the surveys ignored the cultural context of fertility decisions in which women often have no authority, have never viewed themselves or their husbands as able to determine family size, or may change their minds over time.[2]

Moreover, many of the questions were slanted toward positive answers. As Mahmud Mamdani found in his classic 1972 study of a Harvard-sponsored family planning project in an Indian village, the peasants were often willing to comply with the interviewer's biases. "It is sometimes better to lie," one villager told him. "It stops you from hurting people, does you no harm, and might even help them."[3]

The continued use of KAP surveys, despite mounting criticism of their methodology, may have something to do with the fact that they were not only intended to measure demand for family planning, but to serve a political purpose. As Bernard Berelson, former head of the Population Council, stated candidly:

A survey should probably be done at the outset of any national program—partly for its evaluational...use but also for its political use, in demonstrating to the elite that the people themselves strongly support the program and in demonstrating to the society at large that family planning is generally approved.[4]

Today various estimates of the "unmet need" for contraceptives are still used to justify ever greater investment in population programs. But as critics point out, the way unmet need is defined is still problematic. It usually does not include the needs of women outside of marital unions or of adolescents, and fails to address a whole constellation of issues which surround contraception—whether people have an unmet need for abortion, safer contraceptive methods, or more comprehensive reproductive health care, for example.[5] Furthermore, by viewing contraception as a technical fix, the population control approach to fulfilling the "unmet need" can actually undermine the delivery of quality family planning services, as well as divert resources away from basic health care.

A second key assumption of family planning theory is that people can be motivated to practice family planning through information, education, and communication (IEC) campaigns—e.g., through billboards showing an affluent two-child family, messages over the radio and cinema, or lectures in schools and public meetings. Although there certainly is a role for public education on family planning matters, IEC programs are typically beset with a number of problems and biases.

Many programs are based on elitist assumptions, which are reflected in the inappropriate nature of the message itself. In Indonesia, the main motto of the family planning program is that with two children, "We are a happy and prosperous family,"[6] a common refrain in many other countries as well. But for a peasant without land or employment opportunities, limiting fertility hardly brings prosperity or happiness; the cozy image of the Westernized nuclear family belongs to an alien and unobtainable world. Moreover, although women often want to limit or space births, many want more than two children, especially in situations of high infant and child mortality.

As Mamdani points out, the fundamental premise of the IEC approach is questionable:

> The underlying assumption is that the behavior of the population, given the environment and its constraints, is not rational: it is thus susceptible to "education." If education fails, it is a question of not having used the right techniques.[7]

Hence, today, ever more sophisticated techniques are being employed. AID, through the Enter-Educate program of the Johns Hopkins Population Information Program, is buying its way into Third World media. The U.S. government pays popular national actors and singers to promote family planning and specific contraceptives, on radio, television, video, and film. The United States also finances networks of broadcasting agencies such as the Union of National Radio and Television Organizations of Africa.[8] Such funding can jeopardize the independence and editorial autonomy of local media, making them a tool not only of U.S. population policy, but other U.S. national security interests.[9]

The population control message of Enter-Educate is often quite explicit. Take the case of "A Future for Our Children," a U.S.-funded video produced in Liberia, which according to its sponsors "uses visual images from everyday life to demonstrate the effects of too many people on already overburdened social services. Scenes show unemployed young people loitering in the streets, a teacher trying to cope with a class too large for her classroom, and people living in cramped housing."[10] But nothing, of course, is mentioned about the unequal distribution of resources and power.

Enter-Educate projects often provide free advertising for brand-name contraceptives and, in the case of hormonal methods, minimize any safety risks (see Chapter 11). On a deeper level, they promote the consumer ethic itself. The implicit message is that the two-child family is the happy family because it can buy more things; the big family and, by extension, the nation, are poor because they have too many children.

The last assumption, shared by both foreign agencies and many Third World governments, is that there is a neat congruence between the goals of population control and the improvement of individual health and welfare. In practice, however, emphasis on population control profoundly affects how family planning programs are organized and implemented in the field, and means, in a number of cases, that they function *in actual contradiction* to the goal of individual welfare.

In the drive to lower birth rates, the population establishment has developed what Donald Warwick calls the "machine theory of implementation," in which family planning programs consist of mechanical delivery systems on the one hand and program clients, who are "receptacles for the services delivered," on the other.[11] Standard models have been developed and applied irrespective of different cultural contexts, with authority centralized within the national government and passed down through a rigidly defined hierarchy of officials. Success has typically been evaluated solely in terms of numbers of acceptors and of targets met, not in terms of people's satisfaction with the services delivered.

Although the goal of this machine model is above all "efficiency," in practice its top-down organization and target orientation can cause a high degree of bureaucratic bungling. In the Philippines, for example, Warwick describes how during the Marcos era the pressure on family planning workers to meet numerical quotas of acceptors led to unproductive competition between local agencies vying for funds.

A national administrator of the Family Planning Organization of the Philippines complained that the agencies engaged in "acceptor grabbing" to support their claim to be the better agency to implement family planning: "This boils down to their motivation of getting more funds.... They feel that family planning is where the money is, and this is the root of all evil."[12]

Thus mobile clinics from one Filipino religious group who distributed the pill and IUD in slum areas claimed "credit" for all their acceptors, but when some of the women subsequently suffered from adverse effects, the mobile units were nowhere to be seen. Staff members from permanent clinics in the area, run by another organization, were meanwhile reluctant to admit these patients for treatment because they could not count them as acceptors.[13]

While local agencies fought for numerical victories in the field, the centralization of authority in the capital led, in the words of one AID-sponsored evaluation, to "the development of big buildings in Manila, with large, underutilized staff, and with little trickle down of resources to the field where they can be used."[14]

By its very nature, the donor-imposed model of family planning neglects, and sometimes outright disrespects, local culture. This has meant that many family planning programs have lost the opportunity to build on existing fertility control practices such as birth spacing, breast-feeding, and herbal contraceptives, and have failed to address people's other reproductive needs, especially problems of infertility.

Many family planning programs, instead of winning over and involving trusted local healers and midwives, have alienated them. In Egypt, for example, where the traditional midwife is an important figure in rural communities, the Ministry of Health decided that midwives did not have the proper training to operate in the health system as family planning workers. As might be expected, many midwives perceived the government's family planning program as a threat to their positions and authority and worked against it.[15]

On the other hand, the involvement of local midwives, called Traditional Birth Attendants, or TBAs in official jargon, in population control programs has also been problematic. In Bangladesh, for example, they were steered away from their midwifery work into pressuring poor women to be sterilized (see Chapter 12).

The most serious drawback of the machine model of family planning is limitation of choice, whether through subtle pressure or outright coercion. The emphasis on meeting targets means that people are often pushed into accepting contraception or sterilization against their will, so that family planning workers can fulfill the quotas on which their jobs depend. "No program with targets can be completely free of coercion," write demographers John and Pat Caldwell.[16]

Target orientation can also distort the kind of education family planning workers receive, so that they have imperfect information on the relative risks and merits of different contraceptive methods and are thus ill-equipped to meet people's needs. In South Asia, the World Bank notes, "Where it exists, supervision takes the form of enforcing accountability and targets rather than supportive training and advice."[17]

While in theory most programs follow the "cafeteria" approach to family planning, in which the widest choice of contraceptive methods is made available, in practice the drive to bring down birth rates means that only the so-called more effective methods—IUDs, hormonal methods, and sterilization—are promoted. In the Philippines, for example, AID pressure led an agency to circulate this warning to its clinics: "Discourage condom acceptors and encourage more IUDs and pills. The clinic is evaluated on the method accepted by the clients. There will be no more supply of condoms: so convince your condom acceptors to shift to pills and IUDs." [18] We are now reaping the grim harvest of this bias against barrier methods with the spread of HIV/AIDS and other sexually transmitted diseases.

Today even the pill is considered too ineffective because of the potential for "user failure"—instead, injectables like Depo-Provera and the implant Norplant are favored. Such biases are reinforced by incentive systems, where both providers and acceptors are "rewarded" for particular methods.

In order to meet quotas for "effective" methods, family planning workers often consciously decide not to disclose potential adverse effects to acceptors. As one Kenyan field worker explained, "We don't tell them of the major side effects for fear of losing them." [19] In the short run, this may win higher acceptance rates, but in the long run, it can lead to disillusionment with specific contraceptives and family planning in general. Indeed, it is now commonly accepted that the greatest single obstacle to continued use of family planning services is adverse experience with methods adopted. [20]

For these reasons, the machine model of family planning has not only failed to expand reproductive choice, but in many places—notably India, Pakistan, Egypt, and Kenya—has proved inefficient even in terms of its own goal: to lower the birth rate. Nevertheless, critical evaluations have been remarkably rare.

More often than not, any problems are simply attributed to "management" difficulties. The basic assumption is that if officials could only organize things a little better, making use of new management information and training systems, then programs would function more effectively. Computerizing program data thus assumes a higher priority than instituting fundamental changes.

Even in the absence of many critical evaluations, high dropout rates from family planning programs and the persistence of high birth rates in many countries have indicated clearly enough that the family planning machine is in need of repairs. The response of the population establishment has been mixed. More liberal elements have tried to reform family planning programs through integrating them with health, community, and women's development projects, as well as setting standards for greater "quality of care" (see Chapter 8). More hard-line population control advocates, however, have stepped up the pressure on target groups through the use of incentive and disincentive schemes to induce sterilization or contraceptive use. These not only limit choice, but in many cases lead directly to coercion.

THE INCENTIVE DEBATE

Within the population community incentives are a source of much controversy. This is reflected in differences in official policy among population agencies. In principle, the UNFPA and a number of private agencies such as the Pathfinder Fund and the IPPF are against incentives, although in practice they often cooperate with governments who use them. The World Bank, on the other hand, openly supports and finances incentive schemes. Its former senior population adviser, Dr. K. Kanagaratnam, maintained that "Incentives and disincentives are the stock in trade of the business—they help to create a national norm, a milieu."[21] AID also joined the incentive supporters' camp, although it has disguised incentives as "compensation payments" (see Chapter 12).

Supporters of incentives argue that they are a neutral tool of social engineering, designed as "inducements to change behavior." According to this view, the use of incentives in family planning programs helps to spread information about contraceptive techniques, acts as a trigger-mechanism to start people using contraception who are already interested in limiting births, and encourages those not yet interested to accept family planning through financial benefits that alter their "taste" for children. Ostensibly, incentives are voluntary, since people can either choose to accept them or refuse them if they want.[22]

Such views display a fundamental ignorance of the social context in which incentives are introduced. "What is remarkable is that none of them makes room for a more down-to-earth explanation of the effectiveness of incentives in a culture of poverty," writes Marika Vicziany in her classic study of the Indian family planning program, "namely, that the main reason a material incentive works is that it provides an immediate economic gain."[23] For people who are desperately poor, there is no such thing as free choice. A starving person is much less likely to make an informed decision about sterilization if he or she is offered cash and food as a reward. Thus, in practice incentives often have more to do with coercion than with choice.

Even those advocates of incentives who recognize the role of poverty manage to get around it by means of contorted logic. According to a World Bank working paper on "Ethical Approaches to Family Planning in Africa," incentives and disincentives "may have a place in family planning programs, but they should never have discriminatory or coercive effects." But the authors also state that "By their nature, incentives and disincentives are aimed primarily at the poor, since it is mainly the poor who will be susceptible to them." If this is not discrimination, what is?[24]

The most common form of incentives is one-time payment to acceptors and/or providers of sterilization, and occasionally of other contraceptives, especially the IUD. These not only bias contraceptive choices toward specific techniques but all too often trade on the desperation of the poor and lead to profiteering on the part of family planning personnel.

When motivators—people from the community who recruit acceptors—are also paid a fee, this can lead to additional abuses, as local bosses use the opportunity to exert pressure and turn a fast profit. A study of mass vasectomy camps in India's Gujarat State found, for example, that the "most influential" motivators were members of the local revenue department and the police.[25] In Pakistan, when incentives for doctors, motivators, and acceptors were introduced for IUD insertion, an "IUD factory" ensued in which all three groups cooperated to have IUDs repeatedly inserted, then removed, then inserted...[26]

Dr. Zafrullah Chowdhury of the People's Health Center in Bangladesh has likened such systems to prostitution, where the "recipients 'sell' their human pride and dignity":

> The prostitute sells the body to survive, knowing that the person who has used them has no concern for the physical/emotional implications this may have for the prostitute. Similarly, the sterilization acceptor under an incentive scheme is merely a further number of the profiteer. Once the procedure is finished, so is the patient—no one cares about them post-operatively, if they have complications, if further problems arise later. They have served their usefulness.[27]

Such incentive systems also do little to change people's basic attitudes toward family planning, and in fact may make it a very negative experience, leading to a backlash.

In some parts of Thailand, family planning acceptors receive rewards, not in cash but in kind. In one program run by the private Community Based Family Planning Services (CBFPS), women were urged to "space your next pregnancy with a pig." The woman received a piglet, which she fattened for eight to nine months, during which time she agreed not to get pregnant. She then shared the profits of the grown pig with the CBFPS program. If she failed to keep her word, the pig was not taken from her, but she might lose the opportunity to get another.

Says the IPPF's *People* magazine: "There is no need for coercion in [this] program. Thai villagers do not need much 'persuasion' to observe that a neighbor with only two children and two pigs is better off economically than a neighbor with six children and no pigs."[28] But is this necessarily so? Equating prosperity with the number of children one has in relation to the number of pigs is a dubious—and demeaning—way of looking at the more complex realities of Thai rural life.

Community incentives are often deemed less controversial than individual incentives, but are these really any more respectful of basic human rights? In community incentive schemes, whole villages or groups of family planning acceptors are rewarded if they achieve a high contraceptive acceptance rate. In Indonesia, under a World Bank-financed $3 million community incentive scheme sixty villages were eligible for government grants for public works projects if 35 percent of their couples practiced contraception. AID also supports community incentives in Indonesia to "promote intercommunity competition," and Thailand has instituted programs where access to environmental improvements, income-generation funds, and health care is contingent on community family planning performance.[29]

The potential for abuses in these cases is obvious. Powerful local leaders, eager to secure the government grants, could easily pressure poorer families into "accepting" family planning, and then proceed to use the outside resources exclusively for their own benefit. Such schemes also raise the question of why villages do not have access to public works and economic improvements *in the first place*.

Some proponents of community incentives admit the possibility of misuse:

> Relying as they do on peer pressure, community incentives involve persuasion, if not coercion, of the most direct kind—from one's neighbors and community leaders. If local power structures favor an elite, the incentive program may also, possibly to the detriment of the community as a whole.[30]

But local power structures that "favor an elite" are the rule, not the exception.

Even where wealth and power are more equally shared among villagers, community incentive schemes would raise difficult ethical questions. By their very nature, they subject individuals to peer pressure in one of the most private areas of their lives, not necessarily because it is in their own best interest, but because a population control agency has decided to offer the community a substantial bribe. Proponents of such schemes might well ask themselves if they would like to be pressed by their neighbors not to have children because their block could then get a road repaved by the World Bank.

Some countries have gone even further and instituted comprehensive economic incentive and disincentive schemes run by the government (see Chapter 9). In South Korea, for example, low-income "acceptors" of sterilization receive substantial cash payments—$45 if they have more than two children, $110 if they have two, and $330 if they have only one. Only low-income people are eligible.[31]

In Singapore, Prime Minister Lee Kuan Yew's eugenicist belief that the poor remain poor and uneducated because they are genetically inferior led to the implementation of an extremely punitive incentive and disincentive scheme in which families with two or more children faced reduced access to public housing and education, loss of maternity leave, higher income taxes, etc.[32] According to Lee:

> Free education and subsidized housing lead to a situation where the less economically productive people in the community are reproducing themselves at rates higher than the rest. This will increase the total population of less productive people. Our problem is how to devise a system of disincentives, so that the irresponsible, the social delinquents, do not believe that all they have to do is to produce their children and the government then owes them and their children sufficient food, medicine, housing, education and jobs.[33]

In 1983 the Singapore program took a bizarre turn. Worried that educated women were sinking below replacement level fertility, the government introduced a selective incentive scheme, in which uneducated women continued to be penalized for having more than two children, while educated women were given incentives to have more children, including priority access to the best schools and greater tax relief. Unmarried educated women, especially those working in public service, were pressured to marry under threats of withholding job promotion.[34] Popular opposition to the scheme, particularly on the part of educated women, led to its eventual dismantlement. Now the Singapore government is encouraging women in general to have more babies because of the country's low birth rate.

Incentive and disincentive schemes can further widen the gap between rich and poor. When people need children for their immediate economic survival, they are less likely to pay serious attention to long-term disincentives, although these can punish them in the future. Meanwhile the rich, who are often already motivated to have fewer children, take advantage of the scheme, deriving economic benefit.

These schemes also have the impact of punishing children for the decisions of their parents. After all, it is the children who suffer most when they are denied a place in school or medical treatment at a government clinic just because they happen to be the third child instead of the second. In the United States today some states have implemented so-called "welfare reform" measures which deny women additional benefits if they have a child while on welfare.[35] (Contrary to the conventional view of the overbreeding poor, women on welfare have on average two children, the same as the national average.) This measure not only hurts women and children, but totally ignores the role of men in getting women pregnant and the fact that contraceptives can fail.

While critics see in such incentives and disincentives the potential for serious infringement of personal liberty, supporters argue that similar incentives already operate in many walks of life. Tax laws, for example, help to determine how people invest their money, and parking tickets are a disincentive to leaving one's car in restricted places. Without such measures for social control, it is argued, society simply could not operate.

Demographer Kingsley Davis sees nothing wrong with using compulsion to bring down birth rates: "Why does the family planning movement...,which is the predominant approach to population policy, have as its slogan, 'every woman has the right to have as many children as she wants'?" he asks. "We would not justify traffic control by saying that 'every driver has the right to drive as he pleases.'"[36]

Such an argument avoids the central question of why people need to be persuaded or forced to have fewer children in the first place. Isn't it because of the very absence of the most powerful incentive of all: the economic and social security of having fair access to the fruits of development? This is not something that can be handed out in local currency when a person is sterilized; instead it involves major social restructuring. When incentive schemes are substituted for social change, the result invariably discriminates against poor people, especially women, if it does not outright coerce them.

Even if one accepts that, broadly speaking, incentives and disincentives are justified—that there must be limitations to personal liberty for the good of the community—other questions arise: Just *who* defines what is in the pubic interest? Who designs the tax system? Who decides that population control must be a priority, instead of women's rights, land reform, health care, and education? Those who hold the reins of power, of course.

In many, if not most, countries, poor people are cut out of the political process, even if they constitute the majority. They are not the ones designing family planning incentive schemes in the capital cities of the Third World, or in AID's or the World Bank's offices in Washington. Their definition of the public interest differs fundamentally from that of the politicians, technocrats, and generals who rule *over* them, not *for* them.

This basic political fact of life is largely ignored by even the most liberal family planners, who, despite all the evidence to the contrary, persist in believing (or at least maintaining publicly) that governments always operate in their citizens' best interests and mediate between the individual right to choose and greater social goals, between the rights of those living today and those yet unborn. Thus, says the background document to the International Conference on Family Planning in the 1980s:

> When provision of contraceptive information and services does not bring down the fertility level quickly enough to help speed up development, governments may decide to limit the freedom of choice of the present generation so that future generations may have a better chance to enjoy their basic rights.[37]

But sacrificing one generation for the next is a dangerous, and dubious, road to progress. Once basic rights are abrogated, they may be lost for a long time. And forcing people to have fewer children will not "speed up" development. It will only give family planning a bad name, hurt women, and reinforce the authoritarian power structures that prevent development from occurring in the first place.

The next chapter takes a closer look at the experience of two countries, Indonesia and Kenya, where reproductive choice has been subordinated to population control objectives. There are lessons to be learned from both.

5

THE INDONESIAN "SUCCESS" AND THE KENYAN "FAILURE"

INDONESIA: SUCCESS AT WHOSE EXPENSE?

In the last two decades Indonesia, whose estimated population of over 180 million makes it the fifth most populous country in the world, has experienced a significant, though not spectacular, fertility decline. Although the figures are disputed, the crude birth rate, which was between 40 and 45 in the early 1960s, is probably now in the range of 25. Contraceptive prevalence has also increased from 2 percent of married women of reproductive age in 1972 to over 50 percent today. The total fertility rate is somewhere between 2.5 and 3, down from 5.6 in 1969.[1]

Population agencies often credit Indonesia's family planning program for this fertility decline. Indonesia, asserts a U.S. Agency for International Development (AID) document, is a "'success story' unrivaled in family planning history."[2] Demographers are more cautious, however, pointing to a number of broad social and economic changes, such as rising male and female educational levels, reductions in childhood mortality, rural to urban migration, and changing employment patterns in the countryside, as being conducive to smaller families.[3]

Whatever the precise causes of Indonesia's fertility decline, it is true that the country has a strong national family planning program, particularly on the densely populated islands of Java and Bali. The history of family planning in Indonesia dates back to the 1950s, when the Indonesian Planned Parenthood Association first introduced contraceptive services. At that time, however, Indonesia's first president, the nationalist Sukarno, was strongly pronatalist, and family planning received no government support.

Sukarno's independent foreign policy greatly antagonized Western powers, and during his regime international agencies such as the Ford Foundation focused on sending the country's intellectual elite abroad for training, in the hope that one day they would inherit power.[4] Their investment paid off in 1966, when a bloody military coup, which left a million dead, brought the country's current ruler, General Suharto, to power. Under the influence of Western-trained technocrats, Suharto embraced the philosophy of population control. Today he has become one of its most prominent spokesmen in the Third World.[5]

In 1970 Suharto set up the National Family Planning Coordinating Board (BKBBN) to oversee, financially and organizationally, the country's population control effort. During the first years of the family planning program, contraceptive services were delivered mainly through the Ministry of Health's network of rural clinics. Later the BKBBN, with foreign assistance, set up its own network of family planning field workers, who visited individual households and referred acceptors to family planning clinics. In the mid-1970s the BKBBN adopted the Village Contraceptive Distribution Center approach, which, according to the U.N. Fund for Population Activities (UNFPA) official Jay Parsons, was "based on the assumption that the monthly trek by acceptors to the family planning clinic represented an unacceptable burden on women whose motivation to use contraception was tenuous at best."[6]

Under the new approach women contraceptive users were joined together in Acceptor Clubs. The leader of the club, typically the wife of the village headman or another prominent official, acted as the intermediary between the village women and the family planning clinic, helping to ensure a steady supply of contraceptives at the local level. Today the concept of the Acceptor Clubs has been expanded, so that through them women receive access to credit, training, and some basic mother and child health (MCH) services.

What are the pros and cons of the Indonesian approach?

On the positive side, Indonesia has been successful in making certain kinds of contraception widely available. Initially, it emphasized birth spacing rather than sterilization, although this is changing for the worse. It created a contraceptive delivery system that reaches right down to the village level and depends on the participation of local communities to keep it going. Through widespread educational and publicity efforts, Indonesia has also demystified the subject of birth control, so that the vast majority of the population have heard about it and are not afraid to talk about it or use it.

There is another side to these achievements, however, which has to do with the way the Indonesian family planning program has been implemented as a tool of population control. The negative aspects of the program include severely limiting contraceptive choice, using authority and coercion, tolerating a poor quality of acceptance, and undermining health delivery.

Limitations on Contraceptive Choice. Target orientation, one of the central features of the machine model of family planning, is a key component of the Indonesian family planning program. BKBBN officials, for example, are encouraged to out-perform each other in meeting targets, as they compete for performance incentives, such as AID-financed trips and training programs. Their style of work ranges, according to AID, from "calculated, strategic planning characteristic of the military to missionary zeal and a messianic conviction that the program is predestined to succeed."[7] In its Fifth Population Project (1989-90 through 1993-94), the government set a target of reducing the country's growth rate from 2.1 to 1.9 percent, primarily through increasing contraceptive prevalence.[8] This kind of ambitious target easily leads to distortions in the provision of contraceptive services.

The Indonesian program pushes the supposedly more effective contraceptives and targets women. "All methods of contraception are available," claimed the BKBBN in 1989, "but participants are encouraged to accept the more effective ones, namely the IUD, the pill or the injection."[9] The profile of contraceptive use follows accordingly, with the pill, IUD, and injectable the main methods used in 1992.[10] Today, Norplant, the hormonal implant which is effective for five years, is the new technical fix.

In parts of Java, traditional fertility control methods, such as withdrawal and abstinence during breast-feeding, are believed to have been practiced effectively for many generations.[11] Now they are actively discriminated against. An article in *Tempo*, Indonesia's leading weekly news magazine, revealed in 1984 how in one district in East Java, villagers complained that they were being penalized for using traditional methods rather than modern contraceptives distributed by the government. One civil servant was threatened with the denial of his salary if his wife refused the IUD, even though they had practiced traditional methods successfully for four years.[12]

At the same time that the official family planning program pushes the so-called more effective methods, adequate health infrastructure does not exist for the treatment of side effects, routine checks of women with IUDs, or long-term monitoring of hormonal contraceptive users through cervical smear tests for cancer, etc.[13] A long legacy of elitism in the country's medical education system also means, according to Indonesian specialists Terence and Valerie Hull, that "Many doctors treat patients with disinterest bordering on disdain.... This is nowhere more dramatic than in the case of women's reproductive health care...where there is no assurance that health professionals will do internal examinations, take a case history, or schedule a series of follow-up visits to monitor contraceptive use or medical anomalies."[14]

In the early 1980s, as part of an intensification of population control efforts, the BKBBN launched a mass IUD insertion campaign. There was little concern for the fact that the IUD is an inappropriate form of contraception for many women, because of side effects such as heavy bleeding and the risk of infertility, or that mass insertions could easily lead to infection. The campaign included mass IUD "safaris," where thousands of women were brought together, often under pressure from local officials, to have IUDs inserted in a "picniclike" atmosphere. A key element of safari entertainment was the presence of high-level government officials, including occasional appearances of President Suharto himself.[15]

Today the drive to pressure women to use more effective methods is intensifying, with the sanction of the major international donors to Indonesia's program, the World Bank, the UNFPA, and AID. One of the main goals of the Fifth Population Project is to increase the use of permanent and longer-acting methods, notably the IUD, Norplant, and sterilization. The World Bank alone is providing half a million doses of Norplant. The Bank is obsessed with the possibility that Indonesia's family planning effort might slow down, "which could result in higher population growth rates than those targeted or desirable."[16]

The Bank and other agencies choose to ignore how targeting women with Norplant has already had undesirable results. A 1990 internal Population Council report provides chilling evidence of how Norplant has been abused in the Indonesian program. At that point nearly half a million Indonesian women had received Norplant—now the figure is closer to 1.5 million—often without counselling on side effects or other contraceptive options, pregnancy screening, or proper sterilization of equipment. Many were not even told that the implant had to be removed after five years to avoid risk of life-threatening ectopic pregnancy.

Moreover, removal on demand was not guaranteed, not only because of lack of trained personnel, but more importantly to serve the Indonesian government's demographic objectives. According to the Population Council report, "Recent government policy encourages Norplant for the duration of the full five years of effectiveness, which is communicated to the client as a form of commitment." Or as one Indonesian population official put it, "People are told it has to last five years, they give their word...and rural people don't go back on their word. If they request removal, they are reminded that they gave their word."[17]

The report found that many more people had been trained to insert Norplant than to remove it. Given the poor quality of services, it urged a "slowdown in the expansion of Norplant in new areas," especially remote ones where there is little or no health infrastructure.[18] Yet it is precisely these remote areas—Indonesia's outer islands and transmigration zones—which the government and international donors are now targeting. The UNFPA and Asian Development Bank initiated a Norplant "Outer Islands" project in

1989.[19] Once again the demographic objective outweighs any concerns for women's health and informed consent.

Use of Authority. The structure of political authority in Indonesia has profoundly influenced the organization of family planning services. When Suharto first seized the reins of power, he streamlined the bureaucracy by purging suspected leftists and dissenters, placed military officers in key civil service positions to ensure loyalty, and filled the prisons with political detainees.

Such "administrative reforms," as they are euphemistically termed in AID's case history of the Indonesian family planning program, did little for civil liberties, but did facilitate population control. According to AID: "The most ready explanation given for the success of the Indonesian family planning program is the strong hierarchical power structure, by which central commands produce compliant behavior all down the administrative line to the individual peasant."[20]

Today Suharto still brooks no political dissent. Yet many people in the population field applaud Indonesia's "political stability" and "strong political commitment" to population control, without acknowledging that such stability and commitment have been achieved at the price of a repressive military dictatorship.[21]

The extent of direct coercion in the Indonesian family planning program is a matter of some debate, though most observers agree there have been cases. In the late 1970s in East Java, for example, the military became directly involved in promoting IUD insertion during a special drive to meet high targets. A subsequent study of four villages involved in the drive reported that almost half the acceptors said they were coerced, and most admitted that they feared the government.[22]

In 1984, *Tempo* reported that in Jepara District primary schoolteachers were told that their salaries would not be paid if they could not produce certificates of participation in the official family planning program, and in Pati District village women were threatened with heavy fines for becoming pregnant.[23]

Responding to reports of coercion, Dr. Haryono Suyono, head of BKBBN, told *Tempo,* "We have to deal with 20,000 people a day so some people are bound to get trodden on in the process."[24]

In 1990 reports of coercion in the Indonesian vasectomy program hit both the national and international press. In an investigation conducted for the Australian government, Terence Hull suggests such reports were exaggerated, but nevertheless states, "It cannot be denied that some people, at least, were unhappy with the involvement of the police in the family planning program and others felt under pressure to accept a contraceptive measure which they did not want to use." Hull cites AID's role in pressuring the Indonesian government to push sterilization much more aggressively in the mid-1980s in order to meet its demographic goals. AID funding of mass sterilization services allowed the program to expand too rapidly, without due concern for informed consent or quality of services, and encouraged the development of sterilization targets.[25]

Coercion of women is still much more common, however. A case study of Kembangwangi Subdistrict in West Java reveals the role of the military in threatening villagers. (Although Indonesian soldiers are often involved in community development activities, they appear to overstep their boundaries when it comes to family planning.) In one safari in 1990 family planning workers accompanied by the police and army went from house to house and took men and women to a site where IUDs were being inserted. Women who refused had IUDs inserted at gunpoint. In another village those who said no were branded as communists; in others they were threatened with transmigration to outer islands.[26]

In a separate case study of the introduction of Norplant into Lombok, Indonesia, a family planning worker told the foreign researcher, "If the target is still high and has not yet been reached and the people are difficult to reach, the army makes them a little bit afraid so that they are willing to come together for a family planning session."[27]

In general, the Indonesian government relies far less on direct coercion in its family planning program than on more subtle forms of paternalism and social pressure. National, provincial, local, and even foreign authority figures visit safaris and attend village pageants in order to drive home the message that population control is a patriotic duty, and that women who accept family planning are appreciated by those on high. The flip side of this paternalism, of course, is that women who do *not* accept are *not* appreciated.

It is not high-level authority figures who make the crucial difference in the Indonesian program, however, but the ones in closest everyday contact with the villagers. They help create the peer pressure necessary to sustain contraceptive acceptance.

Quality of Acceptance. In his article sympathetic to the Indonesian program, Jay Parsons concludes that despite its great success in recruiting acceptors, it essentially relies on "externally imposed motivation." According to him, program managers at the subprovincial level report that although the majority of couples in their areas are practicing contraception,

> few know or understand why they are doing so except that they have been encouraged to by their village elders or that not to accept family planning is considered in some way treachery against the national good.... Should there be a break in the now externally imposed pressure exerted on couples, it is questionable whether current contraceptive use levels would continue as high as they are at present.[28]

The great *quantity* of acceptors recruited by the program has thus been achieved at the expense of the *quality* of acceptance.

The mechanisms by which people are pressured to accept family planning are intimately tied to the social structures of community life. On Bali, for example, the main form of social organization is the *banjar*, a small community of kin-related families. Every thirty-five days the *male* heads of these families meet to discuss issues of common concern. Working with the heads of the banjars, the BKBBN introduced discussions of overpopulation and family planning into these meetings. Soon each household head had to report publicly the household's family planning status, and detailed maps of the banjar were prominently displayed, where each house was color-coded according to contraceptive use.[29]

In Central and East Java the BKBBN builds on what Parsons calls the "mystical reverence" of the Javanese "common folk" toward authority figures.[30] The BKBBN has displayed great ingenuity in harnessing the support of local village headmen, teachers, religious officials, policemen, wives' associations, etc., in the population control cause. Is it reverence, or is it fear, that motivates poorer and less powerful villagers to accept the message and join the Acceptor Clubs? While the Indonesian program is commonly praised for the extent of community participation, the Hulls point out that few commentators have really analyzed to what extent club member-ship is voluntary or borders on "community exploitation" by virtue of bureaucratic pressure from above.[31]

Once women join Acceptor Clubs, however, there is a steady supply of carrots to help make up for the stick. The provision of credit, training, resources, and awards through the clubs acts as a material incentive for contraceptive acceptance. The UNFPA re-ports that in 1990 there were 12,000 such "income-generating" women's groups in Indonesia, which have contributed to "the shift to more reliable contraceptive methods, mainly the intrauterine de-vice."[32] Critics note that this approach actually reinforces women's inferior status in Indonesia, not only by focusing on their reproduc-tion but by promoting only minor economic activities largely lim-ited to the private sphere: sewing, making handicrafts, gardening, baking cakes.[33]

Youth are the latest target of such schemes. With support from UNFPA, youth clubs are being formed in which participants with "the best performance and positive attitude" will be given money by the government to start income-generating schemes, provided that they commit to late marriage and working as voluntary family planning motivators. A photograph accompanying this an-nouncement shows officers from the National Committee of Indo-nesian Youth and "Family Planning Girl Scouts" inserting Norplant in the arms of two women.[34]

Undermining Health. Defenders of the Indonesian program like to point out that even though community pressure is instru-mental in getting individuals to practice contraception in Indonesia, in the long run those individuals benefit, through the improvements family planning brings to their health and lives. And after seeing these improvements, individuals will eventually develop their own personal motivation to use contraception.[35]

Certainly, there is a role—and demand—for voluntary family planning in Indonesia, but the current population control program has undermined, not improved, health care in the country. This is not just a question of the cavalier attitude toward contraceptive side effects and safety, but of the persistent bias against primary health care in favor of family planning.

Basic health care in Indonesia has not received nearly as much attention or resources as population control. According to AID, this is because

> there is a strong consensus that progress in fertility reduction would have been far slower had family planning services been held back from the rural areas until it had somehow become possible to provide a general village-based health care package of which family planning was part.[36]

As a result, Indonesia has made slow progress on the health front. Its infant mortality rate has remained significantly higher than in neighboring Southeast Asian countries.[37]

In the early 1980s the Indonesian government recognized that the persistence of high infant mortality was acting as a constraint on family planning acceptance. It decided to "piggyback" some basic health measures on to the population program, in order, according to the BKBBN, to "strengthen the motivation of childbearing-aged couples to carry out family planning."[38] These measures included the monthly weighing of children to chart their growth, basic immunization, diarrheal disease control, nutrition education, and MCH services combined in an Integrated Family Health Package. The problem with this approach was that in terms of resource expenditure, the emphasis was still not on family *health*, but on family *planning*. In 1984 the BKBBN received 75 cents per capita just to promote family planning, while the Ministry of Health had only $1.30 per capita for the whole health system including all hospitals, clinics, drugs, doctors, nurses, etc.[39]

Today this bias persists, and it is not only the fault of the government, but also of international donors. There are almost twice as many family planning clinics in Indonesia as primary health care centers.[40] According to the World Bank, during the budget crises of the 1980s spending for family planning was not reduced while "the health sector, on the other hand, continues to face shortages of resources for basic operations and maintenance, and has not enjoyed the same degree of donor support."[41] The Bank is proud of the way it financed BKBBN's "impressive" buildings, which are better appointed than other government offices; this allowed BKBBN "to achieve status in the eyes of the public and its own staff." Only now, with a slight twinge of bureaucratic conscience, does the Bank lament that it did not try to upgrade the health system, too.[42]

While infant mortality has improved somewhat in recent years, maternal mortality is still extremely high in Indonesia, an estimated 450 deaths per 100,000 live births, and some observers put the figure higher.[43] In belated recognition of this fact, Indonesia's Fifth Population Project contains a World Bank-financed "safe motherhood" component, a key feature of which is better training for community midwives. However, the goal is not only to help midwives identify and treat women with pregnancy-related problems, but to increase the number who can deliver more effective clinical family planning methods![44] Stopping births is still a higher priority than ensuring that women give birth safely.

Today Indonesia has become *the* family planning showcase in the Third World. Courtesy of AID, UNFPA, and other international agencies, officials from countries around the world are flown there to observe the program, in the hope that they will carry the model back home. They visit villages, where they are treated to sumptuous meals and elaborate entertainment, where officials tell them about the remarkable progress they have made in reducing birth rates.[45] The key ingredients of Indonesia's "success"–lack of contraceptive choice, authoritarianism, pressure, and disregard for women's health–are thus being exported around the world.

Fortunately, there is a growing women's health movement in Indonesia which challenges this approach. "The policy, the strategy, the organization, and the overall set-up of the family planning program need to undergo a radical reorientation, from a heavy-handed, authoritarian and control-oriented program to a more democratic service-oriented program," write three Indonesian women activists.[46] Unfortunately, theirs are not the voices the foreign visitors are brought to hear.

KENYA: WHOSE FAMILY PLANNING FAILURE?

Until recently the East African nation of Kenya had one of the highest birth rates in the world. Between 1948 and 1991 Kenya's population multiplied almost fivefold to reach 25 million, with the total fertility rate reaching almost 8 million in 1979. Yet in 1967 Kenya became the first African nation south of the Sahara to launch an official population control program. What explains this apparent contradiction?

There are two key elements to understanding the Kenyan experience. First, until recently social and economic conditions have not been conducive to a significant fertility decline. Although Kenya has experienced relatively rapid rates of economic development compared to other African countries, the fruits of that development have been very unequally distributed. At the end of the 1960s, the richest 20 percent of Kenyans received 68 percent of the country's annual income, the bottom 40 percent only 10 percent. In the rural areas, where most Kenyans live, privatization and export-oriented agriculture have led to the concentration of the best land in the hands of a few rich farmers and corporations, and the marginalization of smallholders.[47]

High rates of infant mortality have persisted in the poorest areas of the country, and children are still needed as a source of labor and security in rural society. Women also have a subordinate position within the household and community. Women not only lack opportunities in the modern sector of the economy, but in agriculture they bear most of the workload, providing three quarters of the labor on small holdings.[48]

There are also strong social pressures on women to have children. As an editorial in *Viva*, a Kenyan women's magazine, explains: "Socially and culturally, we women have been made to believe that our primary role in life is to be a producer of children. We have been told again and again that only through marriage, pregnancy and motherhood can we find dignity and respect."[49] Men also have had very little economic incentive to want fewer children, since women bear most of the responsibility for child support.

Despite conditions favoring high fertility, in Kenya, as in most countries, there has been an "unmet need" for contraception, a need the official family planning program largely failed to fulfill.[50] The way the program was conceived and organized is the second element of the Kenyan failure.

In the early 1960s expatriate advisors in the Kenyan Ministry of Economic Planning and Development pressed the government to promote population control. In accordance with conventional development theory at that time, they blamed rapid population growth for the country's economic problems, avoiding the sensitive issues of uneven distribution of land and a capital-intensive industrial strategy leading to high unemployment.

Hoping that accepting the expatriate advice might improve Kenya's credit rating in international banking circles, the government invited the Population Council to study the population problem in 1965. A team of four U.S. consultants spent three weeks in the country and produced the report which formed the basis of Kenya's first population policy. The advice was simple: Declare the urgent need for population control, promote the IUD, and hire more foreign advisors.

The report not only ignored the cultural context of fertility decisions in Kenya but, coming from outsiders, it laid the government open to charges of a white plot of "genocide." Without popular support, the family planning program floundered. As one Kenyan official admitted, the people were reluctant at the outset because "family planning was introduced wrongly, i.e as population control, and people did not like the idea. The wrong introduction to family planning could have been avoided by only mentioning the improvement of the health of the mother and child."[51]

Despite this experience, population control has remained the dominant motif of the Kenyan family planning program. In the mid-1970s the World Bank became the coordinator of a consortium of donors, which included the UNFPA, the United States, Sweden, West Germany, Denmark, and Britain, who have helped fund and organize the Kenyan population program. Since its inception, the main thrust has been the delivery of MCH and family planning services through the expansion of rural health facilities and the training of staff in contraceptive techniques. On paper it sounds fine, but in practice it is a different matter.

A 1980 World Bank evaluation provides some valuable insights as to why the first stage of the program, from 1974 to 1978, produced such dismal results. The project's goal was "to reduce the high annual rate of natural increase...by recruiting 640,000 new Family Planning acceptors and thereby helping to avert some 150,000 births."[52]

While setting such targets can easily distort the nature of any family planning program, in the Kenyan case the targets were not even based on the country's own data (which didn't exist), but on models derived from as far afield as Taiwan. In addition, the target was based on the use of only one method, the pill, which accounted for 80 percent of contraceptives dispensed. Confusion resulted in the field when the various donors gave different brands of pills.

The donors also failed to face up to the weaknesses of the government health services. Although rural health centers were expanding in this period, specialist urban services were still receiving the bulk of resources. Many rural clinics were thus under-funded and under-staffed—given their poor record on delivering even basic health care to rural people, they could hardly be expected to provide adequate family planning assistance.[53] As a result, the Kenyan family planning program, in the words of the World Bank, did not succeed "as well in retaining acceptors as it did in recruiting them."[54] The average client came back to the clinic fewer than four times and then dropped out of the system altogether.

A study cited by the Bank found that one of main reasons for high dropout rates was contraceptive side effects. No effective program evaluation was possible, however, due to lack of data. Furthermore, what little data there was concentrated on the family planning side, neglecting MCH services.[55]

Another persistent problem faced by the Kenyan program, both past and present, is the inability of family planning field educators to communicate effectively with village women. Drawn from the middle classes, they tend to have an attitude of superiority toward the poor. As the editors of *Viva* explain:

> There's no communication between the family planning people and the villagers. The women who go there to talk, like Mrs. ——, she is so painted, everyone just stares at her. She's got eight children. What does she know? In any case they are too elitist. How can you say fewer are better? People see a family of 10 well off, while the one without any child is suffering. How can they think that the second situation is supposed to be better?[56]

In addition, family planning field workers have been paid more than the community nurses to whom they are supposed to report, causing friction where there should be cooperative effort.[57]

Even those health personnel who have a genuine commitment to family planning face real practical difficulties in meeting women's needs. A public health nurse from Nyanza Province writes that because of the shortage of health personnel, "the explanation of the side effects of conventional contraceptives is not done properly, and in the end the users become discouraged when they find themselves experiencing some side effects."[58] Many family planning workers have not been trained adequately and do not know the proper use, contraindications, and side effects of the contraceptives they are promoting.[59]

Another major problem with the Kenyan program—as with many other population programs—has been its almost exclusive focus on women. As researcher Margrethe Silberschmidt points out:

> The lack of a gender approach in population/family planning programs has placed an unequal burden, both physically and psychologically, on women. Moreover putting all the responsibility onto women has the effect of marginalizing men and making them less likely to behave as responsible husbands and partners. And because women in most socio-cultural contexts do not have the decision-making authority or access to resources to be using the services, it has impeded the success of programs.[60]

Silberschmidt also notes the lack of attention to adolescents' needs for birth control.

Throughout the early period of the Kenyan program, the World Bank made a "significant nuisance" of itself by trying to raise "the sense of urgency" with which the Kenyan government approached its "population problems."[61] Concerned by the population program's lack of success, the Bank went a giant step further in 1982, imposing aid conditionality. The release of part of Kenya's Second Structural Adjustment Loan was made contingent on the establishment of a National Council on Population and Development of Kenya (NCPD), whose creation was opposed by the Ministry of Health. The NCPD, a separate executive agency, became responsible for executing Kenya's population projects.

Between 1982 and 1989 Kenya received more than $8 million a year in foreign population assistance, one of the highest per capita amounts in the world. Concurrently, the World Bank pressured the Ministry of Health to offer sterilization services and "liberalize guidelines" for promoting contraceptives—i.e., allowing mass promotion of the pill and Depo-Provera without adequate health back-up—while AID funded large-scale social marketing and community-based distribution of contraceptives. According to the Bank, "Signals were changed that made health center staff give higher priority to the provision of [family planning] services."[62] At the beginning of the 1980s 40 percent of the population lived within one day's travel to a contraceptive delivery site; by the end of the decade almost 90 percent lived within three hours of these services.

Today Kenya appears to be in the process of demographic transition. Fertility began to fall in the latter half of the 1980s; by 1989 the Total Fertility Rate reached 6.7 and fell further to an estimated 5.35 children in 1993. Contraceptive prevalence also rose from 17 percent in 1984 to 33 percent in 1993.

Demographers put forward many complex and interrelated reasons for this fertility decline—increased access to contraception is only one of them. The pressure on land, the greater role of education in social mobility and its high cost, and more economic independence for women have all acted to change family size.[63] To this list the World Bank adds the exposure of the population "to a materialistic, Western lifestyle" as the result of the government's free market policies and the consequent "influx of foreign aid donors, private investors and tourists."[64] Yet the fact remains that "materialistic, Western lifestyles"—even if they were such a worthy goal—remain out of reach of most Kenyans. Half of the country's population still lives in absolute poverty, and there are more poor women than men. The persistence of poverty may well act as a brake on further, sustained fertility decline.[65]

And while the uptake of contraception is increasing, the quality of services leaves much to be desired. Women are overwhelmingly the targets, and high-tech methods, without adequate health back-up, the preferred means. Female sterilization now accounts for 5.6 percent of contraceptive prevalence, male sterilization zero percent. Condom use meanwhile accounts for less than 1 percent of contraceptive prevalence in a country hard-hit by AIDS.[66]

Kenya is no longer the family planning "failure" it used to be, but population control remains a stumbling block in the development of safe and comprehensive reproductive health services for both men and women.

Part Two

POPULATION CONTROL COMES OF AGE

6

BIRTH OF AN
IDEOLOGY

Population control, as a major international development strategy, is a relatively recent phenomenon, dating back to the aftermath of World War II. Yet its origins reach back to the intellectual currents and social movements of the nineteenth and early twentieth centuries, which culminated in an organized birth control movement in Europe and the United States. The conflicts and contradictions in that movement's history presage many of today's debates.

STRANGE BEDFELLOWS

The human race has long sought to control births. Abstinence, withdrawal, and abortion are age-old techniques, sanctioned by many ancient societies. Barrier methods such as vaginal sponges and cervical caps were also used in the Middle East several thousand years before Christ. In seventeenth- and eighteenth-century Europe, condoms (made of linen or dried sheep gut), vaginal sponges, and pessaries were available in some countries. In 1843 the vulcanization process allowed the production of more reliable rubber contraceptive devices, and the diaphragm, or "Dutch cap," gained great popularity in the Netherlands in the late nineteenth century. IUDs and spermicides were also used in Europe at the time.[1]

The availability of contraceptive devices in Europe did not mean that birth control was always socially acceptable in the West, however. In the modern era, the struggle for the legitimization of birth control is a drama spanning two centuries and involving many actors with radically different scripts. The early neo-Malthusians supported birth control as a means of improving the condition of the poor by limiting population growth; feminists and socialists believed it was a fundamental woman's right; eugenicists embraced it as a way of influencing genetic quality. These strange bedfellows combined to give the birth control movement its unique character: It carried within it the seeds of birth control as a liberating force, as well as a means of coercive population control. The following analysis of the birth control movement draws largely on the historical interpretation advanced by Linda Gordon in her book *Woman's Body, Woman's Right*, as well as on research done by Bonnie Mass for her book *Population Target*, one of the first major critiques of population control as an international phenomenon.[2]

The first major public advocates of birth control were the English radical neo-Malthusians. Although Malthus had warned of the dire consequences of rapid population growth, he had *opposed* contraception in principle and had deployed his arguments mainly to justify the wide gap between rich and poor in late-eighteenth-century Britain. According to him, welfare measures such as England's Poor Laws only led to further impoverishment, since they enabled the poor to breed more. The radical neo-Malthusians, by contrast, viewed overpopulation as a cause of poverty and believed that contraception, by enabling the poor to have fewer children, could help to alleviate poverty and improve the condition of the working class. In 1823, in his "diabolical handbills" addressed to the English working class, neo-Malthusian Francis Place advised the use of the vaginal sponge and withdrawal.[3]

These first attempts to publicize the possibility of birth control took place against a backdrop of deep cultural conservatism about sexuality. By the beginning of the nineteenth century, the prevailing view, as filtered through the churches, was that the main purpose of sexuality was procreation within marriage.

Robert Dale Owen, the son of the famous British reformer Robert Owen, brought radical neo-Malthusianism to the United

States in the early part of the nineteenth century. In the United States Owen broke with his English mentors, supporting birth control primarily on the grounds of women's right to self-determination. For him the cause of poverty was unequal distribution of wealth, not overpopulation.

Owen's ideas fell on fertile ground. The United States was a new country, with plenty of land and growing employment opportunities; overpopulation was clearly not a threat. Social reformers at the time were largely utopians, believing in the possibility of a "perfect" society based on a pre-industrial vision of economic independence. Individual reform was the key to social reform, and women's rights, including the right to control reproduction, were a cornerstone of individual freedom.

This emphasis on women's rights helped lay the basis for the growth of a feminist movement in the United States in the middle of the nineteenth century, composed of suffragists, moral reformers (such as temperance advocates), and those who challenged the convention of legal marriage. Although many feminist groups disapproved of contraceptive devices per se as "unnatural," they believed in voluntary motherhood, the right of women to choose when to become pregnant, with abstinence the preferred means.

Motherhood was seen as a skill and a talent, rather than an instinctive practice. Unwanted children, the feminists argued, were more likely to be physically and morally defective. Although voluntary motherhood was an important step forward, feminist thinking of the day failed to address the concerns of the growing proportion of immigrant and working-class women in the United States, since the values it preached were largely white, Protestant, and middle-class.

THE WOMEN REBELS

In the United States two trends combined to make birth control a more broad-based issue in the second decade of the twentieth century. Among the intelligentsia and social reformers, a new philosophy of sex radicalism spread from Europe and increasingly undercut traditional Victorian views. Among these circles, sexuality was now valued independently of reproduction.

At the same time working-class militancy was on the rise, as the International Workers of the World (IWW) and the Socialist Party supported drives for unionization. Women were key actors in these struggles, proving to be militant and persevering strikers in many major industrial disputes. The combination of sexual rebellion with social rebellion produced the spark that ignited the U.S. birth control movement. The famous anarchist Emma Goldman, one of its most outspoken advocates, was arrested for distributing a pamphlet *Why and How, the Poor Should Not Have Many Children*, which described condoms, cervical caps, and diaphragms. But it was a young Socialist activist, Margaret Sanger, who became the main organizer of the movement. Her early writings in the New York Socialist paper *The Call*, under the title "What Every Girl Should Know," were not directly concerned with birth control, but reflected a general concern about women's health.

Sanger's interest in birth control was deepened by visits to France, where it was widely practiced, and to several other European countries, where birth control had become a demand of political activists. As early as 1882 in Holland, a trade union-sponsored birth control clinic had been opened, and in Germany female members forced the Social Democratic Party to give up its opposition to birth control.

Returning to the United States in 1914, Sanger started her own paper, the *Woman Rebel*, supported by the IWW, the Socialist Party, and the anarchists. In its pages she combined her now compelling interest in birth control (a term she coined) with continued support of the working-class movement. Sanger's political militancy started to fade, however, into a romantic philosophy of individual expression. She claimed that birth control could free the "absolute, elemental, inner urge of womanhood."[4] Sanger fled to Europe when the *Woman Rebel* was closed down by the post office and she was indicted on two counts of obscenity.

Spurred by the news of her indictment, the birth control movement continued to grow in her absence. When Sanger returned from Europe, she campaigned for public support for her trial, and in 1916 the charges against her were dropped. Turning to direct action, Sanger and her sister were arrested for opening their first birth control clinic in the Brownsville area of Brooklyn, and Emma Goldman was arrested again for handing out contraceptive information.

After 1916, the alliance between Sanger and the radicals began to weaken. This was to have a decisive influence on the future course of the U.S. birth control movement. Many radicals believed that a focus on women's problems detracted from the more important issue of class conflict, and that revolution, by ushering in a new era of socialist prosperity, would take care of women's problems automatically. Why worry about birth control when under socialism women would be able to support any number of children? Others feared that a focus on birth control and sexual matters could alienate people who might otherwise support a radical economic program. In addition, World War I led to a wave of anti-radical hysteria. Facing severe government repression, socialists were forced on the defensive, and their interest in birth control waned.

Social changes in the 1920s also contributed to the decline of a radical, feminist birth control movement in the United States. As in the 1950s, the postwar economic recovery led to the view of women as consumers, housewives, and beauty objects. Sexual mores loosened among the middle class, making birth control more privately acceptable, if not publicly so. The feminist movement faded after achieving the major victory of the women's suffrage amendment to the Constitution in 1918. Sanger herself, though remaining an ardent birth control advocate, drifted toward political conservatism. Already in 1917 she was considering a new tactical approach. She wrote her sister from jail: "It is true that the fashionable seem far removed from the cause, and its necessity—but we cannot doubt that they and they alone dominate when they get an interest in a thing. So little can be done without them."[5]

By 1917 Sanger had split formally with the radicals over control of her *Birth Control Review*. As the radicals left the cause, professionals and eugenicists came to fill their shoes.

MORE CHILDREN FROM THE FIT, AND LESS FROM THE UNFIT

In 1921 Sanger and her associates set up the American Birth Control League (ABCL). Although she continued direct action tactics, such as setting up clinics, Sanger's quest for respectability led her to court professionals, especially doctors. In the 1920s a few liberal doctors moved toward public support of birth control—as long as they were guaranteed a monopoly over its dissemination. Sanger supported their demands for legislation that would limit the right to prescribe contraceptives to doctors.

Other birth control groups opposed such bills on the grounds that they would limit birth control to that small number of women who had access to clinics and regular medical care. As historian Linda Gordon remarks, "The impact of professionals—particularly doctors—on birth control as a social movement was to depress it, to take it out of the mass consciousness as a social issue."[6]

A more ominous development was the influence of eugenics, the science of improving human heredity. One branch of eugenics maintained that the rich and powerful were *genetically* superior to the poor, and that whites were in general superior to other races. To the United States elite, such a philosophy provided a convenient justification for their privileged position.

In 1904 steel magnate Andrew Carnegie established a center for the study of "hybridized peoples," or racial mixtures. Bonnie Mass quotes a Carnegie researcher who wrote about racial integration in Jamaica:

> The moral disharmony in hybrids may often be due to the even greater contrast between the psychology of the various races, as, for instance, between the ambition, the love of power and the adventurous spirit of the whites, and the idleness, the inconstancy, the lack of self-control and often of adequate intelligence of many colored people.[7]

The wealthy Harriman family funded the Eugenics Records Office and the Kellogg family the Race Betterment Foundation in 1913.

The eugenicist conclusion that the poor were genetically inferior led to calls for compulsory sterilization. Paul Popenoe, a leading eugenics spokesman, estimated that 10 million Americans should be sterilized on the basis of IQ testing. By 1932 compulsory sterilization laws for the feeble-minded, insane, criminal, and physically defective had been enacted by twenty-seven states.

Eugenicists soon joined the birth control movement in growing numbers, providing it with a new direction to replace the discarded one of women's rights. As early as 1919, Sanger's *Birth Control Re-*

view published eugenicist arguments, including her own famous statement, "More children from the fit and less from the unfit—that is the chief issue of birth control." In her book *The Pivot of Civilization*, she warned that the illiterate "degenerate" masses might destroy "our way of life." By 1932 she was calling for the sterilization or segregation by sex of "the whole dysgenic population" (those who are suspected of being producers of "unfit" offspring).[8]

The American Birth Control League now advocated "racial progress" and sterilization. At one period the organization was led by Guy Irving Burch, director of the American Eugenics Society and founder of the Population Reference Bureau, who supported birth control because he had long worked, in his own words, "to prevent the American people from being replaced by alien or negro stock, whether it be by immigration or by overly high birth rates among others in this country."[9]

By 1940 the eugenicists and birth controllers' interests had so overlapped that Henry Pratt Fairchild, former president of the American Eugenics Society, said at the annual meeting of the Birth Control Federation (formerly the ABCL):

> One of the outstanding features of the present conference is the practically universal acceptance of the fact that these two great movements (eugenics and birth control) have now come to such a thorough understanding and have drawn so close together as to be almost indistinguishable.[10]

It was left to a man named Adolf Hitler, however, to carry the racial purity/superiority school of eugenics to its logical—and lethal—conclusion. The German sterilization laws passed in 1933 (based on the Model Eugenical Sterilization Law developed by the U.S. Eugenics Record Office) eventually led to over 200,000 sterilizations of "inferiors," while millions more were murdered in Nazi gas chambers.

Some eugenicists greeted Hitler's initial efforts with enthusiasm. Bonnie Mass notes how the *British Eugenics Review,* for example, wrote that "It would be quite wrong and unscientific to decry everything that is going on in that country.... In Germany, the most advanced eugenics legislation is carried through without difficulty."[11] In 1939 Guy Burch campaigned against the admittance of "non-Aryan" children, Jewish orphans who were refugees from the Nazis, into the United States.[12]

Although the Nazi atrocities helped to discredit this brand of eugenics in the United States, it never completely disappeared. In fact, some of the concepts resurfaced two decades later in the drive for population control.

Meanwhile, racism also infected the birth control movement. In 1939, for example, the American Birth Control Federation designed a Negro Project with the aim of hiring several black ministers with "engaging personalities" to travel through the South enlisting the support of black doctors for birth control. According to Gordon,

> This project was a microcosm of the elitist birth-control programs whose design eliminated the possibility of popular, grass roots involvement in birth control as a cause. "The mass of Negroes," argued the project proposal, "particularly in the South, still breed carelessly and disastrously, with the result that the increase among Negroes, even more than among Whites, is from that portion of the population least intelligent and fit, and least able to rear children properly."[13]

While eugenicists and racists thus turned birth control into an offensive weapon, it was soon to undergo another transformation, into a tool of top-down social planning.

FROM BIRTH CONTROL TO FAMILY PLANNING

The New Deal and World War II ushered in a new era of social planning to the United States, for both required reorganization of the society on a massive scale.

The New Deal involved the government much more directly in the provision of social services to the poor. The impoverishment of many white, middle-class people during the Depression now made it difficult to blame poverty on genetic inferiority. Instead, poverty increasingly came to be viewed as "environmentally" caused, though it could inflict lasting damage on its victims. The solution was social reform through welfare programs, which could improve the position of the individual.

Although birth control was not an explicit part of federal welfare programs, under the New Deal many social workers began to promote it. This had the advantage of spreading birth control infor-mation to many poor women. However, it also placed "birth control in the context of social worker-client, subject-object relations, discouraging mass participation in the programs," as Gordon notes.[14] This legacy unfortunately persists in many family planning programs today. Following the planning trend, the Birth Control Federation of America changed its name to the Planned Parenthood Federation in 1942, and family planning became the new, and more acceptable, euphemism for birth control. Gordon quotes a family planning poster of the time that aptly summed up the new philosophy:

> MODERN LIFE IS BASED ON CONTROL AND SCIENCE
> We control the speed of our automobile. We control machines.
> We endeavor to control disease and death. Let us control the size
> of our family to ensure health and happiness.[15]

The goal was to stabilize the family, even if that implicitly meant stabilizing women's inferior role. However, Planned Parenthood did take the step forward of recognizing mutual sexual enjoyment as a prerequisite for a happy marriage and acknowledging men's role in reproduction. Sex and the need for contraception *outside* marriage remained taboo. Planned Parenthood clinics, in fact, would not serve unmarried women, and the last barriers against services to them did not fall until the late 1960s.[16]

Despite their limitations, Planned Parenthood and the organizations that preceded it did perform the very valuable role of making contraception more accessible and acceptable. They helped free many women from the burden of unwanted pregnancies. At the same time, however, they shifted the focus away from women's rights, embraced eugenicist and elitist views of the poor, and adopted a limited, top-down approach to the delivery of services. Margaret Sanger's movement thus helped pave the way for the coming of population control.

THE POSTWAR POPULATION CONTROL BOOM

During the immediate postwar period in the United States, perceptions of demographic issues began to change. Emerging from World War II as the major world power, the United States had a growing need for access to Third World raw materials in order to assure a steady supply for the country's industries. At the same time population growth rates were on the rise in the Third World.[17]

United States access to Third World raw materials and markets depended on the existence of "friendly" governments, at a time when nationalism was on the rise, often tinged with a radicalism unpalatable to the United States. The success of the Chinese Revolution, Indian and Indonesian nonalignment, independence movements in Africa, economic nationalism in Latin America—all these contributed to growing U.S. fears of the Third World. Population growth, rather than centuries of colonial domination, was believed to fuel the nationalist fires, especially given the increasing proportion of youth.[18]

Although government reports touched on these perils of overpopulation, private organizations and foundations were the main force behind the postwar population control boom. In the 1940s the publications of the Planned Parenthood Federation began to emphasize the problem of overpopulation. In 1948, largely due to Sanger's efforts, the International Planned Parenthood Federation (IPPF) was formed. It was initially funded by the Brush Foundation of Cleveland—Dorothy Brush, one of IPPF's most influential board members, was also on the board of directors of the American Eugenics Society. The English Eugenics Society gave IPPF its first London offices free of charge.

In 1952 population control gained impeccable establishment credentials when John D. Rockefeller III invited thirty prominent U.S. conservationists, Planned Parenthood leaders, demographers, and development experts to a population conference in Williamsburg, Virginia. At the conference the Population Council was born, embodying Rockefeller's conviction that "the relationship of population to material and cultural resources of the world represents one of the most crucial and urgent problems of the day."[19] By 1955 the Council was advising the government of India on setting up a family planning program, and in 1959 another technical assistance mission went to Pakistan, which at that time included East Bengal, now the independent country of Bangladesh.

In 1963 Rockefeller himself visited Bangladesh, accompanied by Frank Notestein of the Population Council and the journalist Lewis Lapham. Lapham described their visit to a riverbank in the city of Dhaka, where they passed through "narrow, dusty streets cluttered with people and animals of all descriptions," smelling of "bad meat, urine, and sweat." On the shaven head of a sick child, the flies "were as thick as caraway seeds on a roll," the few women in the streets "looked like bundles of old rags."

> We reached the west bank of the river at dusk.... The sand swarmed with people. Rockefeller said nothing for at least twenty minutes. He stood beside an over-turned oil drum, confronted by the chaos so remote from the orderly presentations on the 56th floor of the R.C.A. building. Here at last was what he had come to see, the plain reality of the so-called "population explosion." No statistics, no high-flown sentiments, no handsomely-illustrated brochures or predictions of disaster for mankind; just a lot of people pushed down to the edge of a warm river.
>
> "The numbers," he said, "the sheer numbers of it...the quality, you see, goes down."[20]

Another early enthusiast was Hugh Moore, founder of the Dixie Cup Corporation, who set up the Hugh Moore Fund in 1954 to rally U.S. businessmen to the population cause. The Fund distributed T. O. Greissimer's *Population Bomb* (forerunner to Paul Ehrlich's book of the same title), which warned: "The population bomb threatens to create an explosion as disruptive and dangerous as an explosion of the atom, and with as much influence on prospects for progress or disaster, war or peace."[21] Moore's generous financial support brought him clout within the American Planned Parenthood Federation, where he served as vice-chair, and the IPPF, where his former employee Greissimer became head of the New York office.

The 1957 report of an ad hoc committee, consisting of representatives from the Population Council, Laurence Rockfeller's Conservation Foundation, and Planned Parenthood, outlined the emerging strategy of population control. Titled *Population: An International Dilemma*, the report depicted population growth as a major threat to political stability both at home and abroad. In the Third World the solution was not outright promotion of birth control by U.S. interests, but rather the wooing of national elites who, once convinced of the cause, could build support in their own countries.[22]

The private population establishment was to follow this strategy in the years ahead, building links with prominent Third World government officials, medical personnel, academics, and leaders of private organizations through training programs in the United States and the establishment of research institutions here and in the Third World. One of the first steps was to enlist the cooperation of U.S. academics.

Beginning in the 1950s large amounts of money began to flow into U.S. universities from the Ford Foundation, the Population Council, and the Rockefellers to finance population studies, facilitating the development of what some observers have called "a powerful cult of population control" in U.S. academia.[23] Government funding followed soon after, until, with a few exceptions, demography and related social sciences came to serve the population establishment's goal of promoting the machine model of family planning as the solution to the population "crisis." According to demographer Paul Demeny, this has had a devastating impact on the field:

> Social science research directed to the developing countries in the field of population has now become almost exclusively harnessed to serve the narrowly conceived short-term interests of programs that embody the existing orthodoxy in international population policy.... It disdains work that may be critical of existing programs, or research that seeks to explore alternatives to received policy approaches. It seeks, and with the power of the purse enforces, predictability, control and subservience.[24]

The early economic rationales for population control clearly illustrate this process. In the mid-1960s, for example, General Electric researcher Stephen Enke produced the first cost-benefit analysis of population control, which claimed that resources spent on family planning could contribute up to 100 times more to higher per capita incomes than could resources invested in production.[25] In other words, population control was a very profitable investment indeed, more profitable in fact than most any other development expenditure!

Enke's findings exercised a powerful influence over U.S. policymakers. In a speech before the U.N. President Johnson raised the issue of "multiplying populations" and urged his audience to "act on the fact that less than five dollars invested in population control is worth a hundred dollars invested in economic growth."[26]

From private and corporate support to academic respectability to government policy—population control followed this path to the top. For the powerful, population control was "an idea whose time had come," and official U.S. government assistance would soon be forthcoming.

THE OFFICIAL STAMP OF APPROVAL

Official acceptance in Washington of the need to counter the "population threat" dates from the Draper Committee. Set up by President Eisenhower in 1958 to study the U.S. Military Assistance Program and other forms of aid, the committee was chaired by General William H. Draper, a New York investment banker and a key figure in the postwar reconstruction of Europe. Like Draper, many of its members combined high-level defense experience with positions of corporate power.

The committee's mandate did not specifically mention population, but on the day it was established, General Draper received a cable from Hugh Moore, the Dixie Cup magnate, warning: "If your committee does not look into the impact and implications of the population explosion, you will be derelict in your duty."[27]

In the following months, Draper took Moore's message to heart, embracing the population issue with a passionate zeal that would last the rest of his life. He told the Senate Committee on Foreign Relations in May 1959: "The population problem, I'm afraid, is the greatest bar to our whole economic aid program and to the progress of the world."[28]

In July, at a White House press conference publicizing the final recommendations of the committee, Draper's dramatic presentation—complete with an alarming map of world population growth—made headlines around the world. The committee recommended that the U.S. government fund population research as part of its Mutual Security Program, and that aid be given to those "developing countries who establish programs to check population growth."[29]

By the mid-1960s the weight of the U.S. government began to swing behind population control, and new legislation soon embodied growing Congressional enthusiasm. The 1966 Food for Freedom bill, according to the House Committee on Agriculture, recognized "for the first time, as a matter of U.S. policy, the world population explosion relationship to the world food crisis," and allowed food aid revenues to be used to finance family planning programs in the Third World.[30] In 1967 alone Congress directly allocated $35 million to the U.S. Agency for International Development (AID) for population programs.

The population control lobby was impatient, however, with what they saw as the slow pace of government involvement. In 1967 Hugh Moore set up yet another organization, the Campaign to Check the Population Explosion, which financed alarmist advertisements in major U.S. newspapers. The campaign attracted powerful support—among the advertisements' signatories were Eugene Black, former president of the World Bank, and Lewis Strauss, a founding member of the Population Council. The rhetoric of the ads was clearly designed to create a wave of overpopulation paranoia, and their racist overtones were only thinly disguised. "The ever mounting tidal wave of humanity now challenges us to control it," warned one ad, "or be submerged along with all our civilized values." According to another,

> A world with mass starvation in underdeveloped countries will be a world of chaos, riots and war. And a perfect breeding ground for Communism.... We cannot afford a half dozen Vietnams or even one more.... Our own national interest demands that we go all out to help the underdeveloped countries control their population.

Not even the United States was safe from the overpopulation menace. "How many people do you want in your country?" an ad challenged, then painted a picture of cities "packed with youngsters—thousands of them idle, victims of discontent and drug addiction.... You go out after dark at your peril. Birth Control is an answer."[31]

For some people it was the *only* answer.

RAVENHOLT AND THE WAR ON POPULATION

Today the U.S. Agency for International Development (AID) is the largest single funder of population control in the Third World, allocating over a half billion dollars annually to population activities.

Overseeing the agency's entry on the population scene was the colorful and often controversial figure of Dr. R. T. "Ray" Ravenholt, who became head of AID's population branch in 1966. Ravenholt's enthusiasms included the production of red, white, and blue condoms to celebrate the American bicentennial, as well as the promotion of much riskier contraceptives.

Ravenholt's single-minded devotion to the cause of population control not only contributed to AID's "leadership" in the field, but to the specific forms which population control took in the Third World. His approach was simple: Reduce fertility by means of the direct provision of family planning services and the development of new and better contraceptive technology, regardless of social context. And the justification for U.S. involvement? As he explained, "Without our trying to help these countries with their economic and social development, the world would rebel against the strong U.S. commercial presence."[32]

In 1969 President Nixon upgraded Ravenholt's program into a separate Office of Population under AID's Technical Assistance Bureau with a $50 million annual budget, which increased steadily during the next decade. Enjoying unprecedented bureaucratic autonomy, Ravenholt's Office became a personal population control empire.

Ravenholt sought to translate his rising budget into quick results. Progress should be measured, said an AID memo cited by Donald Warwick, "in the only terms which ultimately matter—births averted."[33] A staff member commented, "A core value for the Office of Population is showing that you can spend money faster than other organizations in the field.... Look how quickly we act, how outrageous we dare to be."[34]

Not everyone in the agency agreed with Ravenholt's approach. He had to overcome opposition from senior administrators who resented his independent empire, from economists who disagreed with his single-minded focus on family planning as the key to development, and from overseas mission directors who disliked the pressure to perform on the population front irrespective of cultural conditions.

AID increased its leverage in the population field by funding other organizations. By the early 1970s it contributed over half the budget of the IPPF and the U.N. Fund for Population Activities (UN-FPA); 90 percent of the budget of the Pathfinder Fund, a Boston-based "private" family planning organization; and substantial amounts to the Population Council, universities, and other private agencies.

This strategy not only helped AID to win friends, but to get around some of the political sensitivities involved in the promotion of population control in the Third World. As a top State Department population official explained:

> In all of our assistance, we would do well to maintain a low pro-file. It is probable that we will have to work more and more through international organizations and private voluntary groups since these non-U.S. government entities are rather widely pre-ferred in countries now entering the family planning field.[35]

By the late sixties the United States was putting pressure on the United Nations, where opposition from Catholic and Communist countries had prevented population control from becoming a major concern. In 1969 President Nixon called for the U.N. to take a lead-ing role in population control in his Presidential Message on Popula-tion.

That same year the UNFPA was established, under the direction of Rafael M. Salas, a high-level Filipino government official and busi-nessman. Over at AID, however, Ravenholt had a very clear idea of who was in charge. "I see AID and the U.N. playing essentially com-plementary roles," he said. "The Agency is ahead of the U.N., which will follow trails blazed by AID."[36] In 1970 the U.N. General Assem-bly designated 1974 as World Population Year and began prepara-tions for a World Population Conference to be held in Bucharest.

Confident that it had now built a solid international consensus on the need for population control, the United States government was in for a rude shock.

BUCHAREST: THE PENDULUM SWINGS FORWARD...

Opening the World Population Conference in Bucharest in 1974, U.N. Secretary Kurt Waldheim struck an apocalyptic note, warning that "the problem posed by world population not only con-stitutes a danger, but the world's population is in danger."[37] His tone was echoed in the draft World Population Plan of Action, written in advance with substantial U.S. involvement. The draft set out specific targets for world population "stabilization" and concentrated on population growth as the main obstacle to social and economic development. Instead of being readily accepted, however, the draft plan generated disharmony and debate.

Opposition came not only from traditional Roman Catholic quarters, but also from many Third World countries, which saw the focus on population growth as a way to avoid addressing deeper causes of underdevelopment, such as inequalities in international relations. China called on the conference to remember that "of all things in the world, people are most precious." India argued that "development is the best contraceptive," and criticized the high consumption of resources in the West.[38] Feminists, demographers, and representatives of voluntary agencies also added their voices to the critique of population control.

However, the worst shock to the U.S. population community came with the defection of one of its most senior members. In a speech before a forum of nongovernmental organizations, John D. Rockefeller III, godfather of the population movement, called for "a deep and probing reappraisal of all that has been done in the population field":

> I believe that the place for population planning is within the context of modern economic and social development; I believe that economic growth is truly meaningful to the extent that it enhances the well-being of the people generally; I believe that the developed nations must strive to understand modern development, to be of assistance whenever possible, but to recognize that each nation must solve its development and fertility problems in its own way; I believe that women increasingly must have greater choice in determining their roles in society.[39]

The U.S. delegation, led by Secretary of Health, Education, and Welfare Caspar Weinberger, reacted angrily to these challenges, dismissing calls for a New International Economic Order as rhetoric and denying that Western consumption patterns had anything to do with population issues.

Despite U.S. opposition, the World Population Plan of Action was substantially revised. Explicit targets were dropped, and population growth was placed within the much broader context of socioeconomic transformation. A new view emerged dominant from the conference. Population growth was no longer seen as the main barrier to development; instead development itself could help lower birth rates. "Development is the best contraceptive" became a popular slogan.

However, at least one passage in the Plan of Action left room for considerable ambiguity:

> All couples and individuals have the basic right to decide freely and responsibly the number and spacing of their children and to have the information, education and means to do so; the responsibility of couples and individuals in the exercise of this right takes into account the needs of their living and future children, and their responsibilities toward the community.[40]

In the eyes of population control proponents, acting "responsibly" can be interpreted as conforming to the demographic goals of government family planning programs, which supposedly represent the interests of the "community"—the freedom of "freely" then ceases to be meaningful.[41]

The World Population Conference's emphasis on the "population-development linkage" did not spring from out of the blue. The seventies were a time of much soul-searching about the meaning and purpose of development. The 1960s' unbridled confidence in the "trickle-down" theory—the faith that a narrow focus on economic growth would eventually benefit the poor—gave way to a new focus on "meeting basic human needs" such as food, shelter, education, and health care.

Liberal population experts endorsed the new approach, for not only could meeting basic needs help to lower birth rates by motivating people to have fewer children, but family planning could be an important part of the basic needs package. "Integration" became the new buzzword: Integrate family planning with health, with women's programs, with education.

"Integrated development" meant fighting poverty—and population—simultaneously on all fronts. Except, that is, for the front which was politically most sensitive. Few asked the awkward question of why the basic needs of the poor were not being met in the first place.

The glaring inequalities in the distribution of income, land, and power were discreetly avoided, in the belief that Third World governments, with the backing of international donors, could deliver such goods as health and family planning to the poor, without fundamentally altering the social order in which they live. The Bucharest critique was thus interpreted in a way that fell far short of genuine social reform, and as a result many of the ensuing "integrated" programs were doomed to failure. Local elites once again asserted their control over foreign aid-provided resources, and the New International Economic Order never materialized, as Third World nations sank deeper into debt and the West entered an era of economic recession. And far from being "integrated" into basic needs projects, population control came to dominate those of which it was part.

The Bucharest critique also had little impact on the U.S. government's strong commitment to population control. Only months after Bucharest, the Ford administration produced a confidential National Security Study Memorandum 200 prepared by the CIA, AID, and the Departments of State, Defense, and Agriculture, which was adopted as national security policy in 1975. Recently declassified (and carefully analyzed by researcher Elizabeth Soto), this document supports population control as a way to stem radical dissent and protect U.S. access to strategic minerals in the Third World.

"Younger people, who are more prevalent in high-fertility populations, can more readily be persuaded to attack such targets as multinational corporations and other foreign influences," the study warns. It targets thirteen key countries for population control, including Nigeria, Bangladesh, and Brazil, and advocates using food aid as leverage if necessary. "Mandatory programs," or, in other words, coercion, are put forward as possibilities which should be considered.[42]

The only lessons the study takes from Bucharest are that the United States should co-opt more Third World leaders, using its leverage at the United Nations and other multilateral agencies, and better disguise the ravenous population control wolf in the sheep's clothing of integrated programs:

> Providing integrated family planning and health services on a broad basis would help the U.S. contend with the ideological charge that the U.S. is more interested in curbing the numbers of LDC [less-developed country] people than it is in their future and well-being.... we should recognize that those who argue along

ideological lines have made a great deal of the fact that the U.S. contribution to development programs and health programs has steadily shrunk, whereas funding for population programs has steadily increased.[43]

Compared to the 1980s and 1990s, however, the recognition at Bucharest of the population-development linkage seems a distant memory of a golden age. In the 1980s the basic needs strategy itself went out of style, supplanted by lean and mean "free market" structural adjustments and a few cost-effective "safety net" measures, such as childhood immunization, designed to keep death rates from escalating beyond "acceptable" limits.[44] In the 1990s family planning programs and free trade agreements are supposedly the magic keys which will unlock development, but the sheep's clothing is now the language of women's rights.

7

THE POPULATION ESTABLISHMENT TODAY

Today about 5 billion is spent each year on family planning in the Third World. Around 3 billion is spent by Third World governments, with China, India, and Indonesia the biggest spenders; over 1 billion is donated by governments of developed countries, multilateral institutions, and private agencies that constitute the Western population establishment; and the rest is spent by individual contraceptive users. Although population assistance has risen over time, it accounts for only 1 percent of official development assistance. This small percentage appears more significant, however, when one considers that less than 7 percent of official development assistance is allocated to human welfare concerns.[1] Moreover, population aid and the policies it helps to generate influence many other aspects of development planning.

The population establishment is by no means a monolith—it is made up of a wide spectrum of organizations and individuals, pursuing different and sometimes conflicting activities and goals, some more attuned to women's rights than others. Yet they are loosely joined together by a common sense of purpose, and often more tightly by a common source of funds. Since the U.S. government is the largest single donor, contributing almost half of international population assistance, it is the key actor in the population control drama. However, it generally prefers to play its role behind the scenes.

Following is a list of the major agencies involved in population activities:

The U.S. Agency for International Development (AID). AID population assistance takes two main forms. The first is bilateral assistance to country-level programs, which accounts for about half of the population budget. A few countries, notably Bangladesh and Kenya, have received a disproportionate share of bilateral assistance relative to their population size.[2] In 1993 AID made the policy decision to target assistance on two types of countries: "countries that contribute the most to global population and health problems" and "countries where population and health conditions impede sustainable development," which include places where growth rates "threaten the environment."[3]

The other half of AID's population budget goes primarily to cooperating agencies, which include nonprofit groups, private firms, and universities such as Johns Hopkins. Under Reagan and Bush, U.S. assistance to multilateral agencies was severely reduced because the IPPF and the UNFPA lost funding over abortion controversies. Aid is resuming under Clinton.

AID's new "Sustainable Development Strategy" identifies population growth as a key "strategic threat" which "consumes all other economic gains, drives environmental damage, exacerbates poverty, and impedes democratic governance."[4] Population control is one of AID's four main areas of concentration, and the Clinton administration is requesting $585 million in FY 1995 for population programs, up from $502 million the year before.[5]

Although population programs will also have health care and female education components, family planning will continue to receive the most resources, since according to AID it is the single most effective means to reduce population growth.[6] And it appears that AID will support health and education only to the extent that they serve its population control objectives. In the words of AID administrator J. Brian Atwood:

> Family planning will remain the critical element in our population programs.... Our concern must be to meet the unmet need for

family planning, but to go beyond. Maternal health, prenatal care, safe sex and social education must be part of the total picture. So must the empowerment of women. So must the education of girls. We cannot attack the crisis with a single arrow. We cannot go to war with a single weapon.[7]

Governments of Other Developed Countries. Japan is now the second largest national donor. Recently, it substantially increased its population assistance, earmarking $3 billion for a global initiative on population and AIDS for the seven-year period FY 1994-FY 2000. Women's health activists in Asia are worried about the implications of such a large increase. In the past Japan has had a relatively low profile in population matters, but now it is officially embracing the view that the "population explosion" is causing food shortages, unemployment, urban slums, and environmental degradation.[8] Other major donors are Germany, Norway, Sweden, the United Kingdom, the Netherlands, Canada, Denmark, Finland, Switzerland, and Australia. Most channel at least half their population assistance through multilateral agencies.[9]

Traditionally, European governments have had a more broad-based approach toward population than the United States and, in some cases, have served as an important counterweight to AID's and the World Bank's narrow family planning agendas (see Chapter 12). In the late eighties, however, the UNFPA and U.S. lobby groups such as the Population Crisis Committee put pressure on European governments to increase their support for population control, a strategy which is unfortunately starting to pay off.[10] Parliamentarians have been a special target. In 1994 a British all-party parliamentary group on population and development recommended that the government double its foreign population assistance in the next ten years, and, more ominously, reduce funding to overseas aid charities which fail to make family planning a priority, and increase it to those which do. It also urged NGOs to engage in the social marketing of contraceptives.[11]

The U.N. Fund for Population Activities (UNFPA). With a budget of close to $220 million a year, the UNFPA is the largest multilateral member of the population establishment. Although in theory the UNFPA is supposed to support a wide spectrum of population-related activities, in practice its main emphasis is on funding family planning programs. Between 1969 and 1991, for example, the UNFPA devoted only 1.6 percent of its total assistance to the broader area of women, population, and development, as opposed to over 45 percent to family planning programs. Moreover, many of its women's programs are "small-scale endeavors which simultaneously address women's reproductive and productive roles."[12]

This emphasis on family planning is no accident. According to a UNFPA official interviewed in 1984, before the cut-off of U.S. funds: "AID, which provides about a quarter of our funds, puts pressure on us to focus on family planning." Officially, the UNFPA is committed to the principle of voluntarism and must abide by the U.N. Human Rights Charter. It projects a public image of an organization, in the words of one official, "in business to do what people want, not to tell people what to do."[13] But in effect the UNFPA does not do what people want but what governments want, and what governments want, if it involves pushing population control, can easily conflict with voluntarism.

The UNFPA, in fact, has played a very negative role regarding coercion. It has given awards to the population field's worst human rights violators (see Chapter 9) and has often actively cooperated with them, as in the case of Indonesia. In recent years, it has also produced extensive and expensive propaganda promoting population alarmism, particularly the view that rapid population growth poses the most serious threat to the global environment. It is playing a key role in orchestrating the new population "consensus."

That said, not all UNFPA-sponsored programs are oriented toward population control, and it funds some positive initiatives in the field of women's health. However, its institutional ethos continues to be strongly neo-Malthusian.

The World Bank. In the late 1960s, then World Bank president Robert McNamara became a powerful voice for population control within the international community. It is only in the last few years, however, that the Bank has become a leading financier of family planning, making new loan commitments of around $200 million annually. India, Indonesia, and Bangladesh account for almost half of Bank population assistance, though Africa has more projects.[14]

Bank influence in the population arena extends far beyond financial commitments. By virtue of its leverage over other forms of development finance, the Bank is able to pressure Third World governments to develop population policies. This is done by discussing the adverse impact of rapid population growth in its influential economic reports and through "dialogues" with senior government officials, and by arranging the co-financing of large population projects with other donors, which gives the Bank greater power in its role as coordinator. In the 1980s the Bank increased its leverage by making the release of structural adjustment loans contingent upon adoption of population control policies in a number of countries, especially in Africa.[15] While the Bank sought to free market forces through its privatization strategies, it tried ever more tightly to control population growth, by robbing health budgets and using incentives and disincentives if necessary.

This action reflected a shift in World Bank ideology on poverty and population away from the more liberal view that poverty alleviation through social and economic development was the main key to fertility decline. According to analyst Peter Gibbon, in the 1980s the Bank believed that population problems could no longer wait for socioeconomic development to solve them; their urgency was "increased by the threat of ecological imbalance and by the necessity to succeed with the structural adjustment effort."[16] Despite differences of opinion within the institution, the Bank began to attach greater importance to population than to poverty. Gibbon maintains that this shift reflects a fundamental change in the North's strategy of stabilizing and dominating the South. In the 1970s, when the international economy was awash with petro dollars, multilateral, bilateral, and private donors and lenders competed to give assistance to Southern countries and to build alliances with their ruling elites. They had an optimistic faith that investment would spur modernization and that poverty reduction programs would succeed in bringing political stability.

In the 1980s, with the international economic recession and the decline of the Eastern bloc, Northern concern shifted from making loans to recovering them, from buying alliances with Southern elites to forcing them to comply with austerity programs. The North became more interested in "direct political stabilization" of the New

World Order through selected U.S. military interventions, co-opta-
tion of international nongovernmental organizations (NGOs), and
reduction of population growth. According to Gibbon, this created
the paradox of a weakened emphasis on poverty while poverty was
rising and a renewed emphasis on population control while population growth was actually slowing.[17]

Now in the 1990s the liberal approach seems to be creeping
back, though it is too early to tell whether the transformation is rhetorical or real. Though the Bank's current philosophy holds that
slowing population growth is still a "high priority" in the poorest
countries, it maintains that

> Population policy should be integrated with social policies that
> address a range of poverty reduction and human development ob-
> jectives. Particular emphasis should be placed on better infant
> and child health, education of girls, and overall improvements in
> the status of women. These measures bring important benefits in
> their own right, and experience now shows that they are more ef-
> fective in reducing high birth rates than policies which focus nar-
> rowly on fertility reduction alone.[18]

Belatedly the Bank is beginning to criticize family planning programs that use demographic targets and incentives: "The point is to
provide fertility regulation as a reproductive-health and not a population-control measure."[19]

While such statements are welcome, they are too little too late,
given that the Bank has already set many governments off in the opposite direction. Many problems also remain with the Bank's approach to reproductive health and health care in general, not to
mention its broader economic strategies. Yet this softening of the
population hard line could open more political space for policy
changes. In recent negotiations with the Indian government, for example, the Bank urged the government to abandon targets in its
population program—without success.[20]

The International Planned Parenthood Federation. With
a budget of roughly $100 million a year, the IPPF, headquartered in
London, is the largest international private agency funding family
planning services. Major contributors include the governments of
Japan, Canada, Sweden, Norway, Denmark, and the United Kingdom.[21] In 1985 the IPPF lost U.S. government funding because of its

principled refusal to insist that its 117-member family planning associations stop all abortion activities. That funding is now resuming.

At the same time that the IPPF promotes family planning as a basic human right, it uses overpopulation rhetoric to build support for its programs and takes an incautious attitude toward contraceptive safety. As a result, its member associations have often played a double role: On the positive side, they have bravely introduced family planning programs into hostile environments; on the negative side, they have helped pave the way for population control interventions and programs that neglect women's overall health (see Part Three). Reformers within the organization are now pushing for greater attention to quality of care issues and more work on AIDS.

The Population Council. Located in New York, the Population Council operates on an annual budget of approximately $40 million. Its main funding source is the U.S. government.[22] Since its inception in 1952 the Council has played a key role in the design and introduction of family planning programs, the training of Third World personnel, and the transformation of population studies into a respectable discipline.

Today the Council is a proverbial mixed bag, with staff ranging from population control advocates to academic demographers to feminist reformers of family planning. Its Center for Population Studies does interesting research on the role of women, migration, development, and the determinants of fertility; its International Programs department is more directly involved in setting up family planning programs within a technocratic population framework; its Center for Biomedical Research develops new contraceptives, such as Norplant, often designed to play a major role in reducing population growth. Despite its professed commitment to quality of care and freedom of choice, the Council has actively promoted the mass introduction of easily abusable contraceptive technologies into already abusive population control programs.

The Population Council is the preeminent liberal population organization today, especially since the Ford Foundation has shifted its focus more on to reproductive health. Over the years its good credentials among the upper echelons of the U.S. establishment have given population control a legitimacy it might otherwise lack.

Foundations. From 1952 to 1983 the Ford Foundation committed $260 million to population activities, with major program areas being reproductive and contraceptive research, demographic training, core support for the Population Council, and technical assistance to family planning programs. Ford played a major role in the early design of family planning, greatly influencing—and by many accounts distorting—the structure and goals of India's population program.[23] Some of its early population specialists considered coercion a viable option and suggested nightmarish technical fixes such as "a substance that could be given to an entire population in food or drink which would confer sterility until an antidote is given."[24]

Ford, however, changed faster than the rest of the field and transformed its population program into a reproductive health program in the mid-1980s. It is now an important source of support for many women's health initiatives. The MacArthur Foundation, increasingly active in the population field, has a similar philosophy and is also a key funder of more progressive research and advocacy organizations, with a focus on Brazil, India, Mexico, and Nigeria. Within the international women's health movement there is dissension over the extent to which foundations should be involved in setting the political agenda.

The Hewlitt, Mellon, and Rockefeller Foundations are also key players in the population field, but tend to be more traditional, with less of a link with the women's movement. Along with the Population Council, these five U.S. foundations accounted for over 60 percent of private funding of international NGOs engaged in population-related work from 1989 to 1991.[25]

Private Agencies, Consulting Firms, and Academic Centers. While AID, UNFPA, World Bank, IPPF, Population Council, and large private foundations are at the hub of the population establishment, a multitude of smaller groups help make the wheels go 'round. The Association for Voluntary Surgical Contraception, the Pathfinder Fund, Family Health International, Family Planning International Assistance—these are a few of the private agencies that develop and deliver family planning services to the Third World. Most profess to be working for the double goals of making family planning services available and limiting population growth. Individuals within these agencies often tend to lean toward one goal or the other—there is not always one unified point of view.

A prevalent trend in the development business is the growth and proliferation of consulting firms, which feed off the U.S. government budget. The population field is no exception. Among the main consulting firms involved in population work are Development Associates, the Futures Group, and Westinghouse Health Systems. AID, for instance, funds a project of the Futures Group called RAPID (Resources for the Awareness of Population Impact on Development) which, with sophisticated computer technology, dramatizes the perils of overpopulation with simple graphs, highly selective statistics, and the kind of elementary Malthusian reasoning that attributes almost every social ill to high fertility.

To the tune of over $23 million since 1986, AID also finances the Futures Group's OPTIONS project. The project provides Third World governments with advisors who conceptualize and draft population policies and related legislation, often based on RAPID data. It concurrently indoctrinates key Third World leaders through population training, seminars, "observational travel," and fellowships. Its main targets, mostly in Africa, are "heads of state, ministers, parliamentarians, private sector leaders and others who control the allocation of significant amounts of resources."[26] The OPTIONS project raises serious ethical questions about the nature of U.S. intervention. The fact that national population policies incorporate RAPID data and analysis is also troubling, given how far removed RAPID is from an accurate depiction of reality.

Research and training centers at Johns Hopkins University, Columbia University, University of Michigan, Georgetown University, University of North Carolina, Northwestern University, and Tulane University provide the academic backup to the U.S. population program, each receiving substantial funding from AID.[27]

Although strictly speaking most of these organizations are private, in reality almost all depend heavily on U.S. government funds. This can limit their independence, as in the case of the Pathfinder Fund, which in 1983 was forced to stop all abortion funding, even through private sources, in order to receive its annual appropriation from Congress. It also means that many are reluctant to challenge

AID emphasis on population control, for population money is their lifeblood.

Pressure Groups and Publicists. Public support for population control is vital in order to lubricate the wheel with regular applications of funds. Thus pressure groups and publicists perform an important role in building a U.S. population control constituency, lobbying Congress and influencing the media. They are also spreading their tentacles into Europe. They tend to take an extreme line—the group Zero Population Growth, for example, believes that overpopulation is the second greatest hazard in the world next to nuclear war—but their zeal is tolerated as long as it yields results. In the 1990s their strategy has been to appropriate the language of women's rights in order to make the population message more palatable.

Of all the pressure groups, the Population Crisis Committee, now renamed Population Action International, founded in 1963 by General Draper and Hugh Moore, is the most influential. It exercises leverage far beyond its modest annual budget of several million dollars by using prominent retired military, government, and business leaders to press its case not only on the U.S. public and Congress, but on senior Third World officials. The Population Institute, also based in Washington, D.C., is engaged in a similar mission, but tends to be less sophisticated. In recent years more environmental groups have joined the population control bandwagon. Population agencies have vigorously courted mainstream environmental groups because they see interest in the environment as a way to attract a broader constituency and expand U.S. funding for family planning programs. For a variety of reasons, many environmental groups have proven to be all too open to this marriage of convenience. Of these, the National Audubon Society, the National Wildlife Federation, and the Sierra Club have the most active lobbying operations (see Chapter 8).

The international parliamentary movement on population and development, supported by the IPPF, the UNFPA, the Pathfinder Fund, and Population Action International, among others, is also an important pressure point for the promotion of population control. It brings together parliamentarians from different countries at periodic conferences with the rationale that "Meetings of elected parliamentarians, from donor and recipient countries alike...help form a political safety net for heads of state who want to move aggressively on the population front."[28]

In 1985 the *New York Times* ran a full-page advertisement sponsored by the Global Committee of Parliamentarians on Population and Development, which called for "population stabilization" and blamed "degradation of the world's environment, income inequality and the potential for conflict" on overpopulation. The ad carried the signatures and photographs of thirty-five heads of state, all but one of them men.[29]

It would be mistaken, however, to view this process as simply the Western population establishment putting pressure on recalcitrant Third World leaders, for many are more than willing to cooperate. This is because there is often a common interest between the population agencies and Third World elites. After all, there is generally more in common between an AID official in Washington, for example, and a government family planning minister in India, than there is between the minister and an Indian peasant. Perhaps the AID official and the minister attended the same training course at a university in the United States; they undoubtedly read the same journals, attend the same conferences, and socialize at the same parties when visiting each other's area of the world. Today some liberal Western members of the population establishment complain that Third World colleagues are often much more concerned with rapid population growth and dismissive of human rights concerns than themselves. Ironically, the indoctrination process has proved a little too successful.

Money helps to lubricate the relationship between the population establishment and Third World elites—it is probably no exaggeration to say that foreign support for population control has largely been bought at Western taxpayers' expense. Donald Warwick notes that in the Philippines, for example, AID forged a local population control lobby through the simple strategy: "Buy in, buy out, and buy around."[30] Third World members of the Old Boy population network (for they continue to be mainly upper-class men, though more women are now joining the ranks) are constantly rewarded with scholarships and travel grants, funding for pet projects, prizes, and renown in the international press.

Although these material rewards help to cement the alliance, the identity of interest between foreign agencies and Third World elites goes far beyond the perks. Both are part of the new class of world managers, which has begun to transcend differences in culture. They define most issues as "management problems" rather than as moral dilemmas, failing to question their own values and assumptions and to confront the frequent incompatibility between population control and respect for human rights. And for them, bringing the birth rate down is an enterprise that befits their managerial talents, whereas attacking poverty and inequality head-on would jeopardize their privileged position in the hierarchy of politics and power.

Today the population establishment is truly international—among a small circle of friends.

FROM PRESSURE TO POLICY

The stage is set. The actors are in place. The next step is to finalize the script. This is the job of the technocrats.

Robert S. McNamara is the global manager par excellence. In the 1950s he managed the Ford Motor Company; as Secretary of Defense in the Kennedy and Johnson administrations, he managed the U.S. war in Vietnam; and his years as president of the World Bank saw its transformation into the preeminent international institution managing development in the Third World. Now, upon his retirement, he has determined how to manage population growth.

Writing in *Foreign Affairs*, McNamara blames rapid population growth for a whole catalog of miseries: unemployment, pressure on food supplies, degradation of the environment, an increase in poverty, and even the rise of authoritarian governments.

He warns that if the world fails to bring down population growth rates through "humane and voluntary measures," either the old Malthusian checks of starvation and disease will take their toll, or governments will be forced to take coercive measures and desperate parents to resort to frequent abortion and female infanticide.[31]

What is the way out of such a situation? For McNamara, the answer is simple: Develop and implement a population policy. He outlines some of the essentials of such a policy—political will, administrative capacity, the strength of community institutions. "But the most important single step that any nation can take to reduce its rate of population growth," McNamara states, "is to establish a frame or a plan within which all of these measures can be formulated and against which progress can be periodically evaluated.... As a foundation for such action, country fertility targets must be set for specific time periods."[32]

His is a neat vision of a world in which the policymakers draw up a plan, which the functionaries then implement, and the poor masses respond by limiting their fertility. The chain of command is as clear as a military hierarchy. The technocratic mind, in fact, seeks to manage civil society as it would an army at war.

McNamara's vision is elaborated in the World Bank's *World Development Report 1984*, which lays out a blueprint for developing population policy: First, collect data to document the deleterious effects of rapid population growth. Second, ensure the political commitment of important national leaders. Third, create the right institutions. Fourth, intensify support for family planning services. Fifth, adopt other more stringent measures if necessary.[33]

The Bank draws a clear distinction between population control policy and family planning as an individual right:

> Family planning programs provide information and services to help people achieve their own fertility objectives. By contrast, population policy involves explicit demographic goals. It employs a wide range of policies, direct and indirect, to change the signals that otherwise induce high fertility.... it requires clear direction and support from the most senior levels of government.[34]

To change those "signals" more quickly, the Bank has endorsed incentive and disincentive schemes, such as payments to sterilization acceptors. Carefully designed and administered, these schemes, the Bank claims, "meet the criteria of improving welfare and allowing free choice."[35] Instead, they usually restrict free choice and give the green light to coercion.

Some top population policymakers have openly counselled the use of coercion. In an article published in 1979, Bernard Berelson, the late president emeritus of the Population Council, and Jonathon Lieberson argue for the "stepladder" approach to population policy: Start off with soft measures, such as voluntary family planning services,

MAKING POPULATION POLICY:
SOME UNSALUTARY EXAMPLES

In the 1980s AID, UNFPA, and the World Bank worked closely together to get African leaders to embrace population control. In some cases, especially in francophone Africa, this helped reverse a long colonial tradition of pro-natalism, which prevented women's access to contraception. At the same time, however, the agencies promoted the machine model of family planning and the neo-Malthusian ideology which underlies it. The agencies also bypassed mechanisms for democratic decision-making—the agenda was set largely from outside.

In the case of Senegal the three agencies coordinated efforts to pressure the Senegalese government to formulate a population policy. The Bank and the UNFPA carried out a joint sector mission to document the importance of population control in Senegal, while the AID-funded OPTIONS project financed sending three consultants to the Ministry of Planning and Cooperation to help draft the population policy. It also organized a Senegalese "study tour" to Zaire to learn about Zaire's new population policy. (The corrupt and authoritarian regime in Zaire hardly seems a good model.) Meanwhile, RAPID presentations "demonstrating the impact of rapid population growth on development potential" were given to a cross-section of leaders from ten regions of the country. In a final turn of the screw, Bank staff spoke about population "with high-level officials when discussing terms for a structural adjustment loan (SAL)." As a result, preparation of a population policy statement and action plan became an "agreed condition" of the loan.[1]

In Nigeria the Bank funded Nigerian consultants who "conducted research necessary to suggest a reasonable population policy to the government."[2] This work also provided material which the Futures Group used to update RAPID presentations. These presentations in turn were used to train Nigerian demographers and build support from government officials and religious leaders. The World Bank president at the time, Barber Conable, also met with the president of Nigeria to discuss population matters.

The result was a population policy adopted in 1989 which endorses patriarchal norms and targets women. "The patriarchal family system in the country shall be recognized for stability of the home," it proclaims. It calls for women to reduce the number of children they have in their lifetime from over six to four by the year 2000, while men are only "encouraged to have a limited number of wives

and optimum number of children they can foster within their resources."[3] Not suprisingly, Nigerian women's organizations were
outraged.

Funding for family planning is already outpacing that for basic
health. A 1991 World Bank loan, to be spread over seven years, gives
family planning considerably more money per year than the Health
Ministry has for all its annual recurrent expenditures. A Nigerian
newspaper warns that "the project could divert interest from the
core primary health projects which are meant to improve the health
standards of rural dwellers who are prime targets in the family planning project."[4] Due to structural adjustment, health services are
already in terrible shape, even for the middle class.

To add insult to injury, the Nigerian population policy is based
on seriously inflated population projections. In 1992 the provisional
results of the Nigerian census revealed that there were 88.51 million
Nigerians, 20 to 30 million fewer than originally projected by the
World Bank, the United Nations, and government departments—a
rather large error.[5]

In Latin America the strategy has been less direct. Because of
political sensitivities about population control, the Bank's approach,
for example, is "to focus on reproductive health and safe motherhood as the rationale for family planning" and to downplay "explicit
demographic justification." The Bank, however, urges its staff to
"continue explaining the economic and social value of slower population growth at every appropriate opportunity."[6]

and proceed if necessary to harsher measures, such as disincentives,
sanctions, and even violence. "The degree of coercive policy
brought into play should be proportional to the degree of serious-
ness of the present problem and should be introduced only after
less coercive means have been exhausted," they write. "Thus, overt
violence or other potentially injurious coercion is not to be used before noninjurious coercion has been exhausted."[36]

They are able to condone coercion so easily because they believe there is no such thing as a "correct" ethical system or univer-
sally "approved" ranking of human rights. In their ethically neutral,
morally relative universe one thing is clear, however: They rank
themselves above others. And it is their responsibility, they say, to
make their "best information and policies" known to the "dominant

powers" of other societies.[37] If this is their best policy, what could be worse? On Berelson and Lieberson's stepladder the sky's the limit.

From pressure to policy and ultimately to practice—the population control drama plays on. Sometimes all the actors meet in one location, as occurred in Mexico in 1984.

MEXICO CITY: THE PENDULUM SWINGS BACKWARD

As part of their extensive preparations for the August 1984 Mexico City International Conference on Population, the UNFPA produced a film, *Tomorrow's World*, which depicted the perils of overpopulation and extolled the virtues of modern family planning. Among the more memorable scenes in the film were of a Thai hairdresser giving discounts to customers who buy pills from her and a closing shot of a woman flat on her back, giving birth in stirrups, as an example of what wonders modern medicine can bring.

But the most vivid picture was of a poor, landless Mexican woman who had agreed to sterilization after the birth of her fourth child. "Life without land will never be an easy matter," the narrator tells us, "but at least this mother's problems will stop multiplying."

At the UNFPA headquarters in New York, Dr. Joep van Arendonk, then director of the Program Division, discussed the upcoming conference. "The value of these conferences is that you can reach a number of opinion makers," he explained. "In Bucharest there was not as much awareness, particularly on the part of Africa and Latin America, that there is a population problem. Now there is an awareness, but what action to take? In Mexico, population targets will be a heated issue again, along with contraceptive approaches, the pros and cons of surgical contraception, and the redistribution of population." What about redistribution of wealth? I asked him. "That," he answered, "is not our concern."[38]

The Mexican woman has no land. That is not our concern. Our concern is that she stop having children. Was this the message the UNFPA was bringing to its guests in Mexico?

Certainly in Mexico City the discussion was carefully circumscribed, kept within the narrow bounds of an emerging population control "consensus." The message of Bucharest—that equitable economic and social development is the key to reducing poverty, and hence rapid population growth—had been swallowed, digested, and regurgitated in a much milder form. "The arguments seem to have fused and become two sides of the same coin," wrote the UNFPA's Jyoti Shankar Singh. "Rapid population growth is now accepted as both a cause and an effect of poverty."[39] Development can help bring down birth rates, the argument goes, but population control is equally necessary to bring about development.

After their bad showing in Bucharest when they were attacked by Third World governments, the leaders of the population establishment had also done their homework well. A barrage of pre-conference publications and expert consultations heralded the new "consensus," paving the way for a smooth ride.

The conference scene itself was hardly conducive to challenging the "consensus." Two U.S. women who attended the conference described it in the *Boston Globe*:

> Mexico City played host to an elaborate production by and for an international elite.... That participants were exposed only to the upper echelons of Mexican society and that the conference discussion centered on the ideas of a single world class of administrators raises questions about the international "consensus" which became the watchword of the meeting.[40]

The only real note of discord at the conference sounded when conservative politician James Buckley delivered the official U.S. policy statement of the Reagan administration. The statement not only challenged traditional Malthusian thinking on the impact of population growth (see Chapter 2), but launched a full-scale attack on abortion rights. Since 1974, Congress has prohibited the use of U.S. government funds for the direct support of abortion services overseas; however, private family planning organizations were still able to receive U.S. government aid if they used a segregated, non-U.S. funded account for their abortion work. The 1984 policy went the critical one step further by denying U.S. funds to any private organization which performed or even just promoted abortion (through counseling, for example) as a family planning method. The statement also stipulated that where abortion was legal, foreign governments could only receive U.S. population aid through segregated accounts.[41]

Ironically, the policy statement served to legitimize the position of the population establishment by casting it in the role of the defender of reproductive rights. The press collaborated in this portrayal, for the extremism of the Reagan position made the population control lobby seem moderate by comparison.

Only outside the conference hall were reproductive rights interpreted more broadly, as hundreds of women, men, and children, many from Mexico City's infamous slums, demonstrated on the street. They linked their demands for basic reproductive rights, including the legalization of abortion and an end to forced sterilization, to basic economic rights. Why were Mexico's poorest citizens being forced to pay for the country's debt crisis through austerity measures imposed by the International Monetary Fund? they asked the delegates entering the conference.[42]

No one answered them then, and no one is answering now.

8

BUILDING A "CONSENSUS" FOR CAIRO AND BEYOND

The "consensus" the UNFPA began to create in Mexico City pushed full steam ahead toward Cairo, scene of the 1994 U.N. International Conference on Population and Development (ICPD), and beyond.[1] "Consensus" now rolls off the lips of populationists with the same ease as a common greeting. It is considered so pervasive and all-encompassing that only so-called extremists would opt to stay out.

As the result of feminist pressure, the consensus has broadened to incorporate many women's health and empowerment concerns—to this extent, it represents progress. But it has many drawbacks and contradictions as well. It legitimizes population control at a particularly dangerous moment in world history, when economic, political, and cultural instability is intensifying the search for scapegoats, and fascism is once again on the rise, including a new environmental variant.

The population consensus derives from the New World Order politics of obscuring differences in pursuit of a universal free trade model. The underlying logic assumes that if globalization and the free market are good, then population growth perforce has to be bad, for there is no way advanced capitalism and rampant consumerism can deliver all the goods to all the people and "sustain" both the natural environment and the grossly inequitable distribution of wealth. The best way to shrink the numbers of the poor, reduce the labor supply in a capital-intensive era, and protect the environment is to limit births. Never mind that population growth rates are coming down in virtually every area of the globe already—they must come down much faster.

The consensus puts forward an integrated approach to reducing birth rates, reminiscent of the 1970s. The U.S. State Department describes it as a

> broad agreement that development and family planning can work separately to slow population growth, but that they work most effectively when pursued together. There is also increasing recognition that population growth is part of a constellation of factors that can cause environmental degradation. And it is widely acknowledged that family planning should be provided as part of broader primary and reproductive health initiatives, and that population policy should encompass economic opportunity for women, and elimination of legal and social barriers to gender equity.[2]

To this the World Bank adds that interventions "which are responsive to individual needs and aspirations" are more effective in lowering fertility than programs "driven by top-down demographic targets."[3]

At the same time that the consensus has taken hold in liberal circles, religious fundamentalism and the antiabortion movement are extending their tentacles in every possible direction. For example, the U.S.-based Human Life International now has offices in 18 countries.[4] These forces are taking advantage of the deep cultural malaise generated by economic and political upheavals, the religion of consumerism, and the homogenizing power of corporate media. Viewed against the fundamentalist backdrop on which women's subordination is writ large and clear, the population consensus appears progressive, and some aspects of it undoubtedly are. Appearances can also be deceptive, however, as the following sections reveal.

EMPOWERING ALL WOMEN—AND NO POOR MEN?

The consensus focus on women is the culmination of several decades of increased attention to the role of "women in development" as the result of the convergence of a number of separate currents in the 1970s. First was the growth of feminism in the West and among sections of the educated elite in the Third World. As a new generation of young, upwardly mobile women entered the professions, a few trickled into the field of international development. They began to ask what was happening to "invisible" Third World women and to direct attention toward a previously neglected population. Their efforts helped to identify the problem, although they did not always provide a clear vision of the solution.

Second, as growing numbers of women joined the global assembly line taking low-wage jobs with multinational corporations, they became strategically important to the international economy. Integrating women into industrialization was proving very profitable indeed.

Then, demographic research yielded the information that enhancing women's status was an important key to fertility decline. The population community took heed, integrating family planning programs with women's income generation activities and credit schemes. Unfortunately, many of these programs reinforced women's traditional roles as housewives, bakers, and handicraft makers; proved unprofitable; or made participation contingent on contraceptive use. The basic problem with the income generation approach is that women not only need income, but economic and political power, and challenging the status quo within the family and the community is not a priority.

Such challenges are a priority of many grassroots women's groups all over the world, however, who have loosely coalesced into national and international networks pressing for more fundamental changes. By the late 1980s their collective voices could no longer be ignored. The population establishment took heed again. The education and empowerment of women became high on the consensus agenda, at least rhetorically.

There are a number of problematic aspects to the renewed focus on women and its role in making the consensus more palatable to the public.

First, gender has become a way for population agencies to by-pass politically sensitive issues of class, race, and inequalities between developed and developing countries. Everyone, it seems, is for empowering poor women these days—but not for empowering poor or marginalized men. But many poor men are also "losers" in the development process.

A study in a rural area of western Kenya found that poor men were suffering a serious loss of identity because they could not fulfill their economic obligations to the family due to a lack of decent work. Male activities legitimizing their role as heads of household were also disappearing. Many turned to alcoholism and domestic violence in despair. Although women were the victims of that violence, they still had a stronger sense of identity within both the household and the community—psychologically at least, they were better off.[5]

Clearly, poor men need to be empowered too, but not in the traditional, patriarchal sense. They need education, remunerative work, community, and a sense of opportunity and hope. There are also limits to how empowered women can be if their partners are not, and vice versa—they share the same house, after all, the same economic system.

Beyond a few reforms suggested here and there, transforming economic relations is not central to the consensus agenda. Instead, educating girls is now the main strategy for empowering women. While educating girls is a laudable goal in and of itself, it is also politically safer than advocating other forms of empowerment, such as letting women organize independent trade unions in free trade zones or on plantations. The chief reason population agencies support education for girls is that it is strongly correlated with lower birth rates. If the opposite were true, would population agencies still want girls to be educated?

A more cynical observer might also see the education of girls as a way to incorporate more women into the low-wage, insecure service sector, where most new jobs are being created and where some degree of literacy is required. This is not so far-fetched, given the population establishment's instrumentalist approach toward women's participation in the labor force. For example, a "promising intervention" proposed by the World Bank is "opening up job opportunities for women in occupations that are competitive with child-rearing (e.g., factory or office jobs rather than farm jobs)."[6] Better that she slave ten hours in the factory than grow food on her own plot of land?

This instrumentalist approach extends to the environmental arena as well. The UNFPA puts Women at the very center of its Population, Environment, and Development triangle: Enhancing their status is viewed as the key to reducing population growth, which in turn is the major cause of poverty and environmental degradation. Women are not only expected to solve environmental problems by lowering their fertility, but by being trained to act as "resource managers." But for most poor women, it is greater power over resources which is required, not better management expertise alone. Moreover, in many peasant societies poor women—and men— have long known how to manage environmental resources, though these skills have often been undermined by land dispossession and the spread of corporate agriculture.

The UNFPA views management as a modern phenomenon, however: "Women who are able to manage their environment, instead of simply reacting to it, are likely to be better educated (literate) and have the ability to make decisions about the key aspects of their life."[7] Notwithstanding the value of literacy, it is patronizing to assume that illiterate peasant women simply "react" to their environment. An illiterate peasant woman in Bangladesh, for example, is likely to be a far better manager of environmental resources than a college-educated professional in New York. The latter probably generates more non-recyclable waste in a week than the former does in her entire lifetime.

This brings us to the last point. In many population publications women are presented as an undifferentiated mass which needs to be empowered, with little recognition of the many differences between them—poor or rich, rural or urban, black or white— which in turn impact on their survival and reproductive strategies. Although one can find common agendas among the world's women (for example, most women would probably support an end to domestic violence and forced prostitution), there are also major political differences between them, which include perspectives on population. How many poor women of color, for example, support the position of many rich, white women environmentalists that high fertility is the main cause of the environmental crisis? There is no consensus here, even by the wildest stretch of the imagination.

The same holds true for men. In the population consensus poor men's oppression, while scarcely mentioned, is also not linked in any way to rich men. In a new twist on male bonding, the corporate executive and the landless laborer are both just "men," in the same way that Imelda Marcos and a poor Filipina plantation worker are just "women."

QUALITY OF CARE AND REPRODUCTIVE HEALTH: HITTING THE BOTTOM LINE

As the result of feminist pressure, there have been several important attempts to reform the family planning field in the last decade. The first was the articulation of the "user perspective" by Judith Bruce of the Population Council. Bruce argued that the individual's perspective and experience, rather than being viewed as "discretionary and dispensable items," should be the determining factors in family planning programs.[8] In the late 1980s the user perspective evolved into what is called the "quality of care" approach.

The quality of care approach essentially argues that better quality services—through wider choice of methods, full disclosure of information, technical competence, and respectful interpersonal relations, for example—should be the organizing principle of family planning programs. Not only will high-quality programs better meet clients' needs than ones focused on narrow demographic targets, but they are likely to lead to greater sustained contraceptive use and hence faster falls in fertility.[9] Although many population agencies have embraced quality of care as their motto, it has been harder to translate the theory into practice. In the absence of a functioning health care system, it is difficult, if not impossible, to have a decent family planning program with adequate screening and follow-up. And concurrently with quality of care came a new generation of easily abusable, long-acting contraceptives, such as Norplant, which captured the imagination of demographically driven population programs. Who needs quality when a drug easily stuck in a woman's arm is effective for five years?

Now reformers are calling for family planning to be part of broader sexual and reproductive health services, a position endorsed by the consensus, at least on paper. The reproductive and sexual health approach maintains that family planning, including safe abortion, should be part of a wide array of services. These include pregnancy care (prenatal and postnatal care, safe delivery, nutrition, and child health), STD prevention and treatment, basic gynecological care (screening for breast and cervical cancer), sexuality and gender education, and referral systems for other health problems. It argues that those who want to control population growth should focus more on the "demand" side, creating the economic and social conditions under which people will voluntarily want fewer children, while the "supply" side—family planning within reproductive and sexual health services—should advance people's health and basic rights.[10]

The sexual and reproductive health approach has much to commend it, and is a big step forward. However, there are a number of stumbling blocks in the way of its implementation. These include:

Narrow Interpretations. Population agencies for whom demographic objectives remain paramount will strive to provide the minimum acceptable amount of sexual and reproductive health care in their programs. For example, in suggesting a transitional strategy for the next ten to fifteen years called the "1994 strategy," Anrudh Jain and Judith Bruce of the Population Council propose that family planning programs "pay attention to those aspects of reproductive health that interact directly with the avoidance of unwanted fertility." Their list is limited to safe abortion, treatment of pre-existing conditions which would make particular contraceptive methods unhealthful, and treatment of contraceptive side effects.[11] The World Bank does not consider quality of care measures necessary to implement in "emergent settings," poor countries "which have the strongest interest in speeding up the transition to lower fertility." The implicit message is that they simply do not have the time or money to worry about quality. The Bank recommends it only for "transitional settings" where poor quality in existing programs can act as a brake on contraceptive acceptance and hence demographic effectiveness.[12] In other words, the Bank is still prepared to set countries off on the wrong foot because of narrow population reduction goals. If quality is not an issue from the very beginning, it is very difficult to implement later on.

The Attack on Basic Health. The larger—and often unspoken—issue is how a broad sexual and reproductive health approach can be achieved in the context of deteriorating health conditions and services. The World Bank's structural adjustment assault on health in the 1980s has had a devastating impact in many countries, especially in Africa. Public systems have been dismantled in favor of privatization and the imposition of user fees. Nongovernmental organizations (NGOs) have been encouraged to take up the slack, as if they could ever provide all the needed services to poor people.[13] The strategy has in fact proved such a disaster that the World Bank in 1993 adopted a new approach. It now recommends a two-tier system, private comprehensive health services for the rich, and a publicly financed "essential clinical package" for the poor.[14]

Not surprisingly, the clinical package recommended for low-income countries is extremely limited: prenatal and delivery care, family planning services, management of the sick child, treatment of tuberculosis, and case management of sexually transmitted diseases. According to health researcher Meredeth Turshen,

> This clinical package reduces women's health care to services during childbirth, showing once again that women are valued only for their reproductive role. Governments will subsidize family planning services, but, because little money is intended for physician services (or the training of nurses and midwives in these tasks), women will receive contraceptives without medical supervision.... Sick children are the main beneficiaries of this clinical package, in keeping with the assumptions that families will limit the number of births only after child mortality falls, and that mothers are more likely to accept family planning from health services that care for their sick children.[15]

The World Bank is now developing an "essential package of women's health services," which so far looks much the same.[16]

Like an arsonist's fire, structural adjustment burnt public health systems to the ground, and they are now being reassembled from the ashes from only the cheapest materials and with population control at their foundation. The consensus accepts this situation as a given—it is hard to imagine how successful a sexual and reproductive health approach can be in this context.

In addition to privatizing and restricting health care, the other limiting factor is that ill health is caused mainly by poverty. It takes more than health services to cure malnutrition, which weakens immune systems, or to ensure clean drinking water. It takes economic and environmental measures which directly benefit the poor. Ultimately, any strategy which aims to improve women's sexual and reproductive health must address these underlying issues. No chronically malnourished woman will ever have acceptable reproductive health.

The danger is that the reproductive and sexual health approach will increasingly be defined as a technocratic intervention rather than as part of a more dynamic process of social change. The international women's health movement is currently divided between those who are willing to promote the approach within a population consensus framework and those who insist it be pursued independent of demographic objectives. While the former strategy may be politically pragmatic in the short run, in the long run it may backfire as population agencies squeeze sexual and reproductive health into smaller and smaller "cost-effective" packages à la World Bank.

Funding Priorities. Already, there is controversy over how much money should go to family planning, and how much to sexual and reproductive health. In the first draft of the U.N. Program of Action for the Cairo conference, family planning was slated to receive $10.2 billion in the year 2000, reproductive health care only $1.2 billion. As a result of pressure from women's groups and progressive governments, the latter figure was increased to $5 billion.[17] Though this is an improvement, family planning still has a two-to-one advantage over reproductive health.

ARE NGOS THE WAY TO GO?

A vital part of the consensus is the incorporation of more nongovernmental organizations (NGOs), into population programs. Greater reliance on NGOs is common in other areas of development and stems from a number of causes. On the positive side, NGOs often, but by no means always, have a better record of working at the community level–they can be more responsive to local needs than government bureaucracies with strong vested interests. Progressive NGOs can organize and mobilize exploited groups, such as poor women and landless laborers, to gain greater economic and political power.

On the negative side, NGOs have frequently been used as a weak substitute for public services eroded under structural adjustment, as mentioned above. They can also offer a "grassroots" legitimacy to organizations such as AID and the World Bank, who are striving to improve their image. In some cases, they have been employed as a tool of counter-insurgency, to provide intelligence about radical political movements and diffuse social discontent.

In reality, there is wide variation among NGOs; their effectiveness and commitment to the poor are dependent on their social base, leadership, and funding sources. They are neither inherently progressive nor a good substitute for government.

Pouring money into NGOs for population work could have a number of undesirable effects. First, it could skew their work away from the provision of other needed services and organizing activities. This is already happening in India, where activists are watching AID population money corrupt the NGO health sector. In the state of Uttar Pradesh alone, AID is planning to fund 100 NGOs to provide family planning services in villages as part of a big push to lower the fertility rate.[18]

AID is also turning its eyes toward environmental NGOs in a new initiative "that will draw upon the advocacy skills and networks that environmental groups employ in their efforts to build 'grassroots' awareness around the issue of population and family planning."[19] One can easily imagine a situation in which environmental NGOs cannot get funding for critical work against corporate logging, for example, but money is readily available for spreading propaganda to local populations about the need to reduce their numbers to save the trees.

There are already a number of environmental groups, based primarily in the United States, who have joined the population bandwagon and gravy train. They are playing a vital role in orchestrating the consensus and spreading population paranoia.

MAKING WAVES

The U.S. environmental movement has long been influenced by Malthusian thinking. This stems in part from the American wilderness preservation ethic, which views human civilization as essentially hostile to nature. The wilderness ethic is the product of a unique history and geography—many U.S. conservationists are ignorant of other cultures where densely populated peasant communities have developed a complex and symbiotic relationship with their environments.[20]

In the late 1960s Malthusian undercurrents in the environmental movement rose to the surface with the first big wave of population paranoia. In 1968 the Sierra Club published Paul Ehrlich's *The Population Bomb,* and in 1974 hired its first population program director. The National Audubon Society launched its own program in 1979. In 1981 Audubon sponsored a national conference on population, which became the springboard for the Global Tomorrow Coalition. The Coalition, a network of over 100 population and environmental groups, was the first major effort to bring these two constituencies together.[21] It presaged and helped to generate the second wave of population paranoia at the end of the 1980s.

This second wave arose for a number of reasons. With the end of the Cold War, fear of nuclear annihilation waned and (white) public anxiety was free to focus on other threats to security. Overpopulation was already widely perceived as the other dangerous "bomb" or "explosion," thanks to Paul Ehrlich and colleagues.

The end of the Cold War also created space for policymakers to address other pressing but neglected problems facing humanity, with environmental destruction high on the list. On the positive side this could bring greater international cooperation in the environmental field. On the negative side elites are defining and appropriating environmental concerns in such a way as to leave their power intact.

The old military-industrial complex is giving way to a new environmental-industrial one. It is composed of Northern leaders, the scientific establishment (many previously employed by the military), the World Bank through its management of the Global Environment Facility, and transnational corporations—with various NGOs included to lend legitimacy.[22] Ironically, the very institutions which contributed most to creating the environmental crisis are planning to resolve it. Population control is one of their tools.

Thus, both in the public consciousness (or lack thereof) and at the highest levels of power, population and the environment have become inextricably linked.

One by one, many mainstream environmental organizations, especially in the U.S., have been swept up in the second wave. Their renewed embrace of population reflects the largely white middle- and upper-class composition of both their leadership and constituencies (the upper ranks of these organizations are male-dominated as well), their failure to address the environmental concerns of poor communities and people of color, and a mistaken belief during the Reagan years that by defending population control they were defending reproductive rights. Outside the mainstream there is a much more broad-based and dynamic movement of social justice ecology which is not Malthusian.[23]

In addition to expanded efforts by the Sierra Club and the Audubon Society, the National Wildlife Federation (NWF) launched a full-scale population program in 1990. Many other groups are also involving themselves more deeply in population, for example, the National Resources Defense Council (NRDC), the Cousteau Society, the Worldwatch Institute, and the World Resources Institute, though some are more Malthusian than others.[24] Thousands of dollars have been spent by Audubon alone on the production of slick population propaganda, and rarely a day goes by when the mail does not bring the liberal U.S. citizen a scare message about overpopulation from one group or another. The only consolation is that now one can recycle the paper these messages are printed on.

Scientific associations are also embracing the population and environment cause, giving it an "expert" stamp of approval, despite the fact that many physical scientists have little knowledge of social science and the complexity and variability of demographic dynamics.

Though most of these organizations fall within the liberal tradition, population environmentalism also has a fascistic wing that is gaining credibility through such "respectable" intellectual figures as U.S. biologist Garrett Hardin and British public health pioneer Maurice King. Hardin was the initial architect of "lifeboat ethics"—

the belief that the earth is now a lifeboat in which there is not enough food to go around. The solution is to not let the poor and starving on board: "What happens if you share space in a lifeboat?" Hardin asks. "The boat is swamped, and everyone drowns. Complete justice, complete catastrophe."[25]

More recently, in an infamous piece in the British medical journal the *Lancet*, Maurice King recommended that where there is unsustainable population pressure on the environment, public health systems should not promote such "de-sustaining" simple methods for saving lives as oral rehydration for diarrhea "since they increase the man years of human misery, ultimately from starvation." He calls this genocidal philosophy "Health in a sustainable ecosystem." Instead of responding with an indictment, the *Lancet* ran an editorial entitled, "Nothing is unthinkable."[26] In fact, King has become a popular speaker at academic conferences on population and the environment.

In their desire to save the wilderness and shun "anthropocentrism," many deep ecologists, especially in the United States, have also displayed gross insensitivity to poor communities, in some cases even welcoming AIDS as a check on population growth.[27] Well-known U.S. poet Gary Snyder has called for a 90 percent reduction in human populations to restore the wilderness.[28]

Neo-Nazi penetration of the environmental movement is also occurring in Europe and the United States, with population control part of the white supremacist "environmental" agenda. This agenda also includes a racist assault on immigrants, which overlaps with the anti-immigration stance of a number of environmental groups.[29]

At the same time the Far Right, notably the Ku Klux Klan, has also made inroads into the antiabortion movement.[30] On many different fronts, neo-fascism is a force to be reckoned with. (See Box: The Hydra at Home.)

FORGING A COALITION FOR RIO

The growing identity of interest between the population establishment and the environmental mainstream was evident in their joint planning for the United Nations Conference on Environment and Development (UNCED), or Earth Summit, held in Rio de Janeiro, Brazil, in June 1992.

THE HYDRA AT HOME

In the United States the end of the century is beginning to have eerie parallels with the beginning, when nativism and eugenics became powerful social forces. The country is witnessing a resurgence of elite fear which seeks biological explanations and solutions for deep-rooted social and economic distress. Many politicians and technocrats are seeking scapegoats in the body politic and in the bodies of the poor, particularly poor women of color. The multi-headed Hydra is rearing its ugly heads. Slash one off, and two more seem to grow back in its place.

Judicial and legislative initiatives for mandatory contraception are one of the Hydra's heads—poor women have been sentenced to Norplant, and in some states women on welfare are denied additional benefits if they have another child (see Chapter 11). Adolescent pregnancy is considered an "epidemic", when in fact rates of teenage pregnancy have been declining every year since 1960.[1]

Another head is the crackdown on immigrants. In the new consensus thinking, the population dislocations caused by free trade, war, and maldevelopment create the need for much stricter immigration controls, not a closer look at economic and political priorities. The liberal gospel of free trade goes hand in hand with a conservative siege mentality.

In what one activist calls "border-patrol ecology," a number of population and environment groups are fomenting dangerous resentment of immigrants, and targeting immigrant women's fertility.[2] In the Sierra Club sympathizers of the Federation for American Immigration Reform (FAIR) have been pressing for anti-immigrant policies, leading to important internal struggles within the organization.[3] FAIR receives substantial funding from the Pioneer Fund, whose original founder advocated sending blacks back to Africa and supported the work of Nazi eugenicists. The Pioneer Fund still finances most major eugenics research in North America.[4] The Population-Environment Balance group and Carrying Capacity Network (CCN) are also spreading anti-immigration hysteria within the environmental community, including trying to pit African Americans against Hispanic and Asian immigrants. A recent Carrying Capacity newsletter states that in California, "There is reason to believe illegal immigrants are moving into the state in order to wrest immigration and social service benefits. As increasing numbers of women from Mexico,

China and other areas of the world come to the United States for the purpose of giving birth on U.S. soil, the United States has every right to consider some fundamental changes."[5]

These groups are spreading the false information that immigrants are a net drain on the economy, when in fact serious studies show they are clearly a net asset.[6] Governor Pete Wilson of California has called for a constitutional amendment to deny citizenship to the children of illegal immigrants, and police state measures such as mandatory ID cards are being advocated by other anti-immigration spokesmen. As this book goes to press, there is a referendum initiative in California to deny undocumented workers access to health care, except for emergency services, and to refuse their children public schooling.

Genetic determinism is also on the rise. As research on human genes flourishes, partly because of the profitable tie-in with the biotechnology business, the U.S. popular press is carrying more articles about how alcoholism, criminality, and other socially deviant behaviors may be genetically based. The implicit or explicit assumption is that these defects could become potentially avoidable through fetal genetic screening and/or denying those affected the right of reproduction. The complex interaction between genetic traits and the individual's social and economic environment is once again being grossly oversimplified, as it was in the heyday of eugenics.[7]

Population control also has a punitive crime control variant. Rather than address the underlying causes of crime—poverty and lack of opportunity—the government plans to put a hundred thousand more police on the streets and build more prisons. The death penalty is coming back in style, and a "three strikes and you're out" law means incarceration for life for those sentenced to three felonies, even if they include things like selling marijuana. The U.S. already has one of the highest per capita prison populations in the world.

Among their initiatives were the circulation and signing of a "Priority Statement on Population" within the population and environment communities. It states, "Because of its pervasive and detrimental impact on global ecological systems, population growth threatens to overwhelm any possible gains made in improving living conditions."[31] As of 1994 Zero Population Growth is still distributing this statement in its mass mailings to U.S. citizens, despite the continued opposition of many feminists.

Another joint effort was the formation of the Campaign on Population and the Environment (COPE) in 1990. COPE was a collaborative effort of the Audubon Society, the National Wildlife Federation, the Planned Parenthood Federation of America, Population Action International, and the Sierra Club. Its major objective was "to expand public awareness of the link between population growth, environmental degradation and the resulting human suffering, and to translate this into public policy."[32]

U.S. groups have also been very active in influencing international environmental organizations, such as the International Union for the Conservation of Nature (IUCN), also known as the World Conservation Union, a large and diverse consortium of both governmental organizations and NGOs. After more than a decade of pressure, Audubon claims credit for getting IUCN to embrace population as a key concern in its 1990 General Assembly.[33]

The ultimate example of the merger between the population establishment and the environmental mainstream was the transformation of the International Planned Parenthood Federation's (IPPF's) once autonomous magazine *People* into an inter-agency venture called *People and the Planet*, sponsored by the IPPF, the UNFPA, and the IUCN, in partnership with a host of other population and environment groups. The first issue of the magazine, designed for the Earth Summit, promoted the standard women, population and environment consensus. And, lest feminists should have objected, a concluding essay by UNICEF's Peter Adamson reminded them that family planning is the key to their empowerment, and furthermore, to the salvation of the world:

> Family planning could bring more benefits to more people at less cost than any other single "technology" now available to the human race.... These benefits alone would be sufficient to justify the claim of "family planning for all" to a special priority in a new world order. But it would, of course, also help to resolve one of the other great problems on the human agenda—the problem of rapid population growth.[34]

Despite their extensive preparations, the population/environment lobby did not meet with much success in Rio. The groundwork for challenging them had also been laid in advance.

In formal inter-governmental negotiations, many Southern nations had refused to put population on the UNCED agenda because it would divert attention from Northern responsibility for the environmental crisis.[35] At the same time the nongovernmental Women's Action Agenda 21, endorsed by 1,500 activists from around the world, condemned the idea "that women's fertility rates (euphemistically called population pressures) are to blame" for environmental degradation.[36]

The population/environment lobby portrayed the women's actions as playing into the hands of the Catholic Church, which wanted to avoid all mention of contraception and abortion in the Rio deliberations.[37] But feminist activists at Rio vigorously opposed the Vatican. The NGO Treaty on Population and Environment they drafted strongly supports women's access to safe, voluntary contraception and abortion as basic rights—but not as tools of population control.[38] Feminist activists identified structural adjustment, militarism, and wasteful and unjust production and consumption patterns as the key culprits in environmental degradation, not overpopulation. Representatives of the population/environment lobby found themselves outnumbered and isolated.

Coming out of Rio in defeat, the population/environment lobby had to rethink its strategy in order to secure victory in Cairo. Many members began to pay more attention to women's rights. While for some this represented a genuine change of attitude, for others it was an opportunistic decision.

The "have your cake and eat it too" syndrome also exists—the belief that you can support women's rights on the one hand and still maintain that overpopulation is a major, or the major, cause of the environmental crisis on the other. The Sierra Club, for example, continues in 1994 to pass out its tree diagram which shows overpopulation as the root system of all major environmental ills plaguing the planet.

Such images and analyses, rather than advancing women's rights, perpetuate the notion that women's fertility is to blame, and do nothing to challenge the status quo distribution of wealth and power. Without that challenge, calls for women's rights ring hollow and end up being just another rallying cry for more U.S. international population aid.

MANUFACTURING CONSENT

In the aftermath of Rio, a group of powerful actors from the population/environment lobby launched a campaign to sell the population consensus to the U.S. public and government leaders. The way this campaign has been carefully orchestrated and heavily financed is a classic example of "manufacturing consent"[39] through manipulation of the media and buying institutional allegiances.

The four main players are the Pew Charitable Trusts' Global Stewardship Initiative; the U.S. State Department through the office of Timothy Wirth, Undersecretary for Global Affairs; the UNFPA; and Ted Turner of the powerful Turner Broadcasting System, producer of Cable News Network (CNN), and his wife, former movie star Jane Fonda. The Pew Charitable Trusts, a private foundation based in Philadelphia, is the largest environmental grantmaker in the United States and thus yields tremendous power within the environmental movement. Along with several other big funders, Pew has been accused of trying to set the agenda for the movement, rather than simply providing the financial fuel to keep it going.[40] Population is one of Pew's top priorities, organized through its Global Stewardship Initiative.

Although the Pew Initiative's *White Paper* lists "population growth and unsustainable patterns of consumption" as its two challenges, population growth is by far its major concern. Among Pew's explicit goals are to "forge consensus" and "to increase public understanding of, and commitment to act on, population and consumption challenges." Its targeted constituencies in the U.S. are environmental organizations, religious communities, and international affairs and foreign policy specialists.[41]

Thanks to over $13 million in funding from Pew, the population/environment lobby churned out massive amounts of campaign material in advance of the Cairo conference. The Pew Initiative itself hired three opinion research firms to gauge public understanding of the connections between population, environment, and consumption so as to "mobilize Americans" on these issues.

The researchers found that the public generally did not feel strongly about population growth or see it as a "personal threat." Their conclusion: An "emotional component" is needed to kindle population paranoia. Those interviewed complained that they had already been overexposed to "images of stark misery, such as starving children." Although the study notes that these images may in fact "work," it recommends finding "more current, targeted visual devices." One strategy is to build on people's pessimism about the future: "For women, particularly, relating the problems of excess population growth to children's future offers possibilities."[42]

Pew and the Turner Foundation also sponsored "high visibility" Clinton-style town meetings on population around the country, featuring Timothy Wirth of the State Department, and organized through the U.S. Network for Cairo, a broad coalition of NGOs also funded by Pew. While critics of U.S. policy participated in the town meetings, the main aim was to build an even broader constituency for population and immigration control, and in particular to draw in the African-American community. "The choice of site of the mid-Atlantic meeting, Morgan State College, a historic black college, may have provided some encouragement to minority participation," reported Pew's *Global Stewardship* newsletter.[43]

Opening with footage of starving children in Africa, CNN coverage of the Atlanta town meeting made short shrift of critics while devoting generous air time to Malthusian alarmists, including Jane Fonda, who is also the UNFPA's "Goodwill Ambassador." Fonda attributed the collapse of two ancient Native American communities to overpopulation.

Other media efforts included the ICPD Global Media Project, with the backing of Jimmy Carter, which aired television ads about the Cairo conference on CNN International and other networks, a Pew campaign to place op-eds promoting population control by prominent people in newspapers, and the publicizing of a Pew-sponsored poll which "proved" that the U.S. electorate considers "rapid world population growth a serious problem," rating it on a par with world hunger, the spread of nuclear weapons, and global environmental threats. The poll also found that "Americans"—that all-encompassing term used to obscure differences—believe it is "appropriate and desirable" for the United States to be involved in

slowing global population growth. The pollsters released their findings at the United Nations during the preparatory meetings for
Cairo.[44]

Meanwhile, in the collective psyche of the national security establishment, population growth is now becoming the great scape-
goat and enemy, a substitute for the Evil Empire. A 1992 study by
the Carnegie Endowment for International Peace warned that population growth threatens "international stability" and called for "a
multilateral effort to drastically expand family planning services."[45]
A widely cited article by Thomas Homer-Dixon, Jeffrey Boutwell,
and George Rathjens identifies rapidly expanding populations as a
major factor in growing resource scarcities which are "contributing
to violent conflicts in many parts of the developing world."[46] In
1994, Undersecretary of State Timothy Wirth drew on this analysis,
identifying population growth as a major cause of the political conflicts in Rwanda, Haiti, and even the Mexican state of Chiapas.

In the pages of respectable journals, racist metaphors are acceptable again, as the concept of "noble savage" gives way to that
of postmodern barbarian. In an *Atlantic Monthly* article on the
"coming anarchy" caused by population growth and resource depletion, Robert Kaplan sensationalizes Homer-Dixon's work. He likens
poor West African children to ants—their older brothers and fathers
(and poor, nonwhite males in general) are "re-primitivized" men
who find liberation in violence, since their natural aggression has
not been "tranquilized" by the civilizing influences of the Western
Enlightenment and middle-class existence. Fomenting fear of immigrants, he warns of the "surging populations" who will cross all borders.[47]

This article, despite its implicit and explicit racism, has captured the liberal imagination, even that of President Clinton himself.
The night before a high-level special forum on population co-sponsored by the National Academy of Sciences, the Turner Foundation,
the Pew Global Stewardship Initiative, and Harvard University's
Kennedy School of Government, Clinton delivered an introductory
speech in which he began by thanking Ted Turner and Jane Fonda.

He recalled how when he was in Atlanta for a global press conference, he "got a handwritten note from Jane Fonda that said, well,
you did a pretty good job on that, but don't forget about population."

He had also received Kaplan's article somewhere along the way. "I was so gripped by many things that were in that article," he said, "and by the more academic treatment of the same subject by Professor Homer-Dixon.... You have to say, if you look at the numbers, you must reduce the rate of population growth."[48]

To his credit, Clinton also mentioned a number of other factors which he believed were impeding sustainable development, and argued against any one "silver bullet" approach. But the fact that he took Kaplan's article seriously and was so publicly beholden to Turner and Fonda showed just how powerful the forces behind the consensus are.

It is as if CNN and Pew were a shadow government, and public officials and mainstream environmentalists shadow puppets in a well-staged play.

CAIRO: A VICTORY FOR WOMEN?

At the same time that the consensus has been carefully orchestrated, the need to draw women into the process has created some political space for maneuver. The drafting of the U.N. Program of Action for Cairo was much more democratic than in the past, with a major role played by women's coalitions such as the Women's Environment and Development Organization (WEDO) and the Third World women's network, Development Alternatives with Women for a New Era (DAWN). A number of prominent feminists were appointed to government delegations, including that of the United States. As a result, the Program of Action contains many strong articulations of a women's rights perspective.

Predictably the Vatican, in an unholy alliance with conservative Islamic forces, opposed any reference, no matter how veiled, to abortion, and weakened passages on reproductive and sexual rights. The abortion war dominated the conference, drawing attention away from critiques of the population consensus by Third World women's groups and more progressive governments. (See Box: Statement of the Government of Eritrea, for an alternative voice.) The attention paid to abortion thus served the interests of the population establishment, as it did in Mexico in 1984. The worse the Vatican acted, the better the establishment looked. The final document contains mixed messages on abortion. "In no case

An Excerpt from *The Statement of the Government of Eritrea*

In the case of Africa in particular, it is debatable whether reduced population growth will mitigate its marginalization in the global economic order and accelerate its development. Africa enjoys, on the whole, considerable comparative advantages in terms of territorial expanse and natural endowments. Its population density—even taking into account current rates of fertility—is and will remain low in relative terms for the foreseeable future. The appalling poverty and deprivation that stalk the continent are not certainly due to overpopulation and they will not be eradicated if family planning were to be introduced through attractive palliatives and public education programmes and practiced by 60-65% of the population (the target figure) instead of the current rate of 10-15%. The scourge of ethnic conflicts, massive internal and external population displacement and widespread deprivation will not be healed by the most prudent and comprehensive demographic policy.

In the event, what is required is a much bolder and holistic approach that addresses and tackles the real causes of underdevelopment. Existing imbalances in the terms of international trade must be adjusted to promote rapid and sustainable development in the countries that are lagging behind and in which the economic gap is widening. Technological transfer must be encouraged particularly in the critical productive sectors rather than on few areas—such as those for producing generic drugs—apparently selected because they promote the agenda of demographic management. The effectiveness and scale of external assistance must be increased substanstantially to extricate these countries from perennial dependence and help them stand on their feet. We believe that the donor community is uniquely placed to meet this challenge at this opportune moment.

Furthermore, it is a matter of historical reality that population stabilization is likely to be achieved as a byproduct of rather than an antecedent to overall development. Entrenched cultural and social barriers to family planning can only be dispelled in proportion to societal progress in all aspects of life. The various programmes associated with family planning, and, especially the social safety nets for the elderly, public education programmes for adolescents, empowerment of women, etc. cannot be implemented on a sustainable basis from external funding. Internal development would be essential and indeed a prerequisite for an undertaking of this scale. In brief, the answer does not lie in a compartmentalised and piecemeal approach but on a comprehensive and innovative approach to the crucial issue of development in the Third World.

—Cairo, 1994

should abortion be promoted as a method of family planning," it reads. Then further on: "In circumstances in which abortion is not against the law, such abortion should be safe. In all cases, women should have access to quality services for the management of complications arising from abortion."

The document accepts the current population and development paradigm as a given, offering no substantive critique of the "free market" economic model or its impact on poor women. It only weakly criticizes poorly designed structural adjustment programs, the debt burden, and unequal terms of trade. Redistribution is out; instead, according to the Program of Action, the emphasis should be on "sustained economic growth within the context of sustainable development." To the extent that this vague formulation is defined, it seems to mean population stabilization, strategic temporary labor migration to suit the needs of multinational firms, and further incorporation of peasants and pastoralists into agricultural commodity markets.

In regard to coercion, the document states that coercion has no part to play in family planning programs, though it falls short of calling for the abolition of incentive and disincentive schemes, instead encouraging governments not to use them. Except for the monitoring of abuses, it does not set forth any institutional mechanisms which would apply sanctions to governments and organizations which employ coercive, abusive, or unsafe family planning methods.

Nevertheless, the document does represent a shift away from targets and incentives to other ways of promoting family planning. It strongly supports the use of a multiplicity of media channels in population information, education, and communication (IEC) activities "from the most intimate levels of interpersonal communication to formal school curricula, from traditional folk arts to modern mass entertainment, and from seminars for local community leaders to coverage of global issues by the national and international news media." Hard core coercion is out; the soft sell strategy is in.

The Program of Action also urges the greater use of NGOs in population and development programs and calls for incorporating population concerns "in all relevant national development strategies, plans, policies, and actions." It also calls for building "political commitment" among national leaders. What will this mean in practice? The kind of national "commitment" to population control one finds in Indonesia?

And what will increased commitment mean on the part of the international donors? According to the document, there is a "strong consensus" on the need for the international community to increase financial assistance to population programs. Will more money for population mean less money for other vital human needs? Although the document supports the direction of more national and international funds to "social development," population could receive a disproportionate share of those funds.[49] There was very little discussion at the conference of how programs would actually be financed. What the future brings will depend on how the consensus is translated into concrete population policies, which will no doubt differ from country to country. While women's empowerment will be an accepted rhetorical norm, there is little time for complacency. Women may have won some ground, but the terrain of struggle is shifting, requiring new strategies.

Aside from fighting against narrow interpretations of reproductive health (e.g., Norplant promotion with a few STD tests thrown in), coercion, contraceptive abuse, and the antiabortion movement, activists will have to take IEC programs much more seriously than they have in the past. If the new population strategy makes good its commitment to truly voluntary family planning services, without targets or incentives, then it will have to generate demand through different channels. Female literacy and empowerment, as well as reductions in child mortality, are being set forward as the social reforms necessary to increase demand for smaller families.[50] But these reforms will most likely founder on harsh economic and political realities that the population and development establishments have so far proved unwilling to confront.

Instead, in the absence of real social transformation, the emphasis will probably be on "motivational efforts" to sell the idea of small families. Many of these messages will push the consumer model: With fewer children, you can buy more and degrade the environment less, which of course is a doubtful proposition. Social marketing of contraceptives, rather than the establishment of comprehensive health services, will continue to be the priority.

When birth rates come down, IEC programs will claim victory, although they probably would have come down anyway—the trend worldwide is toward smaller families, for a host of complex reasons (see Chapter 15).

For the Western public IEC programs will mean an intensified ideological onslaught, linking population growth with political and environmental crises, with television the preferred means. Though the main purpose of the campaigns will be to build support for international population assistance, the other agenda will be population control over the domestic poor and increasingly restrictive immigration policies. Though sugar-coated with the language of women's rights, the consensus may help to breed racism and fear.

While feminists may find some space within the consensus to negotiate for higher-quality contraceptive, abortion, and health services and increased access to economic and educational resources, the real political space will remain outside, in an alliance with progressive development agencies, social justice environmentalists, and anti-racism organizers. In the New World Order not only are reproductive rights are at stake, but basic economic survival and political freedoms.

9

CHINA—
"GOLD BABIES" AND
DISAPPEARING GIRLS

Today China has the most drastic population control policy of any country in the world. The goal is to reach replacement-level fertility, an average of 2.1 births per woman, by the year 2000, leading to a population size of 1.3 billion in 2000 and 1.5 billion at mid-century. In 1993 the Chinese government announced that birth rates were declining even faster than anticipated, but this "accomplishment" has come at an immense social cost.[1]

China's one-child policy and periodic campaigns of forced sterilization, abortion, and IUD insertion have provided powerful ammunition to population control hard-liners, who argue that it proves once and for all that population control is not a Western-inspired plot against the Third World poor. China, after all, is a socialist country, as well as the largest nation in the world. If the Chinese are prepared to go to such drastic lengths to reduce population growth, then who dare dispute the need? Indeed, many argue that other countries should follow China's lead.

It is easy to forget that before the one-child family policy, China achieved substantial reductions in its birth rate through economic and social changes. It is also important to challenge the underlying rationales for the current program. Is China really teetering on the

edge of a Malthusian nightmare of overpopulation and limited resources—or is the real nightmare what is happening now, to women
and girls, in the pursuit of rigid demographic targets?

THROUGH THE LOOKING GLASS

Before the 1949 revolution China presented the world with a
picture of impending apocalypse. The country had been ravaged by
colonial powers and civil war, and the feudal land tenure system in
the countryside had blocked agricultural development. The majority
of China's people were impoverished peasants, living on the very
margin of survival. A 1929-31 survey of rural farmers found dire conditions: Infant mortality was 300 per 1,000, life expectancy was
only 24, and the birth rate was over 41.[2] In the words of one Western observer:

> China quite literally cannot feed more people.... The greatest trag-
> edy that China could suffer at the present time would be a reduc-
> tion in her death rate.... Millions are going to die. There can be no
> way out. These men and women, boys and girls, must serve as
> tragic sacrifices, on the twin altars of uncontrolled reproduction
> and uncontrolled abuse of the land and resources.[3]

The above prediction did not come true. Today, for the population as a whole, infant mortality is down to 38, life expectancy is
69, and the birth rate is around 20. With a population of approximately 1.17 billion, over one fifth of the world's people, China's
success in improving basic living standards significantly raises
global averages.

Although in retrospect the Chinese revolution had many negative features, certain of its reforms undoubtedly laid the basis for improved economic conditions and the subsequent decline in
population growth. Land reforms and the accompanying shift to
communal agriculture brought greater security to the peasants.
Working collectively, rather than in a single-family unit, reduced the
need for children as a source of labor. Free health care and welfare
funds organized by the commune or production brigade helped
guarantee old-age security, though sons still remained the chief support for parents.

In the cities, where 20 percent of the population live, labor and
social welfare legislation ensured retirement benefits, and a policy

of restricting migration into urban areas meant there was less pressure on urban employment than in many other countries. While this may have benefited the urban population, however, it restricted peasant mobility. School enrollment greatly increased—today 90 percent of primary-age children enter school—and the position of women improved. Changes in the marriage laws attempted to increase women's status within the family and substantially raised the marriage age, helping, along with education, to speed fertility decline.[4] However, the revolution failed to transform fundamentally women's subordinate role. Women continued to be responsible for the heaviest burdens of domestic work at the same time as they were increasingly incorporated in the rural and urban labor forces. Overwork and underpay were all too common, with male privilege firmly rooted in the structures of authority, from the family up to the national government.[5]

Fertility decline appears to have begun in earnest in the mid-1960s and proceeded rapidly in the 1970s. According to national statistics, the crude birth rate fell by almost half in the 1970s, from 33.6 at the beginning of the decade to 17.9 in 1979.[6]

The process was no doubt aided by an increasingly aggressive family planning program. In the early decades of the revolution, China's population policy fluctuated greatly, vacillating between the belief that a socialist economic system could benefit from and accommodate a growing population to fears that rapid population growth could slow and imperil the socialist transformation of the economy.

Though two brief birth control campaigns were launched in the 1950s and 1960s, it was not until 1971 that a national family planning program was institutionalized. Its motto was "Later, Longer, Fewer," meaning later marriages, longer intervals between births, and fewer children per family, ideally two in the cities and three in the countryside.

This campaign was built on the foundation of an impressive primary health care system, in which "barefoot doctor" paramedical workers provided basic health services to rural communities. Along with their other duties, these personnel were trained to provide contraceptives and to accompany people to commune health centers for birth control operations.

The campaign accelerated in the mid-1970s with the introduction of target population growth rates in each province and individual incentives for sterilization. Increasingly, the decision when to have children became a community affair, with local birth planning units giving permission to couples to become pregnant. Although in theory persuasion was the preferred technique, in practice there were incidents of coercion—in China the line between persuasion and coercion is often very thin.[7]

Given the country's impressive success in raising living standards and reducing birth rates, why did the government feel compelled to move ever more aggressively, culminating in the implementation of the one-child policy in 1979?

Certainly, China has good reasons for encouraging small families. With more than one fifth of the world's population on less than one tenth of the world's arable land, China does face concrete pressures on food production, including the potential ecological costs of intensifying and expanding cultivation. Yet the fact is that Chinese agriculture has kept pace with population growth, experiencing an impressive boom with the introduction of rural reforms in 1979. China now produces adequate grain to meet all requirements for direct human consumption, feed for livestock and poultry, and seed. The Chinese diet is improving—daily per capita caloric intake is one third higher than it was in 1969-71; per capita meat and poultry consumption was three times more in 1992 than it was 1978.[8]

Even more impressive is the country's rate of economic growth, one of the highest in the world. Chinese leaders are in fact worried that they may need to slow the momentum of growth in order to plan it better. For example, some of the main pressures on China's arable land are associated with modernization: highway development, spreading urbanization, and luxury uses such as golf courses and race tracks.[9]

Ironically, while leaders now worry that economic growth may need to slow down, one of the main justifications for cracking down on births was to speed it up. The decision to launch the one-child policy was prompted by the ambitious new economic strategy initiated by the post-Mao leadership, who, among other things, opened up the country to Western investment. Today in China slogans proclaim "It Is Glorious to Get Rich," in marked contrast to the radical egalitarianism of the Mao era. And according to government logic, babies present a serious obstacle to economic growth. "One fourth of the rise in national income each year has been consumed by the new-borns," claims the minister in charge of China's State Family Planning Commission.

According to the minister, the people are in agreement:

> In order to become rich more quickly and build up a society that is comfortably off, many couples would like to have fewer children and delayed childbearing. They prefer "gold babies" to chubby babies [that is, they prefer to get rich before having children].[10]

But in China family size has a lot less to do with the trade-off between "gold babies" and "chubby babies" than with the politics of gender, rural-urban disparities, and the government's own coercive policies.

FEWER CHILDREN, FEWER GIRLS

In 1984 a documentary on China's one-child policy in the model city Changzhou appeared on public television in the United States and Great Britain. In one of the opening scenes, a young woman, Mrs. Chang Kang Mei, describes how she was "persuaded" by family planning workers to abort her second child when she was seven months pregnant. "I did want to have the baby," she tells the interviewer. "Yes, I did want it. But after they came and did their work, I agreed to the abortion."[11]

Despite her initial resistance, she was also persuaded to undergo sterilization several months later. The city's family planning program had scored yet another success in their drive to achieve complete compliance with the one-child policy, but at what human cost?

Instituted in 1979, the one-child policy has gone through several phases. At first its mission was to encourage couples to have one child, but in 1980 encouragement gave way to official mandate. Coercion became more routine, culminating in a mass sterilization drive in 1983 in which 20 million people were sterilized. Facing widespread resistance, especially in the countryside, where couples wanted at least one son, the government was forced to relax the policy somewhat. It adopted more liberal guidelines on second births in 1984, and in 1988 allowed rural couples whose first child was a girl to have a second child, legitimizing son preference. Third births have been proscribed all along. From the beginning, many ethnic minorities have been excluded from the one-child policy.[12]

China's one-child policy is enforced by a system of strong incentives and disincentives with local and regional variations. Incentives for signing a one-child certificate include preferential access to food, housing, health care, and educational benefits. In the countryside couples may receive extra allocations of land; in the cities, salary supplements. Disincentives, which are easier to enforce in urban areas, include financial penalties, denial of free social services, and demotion. In some cases financial penalties are imposed not only on the couple in question, but other family members and co-workers.[13] Party cadres and local officials are also rewarded or punished on the basis of whether they fill their one-child family quotas.

In urban areas the policy is enforced by an efficient reproductive policing operation. In factories family planning workers carefully watch women to make sure they do not become pregnant. "We watch for women who start to eat less or who get morning sickness," explained one such worker in Changzhou. "If a woman isn't as active as she usually is, that's a sign of pregnancy. It's very difficult to escape the attention of us family planning workers.... No one has ever become pregnant without one of us finding out."[14] Women who use the IUD are subjected to periodic X-ray checks to make sure the coil is still in place.

In general, the one-child policy has met with more success in urban areas where desired family size tends to be smaller, though one recent study of 857 employed women in Beijing and Shenyang found that over half wanted two children. The study examines how most of the women interviewed accept the population policy and do not consider it coercive despite their desire for more children— they perceive "control as care" on the part of the family planning workers. This is not only because the workers provide support and services for approved births, but because of broader cultural and political norms.

According to Cecilia Milwertz, author of the study, there are four key features to the perception of control as care:

First, control and monitoring are taken for granted as a basic element of everyday life. Secondly, the women being controlled are aware that birth planning workers are themselves subject to control—they are just doing their job. Third, control as care is based on cultural assumptions of reciprocity. As long as the work unit satisfies the needs of employees, they will in return follow the requirements of the work unit. Fourth, women and their families are willing to act contrary to fertility preferences by following the one-child requirement on the condition that the policy requirement is applicable to all urban residents.[15]

In rural areas there has been far more resistance to the policy. Not only are children of more direct economic benefit in peasant society, as both farm labor and old-age security, but according to demographer Susan Greenhalgh, the de-collectivization and agricultural reforms of the 1970s and early 1980s "loosened cadre control over the peasantry, undermining enforcement mechanisms and greatly expanding the room for resistance to unpopular policies" such as the one-child requirement.[16]

Resistance has taken many forms in rural China, from paying the fines levied if one has another child, to having IUDs removed privately, to escaping to a relative's house in another village before a pregnancy starts to show, to acts of violence against cadres, such as burning their houses down. But while resistance forced a relaxation of the population policy in the mid-1980s, periodic crackdowns, or "shock months," as they are sometimes called, continue. In 1991 the government introduced a new "responsibility system," which has led to human rights violations on a massive scale. Higher-level officials now hold local officials directly responsible for meeting population targets; if they fail, their wages are docked and promotions denied.[17]

Compulsory sterilization campaigns and forced abortions are the main weapons of the recent crackdown—in 1991, 12.5 million people were sterilized, helping to explain the dramatic drop in the birth rate from 19.7 in 1991 to 18.2 in 1992. In some rural areas officials have resorted to destroying the houses of resisters or beating them up: "They often take things, your furniture, your cow, your pig, your chickens, your preserved meat," a woman in Guizhou Province told a reporter. "If you get sterilized, they take your stuff, and if you don't get sterilized, they beat you. Some people have been beaten badly, family members and women. They take electric batons and they hit whomever they see."[18]

Despite its brutality, direct physical coercion is only the tip of the iceberg when it comes to the negative effects of the Chinese program. Violence takes many other forms, such as damage to women's health and the survival prospects of girls.

Women's health has suffered not only because of forced, late abortions—which carry significant physical, not to mention psychological, risks—but because of the contraceptive policy in general. The Chinese discriminate against temporary contraceptive methods, such as the pill and barrier methods, which are also under the user's control. Instead, the policy is to push "the four operations": IUD insertion, tubectomy, vasectomy, and abortion, which together account for almost 90 percent of contraceptive use. Female methods are preferred—there are three times as many tubectomies as vasectomies, despite the fact that the latter is much safer.

The quality of both contraceptive technologies and services is also problematic. Although there has been little official research on contraceptive side effects, case studies identify post-sterilization infection as a problem, which is not surprising given the prevalence of mass sterilization campaigns with rushed operations in inadequate facilities. The main IUD used in China, a stainless steel ring with no string, was purposely designed so that women could not remove it themselves. The absence of a string means its location cannot be checked except by X-rays and ultrasound, subjecting women to unnecessary medical interventions. The steel-ring IUD also has high rates of failure and expulsion compared to the Copper T, for example. A study found that IUD failure accounted for 80 percent of abortions in one county.[19]

While forced sterilization campaigns make a mockery of the very concept of "services," basic health standards required for proper IUD insertion are also lacking. According to recent research, medical screening for IUD contraindications was largely ignored in the counties studied; in fact, "in most of rural China, no facilities or personnel exist to perform laboratory tests for family planning clients." According to the Population Crisis Committee, this gives cause "for grave concern."[20]

Since women are the chief targets of the Chinese program, they are also the main resisters, and as Susan Greenhalgh points out, resistance itself heightens bodily risks:

> The more children a woman succeeded in having, the more likely she was to be labeled a troublemaker and targeted for surgery. The more women contested the implantation of IUDs, the greater the number of insertions, extractions, and reinsertions of the device they had to undergo. Getting pregnant outside the community ideal always entailed the risk of detection and subsequent "mobilized" (i.e., coerced), often late-term abortion.[21]

In the villages she studied, Greenhalgh found that one out of every eight women married in the 1970s had suffered the trauma of a second- or third-trimester abortion by 1987.

Unprecedented in world history, the Chinese population program has also had an unprecedented—and tragic—impact on girls. Superimposed on a patrilocal and patriarchal culture and economy which largely depends on sons to carry on the family line and provide old-age security, the Chinese program has not only sanctioned gender bias but intensified it. China has one of the most skewed sex ratios in the world. In the late 1980s there were approximately 110 to 113 boys for every 100 girls under the age of one, compared to the normal ratio of 105 boys to 100 girls. In absolute numbers, 700,000 to 800,000 fewer girls are being born per year than one would expect with a normal sex ratio.[22]

Demographers and researchers put forward three main reasons for this disparity: female infanticide, sex-selective abortion, and under-reporting of girls' births, though it is difficult to pin precise statistics to any of these causes. Soon after the introduction of the one-child policy, the Chinese press carried a number of reports of parents drowning, suffocating, or abandoning their baby daughters so they would have another chance to try for a boy. The Anwei Women's Federation found that in one village alone forty baby girls had been drowned in 1980-81.[23] Most observers agree that while cases of female infanticide still exist today, they are not the primary cause of the skewed ratios.

Sex-selective abortion probably plays a greater role. Although in theory the practice is illegal in China, enforcement is difficult. Ultrasound technology is spreading rapidly, and the country now has the capacity to produce 10,000 machines a year. Most township clinics already have machines, ostensibly to determine whether a woman is pregnant or has an IUD in place. Although there are no accurate statistics, Chinese officials view sex selection as a growing problem.[24]

The main cause of the skewed ratio, however, is probably under-reporting of female births. On the positive side, this means that many of the "missing" girls are still alive, although not necessarily in the best of circumstances. Many girls are either hidden by their families or fostered or adopted by others. "This enables their parents to continue trying to produce a son and to escape a fine for an over-quota birth, a fine they would probably be willing to pay if they produced a boy," writes Kay Johnson in her study of girls' abandonment in Hubei Province.[25]

Theoretically, one might expect that girls' abandonment would have declined with the 1988 shift to the "one son or two child" policy allowing rural couples to try for another child if their first is a girl. Johnson found that, on the contrary, abandonment escalated after 1988 because the policy was enforced more thoroughly and coercively—the official strategy was "to open a small hole in order to close a large hole." While the 1988 policy probably reduced the risk to first-born daughters, it shifted it to those born after. After the birth of a second daughter, most parents still want a son, but face the prospect of sterilization unless they hide, secretly give away, or outright abandon the daughter.

The "missing" girls suffer discrimination in a number of ways. If they are not officially registered, they lack access to schooling and services. If they are abandoned as infants, they are often weak and ill by the time they reach an orphanage, and it is difficult to find adoptive parents who are willing to finance the medical care needed to save them. In the Wuhan orphanage studied by Johnson, the mortality rate was almost 50 percent, despite the staff's best efforts to provide care. In recent years almost all the children taken in by the orphanage have been girls.

And it is not only infants who are abandoned. In 1991, in the midst of a rural "mobilization campaign" to sterilize all women who had two children, the orphanage received up to ten children a day, many between the ages of two and five. Johnson writes:

These were truly the saddest cases for the orphanage, for these children were old enough to miss their parents and their homes and to show the emotional scars of abandonment. The Director mentioned a miserable five-year-old girl who arrived at the orphanage with a poem written by her parents in her pocket. It lamented the fact that they were giving up their child, bitterly blaming the government's population control policies for forcing them into this act. The parents hoped that someday they could come back and retrieve their daughter, although, as noted, few parents ever do return to claim a child.[26]

The lack of public outcry over the missing girls reflects the urban bias of many Chinese journalists and intellectuals, who blame peasants for China's population problems as well as for the persistence of "feudal culture" which discriminates against girls. But the fact is that the Chinese population policy has created a new hybrid culture of male bias, reinforcing old norms, for example by legitimizing son preference through "relaxations" in the one-child policy, and new norms, such as making women's bodies the targets of its campaigns.[27] This is not an argument for either a stricter one-child-only policy or shifting coercion onto men. Rather, the whole system itself must be challenged, including the population control principles upon which it is based.

SEE NO EVIL, HEAR NO EVIL, SPEAK NO EVIL

Deviating radically from the two-child norm advocated by most members of the population community, China's one-child policy has inevitably stirred much controversy. Population control hard-liners see it as a vindication of their view that drastic measures are required to check population growth and as a warning to countries who delay taking population control measures—in the end, they too may have no choice but to press for the one-child family.[28]

International population agencies, however, tend to be more circumspect. They are pleased, of course, that China has brought down population growth so fast, but are hesitant to endorse coercion openly. Instead, they downplay it, claiming it is a thing of the past or the fault of local officials incorrectly interpreting government policy. "In recent years, Chinese leaders have begun to move the family planning program in positive directions," wrote the Population Crisis Committee in 1992, after the preceding pages of its own report documented systematic abuses. In 1991-92 coercion in fact was probably at an all-time high. Similarly, in 1989 the Population Council ranked China first among developing countries in "family planning program effort," in other words giving it star marks for coercion.[29]

With a few brave exceptions, foreign demographers and social scientists have also been reluctant to criticize the Chinese program openly, fearing loss of access to Chinese research institutions and data. "Some claim that they can exert a moderating influence on Chinese population policies if they maintain good relations with the Chinese authorities," writes John Aird in his book *Slaughter of the Innocents.* "After a decade of opportunity, however, not much moderation has occurred for which they can claim credit."[30] Other demographers accept that individual rights may need to be sacrificed in order to address the population "crisis" in China and elsewhere.[31]

Although external aid accounts for only a small percentage of China's annual $1 billion-plus population budget, it has helped to legitimize the program in the eyes of the outside world. The UNFPA, the main foreign contributor, has been the worst offender. It has not only turned a blind eye toward coercion in China, but has actively rewarded it. In 1983, during the first wave of heavy coercion, China's Family Planning Minister Qian Xinzhong, together with the late Indian Prime Minister Indira Gandhi, received the U.N.'s Population Award for "the most outstanding contribution to the awareness of population questions." (Indira Gandhi was responsible for the compulsory sterilization drive in India in the mid-1970s.) In 1989 Nafis Sadik, UNFPA Executive Director, stated in a speech in Washington, D.C. that the Chinese program was "totally voluntary."[32]

The UNFPA's failure to criticize coercion in China opened it to attacks by anti-abortion forces in the United States, who claimed that the organization was helping to support forced abortion and sterilization in China. As a result of these pressures, the Reagan administration withdrew its annual contribution of $25 million to the UNFPA.

Under the Clinton administration, aid to the UNFPA is being resumed. Although the administration has criticized human rights violations in China, the population policy has not been high on the list, despite the fact that it has affected millions of people. The resumption of China's most-favored-nation trading status in 1994 shows that ultimately commercial interests override the administration's concerns for human rights.

In 1993 the Chinese government issued a new challenge to the international community by announcing proposed eugenics legislation which would mandate government-ordered sterilizations and abortions for certain categories of mentally and physically disabled people. According to China's Minister of Public Health, the country "now has more than 10 million disabled people who could have been prevented through better controls."[33] In a positive move, the World Bank held up a reproductive health loan to China because of the proposed legislation.[34]

In the foreseeable future the strategy of international agencies, most notably the UNFPA, will probably be to promote some small reforms of the Chinese program, while accepting its broader contours. The UNFPA, for example, is helping the Chinese to shift to Copper T IUDs and plan for the local production of Norplant.[35] While coercive use of Norplant may be "preferable" to coercive abortion and sterilization, coercion is coercion nonetheless. A wider array of contraceptives and better training of family planners, another UNFPA goal, will not fundamentally alter the Chinese program, based as it is on rigid birth quotas.

There is no dearth of alternatives to the current program. Taiwan, for example, experienced a demographic transition without recourse to any draconian means (see Chapter 15). Expanded educational opportunities and pension plans in the Chinese countryside would probably do more to reduce son preference and desired family size than any measures which directly target women's wombs.[36] And above all, the population crisis mentality is simply unjustified. China began its demographic transition well before the government crackdown—moreover, agricultural and economic growth have kept ahead of population growth. China may well be the next "Asian miracle."

And even if there were a crisis? How about a "shock" rural pension plan or "forced" redistribution of educational resources from the favored urban areas to the countryside? Why are women's bodies always considered the prime locus of population control policies?

Within the international community, a double standard is also at work, which centers on the concept of "voluntarism." "As I see it, voluntarism is based on the idea that couples should have the right—the basic human right—to determine the number of its children," wrote UNFPA official Walter Holzhausen. "But what is a human right in one country may not be a right in another."[37] There is a sense that Asian peoples, especially, are different, that they are more willing to accept authoritarian control over reproduction and are less concerned than Westerners with individual rights. "A growing problem in the future," predicted Dr. Stephen Sinding, former head of AID's Office of Population, "is likely to be the difference in perspective between Western voluntarism and the urgency Asian countries feel to bring down their population growth rates."

But is the distinction really so much between cultures as it is between the controllers and the controlled? Many Western members of the population establishment are more than ready to infringe on individual rights, even in their own countries, when it comes to population control, and they have exerted powerful pressures on Third World leaders. Asian countries "are taking the action we've urged them all along to take," admitted Dr. Sinding.[38] It is the people on the bottom who have the best appreciation of voluntarism, because they know what it means to be denied it.

Today population control—a philosophy that subordinates people's need for control over their own bodies and lives to dubious economic and political imperatives—knows no borders. Its very universality demands a universal response, a set of ethics that is not relative to race, class, sex, or nationality. Only through respect for basic human rights can family planning be liberated from the yoke of population control and play a liberating role in the lives of women—and men—around the world.

Part Three

CONTRACEPTIVE
CONTROVERSIES

10

SHAPING
CONTRACEPTIVE
TECHNOLOGY

Technological innovations are not "neutral"; instead, they embody the values of their creators. It is no accident that at the end of the twentieth century billions of dollars are spent every year on weapons of destruction and luxury goods, while technologies that could dramatically improve people's lives—nonpolluting energy sources, sustainable agricultural systems, basic health and sanitation measures—receive minimal funding at best. Those who hold the reins of power exercise power over technological choice.

Contraceptive technology is no exception. The contraceptive revolution of the second half of this century has been influenced more by the pursuit of population control, prestige, and profit than by people's need for safe birth control. Millions of dollars have flowed into the development, production, and promotion of technically sophisticated contraceptives such as the pill, injectables, and implants, despite their health risks, while the improvement of safer and simpler barrier methods has been virtually neglected, with tragic consequences in this era of the AIDS epidemic.

The misdirection of contraceptive technology begins in the research phase and culminates in its use as a destructive and even deadly weapon in the war on population. It is mainly women who bear the cost, many paying dearly with their health and lives.

THE SEARCH BEHIND THE RESEARCH

Prior to the mid-twentieth century, the social stigma attached to contraception made the medical profession and the pharmaceutical industry shy away from research and development of new birth control methods. Before 1959, "the word contraceptive suggested rubber goods from a back street shop, not a tablet from a leading pharmaceutical company," commented a representative of the drug manufacturer G. D. Searle & Co.[1]

What then ignited the contraceptive revolution? The catalyst, to a large extent, was the powerful new philosophy of population control. In the search for a quick solution to rising birth rates, members of the population community began to press for the development of new contraceptive methods.

In 1950, at the age of eighty-eight, Margaret Sanger wrote in a fundraising letter: "I consider that the world and almost all our civilization for the next 25 years is going to depend upon a simple, cheap, safe contraceptive to be used in poverty-stricken slums and jungles, and among the most ignorant people."[2] She raised $150,000 for Gregory Pincus, a reproductive scientist based in Massachusetts, to start research on a "universal" contraceptive. Pincus subsequently became a consultant to G. D. Searle, and the company marketed the first birth control pill in 1960. The contraceptive revolution was underway.

Searle's profits were substantial enough to entice other pharmaceutical firms into the contraceptive business, and the private sector dominated contraceptive research and development until the late 1960s. At the same time, however, the Ford Foundation, the Rockefeller Foundation, and the Population Council increased their funding for contraceptive research and urged the U.S. government to do the same. Much of the early impetus came from India, scene of the first government-sponsored family planning program, backed strongly by Ford. U.S. officials blamed the program's poor results on the lack of a "technological breakthrough." One U.S. Agency for International Development (AID) official went so far as to call for a crash program to develop birth control technology akin to the "intensive and coordinated research and development effort which solved the problem of controlled nuclear explosion."[3]

By the late 1960s the U.S. government, through AID and the National Institutes of Health, had become a major funder of contraceptive research. During the next decade, it overtook the pharmaceutical industry in terms of investment in the field. By 1983 the U.S. government provided 59 percent of the $167 million in total worldwide expenditures in basic reproductive research, contraceptive research and development, and the evaluation of the long-term safety of existing contraceptive methods. U.S. pharmaceutical industries contributed another 21 percent and U.S. foundations another 4 percent, for a total U.S. contribution of almost 85 percent.[4]

Today the major institutions involved in contraceptive research and development are:

- U.S. Government Agencies: AID and the National Institute of Child Health and Human Development, Contraceptive Development Branch.
- U.S. Nonprofits: Contraceptive Research and Development Program (CONRAD), Family Health International, the Institute for International Studies in Natural Family Planning at Georgetown University, the Population Council, the Program for Appropriate Technology in Health (PATH), the Program for Applied Research on Fertility Regulation, the Program for the Introduction and Adaptation of Contraceptive Technology (PIACT), and more than twenty-four universities.
- U.S. Companies: Ortho Pharmaceutical Corporation and a number of smaller firms specializing in one or two products.
- U.S. Private Foundations: the Mellon Foundation, the Rockefeller Foundation, and the Berlex Foundation.
- International Agencies: The International Development Research Center (Canada); the UNFPA; the World Bank; the International Organization for Chemical Synthesis in Development; and the WHO Special Program in Research, Development, and Research Training in Human Reproduction (HRP). The HRP, which is co-sponsored by the WHO, the U.N. Development Program, the UNFPA, and the World Bank, is now a major force in the contraceptive field, active

in the introduction of new methods into Third World countries.

- National Research Centers in Developing Countries: the Indian Council of Medical Research and China's National Research Institute for Family Planning.
- Non-U.S. Pharmaceutical Firms: Lamberts Ltd. in England
  (cervical caps), Leiras Pharmaceuticals in Finland (Norplant),
  Organon International in the Netherlands (implants, vaginal
  rings, steroids), Roussel Uclaf in France (RU486), and Schering, A. G. in Germany (steroids).[5]

There are several reasons why private industry's share in contraceptive research is now so much lower than that of public institutions. The costs involved in developing and testing new
contraceptives are very high: To produce a totally new contraceptive for women requires an estimated investment of ten to seventeen years and up to $100 million or more.[6]

Companies are also worried about the risk of high product liability payments. Liability fears have already led two U.S. companies, Upjohn and G. D. Searle, to close down their fertility research
operations, and only one U.S. company, Ortho Pharmaceuticals, is
still doing extensive research in the field.

Even public sector contraceptive researchers are having trouble
getting liability insurance, and as a result, the testing of many new
contraceptives—from spermicides to hormonal implants—is being
delayed.[7] The liability problem, of course, is not limited to the contraceptive field but plagues the entire U.S. medical establishment.
Its resolution depends on safeguarding people's ability to seek effective redress against medical malpractice, harmful drugs, and dangerous contraceptives (the Dalkon Shield IUD, for example) at the
same time that the liability system is overhauled, so that insurance
rates and payments are kept within the bounds of reason.

Despite these obstacles, the fact remains that contraceptives
are highly profitable items. In the mid-1980s the U.S. retail contraceptive market alone was estimated to be almost $1 billion a year;
worldwide sales were probably over twice this figure. Moreover,
oral and injectable contraceptives are among the most lucrative of
all pharmaceuticals.[8]

A more compelling reason for the public sector's domination of contraceptive research lies in the close relationship between the companies and the population establishment.

COMMON INTERESTS

In the contraceptive field, as well as in many other scientific endeavors, there is not necessarily a dichotomy between government and private research. In the United States legal provisions allow private firms to incorporate government-sponsored contraceptive research into their own product development activities, and in some cases public agencies will finance trials of drugs developed by private industry. The companies thus directly benefit from public research funds, and a number of them are strong supporters of the population lobby in Congress.[9] Public research institutions, on the other hand, need the companies to manufacture the contraceptives, since they do not have an industrial capacity.

The common interest between the companies and the population establishment runs much deeper, however. As health researcher Cary LaCheen points out in a critical study, both are interested in maximizing the volume of contraceptives distributed worldwide, and in reaching new consumers or acceptors in the Third World.

Population control programs represent an important market for a number of pharmaceutical companies. AID, for example, has spent an average of $15 million annually on birth control pills since the mid-1970s. From 1972 to 1979 most of this money went to one company alone, the Syntex Corporation, accounting in some years for 25 to 30 percent of Syntex's total oral contraceptive sales. Similarly, between 1982 and 1984, AID bought all of its $6.7 million worth of IUDs from Finishing Enterprises. According to an industry source, Ansell Industries, which produces condoms, would probably go out of business without AID contracts.[10]

Although not all companies rely so heavily on AID sales, the contraceptives they provide to population programs reach untapped markets where the companies would like to expand. Population agencies, in fact, play a vital role in advertising, promoting, and distributing industry products in the Third World.

This is particularly true in the case of Contraceptive Social Marketing (CSM) programs. In these programs, birth control pills, condoms, and sometimes spermicide tablets are sold at subsidized prices through existing marketing channels, typically small village shops. They are also advertised heavily, through, in the words of one organization, "the proven techniques used to sell soap, soft drinks and toothpaste in every corner of the globe."[11] AID and IPPF are among the main supporters of these schemes, which are now an integral part of many Third World population programs. Africa is the latest target.[12] (On the health implications of this approach, see Chapter 11.)

According to LaCheen, "Contraceptive Social Marketing programs have whittled away the distance between population assistance programs and the contraceptive industry—and serve the industry's needs much more completely and directly than other types of population programs."[13] CSM schemes absorb the high costs of market research, advertisement, and distribution in remote rural areas. They accustom poor people to paying for contraception, albeit at reduced prices, and create a general awareness of modern contraceptive methods. In short, the industry gets a free ride down unpaved roads and dusty paths to thousands of Third World villages. In order to maintain the profitable alliance between themselves and the population establishment, industry officials not only lobby Congress on the need for population appropriations, but give donations to population control organizations. According to LaCheen, the Syntex Corporation, for example, gives several thousands of dollars each year to the Population Crisis Committee.[14] Interlocking directorates further cement the alliance.

Take, for instance, Family Heath International (FHI), whose population research is heavily funded by AID. Dr. William N. Hubbard, president of the Upjohn Company, the manufacturers of Depo-Provera, was on the FHI board of directors when in 1983 FHI president Dr. Malcolm Potts testified for the approval of Depo-Provera as a contraceptive before a U.S. board of inquiry.[15]

In a number of ways, then, the interests of the contraceptive industry and the population establishment converge.

Many would argue that there is nothing intrinsically wrong with such a convergence, if the end result is that new and better contraceptives are developed and distributed widely around the globe. Before accepting such an argument, however, it is important to look at how these institutions have helped to bias the direction of contraceptive technology.

CONTRACEPTIVE BIASES

There are three basic biases in contemporary contraceptive research. First, research has focused overwhelmingly on the female reproductive system. In 1978, for example, 78 percent of public sector expenditures for the development of new contraceptives was for female methods, as opposed to only 7 percent for males.[16]

This is not only because women are the chief targets of population control programs but, according to Forrest Greenslade of the Population Council, "because of sexism."[17] From top to bottom, men dominate the contraceptive research field, and many of them hold the view that reproduction is basically a woman's concern. As R. J. Ericsson, an early pioneer in male reproductive research, complained,

> Male contraceptive research has a dismal past. It is almost an illegitimate specialty within reproductive biology. For the most part, the brightest workers avoid it, and those who do work in the area are looked on as rather strange fellows.[18]

This is slowly beginning to change. In the period from 1980 to 1983, for example, male methods accounted for 12 percent of total contraceptive research and development expenditures.[19] However, even though organizations such as the Population Council are now devoting more resources to male reproductive research, people in the field say it will take at least fifteen to twenty years to catch up in building a knowledge base from which to develop male contraceptives.

A second persistent bias is toward systemic and surgical forms of birth control, as opposed to safer barrier methods. Thus, hormonal, immunological, and surgical methods received almost 70 percent of total public expenditures for the development of new contraceptives in 1978, while barrier methods such as the diaphragm and condom received only 2.2 percent.[20]

Today, due to consumer and feminist pressure, and the prevalence of HIV and other sexually transmitted diseases, resources devoted to barrier methods are slowly increasing, both in the public and private sectors (see Chapter 14). From 1980 to 1983 they averaged almost 5 percent of contraceptive research and development expenditures. The overwhelming emphasis is on *female* barrier methods, however—the male condom has been almost totally neglected.

Female hormonal methods in particular have received a disproportionate share of research funds, accounting for nearly 30 percent of contraceptive research and development expenditures from 1980 to 1983.[21] They continue to appeal to many members of the population establishment who are still searching for a "miracle" contraceptive that will solve the world's population problem. Their preference, as we shall see, is for long-acting methods that require little initiative by the user and minimal interaction between the user and provider, reducing both the risk of accidental pregnancy and the need for counseling and support services. Increasingly, the implicit goal is to remove control from the woman entirely, as is the case with Norplant and the new anti-pregnancy "vaccines."

The pharmaceutical industry has concentrated on hormonal methods not only because they are highly profitable—much more profitable than a diaphragm, which can be used for a year or more—but because public research funds have flowed in this direction. For their part, medical researchers are drawn to sophisticated systemic methods, incorporating the latest in biomedical science, since these are more likely to win recognition, prestige, and lucrative contracts.

A third bias, linked to the previous two, is a greater concern for contraceptive efficacy than safety.

SAFETY FIRST—OR LAST?

From 1965 onward less than 10 percent of total expenditures on reproductive research and contraceptive development has been devoted to safety.[22] This relative disregard for safety is the single most important factor underlying contraceptive abuse.

Safety expenditures also remain concentrated in the industrialized countries, which have more financial resources and trained personnel to test and investigate new contraceptives, and where the media and consumer and women's groups play a key role in keeping up public pressure for regulation. In the United States, the Food and Drug Administration (FDA) is the government's main watchdog agency over the pharmaceutical industry. Since many Third World (and other) governments depend heavily on FDA rulings to formulate their own guidelines, its influence extends far beyond U.S. borders.

Just how effective is the FDA in protecting the consumer against contraceptive abuse? FDA approval of a new contraceptive typically takes eight and a half years. The tests are more stringent than for many other drugs, since contraceptives may be used regularly by healthy individuals for a period of up to thirty years. In the case of hormonal contraceptives, the FDA requires pharmaceutical manufacturers to undertake both short- and long-term animal tests and human trials. The burden of proof lies on the manufacturer, who must prove the drug is safe. This contrasts with weaker regulatory procedures in Great Britain, for example, where it is enough to present evidence that a drug is not unsafe. Of course, safety itself is a relative term. According to the authors of a 1990 National Research Council report on contraceptive development in the U.S.:

> All active drugs cause adverse effects in some users. If safety were understood as the total absence of adverse effects, then no drug could be called "safe." Safety of a drug is conceived as a favorable ratio of benefits to risks for the population of users of the drug as a whole.[23]

Although on the surface FDA regulations seem strict, experience has sometimes proved otherwise. Industry pressure can weaken FDA resolve. FDA officials often pass from public service to lucrative jobs with private industry, helping to ensure that pharmaceutical firms have clout within the agency. In 1974 fourteen FDA employees brought charges against the agency, claiming that because of industry pressure, they were removed from positions where they were either holding up drug approvals or preparing cautionary labeling.

Even when the FDA does not bow to industry pressure, the companies do not always play by the rules. An FDA investigation of G. D. Searle, for example, revealed that the company had consistently faked results in drug safety tests, including surreptitious removal of a tumor from a test dog in a study of the oral contraceptive Ovulen. In the aftermath of the investigation, the FDA commissioner conceded that the evidence cast doubt on the believability of all drug safety tests.[24]

Nevertheless, compared to the absence of regulatory procedures in many Third World and even some European countries, the FDA provides an important measure of protection against potentially harmful contraceptives. However, there are currently attempts to weaken its standards.

The National Research Council report, for example, recommends that the FDA assign more weight to contraceptive effectiveness and convenience of use than it does presently. According to the authors:

> Given the potentially serious health consequences of an unwanted pregnancy resulting from contraceptive failure, methods with fewer side effects are not necessarily safer if they have higher failure rates. The social and health risk of pregnancy will be important considerations for users and must be weighed in the calculation of the safety of the methods.

This argument does not take into account the critical back-up of legal abortion, nor does it specify exactly what is the "social risk" of pregnancy. A further recommendation sheds some light, however, on the underlying ideology. The report urges the FDA to approve certain contraceptives—even if they pose health risks—for the use of specific subpopulations that are "not adequately served by other contraceptives." One can easily imagine a double standard developing: Adolescents and Third World populations both at home and abroad would be made to assume greater health risks for the social goal of limiting their births. In general, the report supports the view that too much attention to safe delivery of contraceptives in the United States is hindering the rate of contraceptive development.[25]

Theoretically, FDA protection extends overseas by a law that prohibits U.S. pharmaceutical manufacturers from exporting drugs not approved for sale in the United States. However, many companies have gotten around this restriction by using foreign subsidiaries to manufacture and export unapproved drugs. There has also been considerable pressure on Congress to change existing legislation so that U.S. firms can export new drugs even if not yet approved for use within the United States, if the drugs meet certain minimal safety standards and the specifications of the importing country. In late 1986 Congress passed legislation that allows such exports to twenty-one countries, mainly in Western Europe.[26]

The eagerness of contraceptive manufacturers to circumvent U.S. regulations reflects a basic economic calculation: In contrast to the industrialized countries where near-zero population growth has led to a saturation of the contraceptive market, the Third World presents a large, expanding market. Companies today are also shifting their initial research efforts abroad, where drug regulations are not so rigid.[27]

In fact, in the contraceptive research business, the Third World has long been an important laboratory for human testing. From 1980 to 1983 at least one fifth of contraceptive research and development and safety evaluation projects were located in developing countries, with India, China, Chile, Mexico, and Brazil the major locations.[28] Not only can companies and research institutions get around Western guidelines by initiating or shifting their drug trials to the Third World, but Third World subjects are usually the prime target group for the new contraceptives.

The growing consumers' and women's movements in the West have led to increased public skepticism of the contraceptive industry, coupled with liability lawsuits that have cost the companies millions of dollars. Most Third World experimental subjects have little access to such information, much less to the courts. Their "informed consent"—consent to undergo drug tests with the full knowledge of potential risks—easily becomes a charade, because in a context of poverty and scarce health care, any attention from medical personnel is usually received with gratitude.[29]

Moreover, the protocol of drug trials often leaves much to be desired. For example, one variety of vaginal ring impregnated with hormones, pioneered by the contraceptive research wing of the Population Council, was studied for "field acceptability" among a poor target population in the Dominican Republic and Brazil. The premise of the study was, in the authors' words, that "the Contraceptive Vaginal Ring is a contraceptive method as effective and safe as the pill...which could be used in basic health systems *without di-*

rect medical supervision [emphasis added]." In the course of the study, the users were not advised of any potential disadvantages of the method, since this would "confound the basic hypothesis." This, despite the fact that the rings have produced a number of worrisome side effects, including a high rate of vaginal discharge. Their long-term effect on the vagina and cervix also remains unknown.[30]

Even those contraceptives approved in the West are often marketed in the Third World according to much looser standards. The printed lists of side effects and precautions required to accompany contraceptives are often much more comprehensive in the United States than in the Third World, for example. This applies to pharmaceuticals in general—when the U.S. Office of Technology Assessment evaluated a sample of labeling by U.S. companies in Brazil, Kenya, Panama, and Thailand, it found that half the products had labeling that "diverged significantly and seriously from the standard. Physicians relying on the information provided with those products could put patients at undue risk."[31]

Third World governments and companies are often to blame as well. In the case of the common Mala oral contraceptive pill manufactured in India, the package insert for users lists no contraindications or risks, stating categorically that "There is no harm by this pill." Instead, it only lists the pill's benefits.[32]

These practices imply a double standard: safety regulations for the West, but not for the Third World. Many members of the population establishment justify this double standard in terms of relative risks. They measure the risk of death from a given contraceptive against a woman's risk of dying in pregnancy or childbirth. In the Third World, where maternal mortality rates of over 500 per 100,000 live births are common in poor rural areas, contraceptive risks appear much lower than in the United States or Great Britain, for example, where the maternal mortality rate is roughly 10 per 100,000 live births.

This reasoning led the journal *Population Reports* to claim: "With all methods, family planning in developing countries is much safer than childbearing."[33] Indeed, this is the most common argument leveled against critics of indiscriminate contraceptive use in the Third World. But just how valid is the comparison between maternal mortality and contraceptive risk?

A close look at the logic reveals a number of very serious flaws:

1. The use of high rates of maternal mortality to justify higher contraceptive risk in effect *penalizes the poor for their poverty*. High maternal mortality rates result from inadequate nutrition, poor health care, and other effects of poverty. Addressing these problems first would not only alter the risk equation, but would establish a better foundation on which to build decent family planning services.

2. How can risk be precisely defined when the *long-term* risks of many contraceptives, such as the pill and injectables, will not be known for at least another one or two decades? Moreover, if a particular contraceptive increases the risk of cancer, a woman's life may be shortened, but the contraceptive will not be seen as the cause of death.

3. The measure of contraceptive risk is generally based on data from industrialized countries. *Third World women may actually be at greater risk from certain contraceptives* owing to their lower body weights, lack of sanitary facilities, poor medical care, etc. Moreover, they are rarely adequately screened before or followed up on after contraceptive use.

4. *Why should the measure of risk center solely on women*, when there are male contraceptive methods such as the condom and vasectomy? As Judith Bruce and S. Bruce Schearer of the Population Council point out: "No attempt has been made to take into account the fact that whereas the health risks of *childbearing* are unavoidably sex-specific, the health risks of *contraception* can be assumed by either partner."[34]

5. *Many contraceptives have other harmful effects*, aside from death, which can have a profound impact on a woman's life. For example, contraceptives like the IUD that carry the risk of impairing future fertility may be totally unacceptable to women, in spite of the risks they face from an unwanted pregnancy.

6. *Mortality risks in childbirth and mortality risks from a contraceptive do not necessarily belong in the same equation*. A woman may willingly assume the immediate risk of childbirth, while she may feel quite differently about the longer-term risk of death from the adverse effects of a contraceptive. Instead, the risk of a particular contraceptive should also be measured in compari-

son to other contraceptives, not only to giving birth. In health terms, barrier contraceptives, for example, are much safer than hormonal methods, even if they may be less effective in preventing pregnancy (a matter of dispute). Many women use contraceptives to space their pregnancies, not to end them altogether. An unplanned pregnancy resulting from the use of a barrier method might appear far more favorable to them than risking their lives on a hormonal method.[35]

7. *Illegal abortion is a major cause of maternal mortality in many countries.* Making abortion safe, legal, and accessible would alter the maternal side of the risk equation, as well as reduce the number of births resulting from contraceptive failure. It would also allow women to use safer but less effective contraceptive methods with the knowledge that they have a secure backup.

8. *With rising mortality from AIDS,* the potential of condoms not only to avert births but deaths must figure into any safety evaluation of contraceptives.

The acceptability of contraceptive risk is a personal decision as well as a scientific one. Many women are prepared to take health risks to prevent pregnancy, but each woman has a right to know all the risks and to make the decision for herself. Yet today contraceptive manufacturers and population control programs are making that decision for millions of women.

Some openly suggest that Third World people should be subjected to even greater risks to bring down birth rates. Dr. Carl Djerassi, one of the "fathers" of the birth control pill and a long-time consultant to the Syntex Corporation, called in 1983 for "heroic steps" to speed the development of new contraceptives for the Third World so as to minimize the economic and political consequences of rapid population growth. These steps include expediting clinical research on humans, a priority rating system of studies with a "willingness to tolerate initially greater risks" in the case of especially promising contraceptives, and the establishment of a new international body to approve contraceptive research in order to bypass Western regulatory agencies, which are "currently not risk-oriented." Having called for a reduction in safety standards, Djerassi then says, "I take it for granted that 'informed consent' procedures

are implemented rigorously and realistically—each country establishing its own."[36]

Today the forces shaping contraceptive technology—the population establishment, the pharmaceutical companies, and the scientific community—often are far removed from the individual man or
woman who uses birth control, and operate in the absence of real
democratic accountability. As a result, the technology does not respond so much to individual needs as it does to the biases of its
creators. Female contraception is emphasized far more than male,
systemic and surgical methods receive much higher priority than
barrier and natural methods, and health and safety are frequently a
secondary concern. The next chapters look at the use and abuse of
these technologies in more detail, focusing on their role in population control programs.

11

HORMONAL
CONTRACEPTIVES
AND THE IUD

To millions of women throughout the world, hormonal contraceptives and the IUD have been presented as liberating technologies. In the West they were heralded as the key to the so-called sexual revolution, and in the Third World as the answer to unwanted pregnancies and high birth rates. The enthusiasm which accompanied their introduction helped to obscure, and still obscures, their drawbacks. In population control programs particularly, many women have been denied vital information about the risks of these contraceptives and have not received medical screening or follow-up care while using them. The result makes a mockery of informed consent.

PUSHING THE PILL

The Pill makes your breasts more beautiful and is good for everyone—including the tailors who have to make bigger brassieres.

—Slogan suggested by DR. MALCOLM POTTS, director of the International Fertility Research Program, and colleagues at the 1977 Tokyo International Symposium on Population.[1]

The birth control pill was the first and is still the most widely used of the hormonal contraceptives. Today over 70 million women take the pill worldwide, making it the second most widely used reversible female contraceptive in the world after the IUD. The pill undoubtedly has many advantages. Used correctly, it is very effective in preventing pregnancy and can alleviate menstrual disorders. It is relatively easy to use and does not interfere with sex. Moreover, it is under women's control—a woman must consciously decide to take the pill every day and can stop taking it if she suffers from side effects. This is a particularly important attribute given the recent trend toward taking control away from women.

The most common type of pill contains the synthetic hormones estrogen and progestin, similar to those produced in a woman's ovaries during the menstrual cycle. These affect the pituitary gland, altering the body's hormonal balance so that ovulation does not occur. The pill thus directly intervenes in one of the female body's most important reproductive processes.

Fears of the population explosion, the impetus behind the development of the pill, also determined where the first clinical trials of the method took place. The Caribbean island of Puerto Rico was chosen because, in the words of three pill researchers, it is a "region in which population pressure is a public health problem." In this particular study, undertaken in the late 1950s, one woman died from congestive heart failure and another developed pulmonary tuberculosis, but the researchers confidently asserted that "none of these effects could in any way be attributed" to the pill.[2] (The pill is closely linked to circulatory disorders.) The ethical and scientific standards of the early pill studies in Puerto Rico in fact left much to be desired. One study even blamed most occurrences of side effects such as nausea, vomiting, and dizziness on psychological factors.[3]

Nevertheless, the studies convinced the U.S. Food and Drug Administration (FDA) in 1960 to approve the first birth control pill, produced by Searle and marketed under the name of Enovid. By 1962 Searle had received reports of over 100 cases of thrombosis and embolism (circulatory disorders, notably blood-clotting) associated with use of the Enovid pill, resulting in eleven deaths.

Yet despite such danger signs, the pill enjoyed "a sort of diplomatic immunity" throughout the early sixties. When the World

Health Organization (WHO) organized a meeting of experts to study the pill in 1965, a member of the task force admitted to a reporter: "The people who were concerned with population problems had already decided that we were going to deliver a whitewash."[4]

By 1969 British studies firmly established the link between the pill and blood clotting, but the FDA was slow to act. The FDA Advisory Committee on Obstetrics and Gynecology concluded in 1969 that the pill's benefits sufficiently outweighed its risks to designate it "safe." According to the committee chairman, Dr. Louis Hellman, one of the pill's major benefits was that it "has made the problem of population control immeasurably easier."[5]

Following Senate hearings in 1970, U.S. feminists began to expose how little information on risks women had received. Through Congressional testimony, lawsuits, and other pressure tactics, they eventually forced the FDA to list possible adverse effects in a direct Patient Package Insert, separate from the insert to physicians.[6]

Today the estrogen content of the pill has been reduced, lessening the risk of circulatory disorders, and there is a progestin-only "mini pill." New biphastic and triphastic pills combine very low hormone doses with better menstrual cycle control. These modifications are definite improvements, but the pill still remains a very potent drug. Pill users run a greater risk of circulatory disorders—blood clots, heart attacks, strokes, and high blood pressure—than nonusers. The risk is higher among women over thirty-five, particularly those who smoke. The pill has been associated with nonmalignant liver tumors, which, though benign, are fatal if they rupture. There is also ongoing concern about the pill's adverse effects on nutrition and lactation, and its possible link with breast and cervical cancer. Other "minor" adverse effects include nausea, headache, depression, and weight gain.[7]

The biggest market for pills is now in developing countries, where the majority of users live. Since 1981 pill sales have increased by an estimated 6.4 percent per year there, as opposed to 2.5 percent in developed countries. Third World sales are boosted by government and donor agencies' promotion of the pill in population programs. From 1985 to 1988 the U.S. Agency for International Development (AID) alone provided an average of over 31 million cycles of pills annually; the total donor contribution was close to 75 million.[8]

Since the beginning, population control has shaped the way AID and other agencies have promoted the pill in the Third World. Because of its efficacy in preventing pregnancy, they believe that the pill can have a dramatic demographic impact if distributed on a wide scale. Its adverse effects are shrugged off with references to high rates of maternal mortality, or hardly mentioned at all.[9] A 1979 AID-sponsored evaluation of family planning programs by Westinghouse Health Systems noted the "considerable pressure" AID has put on countries to accept the pill. The evaluation stated: "It is clear that political administrative elites, and not the masses of acceptors, are deciding on the technology to be used."[10]

The use of the pill as an instrument of population control has passed through several stages (see Box: Taking the Pill Is Good for Your Religion for a particularly creative approach).

TAKING THE PILL IS GOOD FOR YOUR RELIGION

In Indonesia, the U.S. Agency for International Development (AID) prides itself on its ability to move fast in funding creative initiatives by local family planning officials. The following account of Dr. Haji Mahyuddin's Pill Ramadhan in West Sumatra, excerpted from an AID evaluation report, raises serious questions about the way modern contraceptives have been introduced into Third World settings. In this instance, certain religious customs (which arguably discriminate against women in the first place) were manipulated and religious leaders bribed in order to get women to take the pill.

THE PILL RAMADHAN

In 1971, while in private practice, Dr. Mahyuddin became interested in giving birth control pills to women in such a way as to prevent menstruation during the month of Ramadhan, when Muslims are to fast from sunrise to sunset. A menstruating woman is regarded as ritually unclean and thus may neither make the fast nor pray in the mosque. According to custom she may "pay back" missed days after Ramadhan is over but receives less *pahala* (grace from God) for days fasted after the month than during it. The people of West Sumatra are relatively devout Muslims, and thus many women among them would like to be able to fast straight through Ramadhan in order to receive the maximum amount of grace.

Around 1976 Dr. Mahyuddin discussed the feasibility of a "Ramadhan pill" with Dr. Malcolm Potts (then with the IPPF) on the latter's visit to West Sumatra. Potts subsequently sent back information on a three-cycle pill being used elsewhere. Dr. Mahyuddin reasoned that many women would be attracted to use the pill to inhibit menstruation during Ramadhan and, having in this way overcome initial reluctance to use it, could be motivated to continue its use—or even switch to the IUD—after Ramadhan was over.

In May 1978 Dr. Mahyuddin took a Ramadhan Pill proposal to BKBBN [Indonesian National Family Planning Coordinating Board] headquarters. Headquarters approved it in principle but all agreed that support of the *ulama* [religious leaders] would be necessary before proceeding with the project—and before headquarters would agree to fund it.

Dr. Mahyuddin decided to hold a "consultation" for the ulama, using funds he would borrow from his DIP [budget] and then subsequently repay once the project had been approved by headquarters and AID funds for it made available to him.

A one-day consultation with the ulama and the *adats* was held on June 29. They were reportedly all pleased to be called to the provincial capital, to receive room and board, transportation, and a per diem, and all agreed to the Ramadhan Pill idea.... Headquarters received funding from AID in late July and funds were available for the project the first week in August.[1]

The "contraceptive inundation" approach was the brainchild of Dr. R. T. Ravenholt, former head of AID's Office of Population. He urged the vigorous promotion of the pill free or at minimal cost through house-to-house visits of nonmedical family planning personnel and through unrestricted sales in small cigarette stalls and shops sprinkled liberally throughout the rural and urban areas of the Third World in the belief that supply would automatically beget demand. "The principle involved in the household distribution of contraceptives can be demonstrated with Coca-Cola," he explained. "If one distributed an ample, free supply of Coca-Cola into each household, would not poor illiterate peasants drink as much Coca-Cola as the rich literate residents?"[11]

However, as AID discovered, the relationship between supply and demand is not so straightforward, and the inundation strategy proved something of a disaster. In Pakistan, for example, it led to no significant uptake of contraception, but instead, in the view of the Westinghouse evaluation, to a waste of time, money, and effort, and to the "institutionalization of failure" in the country's family planning program.[12] "We were burned in enough places where that strategy was wrong," says Dr. Stephen Sinding, former director of AID's Office of Population. "Now there is greater sensitivity at AID to appropriate levels of supply." But is there greater sensitivity to the potentially harmful effects of the pill on women's and children's health?

Today, in a variation on the inundation theme, AID and other agencies such as the International Planned Parenthood Federation (IPPF) and the Pathfinder Fund are promoting the pill through various community-based distribution, retail sales, and social marketing schemes. In such programs, the pill is distributed or sold without a doctor's prescription and with very little, if any, screening or follow-up. This is not surprising, since the overall goal, according to the Pathfinder Fund, "is to decrease the birth rate by increasing the level of contraceptive use,"[13] not to meet women's need for safe birth control.

Safety concerns are dismissed with assertions such as this one in *Population Reports*: "Modern family planning methods are safe. Contraceptive products are not toxic even if used incorrectly—an important consideration for community-based or nonmedical supervision."[14] Social marketing schemes, in fact, have been designed with the explicit goal of avoiding the need for health services.[15]

A real concern for safety would dictate that potential pill users be adequately screened for histories of heart disease and diabetes and for pregnancy, among other things, all of which call for the attention of trained medical or paramedical personnel. Yet population agencies insist, in the words of *Population Reports*, that "anyone can identify the major risk factors for OC [oral contraceptive] use—smoking and older age. The major physical signs of high risk—obesity and high blood pressure—also are fairly easy to detect."[16] IPPF writes that "Women who should not try the Pill at all can be screened out by a simple set of questions which shopkeepers and nonmedical distributors can easily learn."[17]

In reality, however, these questions—and the interpretation of the answers—are not so simple for nonmedical personnel to learn. And *what incentive do they have to ask them when their goal is getting more acceptors or sales?* Moreover, cultural restrictions in many countries mean that the husband, rather than the woman herself, is the one who buys the pills at commercial outlets, and he often lacks knowledge of his wife's health or is reluctant to talk about it, especially when the sensitive issue of contraception is involved.

In Bangladesh, half the couples who use the pill obtain it from the commercial sector, primarily from pharmacies (without a prescription). A study found that these pharmacies "appear to play a minor role in passing on instructions about correct use," for they are typically "small, bustling places where it may be quite difficult to talk privately about instructions, side-effects and problems related to OC use." Moreover, few pharmacists in Bangladesh have any specialized pharmaceutical training. The study found that in regard to commercial sales of the pill, husbands were the main source of instruction and information for women.[18] Considering how little information the husbands themselves receive, one can safely say the women receive hardly any information at all.

Even when women do receive information about pill risks, it tends to be heavily biased. For example, the administrators of a Population Services International social marketing scheme in Thailand explained, "Women are told that the hormonal changes and related effects during pregnancy are 'the size of an elephant' while the changes and side effects of the pill are 'the size of an ant.'"[19] A Bangladesh social marketing scheme promoted a message on the radio stating that concerns about the safety of contraceptive methods, including the pill, were "ignorant tales told by ignorant people."[20]

Dr. Sinding admits that AID "can't guarantee screening through commercial outlets. There is a risk," he says, "but the health risk from unplanned pregnancy is worse. Each country must make its own decision about risk. It must be the country's policy to sell contraceptives without prescription, not our own." Country policy is subject to donor pressure, however, and that pressure has often proved instrumental in the deregulation of the pill.

Lack of screening and follow-up care are often justified on the basis that the serious side effects of the pill are associated with Western lifestyles and health problems.[21] Yet there are very few studies of the pill's impact on Third World women. In fact, there is strong reason to believe that pushing the pill indiscriminately in the Third World actually increases its risks and the severity of its side effects. This can occur in the following ways:

The Risk of Circulatory Disorders. It is commonly asserted that Third World women have a lower risk of developing circulatory disorders from the pill, since most do not smoke, overeat, or experience as much stress as Western women. Yet there is very little reliable comparative data on circulatory mortality rates. Moreover, chronic rheumatic heart disease, which often goes undetected but which is perhaps the most common heart disease among young Third World adults, increases the risk of blood clotting and other circulatory disorders, and thus could increase the risk of the pill.[22] One might also add that a life of poverty can be very stressful.

The Risk of Taking the Pill During Pregnancy. In the United States an estimated 70,000 fetuses are exposed to oral contraceptives annually, according to an estimate in the early 1980s.[23] In the Third World the proportion is likely to be much higher, given inadequate screening and the absence of pregnancy tests. The possibility of the pill's link with birth defects—though not definitively proved one way or the other—raises questions about the wisdom of its indiscriminate promotion.

The Effect on Lactation. This is one of the greatest dangers of pill use in the Third World. Lactating women on the combined estrogen-progestin pill frequently have a reduced supply of milk. Even a low-estrogen pill, taken in the first few months after birth, can reduce the volume of milk by as much as 40 percent in three to six weeks. Since for millions of infants, breast milk is the main or only source of nutrition in the first one or two years of life, the pill can contribute directly to infant malnutrition and hence higher infant mortality rates. WHO guidelines recommend that women not be encouraged to use hormonal contraception for four to six months after birth,[24] but unfortunately many lactating mothers in the Third World are routinely given the pill.

Although progestin-only pills do not decrease the milk supply, the long-term effects of infants' ingestion of hormones secreted in breast milk have yet to be determined. Even the normally cavalier *Population Reports* states that "it is safest not to expose infants to hormones in the first three or four months of development, when they are most susceptible."[25]

Use of the pill while breast-feeding can also have another negative effect. Inadequate supervision in community distribution or retail sales schemes means that many women take the pill irregularly or drop it altogether after developing the first side effects. The WHO has found the incidence of irregular use to be over 50 percent in some parts of the Third World.[26] Dropout rates as high as 80 percent have been reported after only three months in Bangladesh.[27] As a result, although the pill is theoretically 99 percent effective in preventing pregnancy, the failure rate tends to be much higher in the Third World.

Ironically, these factors may be leading to what some observers have called a "pill-induced population explosion."[28] Breast-feeding, as noted in Chapter 1, is one of the world's most effective natural contraceptives because it suppresses ovulation. When breast-feeding women take the pill irregularly, they tend to resume ovulation sooner, and thus lose an important natural defense against pregnancy. Combined pills which decrease breast milk may also lead women to supplement the baby's diet with other foods. As a result, the baby suckles less frequently, and the mother resumes ovulation sooner.[29]

A study in Bangladesh found that lactating women who used the pill had significantly shorter intervals to the next pregnancy than did lactating women who did not use it *or any other contraceptive*. The study concluded that women should not be given the pill while breast-feeding unless it can be ensured that they take it *regularly* for at least nine months after giving birth.[30]

The Effect on Women's Nutrition. Because the pill causes changes in the metabolism of important vitamins and minerals, some nutritionists fear it may contribute to nutritional deficiency diseases in malnourished women. If so, it is a particularly inappropriate contraceptive for use in impoverished communities. There is a pressing need for more research on this subject.[31]

The Risk of Cancer. The most controversial question surrounding the pill is its relationship to cancer. It usually takes many years for a person to develop cancer after exposure to a carcinogen, but since the pill has only been in use for three decades, it is impossible to evaluate the risks fully. The FDA concluded in 1984, however, that the pill may increase the risk of acquiring cervical cancer, and now recommends that women on the pill should be monitored carefully with physical examinations and Pap (cervical smear) tests, *at least yearly.*[32]

Yet such monitoring is often difficult or impossible to obtain in the West, and virtually unheard of for women living in many rural areas of the Third World. Given that cervical cancer is the most common cause of death from cancer among both Latin American and African women, grave doubts arise as to the wisdom of promoting the pill in the Third World in the absence of screening and follow-up. Knowledge about the pill and cancer has been almost totally derived from studies in developed countries. Follow-up, even for research purposes, is extremely rare in the Third World.[33]

In recent years there has been considerable medical controversy over whether the pill heightens the risk of breast cancer, with some studies indicating that it does for certain sub-groups of women, e.g., long-term users, and others finding no link. Although the FDA recommends routine breast examinations for pill users, it has refused to change pill labeling to reflect concerns over breast cancer. Clearly, more high-quality research needs to be done, but unfortunately research on breast cancer itself, which has reached epidemic proportions in the U.S., has been seriously neglected and under-funded.

Many of the pill's risks cited above increase with higher doses of estrogen, and thus the FDA recommends pills with the lowest effective amounts. The most common oral contraceptives in the West use 30 mcg of estrogen, but Third World family planning programs often use higher amounts. A study conducted in 1987, for example, found that 85 percent of the pills bought by pharmacies in developed regions were low-estrogen, as opposed to 60 percent in developing areas.[34] In the early 1970s, AID was accused of "dumping" high-estrogen (80 mcg) pills in the Third World, which were obtained from the Syntex Company at a very cheap price.[35]

What has been the response of the population establishment to such criticisms? "Critics of community distribution only think Anglo-Saxon gynecologists from Westchester [a rich New York suburb] are equipped to give pills to Third World women," said Richard Pomeroy of Family Planning International Assistance. According to Norma Swenson of the Boston Women's Health Book Collective, others go further, accusing women health activists of "imperialist arrogance" when they insist that the same safety standards be applied in the Third World as they have fought for in the West.[36]

Today there is a move on to "resell the pill." AID and others are encouraging the FDA to change pill labeling to stress its possible benefits in helping to prevent ovarian and endometrial cancers, ectopic pregnancy, and benign breast disease. Such a move would mark a major breach in the accepted practice of only listing a drug's benefits which relate directly to the reasons it is prescribed—in the case of the pill, these are preventing pregnancy and alleviating menstrual disorders. The logic behind the reselling of the pill is dubious: What good is added protection against ovarian cancer when you run a higher risk of cervical cancer and circulatory disorders? Women take the pill as a contraceptive, not as a vaccine.[37]

Even more disturbing is the current push, spearheaded by AID, to weaken even further the "medical barriers" to hormonal contraceptive delivery. A leaked 1991 letter from AID to the IPPF reveals a callous disregard for women's health and safety. "All too often," write two senior AID officials, "family planning programs impose numerous medical barriers to service which we are convinced hinder program effectiveness and impact, especially for hormonal contraception."

In AID's eyes these "barriers" include "excessive physical exams (e.g., pelvic and breast)," "holding the oral contraceptive 'hostage' to other reproductive medical care (e.g., Pap smears and STD [sexually transmitted disease] tests)," and "conservative medical thinking (e.g., taking a woman off the pill for a while if she develops a headache just to play it 'safe'...).'' In fact, these are routine medical precautions associated with prescribing the pill.

Going one step further, AID even urges that the term "contraindications" be dropped from an IPPF manual because "it may have very negative connotations and a major inhibitory effect." Instead, health workers should stress the pill's benefits and the fact that the risks of pregnancy are greater than the risks of the pill, even when it is contraindicated![38]

Within the United States, population agencies are also pushing for the pill to be sold over-the-counter, a move opposed by many health professionals. Not only would it weaken basic medical standards, but it would deny poor women one of the only opportunities they have to get Pap smears and other medical screening.

It may be some time before the final verdict on the pill is delivered, but in the meantime, don't women *everywhere* deserve adequate information and medical supervision while taking this powerful drug? It is not imperialist arrogance to insist on equal rights when it comes to safety. It is ethical and humane.

DEPO-PROVERA: KEEPING AN EYE ON THE NEEDLE

> For the average individual in a Western country, depot progestogen [Depo-Provera] preparations have a limited use because of the high incidence of irregular vaginal bleeding, and the slight risks of permanent amenorrhea.... Finally, depot progestogens provide an effective, acceptable and simple method of contraception for the underdeveloped world, which can be easily administered by paramedical personnel.
>
> —D. F. HAWKINS AND M. S. ELDER, *Human Fertility Control: Theory and Practice*[39]

Depo-Provera, an injectable, hormonal contraceptive manufactured by the U.S. pharmaceutical firm Upjohn Co., has often been at the center of contraceptive controversy. The Depo debate has raged in government hearings, among the medical community, population establishment, feminists, and health activists, and in the pages of the popular press. Despite—or perhaps because of—its notoriety, Depo has been used by relatively few women, and most of them are in developing countries. Worldwide, Depo accounts for only 1 percent of contraceptive use. Yet it is currently being promoted heavily in Africa—in Kenya, for example, injectables are the second most widely used contraceptive after the pill.[40]

Like the pill, Depo-Provera has been heavily promoted in population programs, with the IPPF and the UNFPA the main suppliers.[41] Until the FDA approved Depo-Provera in 1992, AID was unable to supply it directly to family planning programs. Upjohn manufactured and exported it from a Belgian subsidiary.

Unlike the combination pill, Depo-Provera contains only progestin. It is usually administered in a single 150 milligram injection, effective for at least three months. Another widely marketed progestin injectable, produced by the German Schering Company under the brand name NET-EN, is usually given every two months. Both work primarily by inhibiting ovulation through effects on the pituitary gland, and are highly effective when used at regular intervals, resulting in a pregnancy rate of less than 1 in 100 per year.[42] Depo is much more widely used. A number of other injectables have also come onto the market, several of which contain estrogen to induce menstrual bleeding. Estrogen, of course, can cause other serious side effects, such as circulatory disorders.[43]

Depo-Provera's advantages lie primarily in the way it is administered. A single shot protects a woman from pregnancy for three to six months, freeing her from the need for continued responsibility for birth control, unlike the pill, which must be remembered every day, or barrier methods, which require application before intercourse. For women whose husbands object to their using birth control, Depo can be given surreptitiously, during a quick visit to or by a family planning worker.

Depo also enjoys the so-called injection mystique. In many areas of the Third World, people associate injections with safe, effective, modern medicine, and are thus eager to receive them. As a Thai study notes: "A contraceptive to be taken by injection seems to make the dreams of most women come true, and has a tremendous initial psychological advantage over other methods."[44]

From the standpoint of population control, the drug has many benefits: The injection mystique reduces the need for motivational efforts; it is easy to administer, long-acting, and effective in preventing pregnancy. And once a woman has had an injection, there is no possibility of user failure.

These advantages can actually be disadvantages when viewed from another perspective. Freedom from responsibility can also mean loss of control: If a woman suffers adverse effects from Depo, there is nothing she can do until the injection wears off. For some women this can mean months of intense suffering, since the side effects of the drug can linger beyond three months. The injection mystique can also lead to abuse, since if people inherently trust injections, it makes it easier to administer Depo without explaining its side effects.

As for keeping injectable use secret from one's husband, the strategy can backfire. A study in Bangladesh cites the case of a woman who was finally forced to tell her husband she was using the injectable because she developed side effects and needed his assistance in getting medical treatment. Another village woman told the researchers, "I did not tell my husband that I have taken the injection. I am afraid he will throw me out of the house when he hears about the problems."[45]

The most common—and noticeable—side effects of Depo-Provera are menstrual disorders. Over two thirds of women using Depo have no regular menstrual cycles in the first year of use.[46] Many stop menstruating altogether, while others experience heavy or intermittent bleeding. Heavy bleeding can be particularly serious for undernourished women, who can ill afford the iron and blood loss. Because menstrual blood is considered unclean in many Third World cultures, women who experience intermittent bleeding suffer not only physical inconvenience but social ostracism.

In addition, in countries like Bangladesh many poor women face practical difficulties in coping with the bleeding, since the only means at their disposal are unsterile rags. As Judith Bruce of the Population Council points out, "Any additional bleeding or irregularities in bleeding patterns attributable to modern family planning methods may complicate the already difficult task of menstrual management,"[47] a fact which is rarely taken into account by population planners.

Other side effects of Depo include skin disorders, tiredness, headaches, nausea, depression, hair loss, loss of libido, weight gain and delayed return to fertility. These are often dismissed as "minor," but as health writer Gena Corea notes, "Depression is a minor side

effect which merely destroys the entire quality of a woman's life."
She also points out how loss of libido can turn intercourse into a
distasteful ordeal for women. Ironically, Depo has proved an effective male contraceptive, but has not been promoted because of
complaints of loss of libido. Although women complain of the same
thing, it supposedly does not matter in their case.[48]

As for weight gain, researchers hypothesize that Depo stimu-
lates the hypothalamic appetite control center in the brain, causing
women to eat more. "In undernourished women this effect would
be beneficial if they can obtain more food," states *Population Reports*. But of course if they could obtain more food, they would not
be malnourished in the first place![49]

Depo's possible long-term adverse effects are similar to those of
progestin pills: the possible risk of birth defects as the result of
women taking the drug during pregnancy; the potentially negative
impact on infant development of ingesting the hormone in breast
milk; and a possible link to breast, endometrial, and cervical cancers. Depo's link with cancer remains an area of controversy, with
some claiming that recent WHO studies have exonerated it. However, the National Women's Health Network opposed the recent
FDA approval of Depo, citing studies which show an increased risk
of breast cancer among young women who use the drug. According
to Upjohn itself, "Women under 35 years of age whose first exposure to Depo-Provera was within the previous four years may have a
slightly increased risk of developing breast cancer similar to that
seen with oral contraceptives."

Another issue of concern is Depo's negative impact on bone
density due to suppression of natural estrogen. This could heighten
the risk of osteoporosis unless bone loss is reversed on discontinuation.[50]

Despite these concerns, the medical boards of both the WHO
and the IPPF have approved the drug for widespread use, with only
a few minor precautions. The WHO recommends administration of
Depo within the first five days of a woman's menstrual cycle to ensure that she is not pregnant. But according to *Population Reports,*
"In some programs, particularly where access to family planning
services is limited, women are given injections at any time during
the menstrual cycle."[51] In considering the perils of fetal exposure to

synthetic hormones during pregnancy, it is worthwhile remembering the women who took the synthetic estrogen DES during pregnancy, whose daughters developed vaginal cancer and cervical abnormalities twenty years later.[52]

Neither the WHO nor the IPPF discourage the use of Depo by lactating mothers, despite the fact that, in the words of the IPPF, "to date no proper, thorough follow-up studies of children breast-fed by mothers using injectable contraceptives have been carried out."[53] The WHO does recommend delaying the injection for six weeks after birth, however, displaying some recognition of the potential risk.[54]

Depo's short-term side effects and possible long-term risks make it questionable whether it should be used at all, but the ways it has been administered, both in industrialized and Third World countries, raise further doubts. In the West Depo has often been used on ethnic minorities and working-class women, with little or no explanation of its effects.

Before it was approved for contraceptive use in the United States, Depo was available as a cancer treatment, and thus individual doctors sometimes gave it to patients as a method of birth control. Low-income black women in the South and Native American women were special targets. A study of Depo-Provera sponsored by Emory University in Atlanta, Georgia, gained notoriety for its treatment of 4,700 black subjects. A 1978 FDA audit of the study found that researchers did not adhere to the protocol approved by the FDA: "FDA investigators said the study was poorly designed, patient records were inadequate, and researchers did not follow patients who dropped out of the study or provide long-term follow-up to assess potential cancer risk."[55]

Mentally retarded women, incarcerated women, and drug addicts were also Depo targets. In fact, one of the members of the FDA's 1984 board of inquiry on Depo, Dr. Griff T. Ross, recommended that the drug be approved for limited use on retarded women and drug addicts, though he admitted its safety was not sufficiently proved for use on "human subjects."[56]

The same logic which justifies giving Depo to these women in the West underlies the drug's promotion among the poor majority in the Third World. Their safety is somehow more expendable—they count, more often than not, mainly as demographic statistics. For example, in its 1986 report on population growth and policies in sub-Saharan Africa, the World Bank urges African governments to relax restrictions on injectable contraceptives and claims that they can be delivered safely by nonmedical personnel outside of a clinic system. In fact, according to the Bank, the only major disadvantages of injectables are "minimal side effects"![57]

Thailand has one of the longest experiences and highest percentages of injectable contraceptive use in the world. Although Depo-Provera is a popular drug, it is unclear how many women using it are actually aware of its potential risks. Thai consumer activist Weena Silapa-archa writes, for example, "The long-acting injection is widespread among people in the rural areas. This is not only because the people don't know the adverse effect of the drug, but also because they are told the drug is good, safe and effective."[58]

Like the pill, Depo is often given without adequate medical supervision. In Mexico it is sold over the counter in pharmacies and given by "injectionists," practitioners with little or no formal training.[59] Many medical personnel in Third World countries have reported that they never saw any physician package insert accompanying the drug, and thus were unable to communicate adequately the risks and side effects to women.[60]

Currently, the push is on to launch Depo-Provera in India, a potentially vast and profitable market. In 1994 the Drug Controller of India approved the marketing of Depo-Provera by the pharmaceutical firm Max Pharma. The license stipulates that Depo-Provera can only be sold by prescription from licensed gynecologists and that a post-marketing survey be carried out to collect data on the experience of Indian users.

Only weeks after Depo's release in India, women health activists confronted the Drug Controller and Max Pharma officials with evidence of flagrant violations of the license. Not only was the drug available over the counter, without prescription, but the package insert only listed seven contraindications—as opposed to over seventy in Upjohn's literature elsewhere. As for the post-marketing survey, the government could provide no substantive information on how it was to be carried out.

As the result of activist pressure, the government agreed to reconsider Depo's licensing. Activists have also fought the introduction of NET-EN into India and have a case pending before the Supreme Court. The next battle will be to stop Cyclofem, a combined estrogen-progesterone injection. As activists point out, given the sorry state of the Indian health system, there is no way women will get the medical attention necessary for the safe and ethical use of these drugs.[61]

South Africa provides a prime example of the selective use of Depo-Provera. The government targeted almost exclusively black and mixed-race women as part of its effort to reduce the growth rate of the African population (and concurrently increase the number of whites). Under apartheid in South Africa family planning was the only free health service available to blacks, and Depo-Provera the main, and often the only, contraceptive offered. Depo was typically delivered through mobile family planning "clinics" without adequate screening and back-up services—actual health clinics were few and far between, inaccessible to the majority of the rural population.

There were many reports of Depo being used coercively in South Africa. Sometimes women were forced to use Depo-Provera in order to keep their jobs in white-owned factories. Many women also received a compulsory injection after birth, in what nurses called "the fourth stage of labor." Coercive use of Depo was also widespread in white-controlled Namibia.

Now that apartheid has been abolished, progressive health workers face the daunting task of reforming both the health and family planning systems. While some feminists are calling for the immediate banning of Depo-Provera, others point out that many women now rely on it, and a phasing in of other methods would be more appropriate.[62]

These cases do not mean that Depo is always misused. There are examples of family planning programs where women are adequately screened, informed of risks, followed up on, and offered other options. Indian feminist doctor Hari John defends her use of Depo in rural South India (she explains the risks and uses the drug herself) on the basis of women's powerlessness and male opposition to contraception: "Using Depo-Provera is the only way these women can have any control over any aspect of their lives."[63]

Many feminists and health activists, however, disagree with Dr. John's position. "In my opinion the use of Depo could not improve the unjust situation of the women in rural South India," writes Weena Silapa-archa.[64] Judy Norsigian of the Boston Women's Health Book Collective points out that the widespread availability of Depo could actually undermine efforts to change the basic social and economic conditions that produce women's powerlessness in the first place. "It's the old Band-Aid approach," she says, "which does nothing to prevent the cuts."[65] Moreover, although Depo may free women from the burden of pregnancy, it does nothing to free them from the pressure to have unwanted intercourse. Others believe that the severity of the drug's side effects and risks means its use is never justified.

Even supposing the drug is used responsibly, in the hands of people whose first concern is women's welfare and not population control, the question remains: Do a few good programs justify Depo's general approval, given its great potential for abuse?

AND NOW NORPLANT...

I believe that the latest Council-developed method, Norplant contraceptive subdermal implants, is the most important new contraceptive system since the pill.[66]

−GEORGE ZEIDENSTEIN, *President of the Population Council, 1983*

In the winter of 1984 the population community was abuzz with the news of Norplant, encapsulated hormones inserted under the skin of the arm which prevent pregnancy for at least five years. In almost every office I visited in Washington and New York, people expressed the hope that Norplant might prove a much-needed technological breakthrough, a long-acting but reversible form of contraception, which could serve as an alternative to sterilization.

At the Population Council, where Norplant was developed, one of its promoters was a walking advertisement for the drug. He had me feel the capsules, minus the hormone of course, inserted in his arm. "The evidence to date indicates that this new method will have significant personal and demographic impact," stated the Population Council, "now that it is ready to be introduced into family planning programs worldwide."[67] The demographic objective is obvious in the very design of the drug: It is effective for five or more years. One wonders why a one- or two-year option was not developed first.

Norplant is the Council's trade name for six capsules (Norplant I) or two rods (Norplant II) containing the progestin levonorgestrel, which is commonly found in oral contraceptives. Insertion and removal of the implants requires local anesthesia and medical skill. Norplant has a very low failure rate and has an advantage over the combined pill and Depo-Provera in its smaller hormonal dose (similar to the mini pill). Studies show no adverse effect on fertility; after Norplant is removed, women return to normal hormonal levels within twenty-four hours.

Norplant was not approved by the FDA until 1990. The Population Council contracted with a Finnish firm, Leiras Pharmaceuticals, to manufacture Norplant and provide it at a low price to Third World governments and family planning organizations. Today Norplant is marketed in over twenty-six countries, and over one and a half million women have used it, mainly in developing countries. Like Depo-Provera, Norplant's most common side effect is disruption of the menstrual cycle, resulting in prolonged bleeding, intermittent spotting, or amenorrhea. Other adverse effects are also common to progestin contraceptives: headache, depression, loss of libido, weight change, nausea, and acne. Although the Population Council claims that Norplant can be used safely by lactating mothers six weeks after birth, two studies showed lower growth rates among Norplant-exposed babies while they were fully breast-feeding. No longer-term study of exposed babies has been carried out, and it will be many years until cancer and birth defect risks can be ruled out. Although Norplant has a low failure rate, 20 to 30 percent of pregnancies due to Norplant failures are ectopic and hence life-threatening, especially in the absence of medical care. Keeping the capsules in the arm beyond the five-year limit is also believed to increase the risk of ectopic pregnancy.[68]

In some clinical and field trials, Norplant has shown high continuation rates, which has prompted great optimism on the part of the Population Council about its acceptability to Third World women. Ecuadorian researchers, however, have pointed out that high continuation rates may result from women's fears of having the implants removed:

> In our view, it would be wrong to be content with the low termination rate due to menstrual problems. We believe that the rate would have been much higher if it had been easier to remove the implants. In other words, there is a balance between distress caused by the menstrual problems and the fear of the removal procedure.[69]

Norplant acceptability studies, moreover, have many shortcomings; for one, the study population is usually unrepresentative of the general population, who will use the method in far from ideal circumstances.[70] Grandiose claims are also made which the data do not support. In one study in San Francisco, half the women stopped using Norplant after two and a half years and almost all experienced unpleasant side effects, yet Norplant was proclaimed a "highly acceptable method of contraception."[71]

Fears of Norplant insertion and removal are well-grounded, for both are far from simple procedures. If sterile conditions are not maintained, infections can result. During insertion special care must be taken not to drive the capsules into the underlying muscles, since they can migrate in muscle and be difficult to remove. Removal is more difficult than insertion, since once capsules are in the body, a layer of fibrous tissue forms around them, which must be cut away. Even under the best medical conditions, such as those which prevail in Finland, doctors have experienced difficulties removing Norplant.[72]

The way Norplant is administered may in fact make it a particularly inappropriate contraceptive technology in many areas of the Third World, where health systems are poorly developed. Even in closely monitored trials, under direct medical supervision, infections have resulted, requiring the removal of the capsules, and these are likely to be more widespread and potentially more dangerous in clinics with inadequate antiseptic standards.[73] The risk of spreading HIV through unsterile implements can also not be discounted. Removal, in particular, can be painful—in Indonesia, for example, 40 percent of respondents to a family planning questionnaire on early removal of Norplant reported "a terrible pain associated with removal."[74]

In literature designed for prospective users, however, Norplant is billed as easy and painless. In response to the question, "Is removal painful?" a Population Council manual resolutely answers, "No." Another booklet designed for rural African women describes the insertion process: "The doctor inserts Norplant. The process takes about 15 minutes. Mama is given a local anaesthetic so she will feel no pain." Shortly thereafter, "Mama can do all of her housework as usual"—pictures show her washing, farming, cooking, caring for the children. Of course Mama might experience a few "minor side effects" such as headaches or dizziness, but what difference do they make in her already overburdened life?[75]

Norplant's greatest drawback is the almost total loss of user control, despite the fact that people at the Population Council like to call it "user soft," i.e., easy to use. Although it is billed as a reversible method, Norplant should only be removed by trained medical personnel if a woman decides to terminate use early because of side effects or the desire to become pregnant. Given the inadequacies of many Third World family planning programs and general lack of access to health care, one would expect that many women would find it difficult, if not impossible, to get the capsules removed without significant delays.

In past Norplant trials, people moving out of the area have been advised to have the implants removed "as no other clinics were trained in the technique of removal." Nevertheless, even under such artificial study conditions, many women have been "lost to follow-up," including 238 women out of a total of 813 participating in one trial in Indonesia.[76] In Brazil researchers abandoned many poor women in Norplant trials—an investigation by the Brazilian Network for the Defense of the Human Species located fourteen women out of 309 women involved in trials in Rio de Janeiro who still had implants in their arms after five years. Irregularities in the Brazilian trials and pressure from the women's movement led the Ministry of Health to prohibit further Norplant trials in 1986.[77]

Some women have also experienced difficulties in getting the implants removed because of resistance from trial investigators, who, according to the Population Council, "may be hesitant to remove the implants out of concern that the scientific data may be rendered incomplete."[78] Concerns over cost-effectiveness can similarly bias practitioners against early removal. As AID states: "The cost for Norplant is largely up-front. Therefore, the longer the method is used, the more cost-effective it will become."[79] The drug's promoters are not blind to these problems and on paper advise that Norplant should be introduced only under certain conditions. The Population Council stresses that if a woman wants the capsules removed, the procedure should be scheduled without delay.[80] According to the council, Norplant is essentially a clinic-based method, requiring "careful training, supervision, information dissemination, logistics and follow-up."[81]

Yet the fact is that such guidelines are essentially meaningless in demographically driven family planning programs where women's needs have never been adequately respected. It is in precisely these kinds of programs that the Population Council and other agencies have recklessly promoted Norplant. Indonesia is but one example (see Chapter 5). Women have been denied removals in Bangladesh and Egypt,[82] and one can easily imagine how "voluntary" Norplant use will be in China and India. Indian activists are currently engaged in a heated battle to stop further introduction of Norplant into India, including its planned promotion in a multi-million-dollar AID-financed population project in the state of Uttar Pradesh.[83]

The United States is the country where Norplant has been most openly touted as the technical fix for the social diseases caused by "too many of them"—especially too many blacks. In 1990, soon after FDA approval, a now infamous editorial in the *Philadelphia Inquirer* suggested that the implant be used as "a tool in the fight against black poverty." "It's very tough to undo the damage of being born into a dysfunctional family," stated the editorial. "So why not make an effort to reduce the number of children?" It recommended that welfare mothers receive incentives for using Norplant.[84]

Although the editors were forced to apologize for their racism, their message reflects a growing view among the U.S. elite that poverty and crime are the fault of single mothers bearing illegitimate children—not of the severe reductions in social expenditures which occurred during the Reagan and Bush administrations. Norplant adds fuel to their fire—mandatory contraception has come back in style.

In January 1991 a judge in California ordered a black woman convicted of child abuse to use Norplant for three years as a condition of probation. It later turned out she had diabetes, a major contraindication. By 1992 thirteen state legislatures had introduced laws offering cash incentives to poor women for Norplant use and/or mandating its use as a punishment for certain crimes, though none so far have been approved.[85]

Lack of proper counselling and screening has also accompanied Norplant use in some minority communities. Native American health activists charge that in South Dakota the Indian Health Service has neglected informed consent procedures and given Norplant to women medically at risk. Getting the implant removed has also proved a problem for poor women in the U.S., not only because doctors sometimes discourage it, but because of its high cost. Except where it is offered free under Medicaid or private insurance, Norplant often costs over $500, with removal costs as high as $150.[86]

Controversy over Norplant now centers on its introduction into public high school clinics in Baltimore, a city with high teenage pregnancy rates. Critics point out that providing Norplant in this context does not address the underlying causes of high pregnancy rates—lack of economic and educational opportunities—and does nothing to protect young women from HIV. Maryland, the state in which Baltimore is located, has one of the highest incidences of AIDS in the country.[87]

By the end of 1992 over half a million U.S. women were using Norplant. Many are using it voluntarily, under medical supervision. Yet the problem of abuse is very real, despite the fact that the Population Council claims Norplant is not being used coercively.[88] Moreover, current welfare "reform" efforts are getting meaner and leaner. Two states now deny additional benefits to women if they have a child on welfare, and others are considering similar options (despite the fact that women on welfare have an average of two children, the same as the national average). Forced to choose between the risk of pregnancy and loss of benefits, poor women may increasingly "choose" to use Norplant.

And according to some commentators, it's no longer racist to view Norplant as the solution to poverty and crime—poor white women should be targeted too since their illegitimacy rates are on the rise. "Maybe, ultimately, welfare for single mothers will have to be abolished," wrote *Washington Post* columnist Richard Cohen in 1993. "In the meantime, however, it's clear that before we can have crime control, we need to have birth control." Norplant is his weapon of choice.[89]

One of Norplant's main developers, Sheldon Segal of the Population Council, has objected strongly to such suggestions, claiming Norplant was developed "to improve reproductive freedom, not to restrict it."[90] But why then its five-year efficacy, or the fact that women cannot remove it themselves? Intentional or not, abuse is built into Norplant's design.

THE IUD STORY

> They [IUDs] are horrible things, they produce infection, they are outmoded and not worth using...[but] suppose one does develop an intrauterine infection and suppose she does end up with a hysterectomy and bilateral salpingooophorectomy? How serious is that for the particular patient and for the population of the world in general? Not very.... Perhaps the individual patient is expendable in the general scheme of things, particularly if the infection she acquires is sterilizing but not lethal.
>
> —DR. J. ROBERT WILLSON *at the First International Conference on Intra-Uterine Contraception, sponsored by the Population Council, New York City, 1962.*[91]

The IUD (or intrauterine device) is typically a small coiled, looped, or T-shaped plastic or copper device inserted inside the uterus with a tail reaching down into the upper vagina. In the early 1980s it was used by an estimated 60 million women worldwide, but over two thirds of them were in China alone. In 1989 IUD use accounted for 24 percent of contraceptive use in developing countries, but only 8 percent in developed ones.[92] The IUD is believed to prevent pregnancy primarily by causing inflammation or infection of the uterus, which in turn leads to expulsion of any fertilized eggs. As a form of contraception, it is almost as effective as hormonal varieties, without the disadvantage of altering the body's hormonal balance. The IUD is by no means hazard-free, however.

The story of the IUD, in fact, presents yet another example of the exposure of women to unnecessary risks in the name of population control and corporate profit. Although modern intrauterine devices date from the 1920s, they were considered dangerous by many members of the medical profession because of the risk of infection.

In 1962, at the First International Conference on Intra-Uterine Contraception sponsored by the Population Council, the IUD was suddenly embraced with an almost missionary zeal, as a way to stem overpopulation and, as one participant put it, to "change the history of the world."[93] The participants were impressed by clinical evidence that two IUD rings—neither of which had tails—had caused very few side effects.

When U.S. researchers set about to make IUDs, however, they added tails, since these would make it easier for paramedical personnel in the Third World to insert and remove IUDs and would allow women to check that their IUDs were still in place and had not been spontaneously expelled. The possible increased risk of infection from the tails was passed over in view of the main goal, a technical solution to the population problem. (Recent research indicates that single nylon thread tails do not pose an increased infection risk.)

The most common IUD complications are heavy bleeding and cramps, which are more likely to occur in women who have never borne a child. Faulty insertion can lead to perforation of the uterus, and in some cases to the eventual escape of the IUD into the abdominal cavity, where it can cause serious damage. Women who become pregnant while using the IUD run a higher risk of potentially life-threatening ectopic pregnancies or septic abortions, so that although the method has a low failure rate (3 to 5 pregnancies per 100 users), each IUD pregnancy is not only a contraceptive failure, but a medical complication. The device is not recommended for use just after childbirth, since it can more easily become embedded in or perforate the uterine wall.[94]

The most frequent serious long-term effect of the IUD is infertility caused by pelvic inflammatory disease (PID), an infection of the upper reproductive tract. Women who use the IUD run a significantly higher risk of developing PID (anywhere from 1.5 times to 9 times, or even more, the normal risk), possibly because bacteria enter the uterus during insertion or move up the IUD tail, and then grow rapidly because of IUD-related inflammation or increased bleeding. The Dalkon Shield IUD is the worst offender—Shield users faced a fivefold increase in the risk of PID compared with women wearing other IUDs.[95] The body fights severe PID by laying down scar tissue, which can eventually block the fallopian tubes connecting the ovaries to the uterus, leading to infertility. In especially serious cases of PID, hysterectomy (removal of the uterus) is necessary. Because of the risk of infertility, the FDA recommends that young women who have not had children should not use the IUD.[96] It is most suitable for women who do not intend to have any more pregnancies and have only one sex partner.

As with the pill, the IUD's side effects were virtually ignored in the United States until Congressional hearings in 1971 finally brought them into the open. At the hearings, Dr. John Madry, an obstetrician-gynecologist from Florida, charged IUD advocates with excluding "uncertainties and minimizing complications in their reports." He stated: "The philosophy of most IUD advocates is more impersonal and population-control oriented, and a high complication rate may be more readily acceptable if their goal of reducing pregnancy on a global basis is accomplished."[97]

The hearings led to the withdrawal of the Majzlen Spring, a particularly dangerous IUD variety, but the IUD scandals were only beginning.

As the hearings took place, U.S. women were already falling victim to another IUD, the Dalkon Shield. The device could rip through the uterine wall, and its wicklike tail, which physically and chemically erodes in the uterus, was an excellent conduit for bacteria. But what attracted the most attention was the number of septic abortions (abortions accompanied by toxic infection) caused by the Shield. By 1974 the FDA had recorded 287 septic abortions from IUDs, 219 of them caused by the Dalkon Shield. Fourteen Shield users had died.[98]

A. H. Robins Co., manufacturer of the Dalkon Shield, was alerted to these dangers as early as 1971, a few months after the product went on the market, when reports of adverse reactions began to come in. The company, in fact, covered up the negative results of its own studies of the Shield. A former Robins' attorney testified that he was ordered to burn hundreds of potentially incriminating documents in 1975, including a number relating to the wicking action of the tail string.[99]

In the expectation of declining U.S. sales, Robins decided to diversify its markets in 1972. According to an exposé by Barbara Ehrenreich, Mark Dowie, and Stephen Minkin in *Mother Jones* magazine, one of its first initiatives was to contact the Office of Population at AID, offering a 48 percent discount on bulk packages of unsterilized Shields. Ravenholt accepted, and the Dalkon Shield was on its way to the "prime target," the women of the Third World.

Although AID maintains that it did not know of the Shield's dangers at the time, its distribution of unsterilized IUDs alone is damning evidence of the contraceptive double standard. In the United States, IUDs are sold in individual sterilized packages, along with a sterile disposable inserter. AID's unsterilized Shields were supposed to be soaked in disinfectant before insertion, but whether this procedure was rigorously followed in poorly equipped Third World clinics is open to question, especially since *only one set of instructions was attached to every 1,000 Shields*. Moreover, these were printed in only three languages—English, French, and Spanish—though the Shield was destined for distribution in forty-two countries.

Field reports from the Third World added to the mounting evidence against the Shield in the United States, but AID and the Robins Company stood firmly behind the product. Then, in 1974, FDA hearings pressured Robins to withdraw the Shield voluntarily from the U.S. market, where an estimated 2.3 million devices had already been sold.

The next year AID issued a recall. By this time 440,000 women were already using the AID-supplied device, and the thousands of Shields in remote family planning clinics were virtually irrecoverable. Ravenholt later admitted that AID "had been hearing about infections" before Robins' withdrawal of the Shield, but he shrugged them off. "Women who frequently change sexual partners have these intercurrent low-grade infections," he explained. "The IUD can't cause an infection. The body tolerates anything that's sterile."[100]

The U.S. courts did not agree. Spurred by publicity and the educational efforts of the National Women's Health Network, almost 10,000 Shield users filed lawsuits, which forced Robins and its insurers to pay $520 million in damages. In 1984, the Honorable Miles Lord, chief U.S. District Court judge of Minnesota, issued a powerful indictment of the company's representatives:

> Mr. Robins Jr., Mr. Forrest, Dr. Lunsford: You have not been rehabilitated. Under your direction your company has in fact continued to allow women, tens of thousands of them, to wear this device—a deadly depth charge in their wombs, ready to explode at any time.... The only conceivable reasons you have not recalled this product are that it would hurt your balance sheet and alert women who already have been harmed that you may be liable for their injuries. You have taken the bottom line as your guiding beacon and the low road as your route. This is corporate irresponsibility at its meanest.[101]

Robins was pressured into launching a campaign in 1984 to locate Shield users in the United States and overseas. In 1985 the company filed a controversial bankruptcy petition in order to limit its liability and set an April 1986 deadline for women filing claims. Over 300,000 claims were made from the United States and fifty other countries.[102]

The Dalkon Shield's notoriety has drawn attention away from the way other much more common IUDs, such as the Lippes Loop, have been misused in Third World population programs. In the late 1960s, for example, with advice and financial assistance from AID and other international agencies, the Indian government promoted the Loop, which can cause heavy blood loss, as *the* mass contraceptive method in a major expansion of the country's family planning program. (The 1967-68 Indian family planning budget was almost as large as the sum of the budgets of the previous fifteen years!)[103] In the mass campaign little effort was made even to tell women about side effects, much less to treat them, and most women were not given a medical examination before IUD insertion. While the drive was initially successful in recruiting acceptors, the Loop soon lost popularity as thousands of women developed adverse effects. The

Indian Health Secretary later said: "As regards the loop, it is correct that under pressure of our foreign advisers, the program was formulated and put into operation without thinking of the effects it would have on women."[104]

Today IUD abuse persists in India, where women are sometimes denied removal, as well as in neighboring Bangladesh and, of course, in China, where it is a favored means of population control.[105] Whether the IUD is purposefully abused or not, the poor health conditions prevailing in many Third World countries exacerbate its risks and complications. The mortality rate from IUDs in the Third World is roughly *double* that in the West because of increased risk from infections, septic abortions, and untreated ectopic pregnancies.[106] Studies also indicate that in countries where malnutrition and anemia are common, the increased menstrual blood loss associated with IUDs leads to iron depletion in many women after twelve months of IUD use.[107]

IUDs can also cause or exacerbate reproductive tract infections, which are rampant in many parts of the Third World. In rural Bangladesh, for example, one study found that IUD users and sterilized women had much greater rates of infection than users of hormonal methods or women who did not use any contraception.[108] This is not surprising, given the poor conditions under which IUDs are inserted (and sterilizations performed). A 1988 WHO investigation in Bangladesh found that "In most of the health centers where IUDs are being inserted asepsis is poor, appropriate instruments are lacking, lighting is not adequate and above all FWVs' [family planning workers] knowledge and insertion technique of IUDs are inadequate."[109]

And what about infertility? PID caused by sexually transmitted diseases is already a major health problem in many countries, and a chief cause of infertility. In parts of Africa, for example, as many as 40 percent of all women suffer from infertility. The decision to introduce the IUD into such a setting is dubious, to say the least, for it can only be expected to worsen the problem.[110] While for most women infertility is a deep personal tragedy, in many societies it can also cause social ostracism, abandonment, and ultimately destitution.

Despite these risks, the IUD continues to be promoted heavily in many Third World family planning programs, not only because of its efficacy in preventing pregnancy, but because women lack control over the device. Getting the IUD removed safely requires a visit to a health clinic, which many women may find difficult to make, and once there, the doctor will not necessarily take it out. Thus high IUD continuation rates, says the journal *Family Planning Perspectives*, "are probably a reflection of involuntary continuation."[111] This, incredibly, is considered one of the IUDs main *advantages*.

In conclusion, an overall pattern emerges from the history of hormonal contraception and the IUD:

- In the development of these contraceptives, the overriding goal of preventing pregnancy has led to a neglect of potential health risks.
- Safety studies have often proved less than rigorous, if undertaken at all.
- When they finally come to light, adverse effects and long-term risks such as cancer are trivialized by population agencies.
- Typically, women are not fully informed of health risks.
- In population control programs, women are not adequately screened or given follow-up care, compounding the dangers of these contraceptives. A double standard is at work that allows the pill, for example, to be distributed freely in Third World village shops, while it is available only by prescription in the West.

This pattern was not predestined. The history of hormonal contraception and the IUD might have been very different if women's welfare had been the primary concern. The time is long overdue to challenge the prevailing mentality that the womb of the individual woman is expendable in the general population control scheme of things.

12

BANGLADESH—
SURVIVAL OF THE
RICHEST

Soon after my arrival in the Bangladesh village of Katni in 1975, I experienced firsthand what the population establishment calls the "unmet need" for contraception. The village women were extremely curious about why I had no children at the ripe old age of twenty-four, and I told them about my use of birth control.

Within a few days, women who had already borne a number of children started approaching me for help—many were desperate to avoid another pregnancy. I succumbed to the pressure and visited the government family planning office in the nearby town, setting in motion a chain of events that dramatically altered my perception of Bangladesh's "population problem."

Three days after my visit to the family planning office, a government jeep sputtered down the path toward the village. Inside were two young women, who were later ushered into a small, dark house, where they were handed bamboo fans and seated in wooden chairs as a gesture of respect. About fifteen village women assembled, not only to learn about birth control but also to see the strange town women with their educated accents and fine clothes.

The family planning workers spoke about the concept of birth control but did not encourage the women to ask questions. They promised they would return in a few days with IUDs and pills for any women who wanted them. After they left, the villagers asked me if they were my sisters from America.

A week passed, then two, then three. There was no sign of the family planning workers. "When will they come back?" women asked. "We want some pills. All government officers care about is their salary. They sit in their offices and drink tea. What do they care about us?"

In response to the women's pleas, I again visited the family planning office. A few days later two women extension workers came to the village. The younger one wore a silk sari and expensive jewelry; the other was an older woman, the wife of a wealthy merchant. Another meeting was called, and this time even more women attended. The family planning workers began by insulting the village women, asking me how I could stand to live in the village, "where everything is dirty and inconvenient." They chided the women for not wearing blouses, unaware that most of them could not afford them.

After this dismal start, the meeting finally turned toward birth control. The family planning workers showed the women pills, told them how to use them, and spoke about the IUD and sterilization. They neglected to tell the women about the side effects of any of these methods or how they actually worked. The village women were confused, but they took the pills the workers distributed.

Then a woman spoke up. "There's a Hindu woman in the next neighborhood who has one of those coils inside her. It hurts, and she bleeds all the time. She got it four years ago, but no one has come to see her since. She wants it taken out."

"Go and get her," the older woman commanded.

Ten minutes later a frail young woman appeared in the company of her mother-in-law. Shaking with fear, she pulled her thin white sari around her bare shoulders. There was a commotion as everyone was moved out of the house, and stray men and children lingering on the outside were driven away. After five minutes the Hindu woman emerged, clearly in pain, covering her face with her sari.

The older of the family planning women laughed. "Well, it was in for a long time," she said. "But she didn't get pregnant. Now she will, and she'll be sorry."

On that note, the family planning workers left Katni. They left behind several cartons of pills for me to distribute and promised that they would return to replenish the stock. "Are these women really Bengalis?" several women asked as the officials pulled away in a rickshaw. "They speak such a strange language."

When I returned to Bangladesh for a visit in 1982, the women to whom I had given the pill jokingly held up their newest offspring. I learned that the family planning workers had never come back. The Hindu woman who had had the IUD removed was dead—no one knew the exact cause.

Despite the millions of dollars flowing into the country for population control, women's unmet need for contraception was still not being met. Yet in other parts of the country, the situation had changed—and not for the better. Under intense international pressure, especially from the U.S. Agency for International Development (AID) and the World Bank, the Bangladesh government had stepped up its population control efforts considerably. Whereas before village women were neglected by Bangladesh's family planning program, now they were the targets of an aggressive sterilization drive that used incentives and intimidation to produce results. Meanwhile, access to safe and reversible methods of fertility control, not to mention basic health care, was still very limited.

And now, in the 1990s, the population establishment is heralding Bangladesh as an exciting new model of fertility decline. Between 1975 and 1990 the total fertility rate fell from seven births per woman to well below five, while there was little, if any, reduction in the country's high death rates. Bangladesh shows, they say, that you can drive down birth rates even in the absence of social and economic development, if you have a "vigorous" and "aggressive" family planning program.

True, Bangladesh is experiencing a fertility decline, but can the family planning program really claim the credit? And what about all the twists and turns the population establishment leaves out of its simple little plot, such as the heavy-handed reliance on sterilization and disproportionate spending on family planning compared to ba-

sic health care? By holding up Bangladesh as a model, the population establishment is turning the whole concept of development on
its head: It's all right if the poor stay as poor as ever, just as long as
there are fewer of them born.

PRIORITY NUMBER ONE

The initial pattern of population control interventions in Bangladesh is a familiar one. It began with the formation of a private
Family Planning Association in the 1950s, founded by a senior police officer and funded largely from abroad, followed by a 1960
Population Council mission culminating in the establishment of a
government National Family Planning Board in the mid-sixties,
which launched a village-level IUD and vasectomy campaign. Bangladesh's bloody 1971 war of liberation from Pakistan led to a temporary lull in these activities, but the aid money that flowed into the
country after the war also washed in a new wave of population advisers.

The new government's First Five Year Plan (1973-78) set an ambitious fertility decline goal and established a National Population
Council, which pursued a variety of strategies: integrating family
planning and health services, women and development activities,
social marketing schemes, and a misconceived contraceptive inundation campaign.[1]

In the end, none proved particularly effective. Administratively,
the program was weak, and family planning workers lacked adequate training, motivation, and supervision. Moreover, economic
conditions in the countryside were hardly conducive to a substantial reduction in the birth rate.

Nevertheless, the government's Second Five Year Plan (1980-
85) aimed to reduce the crude birth rate from 43 in 1980 to 32 by
1985, primarily by increasing the number of sterilizations through
the lure of incentives.[2] Although international donors viewed this
target as overly ambitious, they applauded the government's growing commitment to population control.

Unfortunately, this commitment did not extend to improving
the lives of the target population, the rural poor. In fact, the accel-
eration of population control efforts in Bangladesh has taken place
against a backdrop of declining or stagnating living standards for the

vast majority. Over 40 percent of the population lives under the poverty line, half of rural families are functionally landless, and agricultural wages hardly buy a day's rations. In the mid-eighties over half of rural children were malnourished, 10 percent severely so. The adult literacy rate is only 35 percent, 47 percent for men and 22 percent for women.[3]

As poverty has continued for the majority, a small urban elite and their rural allies—the landlords, rich peasants, and merchants—have tightened their control over the country's land and other resources. Billions of foreign aid dollars, coming to Bangladesh since independence (aid currently finances three quarters of the government's development budget), have primarily benefitted this wealthy minority. Outside resources have also strengthened the hand of the Bangladesh military, which ruled the country from 1975 until 1990, stifling attempts to restore democracy and initiate positive social change.[4]

Blind to their own role in bolstering the inequity that perpetuates poverty—and hence high fertility—in Bangladesh, the main international donors opted to push full steam ahead with population control.

In March 1983, concerned that the government's population performance was not yet up to snuff, donor agencies, including AID, the World Bank, and the UNFPA, circulated a position paper calling for a "drastic" reduction in population growth, the creation of an autonomous National Population Control Board with "emergency powers," and frequent visits by "high-ranking government and Army personnel" to promote family planning in the villages.[5] It also recommended increasing sterilization incentives.

Pressure intensified several months later when World Bank Vice President W. David Hopper sent a letter to Bangladesh's Minister of Finance and Planning, A. M. A. Muhith, instructing him to "outline necessary measures to strengthen the program so that agreed national population objectives could be met on time."[6]

In January 1984 the UNFPA's Dhaka representative, Walter Holzhausen, circulated an even stronger letter, implicitly endorsing compulsion. He wrote the UNFPA headquarters in New York:

> Most donor representatives here greatly admire the Chinese for their achievements; a success story brought about by massive di-

rect and indirect compulsion.... Talking privately to Bangladesh top officials associated with population control...you hear the almost unanimous view that drastic action is needed and that a new dimension needs to be added to the current "voluntary" program.... It is time for donors to get away from too narrow an interpretation of voluntarism and certain governments in Asia using massive incentive schemes, including disincentives and other measures of pressure, still deserve international support.[7]

Heavily dependent on foreign aid, the Bangladesh government responded quickly to these pressures, instituting a "crash program" for reducing the birth rate. It enhanced incentives for sterilization and introduced punitive measures against family planning personnel who failed to meet monthly sterilization quotas. In 1985 President Ershad, the country's martial-law ruler, announced that population control was the country's number-one priority, more important than boosting agricultural production, increasing literacy, improving health care, or feeding hungry children.[8]

STERILIZATION AT STARVATION POINT

The capital city of Dhaka rises from the flat, fertile river delta of Bangladesh like an oasis of affluence. The latest Japanese cars drive along its wide, smooth boulevards, the hum of their air conditioners merging with the beat of stereo cassette recorders. The rich residential areas of Gulshan and Dhanmondi, home to high government officials, businesspeople, diplomats, and aid agency personnel, boast sprawling houses maintained by retinues of servants. If you travel in the right circles, foreign wine and whiskey flow freely, and if you have a color TV, you can watch the latest "soaps" from the United States. Dhaka, in fact, is making itself in the image of Dallas. It is a city on the make.

In 1984 twenty-year-old Rohima had never been to Dhaka, even though her village was only a few hours' bus ride away. She had just made one of her longest journeys ever, to a government hospital in the nearby town, where she had been sterilized the day before. She was hungry—they had given her no food during her twenty-four-hour stay—but at least she now had 175 *taka*, a new sari, and a card which said that, as a sterilization acceptor, she was eligible for relief wheat. The doctor had given her a prescription, and before returning home, she went to the pharmacy.

The medicines cost 80 taka, so she was left with only 95, which she spent on rice and eggs. She was eager to see her four-month-old son, her only child. When she was seven months pregnant, her husband had divorced her and sent her back to her mother's house. She worked for a wealthy family husking rice, but when the floods came, there was no more work, and she had nothing to eat. Her breast milk dried up, and she had to feed her son barley water.

When she approached the Union Council chairman for food relief, he told her, "If you have the operation, you will get wheat." Family planning workers told other destitute women in the village the same thing. No sterilization, no wheat.[9] Rohima's sterilization effectively ended her chances of remarriage, for in Bangladesh few men will marry a sterile woman.

Although Rohima had probably never even heard of the World Bank, she indirectly made her way onto page 22 of a 1985 Bank confidential report.[10] On that page the Bangladesh government's new population targets were matched with a present and projected contraceptive "mix." At that time 34 percent of contraceptive users, or 1.6 million people, had been sterilized in Bangladesh, and the government aimed to increase this statistic to 41 percent, or 3.5 million people, by the end of the decade. (So much for free contraceptive "choice.") According to the World Bank, this goal was "achievable." Achievable, critics might add, only through the use of incentives and at the expense of poor women like Rohima.

Under the government's incentive system, each person—man or woman—who agrees to be sterilized receives 175 taka, equivalent to several weeks' wages. In addition, women receive a sari worth 100 taka and men a lungi worth 50 taka. Doctors and clinic staff get a special payment for each sterilization they perform, and until 1989 government health and family planning workers, as well as village midwives and members of the public, received a fee for each client they "referred" or "motivated" to undergo sterilization, with the emphasis on recruiting women clients. Until the summer of 1985 family planning workers who failed to meet monthly sterilization quotas could have their salaries withheld and ultimately lose their jobs. Although this is no longer official policy, it happens unofficially when targets must be met. Similarly, motivation fees are still sometimes paid, the money coming out of the client's incentive payment.[11]

Until 1988 AID financed 85 percent of these incentives and referral fees as part of its more than $25 million annual contribution to the country's family planning program, the agency's largest bilateral population commitment in the world. AID's funding of incentives contravened Section 104(f) of the 1982-83 U.S. Foreign Assistance Act, which prohibits the use of U.S. funds "to pay for the performance of involuntary sterilizations as a method of family planning or to coerce or provide any financial incentive to any person to undergo sterilization."

In Bangladesh, AID skirted the law by calling the incentives "compensation payments." It maintained that the money was intended to cover transportation, food costs, and wages lost due to the operation. The free saris and lungis were justified as "surgical apparel," since the peasants' clothing was considered unhygienic. "Just look at these people, they're so dirty," said Jack Thomas, AID's former deputy chief of family planning in Bangladesh.[12] In fact, the clothing is often handed out *after* the operation, giving the lie to the surgical apparel argument. Moreover, free clothing is not handed out after other forms of surgery.

In a country where chronic hunger and unemployment are realities for much of the rural population, the distinction between compensation and incentives is no more than semantic sleight of hand. A hungry person can buy many meals for 175 taka, and a new piece of clothing is a powerful inducement for a man or woman who owns only one worn-out garment. In fact, the documents of other donors, as well as of the Bangladesh government itself, freely called the payments "incentives," since they did not have to worry about complying with United States law.[13]

Not surprisingly, government figures in the early 1980s showed that the number of sterilizations tended to increase dramatically during the lean autumn months before the rice harvest, when many landless peasants were unemployed and destitute.[14] Village surveys by Bangladeshi researchers found that the incentives, coupled with continuing pressure from family planning workers, were instrumental in persuading many poor people to undergo sterilization.[15]

The conditions under which sterilizations are carried out are also disturbing. A 1983 study of the program by the World Bank, the World Health Organization (WHO), the Swedish International Development Authority (SIDA), and the Bangladesh government raised a number of serious concerns.

Informed consent is, officially, the basis of the sterilization program, but the reviewers found that "consent forms are not adequately filled in at most of the centers." In more than 40 percent of the centers observed, clients were "not adequately informed about the permanent nature of the operation" or about surgical procedures. The reviewers also discovered shocking standards of hygiene, and felt compelled to prepare guidelines on such basic procedures as "how to scrub the hands for operation."[16]

Under such conditions one would expect a high rate of complications from the operations, but the review team found that "case records are often not written up and complications are not recorded."[17] A Western health adviser put it more bluntly: "If people die during the operation or there is a complication, their record cards will be torn up."[18] As a result the official death rate from sterilization operations in Bangladesh was lower than that of the United States, a finding the review team diplomatically called "surprising."

Other reports suggest that complications are quite common. A survey of 950 sterilized persons in villages scattered throughout Bangladesh, undertaken by the Catholic Commission for Justice and Peace in 1985-86, found that it took over a third of the women forty-five days or more before they could resume normal work. Eighty percent of males and females had to seek some form of medical treatment after the operation, for which most of them had to pay.

The survey also found that over half the men and a third of the women said they did not know of other methods to avoid pregnancy besides sterilization. Although under government guidelines families are supposed to have three children before undergoing sterilization, over 10 percent of the respondents had only one or two children. One man had no children at all and "accepted" because of the incentives; one woman sterilized was sixty-six years old! [19]

A 1984 investigation by the U.S.-based Program for the Introduction and Adaptation of Contraceptive Technology (PIACT) revealed further adverse consequences of the system. According to the study, sterilization and IUD referral fees led to "unhealthy competition" between different categories of health and family planning workers, who vied for clients. Moreover, the lure of the fees meant that other contraceptive methods were neglected; family planning workers spent half their time finding sterilization and IUD clients, local midwives virtually all of their time.

PIACT also reported the existence of male agents, with no family planning background, who scoured the villages for sterilization clients, sometimes "selling" them to family planning workers who needed to fill monthly quotas.[20]

These official studies represent only the tip of the iceberg of sterilization abuse in Bangladesh. In 1983 the Bangladesh Army launched a campaign of compulsory sterilization in the northern district of Mymensingh. Villagers whose names had been listed by local leaders as having more than three children were forcibly rounded up by military personnel and taken in trucks to a local clinic where they were made to sign "informed consent" papers. In the space of a few weeks, over 500 people, mainly poor women, including many from a minority tribal community, had been sterilized against their will. AID officials eventually exerted pressure on the Bangladesh government to halt the Army campaign. "The government knows it won't work with the Army in the long run," said Thomas. "There'll be a backlash."[21]

A year later such overt compulsion gave way to a more subtle strategy. In the course of monitoring flood relief in the autumn of 1984, field workers of British voluntary agencies discovered that emergency food aid provided by the U.N. World Food Program had been withheld from destitute women unless they agreed to be sterilized. Rohima was one of these women.

Cases were reported from Barisal, Jessore, Comilla, and Pabna districts. A pattern emerged of local officials issuing special cards authorizing food relief to women who were sterilized, then reneging on their promises. Meanwhile, older women and widows, who should have been eligible for the relief wheat, received none, since they were not deemed suitable for sterilization.[22]

Official statistics would seem to substantiate these unofficial reports. According to government figures presented by the *Bangla-*

desh Observer, an "unprecedented" 257,000 sterilizations were performed in the flood months July-October 1984, almost one quarter of the total performed in the entire decade 1972-82.[23]

AID, which was supposed to monitor the sterilization program closely, was not aware of the food aid abuses until alerted by outside parties. It then undertook an investigation, which suggested that "some incidents may in fact have occurred but were not widespread."

The World Bank meanwhile maintained that any abuses were probably due to "overzealous local officials" taking "undue advantage of food shortages to improve their family planning records." These agencies did, however, bring the matter to the attention of senior Bangladesh government officials, who responded by issuing a memorandum prohibiting the use of "unapproved inducements for sterilization acceptance," such as "food/grain supply."[24]

While the linking of sterilization and food aid is not official government policy, it is a logical outgrowth of the incentive/disincentive system. In Bangladesh, where millions go hungry every day, food—or the cash to buy it—is the ultimate weapon. Local officials were bound to add food aid to their arsenal sooner or later, especially when *they are under pressure themselves* to meet sterilization targets.

RATIONALIZING DISCRIMINATION

Not all international donors were as complacent about the incentive system as AID and the World Bank. Nor was a coalition of Bangladeshi development activists, solidarity groups, and feminists who mounted an international campaign against the incentives. In 1985 differences came to a head over negotiations for a five-year, $270 million Population III project for Bangladesh, coordinated by the World Bank. The most vocal critic was the the Swedish International Development Authority (SIDA), which expressed concern that incentives and disincentives were leading to "indirect coercion" and competing with other health services, for example, by diverting the attention of health workers away from Mother and Child Health (MCH) services toward sterilization.[25] The British, Dutch, and Norwegian aid agencies, as well as UNICEF, also raised their voices. Pledging dates were postponed again and again, as these donors sought to apply pressure on the Bank and Bangladesh government. Finally, UNICEF and SIDA definitively rocked the boat by pulling out of the project.

While the other donors stayed in, they demanded assurances that the sterilization program would be monitored and reformed, and asked for more attention to be paid to health. The World Bank promised to conduct a study of the incentive system, which was completed in 1987. Co-authored by two big names in the population field, John Cleland and W. Parker Mauldin, the study is a classic example of the technocrats' trick of making everything look rosy when the evidence is grim.[26]

Among the study's findings:

- It is mainly the poor who are sterilized. More recent data confirm this; among contraceptives users, 59 percent of agricultural laborers are sterilized as opposed to only 16 percent of white-collar workers. Sterilization markedly declines as one goes up the income ladder.[27]
- The "compensation payments" act as incentives for about half of all vasectomy clients and a third of tubectomy clients, with these proportions higher among the poor. "The disproportionate attraction of the compensation payment among the poor is the major reason for a strong link between poverty and sterilization, though costs and inconvenience of reversible contraception are probably important subsidiary concerns."[28]
- Fees paid to "motivators" have "fostered a large number of self-employed agents or canvassers who recruit sterilization candidates for profit.... Their clientele tend to be particularly poor with a financial motive for undergoing sterilization in addition to a desire to limit family size."[29]
- There is a significant incidence of sterilization regret, especially among women who had two children or less at the time of the operation, who subsequently lost a child, or who reported that money was their main motive for being sterilized.

Despite these findings, the authors recommended that payments to sterilization clients be continued on the grounds that their abolition would "discriminate against the poor"![30] In spite of the record of abuse, they described fees paid to motivators as a "sociological necessity," filling a gap between the bureaucracy and the illiterate poor who require a "mediator."[31] As one of the authors later stated in an interview, male agents were an effective way of "reaching the poor."[32] (See Box: Reaching the Poor.)

Although the donors unfortunately agreed that "compensation payments" be continued, referral fees were abolished. Now concern has shifted to how to keep sterilization rates up in their absence. The World Bank is currently worried about the decline in sterilization rates in recent years in favor of short-term methods such as the pill, mainly because sterilization is more "cost-effective." In 1993 it exhorted the government to improve the quality of its sterilization services and beef up its population propaganda in order to recruit more acceptors. The target is still that over one third of contraceptive users should be sterilized.

The government meanwhile attributes a large share of sterilization decline to the fact that the World Bank made it abolish referral fees.[33] And so the show goes on, with one side blaming the other, and neither party asking the fundamental questions: What's wrong with poor people choosing temporary methods? Don't they deserve a choice as much as the rich?

"UNCONTAMINATED" OBSERVATION

The blind drive for "cost-effective" population control has not only distorted the family planning system, but severely undermined health delivery. In Bangladesh the shadow of disease and premature death falls especially on the young—approximately one in every five Bangladeshi children dies before the age of five, and the rate is higher for girls than boys. The main causes of death are malnutrition combined with diarrheal disease and acute respiratory infections. Yet Bangladesh has no national nutrition program or effective sanitation program, which would provide clean water to its citizens.

The shadow also falls disproportionately on mothers. Maternal mortality rates in Bangladesh are among the highest in the world, between 600 and 800 per 100,000 live births. Unhygienic birth practices, eclampsia, hemorrhage, and septic abortions are leading killers, helped along by extremely high levels of female malnutrition and anemia. Almost all rural mothers are malnourished when measured in terms of weight for height. Over half of maternal deaths could be prevented by better care, yet most health facilities are inaccessible to poor women.[34]

The result is human tragedy on a massive scale, less newsworthy than the violence of war, but just as devastating.

While this tragedy is enacted in the villages, government offices in Dhaka are the venue for a bureaucratic farce. In Bangladesh's short life as an independent nation, the uneasy relationship between health care and population control has resulted in five major reorganizations of the health system, causing, according to the World Bank, "a legacy of program disruption and staff demoralization."[35] Under the current system set up in 1983, both are joined in the Ministry of Health and Population Control, with family planning and MCH services forming one wing and broader health services the other. At the local level health and family planning are functionally integrated, with various health personnel theoretically assuming aspects of both duties.

The shift toward greater integration of the two stems in part from the emphasis on sterilization and the IUD, which require clinical infrastructure.[36] While the population program has benefitted from the use of medical facilities and personnel, basic health care has suffered. Spending on population control absorbs over one third of the country's annual health budget. "Bangladesh has been so preoccupied with the pressing problem of its population explosion that the general health situation has not received enough attention," comments the World Bank. "Only in family planning does the government appear to have established an effective system for providing services."[37]

What the Bank neglects to mention is how it has not been an innocent bystander in this process. Nor has AID. Foreign aid finances nearly half of the health budget, giving donors considerable influence over its direction. But instead of promoting primary health care, the Bank and AID have pushed population control. A 1983 AID Emergency Plan for Population Control in Bangladesh stated that the integration of family planning with broader MCH services requires unnecessarily costly and long-term efforts to establish a PHC [Primary Health Care] system instead of focusing on a quick delivery of birth control services to meet the unmet demand.... A population control program does not depend on a functioning primary health care system.[38]

This view was echoed by the UNFPA's Dhaka representative, Walter Holzhausen, who wrote that no one seriously believes that "Bangladesh has the money or the time to establish better MCH services and better educational facilities as a precondition for making voluntary family planning more successful."[39]

A second perspective emerged later in response to the poor performance of the family planning program. Donors decided that selected MCH services could be very useful in conferring "credibility" to population control efforts. They set up a human laboratory to test their hypothesis at the International Center for Diarrheal Disease Research in Matlab, Bangladesh (ICDDR,B). The ICDDR,B's "Matlab model" has had considerable influence not just in Bangladesh, but on the international health and family planning fields in general.

The Cholera Research Laboratory (CRL) was the precursor of the ICDDR,B. The CRL was set up during the early sixties by the U.S.-dominated defence alliance, the South East Asia Treaty Organization (SEATO). After Bangladesh gained independence from Pakistan in 1971, plans were set in motion, primarily by the U.S. government, to transform the Cholera Research Laboratory into a major international health institution, the ICDDR,B.

These plans met with a negative response from both Bangladeshi and foreign health activists. Dr. Zafrullah Chowdhury, head of the People's Health Center outside of Dhaka, warned that "Bangladesh people will serve as guinea pigs for experiments from which they may or may not benefit." The main beneficiaries, he pointed out, would be U.S. professionals in the fields of medical and demographic research. John Briscoe, a foreign researcher who had been working at the Cholera Research Laboratory, cautioned that the main aim of population studies at the new center would be to "'prove' that population growth can be reduced without any change in the health conditions, poverty or social (in)justice."[40] Their predictions have proved all too correct. On the population front, the ICDDR,B's Matlab project area is the most thoroughly studied region in Bangladesh, with the highest density of family planning workers (*not* health workers) relative to local population. It has become the prime location for U.S. researchers to undertake social experiments on the integration of MCH and family planning.

ICDDR,B researchers recognize that many villagers distrust family planning workers because they rightly suspect that these workers are less concerned with meeting their health needs than with meeting sterilization and contraceptive quotas. As a result, the ICDDR,B's Family Planning Health Services Project (FPHSP) introduced selected MCH interventions—such as oral rehydration for diarrhea, tetanus immunization of pregnant women, prenatal care, and training of traditional midwives—to its family planning program in different "packages" in order to see which ones had the greatest effect on enhancing field worker credibility and thus increasing contraceptive use.

"Opportunities for researching the integration issue that are comparable to the FPHSP are rare," write the researchers. "Experiments involving the uncontaminated observation of integrated versus single-purpose service systems are usually impossible to carry out, because national integrated programs have long been functioning."[41] In other words, the Matlab area has not been "contaminated" with an integrated national MCH system.

The results of the experiment? Through a series of regression equations, the researchers concluded that only a minimal MCH package achieved the desired result and that further expansion of MCH services to include, for example, prenatal care and midwife training was not essential to increase contraceptive use. In fact, some MCH interventions were deemed harmful to family planning. For example, when oral rehydration therapy was introduced for diarrhea, the study found that this had the "negative" effect of diverting "attention away from family planning to new and complex health education and community organization activities."[42] This was especially true when the locally available salt and molasses rehydration method was promoted, because more training and motivation were required for this method than if the villagers were simply given manufactured rehydration packets. In other words, a local and affordable solution to the serious problem of diarrhea is likely to be passed over because it is "disruptive" of family planning.

The ICDDR,B's priorities are clear: Family planning comes first, and nothing should stand in its way. This single-minded approach has yielded results. Contraceptive prevalence rates in the Matlab project area are much higher and birth rates lower than those in neighboring villages which have similar socioeconomic conditions, but which are served only by the government health program. The reasons are not hard to fathom: ICDDR,B's female family planning workers receive far better training and logistical backup than government workers. As a result, they are better able to meet women's very real demands for family planning.

Measured by narrow population control standards, the ICDDR,B program is a success—but how real is that success for the local people, who are just as poor as ever? For the ICDDR,B, reducing poverty is not the issue. Indeed, as four of its top researchers note, their findings that a well-organized family planning program can reduce birth rates in Bangladesh "have a significant bearing on one of the central questions in the population field: Can family planning programs in the developing world succeed in the absence of extensive socio-economic development?" The implication is that the answer is yes, even in Bangladesh, "a country characterized by static and possibly even deteriorating economic conditions."[43]

In theory, there is nothing intrinsically wrong with providing (voluntary) family planning services to a poor population, but there is something ethically questionable about promoting those services not only in the absence of desperately needed basic health care, but at its expense. When faced with this question, population control advocates usually fall back on the position that their narrow focus on family planning is justified since family planning itself is one of the most important health interventions to reduce infant and maternal mortality.

Lately, however, this assertion has come under increased scrutiny from demographers. John Bongaarts of the Population Council demonstrates, for example, how changes in family building patterns that accompany increased contraceptive use (e.g., a higher proportion of first births and births after short intervals) offset the decline in infant mortality which would be expected as women adopt contraception and have fewer high-risk teenage births and births after the sixth child. As a result, infant mortality rates remain virtually the same with high levels and low levels of contraceptive use. Bongaarts points specifically to the Matlab project area, which has witnessed little improvement in infant mortality despite a dramatic rise in contraceptive use. "What little decline [in infant mortality] that did occur," he writes, "was probably due in large part to maternal and child services introduced at the same time."[44] It is precisely those services that the ICDDR,B is striving to keep to a minimum so as not to interfere with family planning.

Similarly, increased contraceptive use seems to have had only a limited effect on maternal mortality in the Matlab project area. Maternal mortality is typically expressed either as a *ratio* of deaths per 100,000 live births or as a *rate* of deaths per 100,000 women of reproductive age. By reducing the absolute number of pregnancies and births in the project area, the ICDDR,B family planning program has achieved some reduction in the maternal mortality *rate*. However, the maternal mortality *ratio* has remained roughly the same since there has been no reduction in the health risks associated with each individual pregnancy.[45]

ICDDR,B researchers largely attribute this phenomenon to the fact that increased contraceptive use has shifted the distribution of births from one high-risk category, older women who have already borne many children, to another, younger women who are pregnant for the first time. (To their credit, they also recognize that the lack of safe abortion services in the project contributes to the persistence of high maternal mortality.)

At first glance their analysis may seem compelling, but it ignores the ICDDR,B's own role in perpetuating the high risks associated with pregnancy in rural Bangladesh through its conscious decision *not* to provide basic maternity care as part of its family planning program. According to its own study, direct obstetric causes such as postpartum hemorrhage, toxemia, and postpartum sepsis accounted for 77 percent of all maternal deaths in the project area. Many of these could have been avoided with basic maternity care, including the training and equipping of traditional midwives, one of the "packages" the ICDDR,B decided is not necessary to increase contraceptive acceptance. Clearly for the ICDDR,B, preventing pregnancy takes priority over protecting the pregnant woman. One can only hope that a change is in order, for at least this study admits that for real progress to be made in reducing maternal mortality, "family planning must be offered as only one component of a broader intervention strategy, that includes antenatal, delivery and postdelivery care."[46]

The family planning approach toward reducing maternal mortality also fails to take into account the fact that many contraceptives themselves have associated mortality risks. Indeed, many feminists in the population field are calling for a wider definition of maternal mortality ("reproductive mortality"), which would include not only deaths associated with pregnancy, but those related to contraceptives.

They are also challenging the efficiency of family planning alone in reducing maternal mortality. "Provision of health care seems to offer a more certain ability to prevent most fatalities from pregnancy," conclude Beverly Winikoff and Maureen Sullivan in an important article on women's health. They point to the example of Sweden, where they estimate that 97 percent of the reduction in maternal mortality between 1911 and 1980 was due to improved socioeconomic conditions and general health care, including maternity services, while changes in the age/parity distribution of births typically associated with increased contraceptive use accounted for only 3 percent.[47]

In recent years, infant mortality rates have declined somewhat in Bangladesh, mainly due to an extensive childhood immunization program, though they still remain unconscionably high. Maternal mortality rates have shown little or no improvement. Belatedly, the World Bank is taking steps to expand MCH services in the latest Fourth Population and Health Project in Bangladesh (1992-96), but population control still dominates. Over 50 percent of the $600 million allocated for the project will go to family planning, over double that devoted to health. The demographic objective is uppermost: The goal is a 27 percent fertility decline and the conversion of the population program into "a social movement" through intensified propaganda campaigns. Already, Bangladesh radio carries five hours a day of population-related messages, television five hours a month of population shows.[48]

Worst of all, the World Bank is now patting itself on the back for Bangladesh's fertility decline and going to great lengths to show that it is the "tenacious resolve" of the population program—not social and economic changes—which is responsible. Those with a deeper appreciation of Bangladeshi society dispute this claim, pointing in particular to the greater employment of women outside the home as a major cause of the decline.[49]

All sides acknowledge that a latent demand for family planning existed in any case. The village women I lived with wanted access to birth control, but they also wanted access to health care, education, and other opportunities. A primary health system which offered voluntary family planning as only one of its components would have met their needs far better than the aggressive and often coercive sterilization program that was put into place. How can the Bangladesh program be considered a great success, indeed an exportable model, when it was built over the dead bodies of millions of people denied access to the most rudimentary forms of health care? This may sound like hyperbole, but it is not.

"REACHING THE POOR"

The following is excerpted from the *Hotline, Justice and Peace Newsletter* of the Catholic Commission on Human Rights in Bangladesh (CCHRB), August-September 1987.

80 YEAR OLD MAN DIES—
FORCED STERILIZATION IN MYMENSINGH

A CCHRB investigation revealed the operation of a large gang in Mymensingh who persuade, threaten, or force people at the train and bus station and ferry ghat[dock] to go with them to clinics for an immediate sterilization operation. The main center for such operations is located at the Mymensingh Medical College Hospital Model Family Planning Clinic, where an 80-year-old man, Osman Ali, was vasectomized on 11 August and died two days later on 13 August. The victim...came to Mymensingh to visit his brother. On the way home he was persuaded by a government-approved referral agent, Jalauddin, to go with him to get a lungi and Tk. 175. He was told to lie [to] the clinic that he had two wives aged 36 and 22, when actually he had 5 daughters and 2 sons and his only wife had reached menopause. When he came out of the operation theater, his lungi and money were snatched away from him by Jalauddin (who in addition received Tk. 45 as agent). Osman Ali suffered a stroke on the spot and was admitted to the hospital.

For the Model Clinic 58 referral agents are signed up. The total number in Mymensingh is estimated to be about 100. Doctors and clinic workers complained to the CCHRB investigator that the agents often forcibly take money away from clients, who are usually very poor. They also complained that agents often come in with the clients and try to interfere when they are being questioned or are filling in the admission forms. They appealed for protection against such flagrant abuses of human rights.

13

STERILIZATION
AND ABORTION

Sterilization and abortion are the most controversial of birth control methods—sterilization because of its permanence, abortion because it terminates pregnancy. While arguments rage over the ethics of both methods, this does not prevent their widespread use by women all over the world. This chapter looks at the crucial question of why these methods are chosen, and who makes the choice.

BARREN POLICIES

The world has accepted compulsory vaccination against small-pox, which is surely an invasion of the body.... And the state so claims control of the body of its male citizens that it compels them to accept military service, and of the bodies of its children—male and female—as to force their attendance at school.... In this context I do not think that sterilization after an allowable number of births is so revolutionary a restriction on personal freedom as it may first appear to be. I think it is obvious that we should help to discover and to support any system of incentives which would significantly reduce the birth rate in the countries which are in a population crisis.

—JOHN P. ROBIN, *Ford Foundation, Representative for East and Central Africa, 1968*

If some excesses appear, don't blame me.... You must consider it something like a war. There could be a certain amount of misfiring out of enthusiasm. There has been pressure to show results. Whether you like it or not, there will be a few dead people.

—DR. D. N. PAI, *Harvard-educated director of family planning in Bombay, commenting on his plans for compulsory sterilization (New York Times, 1976)*[1]

Today sterilization is the world's most widespread form of birth control, accounting for over a third of contraceptive use worldwide, and almost half in developing countries. Female sterilization is much more common than male—by 1992 an estimated 140 million women of reproductive age had been sterilized, as opposed to 42 million men. Female to male sterilization ratios are higher in developing countries than in developed ones.[2] The concentration on female sterilization raises troubling concerns, since it is a more complicated and riskier operation than vasectomy and can take longer to recover from.

The most common complications of female sterilization are anesthesia-related problems, internal injury, and infection, and there may be long-term side effects such as heavier menstrual periods or lower back pain. The mortality rate probably differs significantly depending on where the operation is done. According to *Population Reports,* in the U.S. the rate is approximately one death in every 70,000 procedures, but it is likely to be much higher in mass sterilization camps and clinics in countries like India and Bangladesh. Nevertheless, new female surgical methods are often billed as easy and safe—Planned Parenthood, for example, calls the "minilap" technique "Band-Aid surgery"—although they all require a high degree of technical competence.[3]

By contrast, male sterilization (vasectomy), is relatively risk-free, yet it is common in only four countries: the United States, Great Britain, India, and China. The mortality rate from vasectomy is virtually zero in the United States, though in those Third World countries where vasectomies are performed in large "fairs" or "camps" under less than sanitary conditions, deaths from infection are not unknown. Bangladesh and India in particular have poor records in this regard.[4] (See Box: Sterilization Side Effects: Unanswered Questions.)

STERILIZATION SIDE EFFECTS:
UNANSWERED QUESTIONS

While doing field work in a village in the Indian Punjab, social anthropologist Joyce Pettigrew discovered that almost every village woman who had undergone sterilization complained of persistent pain in the pelvic area and lower back region. "After this operation we suffer so much," said one woman. "And then when we cannot work the husbands say 'go and die.'"[1]

Such complaints led Pettigrew to the tentative conclusion that the side effects of sterilization are worse for poor laboring women, whose daily tasks involve bending and stretching for long hours and who subsist on an iron-deficient diet. Because they do not have time to rest or the facilities to bathe properly after the operation, their incisions appear to take longer to heal. The spinal anesthesia used during the operation could also contribute to lower back pain. Only one woman, the wife of a better-off farmer who was allowed to rest, had no complaint of side effects.

The conditions under which village women were sterilized also left much to be desired. In visits to government health clinics, Pettigrew found that "innumerable premises had dirty sheets over which flitted a liberal number of flies." One junior official in the health department confided that in one year alone there had been fifty deaths in the Punjab sterilization program.

Other village-level researchers have reported similar findings. In South India, John and Pat Caldwell note:

> The majority of those who have been sterilized report that they have in fact suffered debilitating effects. In their private capacity, all members of the family planning program know this but it is never reported partly because it would be regarded as non-constructive and partly because the doctors do not believe there can be a physical basis for it.[2]

Similar reports have come from places as far afield as Bangladesh and El Salvador.[3]

Yet there appear to be no official studies of the phenomenon, perhaps for the same reasons Pettigrew found in India: "After effects were not their [the Health Ministry's] business because the government's overall aim was a restricted one—control of the birth rate at all costs."

Although vasectomy is much safer than female sterilization, there are many prejudices against it. Many men fear vasectomy will somehow affect their virility and potency, while many doctors find female sterilization more "interesting," not the least because they receive higher fees for it than for vasectomy. Most family planning programs ignore male responsibility for contraception—and hence vasectomy—an attitude that reflects the basic unequal power relationship between the sexes. Nevertheless, there are examples of successful vasectomy programs, where a real effort has been made to educate and communicate with men.[5]

Because of its permanence, sterilization has frequently been employed as a method of population control. However, there is considerable debate over its demographic effectiveness. Couples who opt for *voluntary* sterilization (in the true sense of the word) tend to have completed their family size, and in many cases already have more children than would be commensurate with a reduced rate of population growth. Thus a number of population agencies favor birth spacing methods, such as the IUD and hormonal methods, which appeal to younger couples, who ideally will have fewer children, farther between, with a more pronounced impact on birth rates.[6] Of course, there is a way to make sterilization more demographically effective—that is, to make it *involuntary*—through targeting people who have not completed their family size by means of incentives/disincentives or force.

The United States has played a major role in the introduction of sterilization into Third World family planning programs. In a 1977 interview Dr. R. T. Ravenholt made his now famous statement that the United States was seeking to provide the means by which one quarter of the world's fertile women could be voluntarily sterilized.[7] The U.S. Agency for International Development (AID) funds the Program for International Education in Gynecology and Obstetrics (PIEGO), which brings foreign medical personnel to the United States to learn sterilization techniques along with population indoctrination. In the mid-seventies, the PIEGO center at Washington University Medical School in St. Louis was closed after a community coalition challenged its medical and ethical standards and population control bias.[8] AID also funds the greater part of the Association for Voluntary Surgical Contraception's (AVSC–formerly Association for Voluntary Sterilization or AVS) international program budget.

AVSC, formerly linked with the eugenics movement, works in over sixty countries. "To begin with, the philosophy of AVS had more to do with population control," said International Programs director Terrence Jezowski in 1982, "but now sterilization is viewed primarily as a human rights issue."[9] Both AID and AVSC insist that they support only *voluntary* sterilization programs, and ones in which other contraceptive methods are also offered in order to ensure freedom of choice. But both have worked in and often actively supported incentive-based programs, for example in Sri Lanka and Bangladesh. And they tend to push *female* sterilization, as is presently occurring in Kenya where AVSC, with AID assistance, has rapidly expanded female sterilization sites.[10] Recently, however, AVSC has taken a principled stand against the introduction of quinacrine chemical sterilization. (See Box: Population Controller's Dream May Become Woman's Nightmare, p. 256.)

Incentives are not the only means of restricting individual choice in sterilization programs. As the following Latin American case studies reveal, there are other important social dimensions to the problem.

La Operación: Sterilization in Latin America. The history of U.S. involvement in sterilization abroad began on the Caribbean island of Puerto Rico. In the 1930s, as poverty and unemployment fueled social unrest, U.S. colonial officials labeled overpopulation as a main cause of the "Puerto Rican problem," conveniently ignoring their own role in generating the economic crisis. After the United States seized control of the island from the Spanish in 1898, U.S. sugar interests quickly moved in, evicting farmers and cattle ranchers to make way for large plantations. By 1925, less than 2 percent of the population owned 80 percent of the land, and 70 percent of the people were landless.[11]

In the 1940s, in another wave from the mainland, U.S. manufacturing industries began to locate in Puerto Rico, attracted by tax-free investment incentives and the prospect of cheap labor. Women were an important part of that cheap labor force, and sterilization was perceived as a way to help "free" them for employment, as opposed to, for example, providing good child-care facilities.

Both private agencies, including the International Planned Parenthood Federation (IPPF), and the Puerto Rican government, with United States government funds, encouraged women to accept sterilization by providing it at minimal or no cost. By 1968 one third of women of childbearing age had been sterilized on the island, the highest percentage anywhere in the world at that time.[12]

Many women undergoing *la operación*, as it is commonly called in Puerto Rico, were no doubt eager for birth control, but, as Rosalind Petchesky points out, their choice of sterilization was voluntary only in a narrow sense. Not only were many women unaware that the operation was permanent, but other forms of contraception were either unavailable or prohibitively expensive. Moreover, the Catholic Church's opposition to sterilization was relatively weak compared to its outright condemnation of abortion and other birth control methods. The Puerto Rican medical establishment favored sterilization because, in the words of demographer J. M. Stycos, they "thought and still think that contraceptive methods are too difficult for lower class Puerto Rican women." Puerto Rican women living within the United States also have very high rates of sterilization—in the early 1980s half of Puerto Rican women of reproductive age had been sterilized in Hartford, Connecticut.[13]

Despite the claims of the Malthusians, sterilization and population control did nothing to solve the island's problems. Puerto Rico now faces a serious HIV epidemic on the scale of Washington, D.C.'s, as well as an epidemic of violence, substance abuse, and unemployment. The island's environment has been badly damaged, not by population pressures, but by pollution from U.S. chemical plants. "Today few illusions exist that population control policies will solve the island's environmental, economic or social problems," writes Dr. Helen Rodriguez-Trias, long-time health activist and former president of the American Public Health Association. "Women still struggle for family planning, safe abortions and health care, but resist pressures to end their reproductive lives prematurely."[14]

In the early 1980s Colombia was the scene of Latin America's most vigorous sterilization drive. Female sterilization was the second most popular family planning method after the pill, not surprising since these were the two methods most heavily promoted.

Sterilizations were largely promoted and performed by the private Profamilia family planning organization, supported by AID, AVSC, and IPPF, among others. Profamilia's executive director, Dr. Miguel Trias, famous on the population scene, has lectured the U.S. Congress on the dire consequences of rapid population growth. Miguel Trias justified his organization's accent on female sterilization on the basis that its side effects are "negligible," the cost to the acceptor is "extremely low," and "its irreversibility puts the patient safely beyond any possible social, religious, or marital conflict."[15]

In Colombia, where illegal abortion rates are high and complications common, sterilization is also presented as an antidote to abortion. "If we reduced our surgery program," said Dr. Trias, "we would stimulate an epidemic of illegal abortions."[16]

Do such factors form a solid foundation for a voluntary sterilization program? As in Puerto Rico, Colombian women were not outright coerced into sterilization, but their acceptance must be viewed in context. The view that the side effects of the operation were negligible meant that women were not well counseled about them. According to a British researcher who visited Colombia, "The information given about the operation is very brief; no mention is made about possible side effects or problems. The main emphasis is the economic advantages to be gained by having fewer children."[17]

Because sterilization was heavily subsidized, the cost to the acceptor was low, but this raises the question of whether the poor would have preferred other methods, if they were available and low-cost as well. As Dr. Miguel Trias notes: "Any attempt to increase the recipient's cost brings about an immediate and substantial diminution in demand among the poorest people who are precisely those who need sterilization most."[18]

Not-so-subtle pressures were sometimes exerted on women to undergo the operation, especially right after giving birth. The British researcher found that women in state hospitals were told that if they consented to sterilization after delivery, they could stay in the hospital for three days instead of the normal twenty-four hours, "a great temptation to an exhausted woman with other children at home."[19]

As for abortion, is sterilization really the cure? As Dr. Helen Rodriguez-Trias points out, "Abortion is a principle cause of maternal mortality in Colombia, but instead of providing safe, legal abortion, the population people promote sterilization."[20] This is not to argue that sterilization should be eliminated from the Colombian family planning program, but its aggressive promotion raises serious questions.

The phenomenon of sterilization regret, long unrecognized and understudied, is starting to command attention. A 1985 WHO study of sterilized women in India, Colombia, Nigeria, the Philippines, and the United Kingdom found that from 1 to 6 percent of women regretted having the operation in the twelve-month follow-up interview. (One would expect the percentage to rise as women's circumstances change, children die, etc.) The highest figures were in Colombia and India. A 1987 survey in Mexico found that over ten percent of women who had been sterilized would not have the operation again if they had a choice.[21] Sterilization's irreversibility, instead of placing the patient safely beyond conflict, thus may instead engender deep conflict, if the decision, made in haste or under pressure, leads later to regret.

The situation in Brazil reveals another important aspect of the sterilization debate in Latin America. In the 1970s Brazil became a target of U.S. government population control efforts. The strategy was to work through private family planning organizations, such as BENFAM, the Brazilian IPPF affiliate, since the Brazilian government was officially pronatalist, although in reality it gave free rein to BENFAM and others.

At the same time "a violent process of urbanization" was taking place as many poor peasants were forced to migrate to the cities due to the government's failure to implement land reform. But life in the cities was difficult as well—the inequitable distribution of wealth as well as a capital-intensive industrialization strategy meant there were few jobs. In the cities people could simply not afford to have many children, and a distress-related fertility decline began.

However, good services did not exist to meet people's needs for contraception. BENFAM mainly distributed the pill, usually without adequate counseling and follow-up care, and barrier methods were not widely available. As a result many women turned to sterilization, although it was illegal. By 1986 44 percent of Brazilian women between the ages of fifteen and forty-four had been sterilized. To circumvent the law, many were sterilized after unnecessary Caesarian sections in private clinics—Brazil has the highest Caesarian section rate in the world. In the northeast, the poorest region of the country, BENFAM and other agencies signed agreements with local governments to sterilize women in public hospitals. Sterilization rates are in fact highest in the towns of the northeast—over three quarters of women of reproductive age were sterilized in Sao Luiz.

Brazil's population growth has dropped dramatically in the last two decades—many observers believe it has effectively passed through the demographic transition—but this "success" was achieved at the expense of women's health, with an excessive reliance on female sterilization. On the positive side, the Brazilian women's movement has been very active in campaigning for a more comprehensive program of women's health and reproductive rights and has made many concrete gains in changing government policy.[22]

India: Something Like a War. The continuum between restriction of choice and outright physical compulsion is dramatically exposed in India. From the introduction of targets and incentives in the mid-1960s to the mass vasectomy camps of the early 1970s, India's family planning program, one of the first and largest in the world, consistently treated the poor recipients of its services as second-class citizens. Lack of respect translated into lack of results. Despite massive infusions of foreign and national funds, India's birth rate has come down much more slowly than anticipated.[23]

Then, in 1975, Prime Minister Indira Gandhi declared Emergency Rule. Encouraged by her son Sanjay, she decided to take action once and for all to solve the country's population problem. Civil liberties were suspended in 1975, and in 1976 a variety of laws and regulations on sterilization were enacted, as the central government put pressure on the states to meet sterilization quotas. Public employees' salaries were made contingent on the number of acceptors they brought for sterilization. Fines and imprisonment threatened couples who failed to be sterilized after three children, and food rations and other government services were withheld from the unsterilized.

In some cases, state governments resorted to brute force, with police raids to round up "eligible" men for forcible sterilization. In at least one case, *all* the young men of one village were sterilized.[24] It was the poor who were most often the victims of both the regulations and police violence, since the wealthy were able to buy their way out either with bribes or substitution of poor men in their places.

In the last six months of 1976, 6.5 million people were sterilized, four times the rate of any previous period. Meanwhile hundreds, if not thousands, died from infections associated with the operation, and in riots and protests against the program.[25]

Although the compulsory sterilization campaign received critical coverage in the foreign press, many members of the population establishment were slow to condemn it. When World Bank President Robert McNamara visited India during Emergency Rule, he paid tribute to "the political will and determination shown by the leadership at the highest level in intensifying the family planning drive with a rare courage of conviction." Paul Ehrlich, author of *The Population Bomb*, criticized the United States for not supporting a proposal for mandatory sterilization of all Indian men with three or more children: "We should have volunteered logistic support in the form of helicopters, vehicles and surgical instruments. We should have sent doctors.... Coercion? Perhaps, but coercion in a good cause." The UNFPA's Dr. Joep van Arendonk, who went personally to India in 1976 to investigate the situation, still maintains that compulsory sterilization did not exist "except for a few abuses."[26]

These "few abuses," however, were enough to bring down Indira Gandhi's government in 1977 in a dramatic electoral defeat. There followed a predictable backlash against family planning: The number of sterilizations dropped to 900,000 that year.

Today India's sterilization program is back in full swing. Although direct coercion is rare, other forms of pressures are brought to bear on the poor.

Carrying out research in rural South India, demographers John and Pat Caldwell and P. H. Reddy saw some of these pressures firsthand. Although the rural elite preferred to use the IUD, poor villagers were offered no other birth control alternative but sterilization in the belief that they were too ignorant to cope with anything else and that their fertility had to be controlled at all costs. According to the research team, when health workers, drawn from the elite, suggest

> the operation for the first time to a young woman with two or three children, there is little overt pressure on her or her family, but rejecting such advice.... perhaps 20 or 30 times over a two-year period is much more difficult. This is particularly so in the Hindu society with its concepts of elite leadership and of religious virtue arising from proper social behavior. This moral pressure partly explains the rapidity with which sterilization decisions are often made.[27]

Such pressure is also exerted on India's tribal minorities, even those who are in danger of extinction. While visiting a Rabha tribal village in the Indian state of West Bengal in 1982, I witnessed a government development officer putting pressure on village leaders to send women "10 to 15 at a time" to the hospital to be sterilized. I later learned that the entire Rabha tribe only numbers 2,500 people, out of a total population of over 55 million in West Bengal.

Added to these pressures is the inducement of incentives—a woman receives the equivalent of $22 for submitting to sterilization, a man $15.[28] This differential reflects the government's policy of concentrating on female sterilization after the politically costly vasectomy abuses during Emergency Rule. As analyst Alaka Basu explains: "What better way than to turn to another target group—that of women—which lacked the individual and group capability to protest and which in any case was beginning to display a demand for some form of birth control even if tubectomy was still not its first preference?"[29] In 1989-90, female sterilizations accounted for over 90 percent of total sterilizations.[30]

More than 70 percent of the sterilizations are performed in camps, where hygienic standards are appalling. In the autumn of 1985 India was rocked by yet another sterilization scandal: In a Maharashtran sterilization camp one woman died and seventeen others were in serious condition after being given an antidiabetic drug mistaken for a pain killer. During the sterilization operation itself, the woman who died had screamed with pain since the anesthetic had not taken effect. The doctors had paid no attention. "The family planning program is beginning to resemble a giant, over-developed and hyperactive limb growing out of an inefficient health system which is incapable of supervising and controlling it," commented an editorial in a prominent Indian weekly.[31] A recent documentary on India's population program, "Something Like a War," produced by Dheepa Dhanraj for British television, provides graphic footage of the shocking conditions within sterilization clinics and the heavy-handed methods used by local elites to recruit "acceptors."

The Indian government's capitulation to an IMF structural adjustment agenda in the early 1990s is now leading to an intensification of the population control program. Observers believe external pressure is behind the government's decision to cut health expenditures while dramatically increasing funds for family planning. The UNFPA and AID meanwhile have substantially raised their contributions to the program. The government has set an (impossible) target of reducing the crude rate from 30.5 to 26.7 by 1995.[32] It aims to build a "population control movement by the people" in which local village leaders will be the "kingpins," increasing the risks of abuse.[33]

In New Delhi, a huge population clock has been set up at a central intersection, registering every new birth in order to alarm passers-by—of course, it fails to register the number of children who die each day from malnutrition and simple diseases, or women who die in childbirth. In India, as in Bangladesh, primary health care has been seriously undermined by the sterilization program.[34]

Is there no alternative? One wonders what would happen if the Indian government simply took the sensible and humane step of providing decent health and voluntary family planning services to its people, as well as education and employment opportunities, instead of herding poor women like cattle into sterilization camps. Not only might human suffering be greatly alleviated, but the birth rate might actually come down.

The United States Parallel. Today sterilization is the most widely used method of birth control in the United States,[35] but, as in many parts of the Third World, sterilization "choice" often takes place in a restrictive context. This is especially the case for poor white, black, Hispanic, and Native American women who lack access to other birth control methods and/or who are the victims of racially motivated designs to limit their numbers. Their choice was further restricted in 1977 when public funding of abortion was virtually eliminated, although sterilization continues to be covered in Medicaid programs for up to 90 percent of the cost.[36]

Poor women and women of color were sometimes subjected unnecessarily to hysterectomies, a much more dangerous form of sterilization, with mortality risks fifteen to twenty times higher than those of tubal sterilization and significant long-term ill effects.

Why were these women given hysterectomies? "In most major teaching hospitals in New York City, it is the unwritten policy to do elective hysterectomies on poor black and Puerto Rican women, with minimal indications, to train residents," explained the director of obstetrics and gynecology at a New York municipal hospital.[37] Doctors were also paid more for hysterectomies than for tubal ligations.

Compulsory sterilization also has a long history in the United States, with the focus on the mentally retarded, prison inmates, and ethnic minorities. In the famous Relf case in the early 1970s, when two young black teenagers in Alabama were sterilized without their consent or knowledge, a federal district court found that there was

> uncontroverted evidence in the record that minors and other incompetents have been sterilized with federal funds and that an indefinite number of poor people have been improperly coerced into accepting a sterilization operation under the threat that various federally supported welfare benefits would be withdrawn unless they submitted to irreversible sterilization.[38]

In 1976 the U.S. General Accounting Office revealed that the federally funded Indian Health Service had sterilized 3,000 Native American women in a four-year period using consent forms "not in compliance...with regulations."[39]

These and other abuses led feminists and health activists to campaign for more stringent sterilization regulations in the United States. The first victory was won in New York City in 1975, when stricter guidelines were enacted, which later formed the basis of federal sterilization reform. These include more rigorous informed consent procedures, a thirty-day waiting period between consent and the actual operation, a prohibition on hysterectomies for sterilization purposes, and a moratorium on federally funded sterilizations of minors, the involuntarily institutionalized, and the legally incompetent.[40]

These measures have met harsh opposition not only from medical quarters, where doctors fear loss of control, but from population agencies. In seeking to relax regulations for the sterilization of the mentally handicapped, AVSC, for example, stated, "protection against involuntary pregnancy is as much an individual right as is protection against involuntary sterilization."[41] But to weigh these two rights against each other is highly misleading. There are other ways to avoid pregnancy besides sterilization, and even if an unwanted pregnancy does occur, there are the alternatives of abortion and adoption. Sterilization ends forever the capacity to bear children.

There is a place for sterilization, without pressure or incentives, with full knowledge and informed consent. In the right hands it can be a powerful tool of reproductive freedom. In the wrong hands it is an intrusive act of physical violence, no matter how clean the surgeon's gloves or the consciences of the donors from abroad.

QUINACRINE: POPULATION CONTROLLER'S DREAM MAY BECOME WOMAN'S NIGHTMARE

The most zealous population controllers have long wanted a cheaper and "easier" form of female sterilization, and now many think they have found the answer to their dreams: quinacrine sterilization pellets. Developed in the 1920s, the drug quinacrine was first used to treat malaria and now has a variety of other medical applications. After initial reseach in Chile in the 1970s, quinacrine pellets were developed as a sterilizing agent. Inserted into the top of a woman's womb, the pellets dissolve and cause a low-level inflammation. This produces scar tissue at the ends of the fallopian tubes, preventing the passage of the egg into the uterus.

Both the WHO and the USFDA have refused to approve large-scale human trials of quinacrine sterilization until animal toxicology studies, conducted according to accepted standards, have been carried out. Quinacrine risks include a possible link with cancer, ectopic pregnancy, uterine complications leading to hysterectomy, and vaginal burning and irritation. Nevertheless, two North Carolina-based population agencies, Family Health International (FHI) and the

Center for Research on Population and Security, have supported testing on women. The Center provides free quinacrine pellets to government health agencies and researchers, while FHI has funded research in Chile and two small studies of U.S. women, and is planning a new clinical trial in Vietnam. To date 80,000 women have received quinacrine in eleven countries: Bangladesh, Chile, Costa Rica, Croatia, Egypt, India, Indonesia, Iran, Pakistan, Venezuela, and 30,000 in Vietnam alone.[1]

Within the population community there is mounting controversy over quinacrine, with AVSC taking a leading role in exposing its possible dangers. In late 1993 AVSC issued a highly critical report of a Vietnamese study of quinacrine which had been published in the British medical journal, the *Lancet*. The study's glowing account of quinacrine use by 31,781 Vietnamese women was not only based on seriously flawed statistical techniques but dubious assumptions. Quinacrine "represents our most cost-effective way of lowering maternal mortality," the study states, using the same false logic applied to sterilization in Bangladesh and elsewhere.[2]

Lowering population growth is the underlying agenda, and there are already allegations of coercive use of quinacrine in Vietnam's heavy-handed population program. In 1993 the Vietnamese publication *The Woman* exposed the case of 100 women on the Hoa Binh rubber plantation, who had quinacrine inserted into their uteruses without their knowledge when they thought they were having routine IUD checks.[3] As AVSC notes, "The potential for coercion and abuse in the context of demographic goals may be of greater concern than the medical risk from side effects and long-term health consequences of quinacrine itself."[4]

The drug's chief advocates claim that quinacrine "would increase the prevalence of sterilization in economically depressed regions" because "it can be delivered by any health personnel already trained in IUD insertion." They openly condone its use by physicians as a sterilization agent "under the legal use of an approved drug for an unapproved use." Quinacrine is a common treatment for malaria and giardia, and is thus easily available to doctors. Where malpractice suits are prevalent, they urge that informed consent forms be signed by patients. So much for respecting basic regulatory procedures![5]

Unfortunately, they are not the only ones who have a cavalier attitude toward quinacrine safety. A recent editorial in the *Lancet* implies that "Northern standards" should not be applied to quinacrine sterilization, a valuable "South-South technology." The editorial fiercely attacks the WHO, the FDA, and the AVSC for their criticisms of quinacrine.[6] When a prestigious medical journal so openly supports the contraceptive double standard, it is time for all health advocates to wake up and watch out.

A WOMAN'S RIGHT TO HER LIFE

Abortion is murder.
> —*slogan of the antiabortion movement in the United States*

A woman's life is a human life.
> —*slogan of pro-choice activists*

Despite the controversy surrounding it, abortion should not be viewed in isolation from other contraceptive methods, since it is ideally a complement to them. No contraceptive method is entirely effective. The backup of safe abortion—the termination of a pregnancy by extracting the fetus—provides an important insurance against contraceptive failure and allows women to use safer but sometimes less effective methods such as barrier contraceptives and natural family planning. If all women were guaranteed access to safe, cheap, legal abortion, the profile of contraceptive use might very well shift from riskier but more effective varieties.

Denying women the right to abortion makes women bear all the hardship and blame for unwanted pregnancies, ignoring the fact that men bear responsibility too, and that many unwanted pregnancies result from unwanted intercourse. For many women, and especially for the young, an unwanted pregnancy can alter irrevocably the course of their lives, closing off options, forcing them into marriages they do not want, or making them raise a child without social and material support. No woman wants an abortion if she can help it, but sometimes it is the only way out.

Legal abortion performed within the first three months of pregnancy is relatively safe, with a lower death rate than from the use of oral contraceptives or even from a simple tonsillectomy.[42] Nevertheless, it is not entirely risk-free, and possible complications, especially infection, are likely to be higher where antiseptic conditions are not maintained.

The vacuum aspiration method in particular has a good safety record and appears to have no adverse effect on fertility, for the first or even second such abortion. To avoid the word "abortion," vacuum aspiration is euphemistically termed menstrual regulation (MR) when its use is limited to the first few weeks after a missed period and smaller instruments are used. MR has become very popular in a number of Third World countries, where, strictly speaking, abortion is illegal.[43] Although it is the safest of all methods, MR is not mentioned in most medical textbooks in the United States and is unavailable in most hospitals.

The controversy surrounding abortion is a relatively recent phenomenon. In most societies, abortion has been used for centuries as a common fertility control method, tolerated implicitly, if not explicitly, by social custom and law. Traditional European, British, and U.S. common law, for example, allowed abortion before "quickening," the noticeable movement of the fetus, which usually occurs during the fifth month of pregnancy. Even the Catholic Church was relatively tolerant of early abortion—not until 1869 did Pope Pius IX declare all abortion to be murder.[44]

Historically, society's view of abortion has reflected changing perceptions of the medical profession and the role of women. In the United States, for example, as medical practice became more institutionalized in the late nineteenth century, doctors sought to secure a monopoly over the practice of medicine and medical technology through an attack on irregular practitioners, such as midwives and women healers, who provided abortion services. At the same time Victorian morality was gaining ground: Middle-class women were relegated back to the home, where their main mission in life was to produce children. Abortion became criminalized, separated from its original context of birth control.[45]

Today, as a conservative backlash sweeps many countries, women are once again being told that their place is at home with their families, though "home" is hardly the safe refuge it is made out to be. Denying women access to abortion is part of that process;

even where abortion is legal, women are made to feel it is a crime. There are many people, of course, who have sincere moral and religious objections to abortion, but it is important to point out that not all of them are Right to Lifers. Many feel that, although they would not choose abortion personally, it must be up to each individual woman to make that choice.[46]

On the international stage, the U.S. government led the attack against abortion in the 1980s, despite its legality in the United States. Under the Reagan and Bush administrations, all foreign nongovernmental organizations that received funds originating from AID had to sign an infamous clause certifying that they would not perform or actively promote abortion as a family planning method. This extended to counseling and referral services as well. A "gag rule" within the U.S. also prevented publicly funded family planning clinics from even counseling women about abortion. The Reagan and Bush administrations' attack on abortion resembled the German book burning of the 1930s and reflected a deep political cynicism. In order to win the domestic antiabortion vote, the White House and conservative Congressmen were willing to deny Third World women access to desperately needed safe abortion facilities.

While President Clinton takes a more liberal stand on abortion, AID's current policy on abortion funding overseas is still very restrictive. The Helms Amendment to the Foreign Assistance Act stipulates that AID funds cannot be used for the "performance of abortion as a method of family planning." The Clinton administration has interpreted this to mean that AID can fund abortion only in cases of rape, incest and life endangerment, and for the treatment of complications caused by unsafe, incomplete or septic abortions. According to the Center for Reproductive Law and Policy, "the policy remains surprisingly close to the positions of the Reagan and Bush administrations."[47]

In many countries, illegal abortion is a leading cause of death for women in their childbearing years. Could it not be said that denying women the right to safe abortion is itself a form of murder?

Abortion and Fertility Control. Despite the development of social sanctions against abortion, it continues to play a major role in fertility control the world over. Abortion has been an important factor in the initial stages of most demographic transitions, in countries as diverse as the United States, the former Soviet Union, and Korea. In fact, according to one text on abortion, "No human community has ever shown a marked fall in its birth rate without a significant recourse to induced abortion."[48]

In many places its incidence declines over time as other contraceptive practices become more widely available, though it remains an important recourse in the event of contraceptive failure or lack of access to alternatives. In some areas, notably Japan, the former Soviet Union, and Western Europe, it continues to be a chief means of fertility control. Even in Sweden where contraception is freely available and sex education is widespread, up to a quarter of all pregnancies end in abortion.[49] Keen to distance themselves from the abortion controversy, many population agencies claim that their promotion of contraception will help prevent abortions from taking place. While there is some truth to this, abortion will be needed for a long time to come. The courageous path is to defend it as a basic right and a method of family planning.

Today 20 percent of the world's population live in forty-nine countries where abortion is prohibited except in some cases to save the woman's life. Forty percent live in twenty-three countries where abortion is legal without mandated conditions. In between are countries where women are allowed abortions for certain social and medical reasons.[50] Although the trend has been toward greater liberalization, this is not the case in a number of countries in Eastern Europe, where women are fighting to retain the right to abortion that they had during Communist rule.

Whether or not abortion is legal has remarkably little to do with its incidence, however. From 25 to 45 percent of the annual 40 to 50 million abortions worldwide are estimated to be illegal,[51] and many of these are in conservative Catholic countries. Women have traditionally sought abortion when they need it, regardless of the law. The crucial difference legality can make is in *safety*.

In some places, such as South Korea and Hong Kong, high illegal abortion rates appear to have resulted in very few casualties, but in general legalization of abortion leads to significant reductions in mortality. In the United States, for example, prior to legalization in 1973, an average of 292 women died per year from induced abortion. In 1973 the figure fell to 36.[52]

Legalization does not automatically guarantee access to safe abortion for all sectors of the population, however, because of geographical, political, and financial constraints. In many Third World countries as well as in the West, abortion facilities are few and far between. Many hospitals and physicians refuse to provide abortion services, and even if they are available, poor people often cannot afford them. In the United States, abortion, which costs on average $250, was put beyond the reach of many women with the passage of the Hyde Amendment to health appropriation legislation prohibiting federal Medicaid funding of abortion. Just one month after the amendment went into effect in 1977, a young Mexican American woman, Rosie Jimenez, died with her Medicaid card in her purse from a cheap illegal abortion performed in Mexico.[53]

The conservative assault on abortion rights in the United States has made it even more inaccessible in recent years. Today one in five U.S. women seeking an abortion cannot obtain one. Lack of government funding is only one obstacle. Others include decreases in available services and providers, attacks on clinics and providers, and restrictive legislation such as parental consent laws and 24-hour waiting periods.[54]

Legalization is thus only the first step in making safe abortion a real option; spreading low-cost services is the other.

Although most women who have abortions choose to do so voluntarily, like other contraceptives, abortion can be used as an instrument of population control. The most dramatic case is China, but there are many others as well. In England and the United States, poor women seeking abortions have sometimes been sterilized at the same time, without their full informed consent. "Unless we get those tubes tied before they go home," said one U.S. doctor, "some of them will change their minds by the time they come back to the clinic."[55] Rates of sterilization regret and physical complications are typically higher in post-abortion sterilization.

In some Third World countries, IUDs are inserted in women appearing in hospitals because of complications from illegal abortion. Although at such times contraceptive counseling would no doubt be useful, inserting an IUD, with its high risk of uterine infection, is a very questionable procedure, to say the least. In India it is a relatively common practice to deny women abortions in clinics unless they first agree to the IUD or sterilization.[56]

In Indonesia the Indonesian Planned Parenthood Association (IPPA), the IPPF-affiliate, insists that women agree to either Norplant (if they have fewer than two children) or vasectomy for their husband (if they have two or more children) as a condition of abortion. The IUD, the pill, and condoms are considered too ineffective in terms of the overall objective of reducing birth rates.[57]

In Bangladesh, however, Menstrual Regulation is one of the few positive developments in the country's family planning program. Although abortion is still illegal in Bangladesh, MR is allowed, and has proved very popular with women. According to one estimate, an estimated quarter of a million MR procedures take place each year. Given very high rates of maternal mortality from illegal abortion in Bangladesh, MR has undoubtedly saved many women's lives.[58] The challenge remains to ensure that MR is not used coercively, i.e., making its availability contingent on sterilization or IUD use, and ensuring that family planning workers get adequate training in the technique.

RU486 WILL NOT SOLVE THE ABORTION PROBLEM

After years of controversy and opposition from the antiabortion movement, RU486, often called the "abortion pill," is now entering the United States. Roussel Uclaf, the drug's French manufacturer, is giving the pill's patent and technology free of charge to the Population Council for U.S. research, and it is expected to be in use in the U.S. by 1996.[1]

Invented by Professor Etienne-Emile Baulieu, RU486 is a steroidal derivative that inhibits the action of progesterone, one of the hormones necessary for sustaining pregnancy. In conjunction with a prostaglandin, RU486 can be used as an abortifacient up to nine weeks after a woman's last menstrual period. To date it has been used by approximately 150,000 women, mainly in France and the United Kingdom.

When RU486 first appeared on the scene in Europe, it was heralded by some U.S. family planning advocates as the solution to the abortion problem, since women would no longer need to attend abortion clinics, focal points for antiabortion demonstrations, but could have an abortion at home. Groups such as the Feminist Majority Foundation have also uncritically pushed for its introduction into poor countries. "RU486 is a safe and inexpensive alternative for women in poor nations who lack fertility control options," states the Foundation. "Minimal time from skilled practitioners is needed to administer RU486. Its use would free up scarce and valuable medical personnel to attend to other work."[2]

RU486 is hardly a such a magic bullet or technical fix, however. While its advantages include a 96 percent success rate, more privacy and accessibility, and the fact that it is a non-invasive procedure, surgically speaking, it also has a number of disadvantages compared with surgical abortion. It must be used early in pregnancy, requires three to four trips to a trained provider, and causes cramps and bleeding similar to that of a heavy menstrual period for seven to ten days, as well as prostaglandin-related vomiting, diarrhea, and abdominal cramps. Prostaglandins also can have serious cardiovascular side effects, so that RU486 is no longer recommended for women older than thirty-five or women who smoke or have heart problems or asthma. Hemorrhages requiring transfusions occur much more frequently with RU486 than with surgical abortion, and when the drug fails in 4 to 5 percent of cases, the woman needs a surgical abortion. The drug's impact on the fetus is not known; there are also concerns about its long-term impact on women's health.[3]

Within the international women's movement, there is considerable debate over the pros and cons of RU486 and the wisdom of its rapid introduction into developing countries. What emerges very clearly, however, is that RU486 will not reduce the need for trained surgical abortion providers—not only may many women prefer a surgical abortion to the prolonged and often painful RU486 experience, but it is a critical back-up in the event of an incomplete RU486 abortion. Moreover, safe use of RU486 depends on the existence of adequate medical infrastructure for screening, treatment of side effects, and emergency resuscitation and transfusion equipment. It is neither a simple drug nor a simple solution.

Population "Quality" Control. Today the abortion issue has taken on a new dimension with the development of reproductive technologies—amniocentesis, ultrasound, chorionic villus sampling—that can identify the fetus' sex and certain genetic defects such as Downs Syndrome and spina bifida in the early stages of pregnancy.

Sex-selective abortion of girls is not only a serious problem in China, but in India too, especially in the north and west. Sex-selective abortion, mainly in private clinics, has reached what some observers term "epidemic proportions"—even poor villagers are saving up money for amniocentesis and ultrasound. Sex selection must be seen in the context of "son preference" and the widespread oppression of Indian women of all classes.

The women who decide to undergo it usually do so because they are under intense pressure themselves, threatened by the ongoing hostility of their in-laws or the prospect of divorce if they bear yet another daughter or fail to conceive a son. Rising dowry demands, largely as a result of growing consumerism, are a major factor—many families can simply not afford to pay for the marriage of their daughters if it means buying the prospective groom a refrigerator, motorcycle, or TV.[59]

Traditional son preference and female neglect, coupled with the spread of a smaller-family norm and sex-selection technology, are leading to a serious decline in the sex ratio. In 1991 there were an estimated 929 women for every 1,000 men in the Indian population, the lowest level in this century. The average obscures differences between states—the north tends to have worse ratios than the south, but in only one state, Kerala, does the number of women exceed that of men.[60]

Direct female infanticide is also a serious problem in some locations. A study of Salem District in Tamil Nadu state found a high incidence of infanticide related to the growth of consumerism, high dowry demands, and the internalization of the small family norm as the road to prosperity. According to the authors, "When the strong preference for sons and negativism about daughters impinges on the strongly internalized small-family norm, the daughters are eliminated! ...The internalization of the small family norm...is itself one of the sources of female infanticide."[61] These findings raise serious questions about the wisdom of Information, Education and Communication (IEC) programs promoting the two-child family as the happy, prosperous family in a context of deep-rooted male bias and rampant materialism.

There is also a very real danger that in countries like India sex selection could become an established method of population control. In a 1984 seminar in Bombay one family planning official stated that "desperate measures" were needed to address India's "explosive" population problem, and condoned sex-selective abortion. In 1994, a *New York Times* reporter blamed India's poverty on population growth and stated that "by pressing for the elimination of sex-determination tests, women's groups are calling for curbs on a practice that has been one of few factors holding down a population increase."[62]

Although instances of sex selection are not unknown in Western countries, amniocentesis and other new reproductive technologies are more typically used to identify genetic defects, with the expectation that women will abort any defective fetuses. These technologies pose very difficult ethical dilemmas.

As women with disabilities have pointed out, the decision to abort a disabled child is influenced by a number of factors besides purely personal ones. In a society like the United States, for example, where the media sells an image of health that only the affluent young can hope to fulfill, fears about raising a disabled child may be way out of proportion to the facts, or far greater than they would be in a more compassionate environment. As one disabled woman describes:

> There is tremendous pressure upon us to have "perfect" babies. Do we want a world of "perfect people?" I really wonder what are the human costs of attempts to control our differences, our vulnerability. I believe that if women are to maintain our "choice" we must include *the choice to have a disabled child.*[63]

The new reproductive technologies and medical advances in prenatal and neonatal care are bringing the issue of eugenics back into the population arena.

In the last analysis, today's controversy over abortion is misplaced. Whether or not abortion should occur is really not the issue. It will occur, no matter how many bombs are thrown at abortion clinics, how many times the Pope condemns it, or how widely other forms of contraception are distributed. Unwanted pregnancies may decline, but they will not vanish altogether.

Instead, the vital issues regarding abortion are these:

- whether it is legal, safe, and accessible, or illegal, dangerous, and out of reach geographically or financially.
- whether it is abused as an instrument of population quantity or quality control, or used as a tool of reproductive choice.

Properly performed, abortion is a woman's safety net and one of the most important reproductive rights of all.

14

BARRIER METHODS, NATURAL FAMILY PLANNING, AND FUTURE DIRECTIONS

The contraceptive revolution of the 1960s and 1970s brought the pill, the IUD, the injectable, and the implant, all extremely effective forms of reversible contraception if used correctly. Yet despite the millions of dollars poured into research, that revolution did not bring many improvements in contraceptive safety. On the contrary, the health risks of these methods are considerable and are compounded by their misuse in population programs. They also do not guard against sexually transmitted diseases such as HIV/AIDS.

Today there is a need for a second contraceptive revolution. "Without giving up the high effectiveness, convenience, and relatively low cost of today's contraceptives," write Judith Bruce and S. Bruce Schearer, "tomorrow's contraceptives must be safe in both the short- and long-term; fully reversible and free of effects on future fertility...on breast-feeding infants and on lactation."[1]

The irony is that such methods *already* exist, in the form of barrier contraceptives–spermicides, condoms, diaphragms, cervical caps–though there is great need and scope for their improvement. Yet with the exception of the condom, these safe, simple, reversible contraceptives are unavailable in many, if not most, Third World family planning programs, and in Western countries people are also often discouraged from using them. Less than 2 percent of contraceptive users worldwide use female barrier methods, and only 6 percent use condoms.[2]

Within the population community, the prejudice against barrier contraceptives runs deep. "The diaphragm was useful in the Western world when services had to be based in clinics and before IUDs or pills were invented," wrote Dr. Malcolm Potts, one of the most prominent researchers in the field, in 1976. "It is a Model-T Ford, still running in a few places, but insignificant at a world level."[3]

Are barrier methods really so anachronistic and insignificant—or could they be the foundation of a second contraceptive revolution, in which health and safety come first?

BARRIER METHODS REVISITED

> The needs of millions of men and women throughout the world are being neglected because of a one-sided concentration on high technology birth control methods.
>
> —JUDITH BRUCE *and* S. BRUCE SCHEARER, *1984*[4]

Unlike antique cars, barrier methods are still a very useful technology. During the first half of the twentieth century, the diaphragm and condom were the most common forms of contraception in the United States. Although their use declined with the development of the pill and IUD, barrier methods are gaining favor again as more people grow wary of the side effects of modern methods and want to protect themselves against sexually transmitted diseases (STDs), especially AIDS. Condom use is especially high in Scandinavian countries, and is highest of all in Japan, where nearly 70 percent of all contraceptive users rely on condoms.[5] Barrier use, however, remains considerably lower in developing countries than in developed ones.

What are the advantages of barrier methods? Unlike hormonal contraceptives and the IUD, they cause no known major side effects. When used with the backup of legal abortion, *they are the safest by far of all reversible contraceptives in terms of mortality risks.*[6] They do not cause any delay in or risk to fertility after cessation of use and, in addition, help to protect users from a number of sexually transmitted diseases, which are a primary cause of infertility and morbidity in many parts of the world. Barrier methods also reduce the risk of acquiring cervical cancer—a major killer of women, while hormonal methods may increase it. (See Box: Barriers to AIDS.)

BARRIERS TO AIDS

Barrier methods have a vital role to play in the fight against AIDS. Although condoms are the main defense against sexual transmission, not only do they sometimes fail, but men often fail to use them. This has grave implications for women, who face a higher risk of acquiring HIV though heterosexual sex than do men. By the year 2000 as many or more women will be infected with HIV than men, and according to the World Health Organization (WHO), the primary mode of transmission is now heterosexual sex.

For many women getting men to wear condoms is difficult, if not impossible. Within relationships women can suffer harassment, abandonment, or physical violence if they insist on condom use, and forced sex is all too common. Women-controlled methods are thus an essential option, though questions remain regarding their efficacy.

For example, recent research is contradictory as to whether nonoxynol 9, a common ingredient of spermicides, reduces the risk of acquiring HIV. A study of sex workers in the Cameroon found that consistent use of nonoxynol 9 vaginal suppositories reduced their risk by 90 percent compared to women who used the suppositories infrequently; on the other hand, a study of sex workers in Kenya found that daily use of contraceptive sponges that contained nonoxynol 9 may have increased their risk of HIV infection, probably because the frequent use of the chemical caused cervical and vaginal abrasions which speed HIV transmission. As a result, public health advocates are unsure what message to convey to women. The New York State Department of Health recommends condoms or abstinence as the best prevention against HIV, followed by the diaphragm used with a spermicide containing nonoxynol 9, with nonoxynol 9 alone the last resort.

Another possible line of defense against HIV would be the development of an intravaginal microbicide, which would kill the virus. It could take a number of forms: foam, suppository, or film, and could be used secretly if it had no taste or scent. There could also be a non-contraceptive version for women who wanted to get pregnant but protect themselves at the same time. Currently, a coalition of researchers and women's health activists are pushing for more funds to be allocated to developing microbicides.[1]

In general, women's needs have been neglected in AIDS research, detection, and treatment, or else women have been scapegoated, as in the case of prostitutes, who are far more likely to acquire HIV from their male partners than the other way around.[2] Population control programs can also stand in the way of HIV prevention. Not only do they push contraceptives which do not protect women from HIV and other STDs, but methods which involve the use of needles and trocars, such as Depo-Provera, Norplant, and the new "vaccines," could be an additional risk factor in settings where instruments are not adequately sterilized. And the persistent targeting of women means that men do not learn to act responsibly—by using condoms, for example.

Privately some contraceptive researchers admit they made a big mistake twenty to thirty years ago when they decided to neglect barrier methods and STD prevention in the quest for ever more effective and technologically sophisticated means to prevent births. We are now reaping the grim harvest of that neglect.

The WHO has endorsed barrier methods as particularly suitable for lactating mothers, since they do not affect either milk quality or quantity. They may also be especially appropriate for the increasing numbers of sexually active unmarried young people throughout the world, who are either unwilling or unable to get contraceptives through formal channels and who face a high risk of sexually transmitted disease.[7]

And the disadvantages? Minor side effects include allergic reactions to spermicides or latex. More serious ones are incidences of toxic shock syndrome in women who have left the diaphragm or contraceptive sponge in place for extended periods of time, and higher rates of urinary infections among diaphragm users. Earlier studies suggested that spermicides may cause a higher rate of miscarriage and birth defects among women who continue to use them after conception, but these have been discredited.[8]

The primary criticism leveled against barrier methods, especially from population control quarters, is their high failure rate. According to *Population Reports,* for example, female vaginal methods "are less effective than oral contraceptives, IUD's, and voluntary sterilization."[9]

Yet, in reality, the clinical data on the performance of barrier methods varies widely, ranging from a pregnancy rate of 2 per 100 users per year, comparable to the pill and IUD, to a high of 30. What accounts for such a difference?

Most studies show that long-time, experienced users of barrier methods have more success in preventing pregnancy. According to Bruce and Schearer, successful use also depends on "full information, competent instruction and follow-up support."[10] Because barrier methods must be used with each act of intercourse, their efficacy requires cooperation between partners.

When comparing how effective barrier methods are in relation to other reversible contraceptives, it is important to remember that in many Third World countries high pregnancy rates result from improper use of the pill. And in terms of continuation rates, the side effects of the pill, IUD, and injectables cause from 40 to 70 percent of users of these methods to abandon them within two years. In fact, fear of adverse effects prevents from one quarter to one third of married women of reproductive age from using any contraceptives at all![11] Even in population control terms, the modern "miracle" methods are not that effective, so why then are barrier methods the subject of so much scorn?

The prejudice against barrier methods has several roots. First, poor people, especially the illiterate, are alleged to be too embarrassed and ignorant about their bodies even to attempt to use them. Second, the methods are deemed "inconvenient," "awkward," and "intrusive." In many settings they may be difficult to wash, store, and dispose of. Third, their use requires that a couple be willing and able to cooperate with each other; a woman cannot use barrier methods surreptitiously, like Depo-Provera. Last, but not least, many population people argue that it takes too much time and resources to educate people about them and to provide adequate follow-up.

Do these arguments really add up to a decisive case against barrier methods? Many problems could be overcome if the methods were introduced with sensitive instruction and follow-up and a stress on joint male-female responsibility for contraception. Sanitation, storage, and disposal problems, though difficult, are not insurmountable. As for costly education and follow-up, shouldn't family planning programs devote resources to these crucial activities in the case of all contraceptives?

To the limited extent that barrier methods have been introduced in Third World family planning programs, it is not surprising that they have sometimes proved less effective than the so-called modern techniques. As Bruce and Schearer explain, biases against barrier methods tend to be self-fulfilling:

> The policymakers' prophecies of the incompetence of poor women are confirmed by the results that occur when barrier methods are introduced with little or no understanding of rural women's culture, and without thorough education and follow-up.[12]

More often than not, barrier methods are simply not made available or are promoted with far less enthusiasm than the pill, IUD, or sterilization. *Population Reports* notes that negative "providers' attitudes" are instrumental in restricting access to them, and that their popularity might well increase if their benefits were stressed.[13]

Indeed, there are a number of encouraging examples of the successful promotion and use of barrier methods in Third World settings. A Bombay clinic achieved an effectiveness rate of 90 percent for the diaphragm among women who maintained contact with the clinic, and success was not correlated with variations in income level, education, or availability of tap water.[14] In Brazil the Colectivo Feminista Sexualidade e Saude in Sao Paulo provides diaphragms to 40 percent of its 2,000 contraceptive clients with supportive sexuality education, training, and follow-up. Continuation rates are high, and accidental pregnancies appear to be few.[15]

In a number of countries, the vigorous promotion of condoms through both commercial channels and family planning programs has led to a significant increase in use.[16] Unlike the pill, condoms and spermicides are well-suited to mass distribution and social marketing schemes, since they do not require medical supervision.

Even if barrier methods were to prove only moderately effective or personally acceptable, they could be an important option for women who want to space births, who have access to safe abortion, or who are disillusioned with other contraceptives. At the very least, people should have the *choice*.

Donor agencies have played an important role in restricting that choice, particularly when it comes to female methods. For example, AID gave an average of only 25 *thousand* diaphragms per year between 1978 and 1982, as opposed to providing an average of 8.5 *million* women with oral contraceptives annually during the same period. AID's record is much better on the condom—it now provides over a half billion a year.[17]

The rationale given for this bias is that AID and other agencies are simply responding to requests from Third World family planning programs, and if there is not much demand for barrier methods, then why should they provide them?

As we have seen, however, contraceptive demand is heavily influenced by the donor agencies themselves. If barrier methods were promoted with the same determination as the pill, IUD, injectable, and sterilization to governments and family planners, the contraceptive experience of many people might be very different indeed.

The bias against barrier methods in family planning programs is matched by their relative neglect in contraceptive research. Two of the major research institutions, the Population Council and the WHO Human Reproduction Program, do virtually *no* research on barrier methods. Since 1987 the U.S. National Institute of Child Health and Human Development has devoted 10 percent of its contraceptive research budget to barrier methods, and AID's Contraceptive Research and Development Program almost 15 percent.[18] Systematic exclusion from research programs has led to stagnation in barrier technology: Many of its current drawbacks reflect what Bruce and Schearer call an "unnecessary obsolescence."[19]

Yet in the field of barrier technology, even minor improvements could make a major difference in terms of acceptability. Despite the low level of resources, new products have been developed and old products refined and improved. These include the contraceptive sponge, with research funded by AID and the National Institutes of Health; the cervical cap, whose introduction and testing in the U.S. were initiated by the feminist health community;[20] the female condom, only recently brought to market; improved male condoms, e.g., condoms made from polyurethane; and varieties of spermicide foams and tablets. Unfortunately, it is doubtful these products will reach developing countries in any sizeable quantity in the near future given the population community's current obsession with Norplant and other long-acting technologies.

Yet there are some grounds for hope. In the past ten years, public pressure, especially from the women's health community, consumer demand, and the threat of AIDS have helped to increase funding for barrier research from a few isolated drops to a slow trickle.[21] Although these are hopeful signs, much more positive action is needed now, if the tide is to be turned and barrier methods are to occupy the prominent place they deserve in contraceptive technology.

THE NATURAL WAY

Like barrier methods, natural family planning (NFP), or periodic abstinence, as it is also called, provides an important alternative to hormonal and surgical forms of birth control. Natural family planning involves a woman identifying the fertile and infertile periods in her monthly cycle by employing the following techniques: the calendar or "rhythm" method, which charts the time of ovulation according to the pattern of a normal menstrual cycle; the temperature method, which identifies ovulation by a rise in body temperature; the mucus or Billings method, which both predicts and identifies ovulation by changes in the consistency of cervical mucus; and the symptothermal method, which combines elements of the other three and which in several studies has proved the most effective.[22] Because all these methods help to pinpoint the fertile period, they can be used to increase the chances of getting pregnant as well as to prevent pregnancy.

An estimated 7 percent of contraceptive users worldwide employ some technique of natural family planning. In only six Third World countries—Haiti, Mauritius, Peru, the Philippines, South Korea, and Sri Lanka—are more than 5 percent of married women of reproductive age known to use the method. Ireland and Poland are the two industrialized countries with the highest use.

NFP has been promoted primarily by the Catholic Church, which sanctions the method as the only acceptable form of contraception, stressing the moral value of abstinence during the fertile period. The two main international organizations that teach and promote NFP are the International Federation for Family Life Promotion (IFFLP) and the World Organization of the Ovulation (Billings) Method (WOOMB). WOOMB only promotes the mucus method and is hostile to the others.[23]

NFP's success in preventing pregnancy largely depends on training, motivation, and cooperation between partners. Failure rates are quite high in some studies—up to 30 percent—whereas in others they are comparable to the more effective contraceptives. In one project in India where close follow-up was top priority, only three pregnancies were reported among 813 women in the first year.[24] Among the advantages of the method are that it is cheap, demands no regular source of supply, causes no side effects that require medical supervision, and encourages active participation by both partners.

If used without any contraceptive backup, NFP has the major drawback of requiring abstinence during the fertile period. Many of the pregnancies that do occur result from couples deciding not to abstain, or husbands forcing their wives to have intercourse. Audrey Bronstein describes some of the "sexual politics" which emerged in an NFP training course she attended in El Salvador:

> A number of women said that abstinence didn't work, because the husbands often came home drunk and would beat them if they didn't agree to have sex. They also said that if the women tried to refuse too many times, the men would go off, and find other women. On the positive side, they felt that where there was a small understanding between the couple, practicing abstinence increases the man's respect for his wife, and will help create a "dialogue" between the two.[25]

In Kenya a missionary teaching the method reported, "Women show up by the hundreds, but the men do not want to make the effort to keep the rules, even if they see the need to limit their families."[26] To some extent, the problem of abstinence can be overcome by the use of barrier methods on fertile days (especially the condom, which does not interfere as much with mucus symptoms).

However, many NFP promoters are against these "artificial" methods for religious reasons, just as they are against abortion in the event of method failure.

Like barrier methods, NFP has been neglected by population agencies, though NFP organizations have received small amounts of funding from AID, UNFPA, WHO, and the British, Canadian, and German governments. Under Reagan, AID increased its support of NFP, mainly under pressure from antiabortion forces in the United States. In FY 1985 AID devoted over $7 million to NFP activities, as opposed to only $400,000 in 1980.[27]

Population agencies typically base their case against NFP on three main grounds: effectiveness, the need for careful counseling, and cost. "Where competition for scarce government family planning dollars and an urgent need to promote fertility control require strict attention to cost- and time-effectiveness," wrote the Population Crisis Committee, "experts usually assign NFP a lower priority than other, more effective methods."[28]

As we have seen, however, the more "effective" contraceptives also have high failure and low continuation rates when introduced improperly. NFP's success does depend on careful counseling, but so do the effectiveness and ethical use of almost all contraceptives. According to the WHO, the once-a-month follow-up required by NFP "is greater than could be provided in national family planning programs," and the cost often prohibitive.[29] Yet otherwise natural family planning is *free* aside from the cost of a thermometer or charts.

Surely, when everything is added up, teaching one woman NFP is not more costly than providing that person with many cycles of pills, the IUD, or sterilization and treating their side effects. One wonders if the issue is not really costs but *profit,* for NFP is the one contraceptive method where no profits accrue to either the pharmaceutical industry or the medical profession.

NFP research also suffers from lack of funds. From 1980 to 1983 it received only 0.6 percent of expenditures for contraceptive research and development, for example.[30] However, research is underway on more accurate ways of determining ovulation, through better thermometers, tests on urine, mucus, and saliva, and even a way to monitor temperature changes in the hands.[31] The development of a foolproof, convenient way to identify the fertile period would greatly enhance both the acceptability and reliability of natural family planning.

The attitude of the population establishment is not the only obstacle to more widespread promotion of natural family planning. Since many of NFP's advocates oppose other forms of birth control, they are against NFP's inclusion in comprehensive family planning programs. Affiliates of WOOMB, for example, issued this declaration:

> A fundamental concept of the philosophy of WOOMB is the acceptance of periodic abstinence and the rejection of artificial contraception, abortion and sterilization, each member [of WOOMB] undertaking not to counsel for or dispense such methods of birth control.32

This approach to NFP not only limits its availability, but ultimately restricts women's choice. Many women, for example, might be willing to use natural family planning with the backup of barrier methods and/or abortion, but in their absence are worried about high failure rates. Others may choose NFP only at certain times during their reproductive years, when they are more concerned with spacing births and are willing to accept an earlier than expected pregnancy. At other times they may well want access to other contraceptives.

Fortunately today, in addition to support from more traditional advocates of natural family planning, support is also building among women disillusioned with the side effects of other contraceptives and interested in a more holistic approach to birth control, in which a woman's knowledge of her own body and male cooperation are key. Such advocacy could help change the tenor of natural family planning, so that it is both more acceptable and accessible in the future.

ON THE HORIZON: DARK CLOUDS AND GLIMMERS OF LIGHT

> Years ago, when I was myself working in endocrinological research, vaccination ideas like this were raised and promptly dismissed as unethical and dangerous; I do not think the balance of argument has changed, except that the threat has come closer, and people are now actually being exposed.
>
> —GRAHAM DUKES, *World Bank advisor on pharmaceuticals, commenting on current contraceptive "vaccine" research*[33]

Although public pressure and the AIDS epidemic have led to some shift in direction, the biased pattern of contraceptive research, development, and promotion we have witnessed in recent decades is likely to continue, especially given the resurgent population crisis mentality of the 1990s. One of the most worrying areas of research is on "fertility regulating vaccines," as they are commonly called in the literature. Feminist researcher Judith Richter prefers to use the term "immunological contraceptives" to distinguish them from vaccines against diseases.[34]

As health activists point out, "Vaccination against disease works by stimulating a person's body to defend itself against a specific type of germ.... Pregnancy, however, is not a disease but a natural body process. Immunological contraceptives cause the immune system to attack a body function which would otherwise be protected."[35]

Immunological contraceptives differ according to whether they are targeting reproductive hormones, eggs, sperm, or early embryos. The most advanced methods are directed at the pregnancy hormone human chorionic gonadotrophin (hCG) and are designed to be effective for one to two years. Part of the hormone hCG is combined with a foreign substance, typically part of a tetanus or diphtheria toxoid, and injected into a woman. When her immune system defends itself against the toxoid, it also attacks hCG produced by her own body, thus preventing pregnancy from taking place.

Immunological contraceptives currently account for an estimated 10 percent of worldwide public spending on contraceptive research—in 1992, the WHO's Human Reproduction Program spent almost one million dollars, or 16 percent of its annual contraceptive research budget, on them. Other agencies conducting research are the Population Council, the U.S. National Institute of Child Health, Contraceptive Research and Development Program (CONRAD), and the National Institute of Immunology in India.

Population control is a key motivation behind immunological contraceptive research. In 1982 Rodney Shearman, a contraceptive researcher, wrote that immunological contraceptives would be an "antigenic weapon" against "the reproductive process, a process which left unchecked threatens to swamp the world." Similarly,

Vernon Stevens, one of the most prominent scientists working in the field, described them as "a new method for more effectively meeting the challenge of ever-increasing global population expansion."[36]

Immunological contraceptives pose a number of problems and serious health risks which make it questionable whether they should be developed at all. In the case of hCG methods, these include:

1. *Temporary irreversibility.* So far there is no way to halt the immune reaction if a woman experiences side effects, is pregnant when she receives the vaccine, or becomes so while the reaction is still occurring.

2. *Unpredictable effectiveness.* It typically takes over five weeks for a woman to develop an effective immune response after taking the vaccine, and this "lag time" differs considerably for different women. In the meantime another contraceptive method must be used. There is also no one standard time when the immune response declines to the point where a woman can get pregnant. Blood must be drawn to determine the beginning and cessation of the immune response. As women health activists have pointed out, the vaccine is actually much less reliable than other contraceptive methods.

3. *Risk of birth defects.* The impact of the vaccine on the developing fetus is not known. This is a critical gap in knowledge, given the high risk of accidental pregnancy associated with the vaccine.

4. *Allergic reactions.* Reactions, sometimes severe, can occur to the diphtheria and tetanus toxoids used in vaccine formulations. This necessitates the availability of advance screening and emergency medical treatments.

5. *Risk of permanent sterility and auto-immune disorders.* No one knows whether or not long-term use of the vaccine could lead to permanent sterility. Equally troubling is the vaccine's potential for causing or worsening auto-immune disorders, in which the immune system reacts against body organs or cells. Such disorders, which include rheumatoid arthritis, lupus, and diabetes, are already more common in women than in men.

6. *Cross-reactivity.* The vaccine formulations used by the Population Council and Indian researchers cross-react with another im-

portant reproductive hormone, hLH (human luteinizing hormone), produced continually by the pituitary gland. Possible risks include menstrual disorders and inhibition of ovulation, as well as auto-immune disorders. The WHO itself is concerned about the long-term impact of these formulations, and uses a different one which does not cross-react with hLH.[37]

7. *Interaction with AIDS.* Vaccines offer no protection against HIV and other sexually transmitted diseases. They are likely to be less effective in people with damaged immune systems as the result of HIV infection and could possibly aggravate HIV-related illnesses by putting an additional demand on the immune system.

8. *Potential for abuse.* As Judith Richter and Faye Schrater have pointed out, immunological contraceptives could easily be used coercively. Moreover, offering them as "vaccines" gives a false sense of safety. If people have negative experiences with them, it could give all vaccines a bad name, a potential public health disaster.

Already, documented violations of medical ethics have occurred in clinical trials in India, where misinformation and inadequate informed consent procedures have even been captured on film. German film-makers Ulrike Schaz and Ingrid Schneider show an Indian woman enrolling in a vaccine trial being told:

> We have got a new injection...the effect of the injection stops children for one year... You need not be afraid of this. The injection has no side effects. You see, this injection is absolutely 100 percent effective...we'll also put in a copper-T [for use during the lag period]. Continuous copper-T is not very good. If you have it 3 years, 6 years, then there is the risk of cancer. That's why we want you to change.[38]

Women were asked to sign the consent forms in English, even though few understood the language.

As a result of these concerns, in 1993 a coalition of community groups, women's organizations, and health activists issued an open letter to researchers, funders, and the press calling for a halt to immunological contraceptive development and redirection of funds towards safer methods which people can control themselves.[39] The research nevertheless continues, with Phase II trials of the WHO hCG vaccine now underway in Sweden.

Meanwhile research on males continues to lag behind, though it is now receiving more attention than in the past. Not surprisingly, concern about safety and side effects appears to be higher in male contraceptive research than in female. "We want to go very slowly," said one researcher at the University of California. The female pill "was applied very rapidly, and later we found a series of very serious complications."[40] The WHO also found greater reluctance among men than women to volunteer for clinical trials.[41]

Hopes that a pill for males (made of Gossypol, a derivative of cottonseed oil) was just around the corner were dashed when clinical trials in China revealed a number of serious side effects, including temporary paralysis and heart ailments caused by a severe drop in blood potassium levels, and a high rate of permanent sterility. The WHO withdrew all funding of Gossypol research in China, but the Chinese government is pressing on.[42]

Other avenues of male contraceptive research include testosterone injections, combined androgen-progestogen injections (some of which contain the same hormone used in Depo-Provera), male immunological contraceptives, simpler forms of vasectomy, reversible plugs which block the passage of sperm in the vas deferens, and simpler heat-based methods, such as application of hot water and insulated underwear, since heat has long been known to depress sperm production.[43]

In the "better late than never" category, support is building for promoting breast-feeding as a fertility control measure in family planning programs.[44] And it is important to mention here that despite the population establishment's bias against traditional methods, withdrawal continues to be a major form of fertility control, utilized by 8 percent of contraceptive users worldwide.[45] Unfortunately in 1988 the WHO stopped its research on indigenous plants and herbs used for contraception—this remains a seriously underfunded (practically nonexistent) branch of contraceptive research.

COOPERATION OR COOPTATION?

In recent years women's health advocates have been invited to engage in dialogues with contraceptive researchers to share concerns and ultimately to create a "common ground," a "collaboration between the users of technology and the creators of it."[46] The

WHO's Human Reproduction Program and the New York-based International Women's Health Coalition are among the chief initiators of this strategy.

On the positive side, these dialogues attest to the growing power of the international women's health movement and the willingness of some scientists to incorporate feminist approaches in their work. For example, the 1993 Declaration of the International Symposium on Contraceptive Research and Development for the Year 2000 and Beyond contains a number of recommendations addressing women's concerns, such as including women's health advocates in all decision-making and advisory bodies that guide contraceptive research and placing emphasis on methods which are user-controlled and protect against STDs.[47]

On the negative side, dialogues have sometimes muted dissent and served to legitimize the contraceptive research agenda without altering it in any significant way. Words are cheap; action is not.

For example, in 1989 the WHO invited a handful of critics to a symposium on contraceptive vaccines attended mainly by scientists who had a direct interest in the research. Although the critics—women's health advocates and social scientists among them—voiced serious concerns about the vaccine's health risks and the potential for abuse, their comments were sanitized in the final report. According to the WHO, the outcome of the meeting was a grand hurrah for further vaccine research.[48]

Another WHO-sponsored meeting in 1992 invited many more women health advocates to dialogue with vaccine researchers. In the final document, their critical comments are reported more comprehensively, including their concern "that their names and presence would be used to legitimize both the content and the process of research in an area about which many were doubtful."[49] Their doubts—and in some cases outright opposition—have led to no major changes in the research agenda, however.

There have also been attempts to involve women's health advocates in the introduction and monitoring of Norplant. Referring to a series of such meetings in India, an activist writes that although they were ostensibly designed to open up a dialogue, their main purpose was to "to divine [women's] arguments, appropriate their language and finally exhaust them."[50]

As a result of these experiences, many women's health advocates are arguing for a more strategic approach to involvement with the research establishment. They acknowledge that meetings can offer opportunities for gaining access to important information and in some cases for pushing policy reform, but recognize the fundamental power imbalance between the agencies who control the funds and the activists whose voices are heard only at the agencies' discretion. Precautionary measures, such as reserving the right to make dissenting comments which will be published, unedited, in official reports, are one way to address this imbalance.

The situation becomes even trickier when women's groups are asked to monitor contraceptive trials. Not only could their involvement serve to legitimize the introduction of a drug like Norplant, but it also could take time and energy away from other pressing work. On the other hand, access to the trials means access to the women subjects and to vital information. Do you or do you not agree to participate? There are no easy solutions to these dilemmas, and they are only likely to get more problematic as the new population "consensus" seeks to dull the edge of the women's movement by drawing activists into the fold.

And if you're not in, you're out. A marginalization process is already occurring in which a sharp line is drawn between those women who are willing to cooperate with the establishment and those who, for whatever reason, are not. Women who are opposed to a particular technology—Norplant or the vaccine, for example—are often branded as extremists who oppose all technologies, when in reality they do not. This false dichotomy makes it more difficult to maneuver, to choose strategically when and how to cooperate, since once a woman is branded as an extremist, most doors are shut. To be acceptable to the establishment one must buy the line that more funding for contraceptive research is a high priority. But shouldn't the house be put in order first before it is expanded? Population control, prestige, and profit still largely guide contraceptive research, determining the nature of the technologies produced. Although men and women could use more contraceptive choices, one must be vigilant about who is doing the choosing.

Priorities also need to be questioned. Why is there more interest in contraceptive research than in reducing maternal mortality?

The Swedish International Development Authority (SIDA) recently took the courageous step of redirecting 30 percent of its funds for contraceptive research to a large maternal mortality study.[51] This is a small but important challenge to the status quo.

In the end, increasing access to safe, voluntary contraception is more a social problem than a technical one. It may be a long time—or forever—before the "perfect" contraceptive is produced. Meanwhile, greater equality between men and women, emphasis on health, safety, and the prevention of sexually transmitted diseases, rather than demographic effectiveness, and safe, accessible abortion services would go a long way toward improving women's experiences of birth control. If there is to be a second contraceptive revolution, let it start with a revolution in values.

Part Four

THE WAY

FORWARD

15

THE LIGHT AT THE
END OF THE
DEMOGRAPHIC
TUNNEL

In this last decade of the twentieth century, population growth rates are declining all over the world, yet in national and international policy circles the obsession with population persists. Despite both historical and statistical evidence to the contrary, researchers closely linked to the population establishment are now claiming that family planning programs are the most effective way to bring about a demographic transition from high to low birth rates. Development is no longer the best contraceptive, they argue, "contraceptives are the best contraceptive."[1] Their underlying agenda is clear: massive spending increases on population programs. The technical fix approach is back in vogue, if it ever went out of style.

In reality, the demographic transition is much more complex than such simple reasoning suggests. There is a much brighter light—powered by social justice—at the end of the demographic tunnel.

THE DEMOGRAPHIC TRANSITION

The value of children as a source of labor and security, son preference, high infant mortality, and the subordination of women all help to explain why people have large families. What motivates them to have fewer children?

Demographers have long searched for clues in the decline in birth rates in Europe over the last few centuries, which could be applied to population trends elsewhere in the world. The European demographic transition used to be thought of in fairly simple and straightforward terms: declining mortality rates as the result of the spread of modern medicine, public health measures, and better food supply led, after a lag, to falling birth rates, while economic development reduced the value of children; education and outside employment of women raised the marriage age; industrialization, urbanization, and the spread of communications challenged traditional cultural values, increasing the acceptance of fertility control.

Today, however, demographers have discovered that the wide variation between countries and regions defies simple formulas. Fertility fell more slowly in England than in France, for instance, despite England's faster industrialization and mortality decline. In Hungary and Poland small landowners—usually the most tradition-bound—began to limit their families in the nineteenth century in order that their children could inherit a viable piece of land.

Yet, while country-specific economic, social, and cultural circumstances have certainly determined the shape of fertility decline, by the beginning of the twentieth century the demographic transition was well underway throughout Europe and in North America as well.[2] The Soviet Union and Japan were to follow suit, experiencing even faster fertility declines over a span of forty-five and twenty-five years respectively. Whatever the smaller flourishes, the broad stroke of economic development dominates the picture of demographic transition in these societies. And this transition was achieved *without* any explicit government population control policies and often without modern contraception.

How relevant is this experience to the Third World today? This question is a subject of much debate. According to demographer John Caldwell, important differences in culture confound attempts to generalize from one to the other. In Europe, for example, well before the onset of the demographic transition, family and social structures made children far more of an economic burden than they are in the typical extended family in the Third World today.[3] For the World Bank, the experience of the now industrialized countries is largely irrelevant: High population growth rates in many Third World countries are "a phenomenon for which economic and demographic history offer no real precedent."[4]

Theories abound as to what key will unlock the door of demographic transition in the Third World. Caldwell maintains that mass education and the penetration of Western values will hasten fertility decline, even in the absence of widespread industrialization. Demographer Mead Cain believes that the issue of security is paramount, and that the provision of alternative forms of insurance and improvements in the "environment of risk" could help reduce people's need for children.[5]

Hard-line population control advocates argue that most Third World countries simply do not have the resources to attain the economic level at which the West passed through the demographic transition, and what resources they do have are being eaten away by population growth. Thus population control, not improvement in living standards, they reason, is the only hope for bringing the birth rate down.

But do Third World countries have to come up to the same income levels of the West to achieve a demographic transition? Birth rates in a number of places—China, Korea, Sri Lanka, Taiwan, and the Indian state of Kerala—started to drop when per capita incomes were still only several hundred dollars. What does the experience of these countries reveal?

Let's go back to the initial premise that economic development is the basic force behind the demographic transition. If one measures development simply in terms of GNP per capita, then one finds that countries with higher per capita incomes generally have lower birth rates, though there are important exceptions to this rule. A number of upper-middle-income countries have relatively high crude birth rates, notably South Africa (31), Gabon (42), Oman (41), Saudi Arabia (37) and Venezuela (29), while two of the world's poorest nations, China and Sri Lanka, have crude birth rates of 22 and 21 respectively.[6]

Is this simply a statistical anomaly, or is the problem with the concept of development? If one defines development differently, in terms of the number of people who actually benefit from economic growth, then one discovers that more equitable distribution of resources can lead to lower birth rates, even at relatively low levels of GNP per capita. Such is the case with China (well before the draconian one-child policy) and Sri Lanka.

First of all, this is a matter of income distribution. A raised standard of living across the population leads to better overall access to health, education, and jobs, all factors that allow people to choose smaller families. Many countries that have more equitable income distribution policies also consciously gear services toward the poor majority, emphasizing mass primary education, for example, rather than expensive higher education for a privileged few. Similarly, countries such as Sri Lanka, China, and Cuba, which have developed extensive public health systems, have managed to bring down infant mortality rates at relatively low levels of GNP per capita, while much richer countries, for example the former apartheid South Africa, have failed.

Also of critical importance is how equitably resources are distributed between men and women. One of the reasons many relatively rich Middle Eastern countries have such high birth rates may be the restrictions imposed on women's participation outside the home, whereas in Asian countries such as Sri Lanka and Thailand, women's education and employment not only give them greater control over financial resources but over their own reproduction.

The recognition of these factors has led to a recasting of traditional demographic transition theory, in which social and economic justice plays a major role.

RETHINKING THE TRANSITION

Traditional demographic theory identifies three basic stages in fertility decline:

High Mortality and High Fertility. In preindustrial societies, high death rates, caused by the absence of medical care and poor nutrition, offset high birth rates so that a basic population equilibrium is maintained.

The Lag: Low Mortality and High Fertility. As societies start to develop, modern technology reduces deaths. At the same time birth rates remain high because of the persistence of traditional attitudes toward childbearing and the lag time between the fall in mortality and people's actual recognition that their children stand a better chance of surviving. The result is rapid population growth. Many Third World countries are stuck in this stage.

Low Mortality and Low Fertility. Equilibrium is restored when a stage in industrial development is reached in which people choose to have small families because of new values, opportunities for women, and the increasing cost of raising children.

In his "Social Justice Theory of Demographic Transition," Dr. John Ratcliffe challenges this traditional view and recasts the three stages of fertility decline:

High Mortality and High Fertility. This is not a natural state of affairs but instead "the demographic pattern typical of highly stratified societies within which social resources are distributed very unequally,"[7] including the vast majority of societies under colonial rule. In these societies, social institutions such as health and education facilities only serve a small ruling elite. Consequently the vast majority of the population suffer from high death rates. The unit for survival is the family and high fertility is a necessity in the subsistence economy.

Falling Mortality and High Fertility. This pattern applies to many Third World countries today. It does not result, as traditional demographic theory maintains, from the introduction of modern medical techniques, but instead from the extension of the formal governing system to more—but not all—members of society. This usually occurs with national independence from colonial role. The new nationalist ruling groups come to power promising basic social reforms, but in the end adopt many of the old colonial policies, such as concentrating resources on higher education for the elite rather than mass primary education and emphasizing Western curative medicine for urban areas rather than primary health care for the rural poor.

However, progress is made in terms of building modern communications infrastructure, increasing agricultural production, and providing basic public health measures such as immunization. Since government services reach more people than during colonial times, mortality rates tend to fall, especially in urban enclaves and among the advantaged classes. Those who work in the formal sector also tend to have fewer children.

For the vast majority of the population living in the rural areas, however, life conditions do not change dramatically. Death rates come down somewhat, but fertility levels remain high because the family is still the basic unit of survival. The lag between low mortality and high fertility is thus really a social gap between the haves and have-nots.

Low Mortality and Low Fertility. This occurs when governments implement wide-ranging social reforms, including land and income redistribution, educational reforms, the provision of primary health care, and improvements in women's status. People no longer have to rely on the family as the unit of survival because the government and other institutions provide security and employment.

What are the implications of this view of the demographic transition? Clearly, it is not population control programs that reduce population growth, but the transformation of the social and economic institutions that perpetuate poverty and make people dependent on children for survival. The following examples of Cuba, South Korea, Sri Lanka, and Kerala illustrate concretely how this social-justice demographic transition takes place.

CUBA: THE UNSUNG SUCCESS STORY

Most population control literature is strangely silent about Cuba, the country which experienced perhaps the greatest decline in birth rate in the shortest amount of time, and once again at relatively low levels of per capita income. Between 1965 and 1980, Cuba's birth rate fell by nearly half. Shortly after the 1959 revolution, its crude birth rate was 35 births per 1,000 people; today it is only 17, only 2 points higher than the United States, though Cuba's per capita income is roughly one tenth as much. Cuba in fact has one of the lowest birth rates in Latin America.[8]

Before Cuba's revolution, most Cubans had the same poor living standards as the majority of Latin Americans: Life expectancy was low, infant mortality was high, and over half the children were malnourished. Economic and social reforms, combined with a highly effective public health system, led to dramatic improvements in the quality of life.

Today Cuba has one of the lowest infant mortality rates in Latin America, a life expectancy only two years less than the United States, and high employment and adult literacy. Income differentials are modest, and although sexism is still strong, women are much more emancipated than in many other Latin American countries. Cuban Family Code legislation even specifies that men should share equally in household tasks.

Within Latin America, Cuba stands out as an example of how equality can affect fertility. Moreover, Cuba achieved its low birth rate without ever once having a population control campaign. Instead family planning services are freely available through the health system to all who want them. Unfortunately, the basic health of the Cuban people has been seriously eroded partly as the result of the U.S. trade embargo designed to topple Castro.

Whatever one thinks of the Cuban political system, one cannot ignore the strength and breadth of its social welfare policies.

THE KOREAN "MIRACLE"

South Korea also boasts one of the fastest demographic transitions in history, from a crude birth rate of 41 in 1960 to 24 in 1974. (It is presently 16.) In Korea the key appears to be economic and social changes after World War II, which led to advances in equality. These were not the result of a popular revolution, however. As economist Robert Repetto explains:

> The high degree of equality was achieved not through a particularly strong commitment to popular welfare, but through the disruption and devastation of war; through a land reform which was legislated in an atmosphere of fear of Communist intervention and carried through mostly by private land sales or by the U.S. military government; and through an education reform which was also initiated by the U.S. military government.[9]

When Korea was occupied by the Allies at the end of World War II, a feudal system of land tenure prevailed in the countryside, with large landlords controlling much of the land. In 1938, for example, only 19 percent of Korea's farm household heads were full owners of the land. After the United States-sponsored land reform, this figure rose to 72 percent.

At the same time educational reform led to mass access to formal schooling. In 1945, 64 percent of children attended primary school, in 1960, 95.3 percent, and there was steadily increasing attendance in middle school, high school, and college over the period. In 1960 over a quarter of all children could expect to receive a college education, a high figure relative to most societies. These new educational opportunities served as a form of social mobility for poorer families, helping to reduce income disparities.[10]

As the result of the general rise in the standard of living, fertility declined in all regions and across all classes in Korea. Family planning programs had little to do with the initial fall: As late as 1964, well after the decline was underway, only 12 percent of women of reproductive age reported ever using contraceptives, though by 1973 the number had risen to 55 percent. Instead, illegal, though relatively safe, abortion was the most common method of birth control. Education and employment of women also had an impact on fertility, since both raised the marriage age.[11] (Unfortunately, today Korea's family planning program utilizes sterilization incentives, as part of the government's embrace of Western population control philosophy.)

In the 1960s and 1970s, Korea also experienced "miracle" economic growth through the development of export-oriented, manufacturing industries, based on cheap labor. While the conventional view is that this growth also furthered social equality, there is compelling evidence that, on the contrary, it has heightened income disparities.[12] Nevertheless, because of the post-World War II reforms, the gap between rich and poor is still less pronounced in Korea than in many other Third World countries.

Taiwan also experienced a similar fertility decline. Its postwar history has much in common with Korea: a United States-sponsored land reform, widening access to education, and rapid industrial growth through export manufacturing. In stark contrast to China, Taiwan's family planning program is largely voluntary.

SRI LANKA: ONCE UPON A WELFARE STATE

Sri Lanka is not a rich country. Its 1991 per capita income of only $500 reflects a long history of economic stagnation, stretching back to British colonial rule when the country became dependent on a few cash crops for income. Although Sri Lanka has not been very successful in terms of economic development, it has made great strides in human development. Prior to the election of a conservative government in 1977, Sri Lanka was one of the Third World's few welfare states.

Through sweeping social policies, including free supplementary rice rations, job and old-age security provisions, a progressive tax structure, and free education and health care, Sri Lankans have enjoyed a quality of life far superior to other low-income and even middle-income countries. The infant mortality rate dropped from 150 in 1946 to 18 in 1991, life expectancy is now 71, and there is virtually universal literacy, except among the exploited Tamil minority on the tea plantations.

Women have also enjoyed real improvements in their lives. By 1977 girls actually outnumbered boys in universities, and many women work outside the home. As a result, late marriage at around twenty-five years is the norm.

The impact of these measures on fertility is predictable. The crude birth rate dropped from 29 to 21 from 1970 to 1991—Sri Lanka in fact has one of the lowest birth rates in the Third World.

Under pressure from the International Monetary Fund and the World Bank, the Sri Lankan government dramatically cut back welfare measures in the late 1970s and is pursuing a strategy of export-oriented economic growth through the establishment of free trade zones for foreign investment. The rationale is that the welfare programs acted as a drain on government resources and a brake on economic development.[13] But would Sri Lanka be where it is today if it had not been a welfare state? Probably not. Instead, infant mortality and birth rates would probably be high, life expectancy low, and the World Bank and IMF would be advising the government to implement harsh population control policies à la India or Bangladesh. Indeed, Sri Lanka's sterilization program already relies on incentives to achieve results.

KERALA: THE EXCEPTION TO THE INDIAN RULE

Anyone who visits India's Kerala state is struck at once by its physical beauty: its lush coconut groves and rice paddies, scenic sea coast and inland waterways. This tropical paradise is also a human paradise in comparison to much of the rest of India. In Kerala people do not seem as weighed down by poverty as their compatriots. Hunger and disease are much less visible on the streets, most children are in school, and women walk with a pronounced air of self-confidence.

Yet by standard measures, Kerala is poor. Its per capita income is among the lowest in India, while its population density is 550 persons per square kilometer, similar to that of Bangladesh.[14] Other quality-of-life indicators, however, are unusually high. Almost 90 percent of Kerala's people are literate, compared to the all-India average of 52 percent. Kerala's life expectancy of close to 70 is considerably higher than the national average, and its infant mortality rate of 17, compared to India's 80, is the lowest in the country and one of the lowest in the Third World. According to the 1991 census, Kerala's sex ratio of 104 females to every 100 males makes it the only state in India with a sex ratio favorable to females.

In Kerala quality of life has also affected family size. Population growth rates for most other Indian states still remain high, yet Kerala is passing through a demographic transition. In 1991 its crude birth rate was estimated at 18.1, compared to the all-India average of 29.3.[15] What has made the difference?

In his work on Kerala, Dr. Ratcliffe describes how mass popular movements brought to power progressive state governments that initiated social reforms. Land reform legislation in the late 1950s and early 1960s, for example, helped to redistribute wealth. On paper these reforms were not much more radical than agrarian legislation in other Indian states, but in Kerala popular pressure ensured their actual implementation. As Indian economist K. N. Raj notes, "Kerala happens to be the only state in India where political pressure based on mass organization and support has been a major factor forcing the pace of land reform and where such reform has constantly received sustained attention."[16]

In addition, strong agricultural labor unions and a relatively high demand for labor have meant that even the landless in Kerala are generally better off than their counterparts elsewhere in India. A 1974 act legislated security of employment for agricultural laborers, as well as welfare and pension funds. Land reform also brought a nutritional improvement through better food distribution and increased production. Moreover, government ration shops selling food at controlled prices are open to all social groups, unlike in other states where urban and professional classes are the chief beneficiaries of subsidized food.

In the period 1961-1971, in India as a whole the highest income groups increased their proportion of asset holdings by 5 percent. Only in three states did the poorest groups gain on the rich, and it was Kerala that had the largest recorded gain. Along with redistribution of wealth came improved access to education and health. Primary and secondary schooling receive the lion's share of Kerala's education budget, and today illiteracy among the young has virtually been wiped out. Kerala also has the highest utilization of health facilities in India, even though eight states spend more per capita.

According to Dr. Ratcliffe, better distribution of health services between urban and rural areas is not the only explanation: The politically conscious Kerala populace "uses the power of the press and the vote to force the system to be responsive to their demands." This is unlike most parts of India where "those who lack a clear understanding both of their rights of access to public services and of the political process are easily manipulated and bypassed, and are thus powerless to enter or influence the system."[17]

Kerala's birth rate decline not only reflects general social development, but the improved status of women. Education has brought more women into the labor force, so they have real alternatives to childbearing. Kerala's average female age at marriage is the highest in India. Unfortunately, there have been instances of excesses in Kerala's family planning program, which relies heavily on sterilization.[18]

Of the many lessons Kerala holds for the rest of India, perhaps the most important is that *the foundation of equity rests on the political power of the poor*. Sadly, in most other states politics is largely the prerogative of the rich, and popular movements are routinely repressed. Inequality meanwhile perpetuates the poor's need for children, and they are then held responsible for rapid population growth. The result is mass population control campaigns, instead of the kinds of social and economic developments that would give people more control over their lives.

What lessons are to be drawn from these case studies?

In neither Cuba, Sri Lanka, Korea, nor Kerala was an intensive population control effort responsible for the demographic transition. Instead, by moving forward on a number of economic and social fronts, these societies, despite their different political systems, created the conditions under which people themselves wanted smaller families. The vital ingredients in their recipe for demographic transition are these:

- income and land redistribution.
- employment opportunities and social security.
- improvements in the position of women, including a later age of marriage.
- reductions in infant mortality.
- accessible health care and education.

It would be simplistic to say that this is the only way birth rates come down—the precise nature of the demographic transition obviously varies temporally, geographically, and culturally, and is not always due to positive factors. The Central American nation of Costa Rica, for example, has had a mixed experience. A sharp decline in birth rates prior to 1975 was largely caused by the introduction of an extensive state social security and welfare system which benefitted the majority of the population. During the severe economic crisis of the 1980s, the demographic transition stalled and fertility rose, although it began to slow again by the end of the 1980s. However, the current decline in fertility may be due less to positive factors than the "increasing number of working class women participating in the labor force under conditions of continuing economic and social insecurity."[19] A similar phenomenon is occurring in many other countries in Latin America, where urban poverty, not popular empowerment, is dictating smaller family sizes.

THE MAGIC BULLET APPROACH

In current considerations of the demographic transition, a crucial distinction exists between:

1. Those who view human welfare as the main goal of development, with fertility decline simply one of many aspects (essentially a by-product) and not necessarily the most important one in terms of improving the quality of people's lives; and

2. Those for whom fertility reduction is the sine qua non of development and family planning the most effective way to achieve it.

This latter view is put forward in a 1993 *Scientific American* article by Bryant Robey, Shea Rutstein, and Leo Morris which heralds the evidence "that birth rates in the developing world have fallen even in the absence of improved living conditions."[20] Bangladesh is one of their success stories. The authors challenge traditional demographic transition theory, claiming that strong family planning programs and new contraceptive technologies backed by the "educational power of mass media" are the most powerful factors now causing fertility decline in the Third World.

This "family planning first" approach has been around ever since population control became U.S. national policy in the 1960s and generated a subservient research establishment to support its claims.[21] What is interesting now is the speed with which the message has been taken up by the popular press. The *Scientific American* piece made the front page of the *New York Times*, and you could hear about it over dinner on National Public Radio. It not only provided a scientific rationale for the Clinton administration's renewed commitment to population control, but rode the larger wave of liberalism's retreat from social welfare: Let them eat contraceptives.

Fortunately, critics of the approach include demographers and economists who are challenging the statistics and assumptions on which it is based. World Bank economist Lant Pritchett, for example, disputes the view of Robey and colleagues that differences in contraceptive prevalence between countries account for 90 percent of the variation in fertility rates. Instead he maintains that high fertility largely reflects desired births, and that it is social and economic factors, not family planning access, which determine how many children people want. Obviously, once people want to control births, they are more likely to avail themselves of contraception, and their demand operates to increase the supply.

According to Pritchett, contraception is not important as a *causal* or *independent* determinant of fertility. Contraceptive use is higher where fertility is lower primarily because desired fertility is lower, which leads to both lower fertility and higher contraceptive demand, and hence higher contraceptive use.[22]

By his calculations, variations in contraceptive prevalence account for two percent, at most, of the difference in fertility rates between countries, after controlling for fertility desires, as opposed to the 90 percent figure put forward by Robey, et al. In the end, it may be impossible to pin a precise statistic on the role of either supply or demand in fertility decline, since it is a complex process where many different development factors interact.

Pritchett also takes on the contention of Robey and colleagues that access to family planning explains why the demographic transition has occurred much faster in many Third World countries than it did in Europe where modern contraception was not available. As Pritchett points out:

> Most of the intuitive appeal of an argument based on the speed of the current demographic transition is lost once it is recognized that differences in respect of family planning programs—active today, absent in the past—are just one small aspect of differences between today's fertility transitions and Europe's historical fertility transitions. In many developing countries that experienced rapid fertility decline, everything happened faster than for the now-developed countries: mortality fell faster, incomes rose faster, education expanded more rapidly.[23]

To isolate family planning as the main cause of current demographic transitions requires an ahistorical reductionism, a sort of family planning fundamentalism: "In the beginning, there was family planning..."

Proponents of the "family planning first" view often use the Matlab experiment in Bangladesh (described in Chapter 12) as their ultimate defense, since fertility rates fell faster in the project area, which was saturated with family planning services, than they did in a neighboring area despite the fact that desired family size was the same in both places. But according to Pritchett, Matlab is simply not replicable on a national—never mind international—scale given its extraordinary expense. Pritchett estimates that the cost per birth averted by the Matlab project was $180 in 1987, which is about 120 percent of Bangladesh's GDP per capita.[24]   And as we have seen, this huge concentration of resources was ethically unjustified. As long as health care was excluded from the Matlab package, the program did little to improve the quality of people's lives, since its main intention was controlling the quantity of births.

Criticizing the magic bullet approach does not mean one is against family planning, but rather for its liberation from a narrow demographic interpretation, which is not even scientifically sound. And as this book has shown throughout, placing family planning within a population control framework undermines the quality and voluntary nature of services. It demeans women and gives family planning a bad name.

There are plenty of compelling reasons besides population control to make family planning, including safe, legal abortion, available to people: so that they can space their children and more easily attain their desired family size, so they can protect themselves against sexually transmitted diseases, so they can free their sexuality from procreation.

From a practical and ethical standpoint, the best population policy is to concentrate on improving human welfare in all its many facets. Take care of the people and they will take care of themselves, the old adage goes. Take care of the population and population growth will come down. In fact, the great irony is that in most cases population growth comes down faster the less you focus on it as a policy priority, and the more you focus on women's rights and basic human needs.

16

THE POPULATION FRAMEWORK: INSIDE OR OUTSIDE?

In my wildest dreams I wish "population" could be dropped all together from the development lexicon and replaced by concern for real people, real environments, not the fixed images of dark babies as bombs, women as wombs, statistical manipulations as absolute truth. Human welfare, yes: education, employment, health care, social and economic justice, reproductive rights, and the long-awaited peace dividend. (See Appendix: Call for a New Approach) Environmental protection, yes: curbs on pollution and waste, demilitarization, support for alternative technologies, farming systems and values which strengthen a sense of democratic community, not crass materialism.

Population Control, No!

This was the slogan of the Women's International Tribunal and Meeting on Reproductive Rights held in Amsterdam in 1984, where 400 women from around the world came together in a powerful condemnation of both population control and antiabortion forces. That meeting solidified my own activism in the international women's health movement. It was held at a time when the movement, particularly its reproductive rights wing, was coming into its own. On the local level feminist initiatives were defining birth control in very different ways than the population establishment. They were responding to women's needs not only through the provision of more comprehensive reproductive health services and sexuality education, but through grassroots organizing around women's economic and political rights.[1]

On the national level, in countries such as Brazil, the Philippines, and India, coalitions of women's groups were exerting pressure on the state to reform health policy, while internationally, the movement was expanding. The centralization of power in Northern countries was eroding, as the movement became more democratic and geographically diverse.

At the same time feminists within the population establishment were engaged in their own reform efforts, mainly through articulating a quality of care agenda. As the antiabortion movement gained strength, finding a powerful political ally in U.S. President Ronald Reagan, other members of the population establishment recognized the value of a strategic alliance with the international women's health movement. In the mid-1980s, dialogues began between representatives of the two groups, often organized by the New York-based International Women's Health Coalition (IWHC) which acted as a political broker. IWHC maintained that it was possible to "balance the scales" between population control and women's health.[2] The first stones had been laid in the foundation of the Cairo consensus.

Who has gained most from the deal is still an open question. Without the participation of the women's movement, the Cairo consensus would no doubt be less attentive to women's rights and more Malthusian than it already is. But have women's organizations given up too much in the process? In particular, should they accept working within a framework which still blames population growth disproportionately for economic and environmental problems, sets targets for population stabilization and scarcely addresses the much more salient issues of unequal terms of trade, debt and structural adjustment, income distribution, and arms control?

This question now divides the movement. A number of groups have agreed to work within a population policy framework, although they have tried in the process to expand it. According to the

Women's Declaration on Population Policies prepared in advance of Cairo:

> Population policies...need to address a wide range of conditions that affect the reproductive health and rights of women and men. These include unequal distribution of material and social resources among individuals and groups, based on gender, age, race, religion, social class, rural-urban residence, nationality and other social criteria; changing patterns of sexual and family relationships; political and economic policies that restrict girls' and women's access to health services and methods of fertility regulation; and ideologies, laws and practices that deny women's basic rights.[3]

Despite this opening, the Declaration essentially sets forth a reproductive health agenda, with calls for more "women decision-makers" and financial resources for meeting program requirements. There is no fundamental challenge to the population paradigm, and government and international agencies, despite mention of their past shortcomings, are perceived as basically benign.

There are two key reasons women's organizations have agreed to work within the population framework. Some reproductive rights activists genuinely believe in the urgency of slowing population growth. Marge Berer, for example, writes that the women's movement should "acknowledge that the world cannot sustain an unlimited number of people, just as women's bodies cannot sustain unlimited pregnancies."[4] Likening the planet to a woman's body, however, is a comparison fraught with peril.

For others it is more of a strategic choice—they would argue that accepting the legitimacy of a population framework allows women greater access to decision-makers, or in some cases, the opportunity to be decision-makers themselves. It reflects the movement's growing sophistication and professionalization, with some kind of compromise as the inevitable price of success.

But does influencing and interacting with the establishment necessarily depend on articulating women's concerns within a population framework? No, write Judith Richter and Loes Keysers, who set forth an alternative agenda of engagement. They note that more liberal people in the establishment may welcome support from the women's movement in their struggle against coercive

population control, on the one hand, and the Vatican and funda-
mentalists, on the other.

> Women's advocates are thus in a relative position of strength.
> Could the splits in the population field not be used differently?
> Why not—instead of embracing a population agenda—enroll the
> population soft liners and family planners, for example, into a
> people's alliance for reproductive rights and health? This would
> allow feminists to set the terms of reference. It would create
> space for a shift of paradigm, rather than a shift from hard to soft
> population control.[5]

The Declaration of People's Perspectives on "Population," issued by women from 23 countries meeting in 1993 in Comilla,
Bangladesh, strongly rejects the population framework:

> Women's basic needs of food, education, health, work, social and
> political participation, a life free of violence and oppression
> should be addressed on their own merit. Meeting women's needs
> should be de-linked from population policy including those ex-
> pressed as apparent humanitarian concerns for women.

The Comilla Declaration also makes clear its support for
women's access to safe contraception and legal abortion as part of
general health care. "Our resistance to population control policies
must never be confused with the opposition of the religious and political right to the same policies."[6]

Nevertheless, women who insist on remaining outside of the
population framework are often accused of playing into the hands
of the Vatican. There are also debates on which is the greater enemy of reproductive rights: religious fundamentalism or population
control. Clearly, this depends on one's specific situation—whether
one is fighting restrictive abortion legislation in Latin America and
Eastern Europe, for example, or sterilization abuse in India and
China. In many places, including the United States, both are ene-
mies, both must be confronted simultaneously.

So far the movement has managed to maintain an uneasy unity
and some sense of common identity—its strength is its members'
ability to discuss and debate openly, to accept difference and het-
erogeneity, to insist on democratic processes and leadership. But
the road ahead will be difficult. Besides the debate over population,
there are many other unresolved issues: If it is politically pragmatic

for some members to work within mainstream institutions, how can they remain accountable to the outside movement? Power doesn't necessarily corrupt, but it often separates and isolates. Does participation in official processes, such as U.N. conferences, siphon too much energy away from grassroots organizing? How can the movement, especially at the international level, maintain any grassroots authenticity? In an era of scarce resources, will the agenda conform too much to the funders' priorities? Where will funding come from?

I myself would argue for a strategy of principled pragmatism. While it makes political sense to dialogue and interact with the establishment periodically, as well as to have sympathetic women in positions of power within it, I believe the international women's health movement should not accept—and does not need to accept—the population framework in its efforts to reform health and family planning policy. When the movement does accept the framework, it loses its critical edge, dulls its tools of analysis, and ends up endorsing narrow technocratic agendas, rather than a broader politics of social and economic transformation. It divorces itself further from the poor women it is supposed to represent and places too much faith in official rhetoric. After Cairo, when the consensus snake begins to shed its skin, its progressive trappings will probably be the first to go. Already, Bangladesh and Indonesia are being put forward as the models which other countries should follow.

Stripped of all the economic arguments, political justifications, and soft-sell marketing, population control at heart is a philosophy without a heart, in which human beings become objects to be manipulated. It is a philosophy of domination, for its architects must necessarily view people of different sex, race, and class as inferior, less human than themselves, or otherwise they could not justify the double standards they employ.

Population control profoundly distorts our world view, and negatively affects people in the most intimate areas of their lives. Instead of promoting ethics, empathy, and true reproductive choice, it encourages us to condone coercion. And even on the most practical level, it is no solution to the serious economic, political, and environmental problems we face at the end of the century.

In saying no to population control from a prochoice, feminist perspective, one often feels like a voice in the wilderness, especially in the United States where Malthusianism is a popular religion, a veritable article of faith. But inhabiting the political wilderness is preferable to accepting conventional wisdom that is unwise. And if one listens closely, one can hear many other voices raised in protest and one can join them until collectively, they are too loud and clear to ignore.

APPENDIX

CALL FOR A NEW APPROACH

The Committee on Women, Population and the Environment is an alliance of women activists, community organizers, health practitioners, and scholars of diverse races, cultures, and countries of origin working for women's empowerment and reproductive freedom, and against poverty, inequality, racism and environmental degradation. Issued in 1992, their statement, "Women, Population and the Environment: Call for a New Approach" continues to gather individual and organizational endorsements from around the world.

Call for a New Approach

We are troubled by recent statements and analyses that single out population size and growth as a primary cause of global environmental degradation.

We believe the major causes of global environmental degradation are:

- Economic systems that exploit and misuse nature and people in the drive for short-term and short-sighted gains and profits.
- The rapid urbanization and poverty resulting from migration from rural areas and from inadequate planning and resource allocation in towns and cities.
- The displacement of small farmers and indigenous peoples by agribusiness, timber, mining, and energy corporations, often with encouragement and assistance from international financial institutions, and with the complicity of national governments.
- The disproportionate consumption patterns of the affluent the world over. Currently, the industrialized nations, with 22 percent of the world's population, consume 70 percent of the world's resources. Within the United States, deepen-

ing economic inequalities mean that the poor are consuming less, and the rich more.
- Technologies designed to exploit but not to restore natural resources.
- Warmaking and arms production which divest resources from human needs, poison the natural environment and perpetuate the militarization of culture, encouraging violence against women.

Environmental degradation derives thus from complex, interrelated causes. Demographic variables can have an impact on the environment, but reducing population growth will not solve the above problems. In many countries, population growth rates have declined yet environmental conditions continue to deteriorate.

Moreover, blaming global environmental degradation on population growth helps to lay the groundwork for the re-emergence and intensification of top-down, demographically driven population policies and programs which are deeply disrespectful of women, particularly women of color and their children.

In Southern countries, as well as in the United States and other Northern countries, family planning programs have often been the main vehicles for dissemination of modern contraceptive technologies. However, because so many of their activities have been oriented toward population control rather than women's reproductive health needs, they have too often involved sterilization abuse; denied women full information on contraceptive risks and side effects; neglected proper medical screening, follow-up care, and informed consent; and ignored the need for safe abortion and barrier and male methods of contraception. Population programs have frequently fostered a climate where coercion is permissible and racism acceptable.

Demographic data from around the globe affirm that improvements in women's social, economic, and health status and in general living standards, are often keys to declines in population growth rates. We call on the world to recognize women's basic right to control their own bodies and to have access to the power, resources, and reproductive health services to ensure that they can do so.

National governments, international agencies, and other social institutions must take seriously their obligation to provide the essential prerequisites for women's development and freedom. These include:

1. Resources such as fair and equitable wages, land rights, appropriate technology, education, and access to credit.

2. An end to structural adjustment programs, imposed by the IMF, the World Bank, and repressive governments, which sacrifice human dignity and basic needs for food, health, and education to debt repayment and 'free market', male-dominated models of unsustainable development.

3. Full participation in the decisions which affect our own lives, our families, our communities, and our environment, and incorporation of women's knowledge systems and expertise to enrich these decisions.

4. Affordable, culturally appropriate, and comprehensive health care and health education for women of all ages and their families.

5. Access to safe, voluntary contraception and abortion as part of broader reproductive health services which also provide pre- and post-natal care, infertility services, and prevention and treatment of sexually transmitted diseases including HIV and AIDS.

6. Family support services that include child-care, parental leave and elder care.

7. Reproductive health services and social programs that sensitize men to their parental responsibilities and to the need to stop gender inequalities and violence against women and children.

8. Speedy ratification and enforcement of the U.N. Convention on the Elimination of All Forms of Discrimination Against Women as well as other UN conventions on human rights.

People who want to see improvements in the relationship between the human population and natural environment should work for the full range of women's rights; global demilitarization; redistribution of resources and wealth between and within nations; reduction of consumption rates of polluting products and processes and of non-renewable resources; reduction of chemical dependency in agriculture; and environmentally responsible technology. They should support local, national, and international initiatives for democracy, social justice, and human rights.

NOTES

Notes to boxed material will be found at the end of the notes to each chapter.

1. SECURITY AND SURVIVAL

1. See, for example, Marc H. Dawson, "Health, Nutrition, and Population in Central Kenya, 1890-1945," in Dennis D. Cordell and Joel W. Gregory, eds., *African Population and Capitalism: Historical Perspectives* (Boulder: Westview Press, 1987). Basic demographic statistics taken from U.S. Bureau of the Census, Report WP/94, World Population Profile: 1994 (Washington, D.C.: Government Printing Office, 1994) and William K. Stevens, "Feeding a Booming Population Without Destroying the Planet," *New York Times,* 5 April 1994.

2. Mead T. Cain, "The Economic Activities of Children in a Village in Bangladesh," *Population and Development Review,* vol. 3, no. 3 (September 1977).

3. John C. Caldwell, *Theory of Fertility Decline* (London: Academic Press, 1982), p. 69.

4. Thais Corall, "Brazil: A Failed Success Story," paper presented to the Conference on Multilateral Population Assistance, Oslo, Norway, 25 May 1994.

5. See Mead T. Cain, "Risk and Insurance: Perspectives on Fertility and Agrarian Change in India and Bangladesh," *Population and Development Review,* vol. 7, no. 3 (September 1981) and, by the same author, "Fertility as an Adjustment to Risk," Population Council, Center for Policy Studies Working Papers, No. 100 (New York: October 1983). Also see Caldwell, *Theory of Fertility Decline.*

6. Nancy Folbre, "Of Patriarchy Born: The Political Economy of Fertility Decisions," *Feminist Studies,* vol. 9, no. 2 (Summer 1983), p. 274. For more on the costs of children—and the political economy of who bears those costs, see Folbre, *Who Pays for the Kids: Gender and the Structures of Constraint* (London and New York: Routledge, 1994).

Also see Caldwell, *Theory of Fertility Decline,* for more on how education changes the value of children. Japan provides an interesting example of how the role of children as a source of security changes. In 1950, at the beginning of Japan's industrial boom, a survey showed that over half the population expected to be supported by children in their old age. By 1961, after a decade of rapid growth, this figure had already declined to 27 percent, and the birth rate had also fallen dramatically. Japan example from William W. Murdoch, *The Poverty of Nations: The Political Economy of Hunger and Population* (Baltimore: Johns Hopkins University Press, 1980), p. 29.

7. Folbre, "Of Patriarchy Born."

8. Indian example from Frances Moore Lappé and Joseph Collins, *Food First: Beyond the Myth of Scarcity* (New York: Ballantine Books, 1979), p. 32.

9. Amartya Sen, "More Than 100 Million Women Are Missing," *New York Review of Books,* 20 December 1990.

10. United Nations Development Program (UNDP), *Human Development Report 1993* (New York: Oxford University Press, 1993), Tables 3 and 4, pp. 140-143.

11. José Villar and José M. Belizan, "Women's Poor Health in Developing Countries: A Vicious Circle," in Patricia Blair, ed., *Health Needs of the World's Poor Women* (Washington, D.C.: Equity Policy Center, 1981).

12. Isabel Nieves, "Changing Infant Feeding Practices: A Woman-Centered View," in Blair, ed., *Health Needs.*

13. Ann Wigglesworth, "Space to Live," background article, *The State of World Population 1983* Press File, prepared by the New Internationalist Publications Cooperative for the UNFPA (Oxford: 1983); Lappé and Collins, *Food First,* p. 337.

14. Beverly Winikoff, *The Infant Feeding Study: Summary,* report submitted to AID by the Population Council (New York: Population Council, n.d.).

15. Maggie Jones, "The Biggest Contraceptive in the World," *New Internationalist,* no. 110 (April 1982).

16. See Wigglesworth, "Space to Live"; James P. Grant, *State of the World's Children 1982-83* (New York: UNICEF, 1983); and Kathleen Newland, *Infant Mortality and the Health of Societies,* Worldwatch Paper No. 47 (Washington, D.C.: Worldwatch Institute, December 1981).

BOX. THE IMPACT OF AIDS

1. World Population Profile: 1994.

2. THE MALTHUSIAN ORTHODOXY

1. Richard D. Lamm, "Linking Third World Aid to Population Control," *International Herald Tribune,* 22 April 1985.

2. Thomas R. Malthus, *An Essay on Population,* Vol. I (New York: E. P. Dutton and Co., 1914), p. 6.

3. Douglas C. North and Robert P. Thomas, *The Rise of the Western World: A New Economic History* (Cambridge: Cambridge University Press, 1973), p. 8.

4. Environmental Fund, *Statement on the Real Crisis Behind the "Food Crisis"* (Washington, D.C.: 1975).

5. Quoted in John Tierney, "The Population Crisis Revisited," *Wall Street Journal,* 20 January 1986. Also see Dennis Meadows and Donnella Meadows, *The Limits to Growth* (New York: Universe Books, 1972).

6. Ann Critenden, "Poverty, Not Scarcity Called Chief Cause of World Hunger," *New York Times,* 7 December 1982.

7. Colin Clark, *Population Growth and Land Use* (London: Macmillan, 1967), pp. 137-38. Also see Ester Boserup, *The Conditions of Agricultural Growth: The Economics of Agrarian Change Under Population Pressure* (London: George Allen and Unwin, Ltd., 1970).

8. Tim Dyson, "Population Growth and Food Production: Recent Global and Regional Trends," *Population and Development Review*, vol. 20, no.2 (June 1994), p. 407. Also see World Resources Institute, *World Resources 1992-93* (New York: Oxford University Press, 1992), pp. 94-96.

9. Amartya Sen, *Poverty and Famines: An Essay on Entitlement and Deprivation* (Oxford: Clarendon Press, 1981), p. 118.

10. Sylvia Nasar, "It's Never Fair to Just Blame the Weather," *New York Times,* 17 January 1993.

11. World Resources Institute, *World Resources 1992-93*, p. 96. According to Bill Rau, *From Feast to Famine: Official Cures and Grassroots Remedies to Africa's Food Crisis* (London: Zed Books, 1991), p. 104, official figures may underestimate current food production in Africa, since they are largely based on formal sales, and many farmers are now marketing crops through "unofficial" channels. "Thus, it is not possible to assess levels of agricultural production effectively from the commonly used data, nor to claim a spreading crisis of declining food availability."

12. See Rau, *From Feast to Famine*; Michael F. Lofchie, "Political and Economic Origins of African Hunger," *Journal of Modern African Studies,* vol. 13, no. 4 (1975), p. 554; Richard W. Franke and Barbara H. Chasin, *Seeds of Famine: Ecological Destruction and the Development Dilemma in the West African Sahel* (Montclair, NJ: Allanheld, Osmun and Co., 1980), and Carl F. Eicher, "Facing Up to Africa's Food Crisis," *Foreign Affairs,* Fall 1982.

13. Rau, *From Feast to Famine* and Lloyd Timberlake, *Africa in Crisis: The Causes, the Cures of Environmental Bankruptcy* (London: International Institute for Environment and Development (1985).

14. *World Resources 1992-93*, pp. 97-98.

15. Walden Bello, *Dark Victory: The United States, Structural Adjustment and Global Poverty* (London: Pluto Press with Food First, 1994), pp. 36, 47. This book gives a good overview of the impact of structural adjustment.

16. Richard W. Franke, "Mode of Production and Population Patterns: Policy Implications for West African Development," *International Journal of Health Services,* vol. 11, no. 3 (1981).

17. Rau, *From Feast to Famine*, p. 92.

18. Mary Tiffen, Michael Mortimore and Frances Gichuki, *More People, Less Erosion: Environmental Recovery in Kenya* (London: Overseas Development Institute and J. W. Wiley, 1994). For an account of a similar study in Nigeria, see Charles Mann, "How Many is Too Many?," *Atlantic Monthly*, February 1993.

19. Timberlake, *Africa in Crisis*, p. 209.

20. Lester R. Brown et al., *State of the World 1984, A Worldwatch Institute Report on Progress Toward a Sustainable Society* (New York: W. W. Norton and Co., 1984), p. 209. Brown's writing continues in this vein. Also see Paul R. Ehrlich and Anne H. Ehrlich, *The Population Explosion* (New York: Simon and Schuster, 1990).

21. See Rau, *From Feast to Famine*, Part III, for examples, and also Ben Wisner, *Power and Need in Africa* (Trenton, NJ: Africa World Press, 1989).

22. Ehrlich and Ehrlich, *The Population Explosion,* Chapter 1.

23. Ibid., pp. 38-39.

24. Ibid., pp. 72, 75.

25. Ibid., p. 58.

26. Anuradha Vittachi, "Sex, Lies and Global Survival," *New Internationalist*, no. 235 (1992), p. 19.

27. Laurie Ann Mazur, *Population and the Environment: A Grantmaker's Guide* (New York: Environmental Grantmakers Association, 1992).

28. Barry Commoner, "Rapid Population Growth and Environmental Stress," *International Journal of Health Services*, vol. 21, no. 2 (1991).

29. Barbara Duden, "Population," in Wolfgang Sachs, ed., *The Development Dictionary* (London: Zed Books, 1992), p. 149.

30. H. Patricia Hynes, *Taking Population Out of the Equation: Reformulating I=PAT* (Amherst, MA: Institute on Women and Technology, 1993), p. 23. Hynes puts forward a new equation which directly addresses the role of human agency, the military, and patriarchy.

31. *Human Development Report 1993,* pp. 11, 27.

32. Paul L. Wachtel, "Overconsumption: Lessons from Psychology for Politics and Economics" (brief version for oral presentation), paper presented to the Global Political Ecology Conference, York University, Toronto, Canada, 3-6 March 1994, p. 5.

33. Ibid., p. 8. See also Juliet Schor, *The Overworked American* (New York: Basic Books, 1991).

34. Hynes, *Taking Population Out of the Equation*, p. 20.

35. Joni Seager, *Earth Follies: Coming to Feminist Terms with the Global Environmental Crisis* (New York: Routledge, 1993), Chapter 1. Also see Hynes, ibid.

36. UNFPA, *State of the World Population 1992* (Oxford: Nuffield Press, 1992), p. 11.

37. UNFPA, *Population, Resources and the Environment: The Critical Challenges* (New York: UNFPA, 1991), pp. 18-19.

38. Solon Barraclough and Krishna Ghimire, "The Social Dynamics of Deforestation in Developing Countries: Principal Issues and Research Priorities," Discussion paper 16 (Geneva: UNRISD, 1990), p. 13.

39. Nicholas Guppy, "Tropical Deforestation: A Global View," *Foreign Affairs*, vol. 62, no. 4 (1984).

40. Lappé and Collins, *Food First,* pp. 48-52.

41. Fatima V. Mello, "Trends in Population Policies in the 90s," in Rosiska Darcy de Oliviera et al., eds., *Population Danger: Sex, Lies and Misconceptions* (Rio de Janeiro, Brazil: IDAC/REDEH/IBASE, 1993), pp. 17-18.

42. Douglas R. Shane, *Hoofprints on the Forest: Cattle Ranching and the Destruction of Latin America's Tropical Forests* (Philadelphia: Institute for the Study of Human Issues, 1986).

43. Daniel Faber, "Imperialism, Revolution, and the Ecological Crisis of Central America," *Latin American Perspectives,* vol. 19, no. 1 (Winter 1992), p. 25.

44. UNFPA, *Population, Resources, and the Environment,* p. 20.

45. David M. Kummer, *Deforestation in the Post-War Philippines* (Chicago: University of Chicago Press, 1992).

46. Gregg Jones, "Marcos Profited from Smuggling $ lb in Timber, Officials Say," *Boston Globe,* 22 May 1986. For more on the Marcos era and the support of the World Bank and AID, see James K. Boyce, *The Philippines: The Political Economy of Growth and Impoverishment in the Marcos Era* (London: Macmillan, 1993).

47. Guppy, "Tropical Deforestation."

48. Faber, "Imperialism."

49. Kenneth Freed, "Salvador's Ecological Nightmare," *Los Angeles Times,* 15 June 1991.

50. Lappé and Collins, *Food First,* p. 43.

51. Faber, "Imperialism," p. 27.

52. Ibid., p. 32.

53. World Bank, *World Development Report 1984* (New York: Oxford University Press, l984), p. 79.

54. Population Crisis Committee, "Third World Population Growth from a Business Perspective," *Population,* no. 8 (June 1978).

55. *World Development Report 1984,* p. 81.

56. World Bank, *World Development Report 1993* (New York: Oxford University Press, 1993), Tables 1, 26.

57. AID, USAID Strategy Papers, LPA Revision (Washington, D.C.: USAID, 5 October 1993), p. 29.

58. *Human Development Report 1993,* pp. 10, 177.

59. Ibid., p. 7.

60. Inter-Church Coalition on Africa, *Beyond Adjustment: Responding to the Health Crisis in Africa* (Toronto: ICCAF, 1993).

61. USAID Strategy Papers, p. 29.

62. Teresa Hayter, *The Creation of World Poverty* (London: Pluto Press, 1983).

63. World Bank, *World Debt Tables 1992-93*, vol. 1, pp. 13-19; on Africa, Bello, *Dark Victory*, p. 68. Also see ICCAF, *Beyond Adjustment.*

64. Peter Roger, "$55 Billion 'Spirited Away Overseas,'" *Guardian*, 19 June 1984.

65. See, for example, UNFPA, *State of World Population 1992.*

66. Population Crisis Committee, "Population Pressures: Threat to Democracy" (fold-out) (Washington, D.C.: PCC, 1991).

67. U.S. Congress, House of Representatives, Population and Development in Latin America and the Caribbean. Hearing before the Subcommittee on Inter-American Affairs of the Committee on Foreign Affairs, 97th Cong., 2d sess., 8 September 1982, p. 45.

68. Malthus, *An Essay*, Vol. II, p. 260.

69. Julian L. Simon and Herman Kahn, *The Resourceful Earth* (Oxford: Basil Blackwell, 1984), Introduction.

70. Julian L. Simon, "Myths of Overpopulation," *Wall Street Journal*, 3 August 1984; and Simon, *The Ultimate Resource* (Princeton: Princeton University Press, 1981).

71. "U.S. Policy Statement for the International Conference on Population," reproduced as Attachment A in the Ford Foundation, *The Ford Foundation's Work in Population* (New York: August 1985), pp. 45-46.

72. For an account of the report, see Constance Holden, "A Revisionist Look at Population and Growth," *Science,* vol. 231, no. 4745 (28 March 1986).

3. A WOMB OF ONE'S OWN

1. Peruvian quotation from Audrey Bronstein's interview notes for *The Triple Struggle: Latin American Peasant Women* (London: War on Want Campaigns Ltd., 1982); Senegalese quotation from Mariama Kamara, "Bearing the Brunt," *People* (IPPF), vol. 10, no. 4 (1983), pp. 17-18; Sri Lankan quotation from "Population Control Practices on the Tea Plantations of Sri Lanka," statement delivered at Women's International Tribunal and Meeting on Reproductive Rights, held at Amsterdam, 22-28 July 1984; U.K. letter from Marge Berer, *Who Needs Depo-Provera?* (London: Community Rights Project, July 1981), p. 25.

2. For a discussion of the impact of colonialism on women, especially in Africa, see Barbara Rogers, *The Domestication of Women: Discrimination in Developing Societies* (New York: Tavistock Publishers, 1981) and Ester Boserup, *Woman's Role in Economic Development* (London: George Allen and Unwin Ltd., 1970).

3. Ronald S. Waife, M.S.P.H., *Traditional Methods of Birth Control in Zaire*, Pathpapers No. 4 (Pathfinder Fund, December 1978), p. 4.

4. See Lars Bondestam and Staffan Bergström, *Poverty and Population Control* (London: Academic Press, 1980), pp. 43-44; Murdoch, *The Poverty of Nations*, p. 28; and Rogers, *The Domestication of Women*, p. 111.

5. See Marilee Karl, "Women and Rural Development," in ISIS Women's International Information and Communication Service, *Women in Development: A Resource Guide for Organization and Action* (Geneva: 1983). This is a crucial source for anyone interested in women and development. Also see *Follow-Up to WCAARD: The Role of Women in Agricultural Production*, Expert Consultation on Women in Food Production (Rome: FAO, 1983), and other papers in this series.

6. See Ester Boserup, "Economic and Demographic Interrelationships in sub-Saharan Africa," *Population and Development Review*, vol. 11, no. 3 (September 1985).

7. *The Need for Improved Agricultural Extension Services for Women Engaged in Agriculture*, Expert Consultation on Women in Food Production (Rome: FAO, December 1983).

8. See Kathleen Newland, *The Sisterhood of Man* (New York: W. W. Norton and Co., 1979), p. 171.

9. *Human Development Report 1993*, Table 9.

10. On women in the labor force see Rogers, *The Domestication of Women*; and Newland, *The Sisterhood of Man*.

11. See Barbara Ehrenreich and Annette Fuentes, "Life on the Global Assembly Line," *Ms.*, January 1981.

12. M. Patricia Fernandez Kelly, "Broadening the Scope: Gender and International Economic Development," *Sociological Forum*, vol. 4, no. 4 (1989). This is a good overview article.

13. See, for example, Nancy Folbre, "Hearts and Spades: Paradigms of Household Economics," *World Development*, vol. 14, no. 2 (1986).

14. See Helen Ware, *Women, Demography and Development*, Development Studies Center Demography Teaching Notes, No. 3 (Canberra: The Australian National University, 1981), p. 61; and Amartya Sen, *Family and Food: Sex-Bias in Poverty* (All Souls College, Oxford: November 1981).

15. Vina Mazumdar, "Another Development with Women: A View from Asia," *Development Dialogue* (Uppsala), nos. 1-2 (1982).

16. Itziar Lozano Urbieta, *Women, the Key to Liberation* (New York: Women's International Resource Exchange Service, n.d.).

17. Boston Women's Health Book Collective, *The New Our Bodies, Ourselves* (New York: Simon and Schuster, 1992), p. 131.

18. Newland, *The Sisterhood of Man*, p. 202.

19. Rashid Faruquee and Ravi Gulhati, *Rapid Population Growth in Sub-Saharan Africa: Issues and Policies*, World Bank Staff Working Papers, No. 559 (Washington, D.C.: World Bank, 1983).

20. Mead Cain, Syewda Rokeya Khanam, and Shamsun Nahar, "Class, Patriarchy and Women's Work in Bangladesh," *Population and Development Review*, vol. 5, no. 3 (September 1979), p. 432.

21. World Resources Institute, *World Resources 1994-95* (New York: Oxford University Press, 1994), p. 52.

22. D. Mandelbaum, *Human Fertility in India* (Berkeley: University of California Press, 1974), quoted in Ware, *Women, Demography and Development*, p. 84.

23. *Human Development Report 1993*, Tables 5 and 9.

24. *World Development Report 1984*, p. 110.

25. Robert Lighthouse, Jr. and Susheela Singh, "The World Fertility Survey: Charting Global Childbearing," *Population Bulletin*, vol. 37, no. 1 (March 1982), pp. 42-43. See also ibid., p. 130.

26. Stephen Sinding, "A Plan for Renewed United States Leadership on International Population Issues," 1992, p. 5.

27. Ruth Dixon-Mueller, *Population Policy and Women's Rights: Transforming Reproductive Choice* (Westport, CT: Praeger, 1993), p. 163.

28. Patricia Smyke, *Women and Health* (London: Zed Books, 1991), p. 17.

29. World Health Organization, Division of Family Health, *Health and the Status of Women* (Geneva: 1980); and "Healthier Mothers and Children Through Family Planning," *Population Reports*, Series J, no. 27 (May-June 1984), p. J661. Also see *Human Development Report 1993*, Table 8.

30. Newland, *The Sisterhood of Man*, p. 52.

31. Dixon-Mueller, *Population Policy*, p. 163.

32. WHO, "Health and the Status of Women." Bolivian figures from Newland, *The Sisterhood of Man*, p. 61.

33. Population Crisis Committee, "World Abortion Trends," *Population*, no. 9 (April 1979).

34. Perdita Huston, *Message from the Village* (New York, Epoch B Foundation, 1978), p. 119.

35. See Christine Oppong and Elina Haavio-Mannila, "Women, Population and Development," in Philip M. Hauser, ed., *World Population and Development* (Syracuse, NY: Syracuse University Press, 1979), p. 480.

36. See World Bank, *World Development Report 1993* (New York: Oxford University Press, 1993).

37. Dr. S. Okun Ayangade, *International Journal of Obstetrics and Gynecology*, vol. 15, no. 6 (1978), p. 499.

38. Nawal El Saadawi, "On Women's Shoulders," *People*, (IPPF), vol. 6, no. 4 (1979). This article is an excerpt from her book *The Hidden Face of Eve: Women in the Arab World* (London: Zed Press, 1979).

39. Gavin Jones, "Towards an Optimum Population: The Malaysian Case," *People* (IPPF), vol. 12, no. 4 (1985). For a recent analysis of the Malaysian case, see Rashidah Abdullah, "Changing Population Policies and Women's Lives in Malaysia," *Reproductive Health Matters*, no. 1, May 1993.

40. Peru information from Rosa Domingo Trapasso of the Peruvian women's group Promoción Cultural "Creatividad y Cambio."

41. See Robin Morgan, ed., *Sisterhood Is Global: The International Women's Movement Anthology* (New York: Anchor Press/Doubleday, 1984), p. 2; and Newland, *The Sisterhood of Man*.

42. See Joe Joyce, "Dublin Scents Victory in Fight to Legalize Condoms," *Guardian*, 18 February 1985.

43. Rosalind P. Petchesky, "'Reproductive Choice' in the Contemporary United States: A Social Analysis of Female Sterilization," in Karen L. Michaelson, ed., *And the Poor Get Children: Radical Perspectives on Population Dynamics* (New York: Monthly Review Press, 1981), p. 69.

44. Tatyana Mamonova, "The USSR: It's Time We Began with Ourselves," in Morgan, ed., *Sisterhood Is Global*, pp. 684-85.

4. THE PLAN BEHIND FAMILY PLANNING

1. See Donald Warwick, *Bitter Pills: Population Policies and Their Implementation in Eight Developing Countries* (Cambridge: Cambridge University Press, 1982), for a fascinating account of these interventions. On recent World Bank policy see Fred T. Sai and Lauren Chester, "The Role of the World Bank in Shaping Third World Population Policy," in Geoffrey Roberts, ed., *Population Policy: Contemporary Issues* (New York: Praeger, 1990).

2. Warwick, *Bitter Pills*, pp. 114-22.

3. Mahmood Mamdani, *The Myth of Population Control: Family, Caste and Class in an Indian Village* (New York: Monthly Review Press, 1972), p. 19.

4. Bernard Berelson, "National Family Planning Programs: A Guide," *Studies in Family Planning*, No. 5, Supplement, 1964, p. 11, quoted in Warwick, *Bitter Pills*, p. 35.

5. Ruth Dixon-Mueller and Adrienne Germaine, "Stalking the Elusive 'Unmet Need' for Family Planning," *Studies in Family Planning*, vol. 23, no. 5 (Sept.-Oct. 1992).

6. BKBBN, *Basic Information on Population and Family Planning Program* (Jakarta: 1982), p. 52.

7. Mamdani, *The Myth of Population Control*, p. 40.

8. "Lights! Camera! Action!: Promoting Family Planning with TV, Video, and Film," *Population Reports*, Series J, no. 39 (1989).

9. Information Project for Africa, "Propaganda, Cultural Imperialism and Population Control: Ideological Communications in the Southern Hemisphere," Working Paper no. 3, IPFA Foreign Policy Series (Washington, D.C.: 1993).

10. *Population Reports*, Series J, no. 39.

11. Warwick, *Bitter Pills*, p. 40.

12. Quoted in ibid., p. 131.

13. Ibid.

14. Westinghouse Health Systems, "Family Planning Program Effectiveness Study," 29 September 1978, in AID, *Family Planning Program Effectiveness: Report of a Workshop*, AID Program Evaluation Report No. 1 (Washington, D.C.: December 1979), p. 52. According to a former population official, corruption was also rife in the Filipino program. When the Filipino Family Planning Association's warehouse burned down, destroying its contraceptive supplies, members reportedly used donated money on luxurious new offices rather than on replacing the lost stocks. This same official comments: "Bribery, nepotism, tax evasion and outright theft are probably as prevalent in family planning programs as anywhere else in the aid world."

15. Warwick, *Bitter Pills*, pp. 154-55.

16. John C. Caldwell and Pat Caldwell, "Family Planning in India: A Worm's Eye View from a Rural Area in South India," *South Asia*, vol. 5, no. 1 (June 1982).

17. *World Development Report 1984*, p. 176.

18. Quoted in Warwick, *Bitter Pills*, p. 139.

19. Ibid., p. 167.

20. According to the *World Development Report 1984*, p. 135, follow-up surveys of women who have accepted contraception find that discontinuation is largely due to medical side effects. One survey in the Philippines found this reason cited by 66 percent of women who stopped taking the pill and 43 percent who discontinued the IUD.

21. Personal interview, February 1984.

22. This description of the classic incentive model is from Marika Vicziany's excellent critique of the Indian family planning program, "Coercion in a Soft State: The Family Planning Program of India, Part I: The Myth of Voluntarism," *Pacific Affairs*, Fall 1982, p. 393.

23. Ibid.

24. Fred T. Sai and K. Newman, "Ethical Approaches to Family Planning in Africa," Working Paper (Washington, D.C.: World Bank Population and Human Resources Division, Dec. 1989), p. 11.

25. Judith Jacobsen, *Promoting Population Stabilization: Incentives for Small Families*, Worldwide Paper 54 (Washington, D.C.: Worldwatch Institute, June 1983), p. 12.

26. Personal interview with Alex Marshall, UNFPA, February 1984.

27. Dr. Zafrullah Chowdhury, "Cash Incentives Degrade Both Parties," *People* (IPPF), vol. 9, no. 4 (1982).

28. Henry David, "Mechai's Way," *People* (IPPF), vol. 9, no. 4 (1982).

29. Indonesia: World Bank project from Jacobsen, *Promoting Population Stabilization*, p. 20; AID quote from AID Office of Population and Health, *Indonesia: Family Planning Program*, Orientation Booklet (Jakarta: June 1984), p. 11; Thailand from David, "Mechai's Way."

30. Jacobson, *Promoting Population Stabilization*, p. 20.

31. John A. Ross and Stephen L. Isaacs, "Costs, Payments, and Incentives in Family Planning Programs: A Review for Developing Countries," *Studies in Family Planning,* vol. 19, no. 5, (Sept.-Oct. 1988).

32. See ibid. and Jacobsen, *Promoting Population Stabilization.*

33. Quoted in Chee Heng Leng and Chan Chee Khoon, *Designer Genes: I.Q., Ideology and Biology* (Selangor, Malaysia: INSAN, Institute for Social Analysis, 1984), p. 7. This booklet presents an excellent critique of eugenics.

34. See ibid.; Nicholas Cumming-Bruce, "Lee's Brighter Babies Plan Angers Wives," *Guardian,* 22 February 1984; Nuray Fincancioglu, "Singapore's Controversial Incentives," *People* (IPPF), vol. 11, no. 3 (1984); and C. K. Chan, "Eugenics on the Rise: A Report from Singapore," *International Journal of Health Services,* vol. 15, no. 4 (1985).

35. Kimberly J. McLarin, "Trenton Welfare Change Being Felt," *New York Times,* 5 December 1993.

36. Kingsley Davis, "Population Control Cannot Be Painless," *People* (IPPF), vol. 9, no. 4 (1982).

37. UNFPA, Population Council and IPPF, *Family Planning in the 1980s: Challenges and Opportunities,* prepared for Report of the International Conference on Family Planning in the 1980s, Jakarta, Indonesia, 26-30 April 1981 (U.S.: 1981, pp. 97-98.)

5. THE INDONESIAN "SUCCESS" AND THE KENYAN "FAILURE"

1. Figures from World Bank, *Staff Appraisal Report: Indonesia, Fifth Population Project* (Washington, D.C.: Population and Human Resources Division, Asia Country Department V, 8 February 1991), and UNDP, United Nations Population Fund: Proposed Programmes and Projects, Recommendation by the Executive Director, *Assistance to the Government of Indonesia, Support for a Comprehensive Population Programme,* DP/FPA/CP/69 (New York: UNDP, 5 March 1990).

For background see Geoffrey McNicoll and Masri Singarimbun, *Fertility Decline in Indonesia: I. Background and Proximate Determinants,* Center for Policy Studies Working Papers, No. 92 (New York: The Population Council, November 1982). Also see T. H. Hull, "Fertility Decline in Indonesia: A Review of Recent Evidence," *Bulletin of Indonesian Economic Studies,* vol. 16, no. 2 (1980), and by the same author, "Indonesian Population Growth 1971-1980," *Bulletin of Indonesian Economic Studies,* vol. 17, no. 1 (1981). On reliability of Indonesian statistics, see Peter Kim Streatfield, *The Reliability of the Contraceptive Prevalence Statistics of the Indonesian Family Planning Program,* Research Note No. 23, International Population Dynamics Program (Canberra: The Australian National University, 1 August 1984). Thanks to Dr. Peter Hagul of the Gadjah Mada University Population Studies Center for making this and other publications available to me.

2. *AID's Role in Indonesian Family Planning: A Case Study with General Lessons for Foreign Assistance,* AID Program Evaluation Report No. 2 (Washington, D.C.: December 1979), p. 1.

3. McNicoll and Singarimbun, *Fertility Decline in Indonesia: II. Analysis and Interpretation,* Center for Policy Studies Working Papers No. 93 (New York: Population Council, December 1982).

4. For the role of the Ford Foundation and other U.S. institutions, see David Ransom, "Ford Country: Building an Elite for Indonesia," in Steve Weissman, ed., *The Trojan Horse: A Radical Look at Foreign Aid* (San Francisco: Ramparts Press, 1974). On influence of Western-trained technocrats, see *AID's Role in Indonesian Family Planning,* pp. 33-34.

5. See *Family Planning in the 1980s,* p. 34.

6. Jay S. Parsons, "What Makes the Indonesian Family Planning Program Tick?" *Populi,* vol. 11, no. 3 (1984). See this article for a history of the program.

7. *AID's Role in Indonesian Family Planning,* p. 44.

8. UNDP, *United Nations Population Fund,* p. 4.

9. Republic of Indonesia, *Saving Life and Making It Better: The Evolution of the Indonesian Family Planning Program,* 1989, p. 20.

10. Adrina, "Family Planning Programme in Indonesia and Its Impact on Women," paper delivered at Hearing on Multilateral Population Assistance, Failures and Successes in Population Policies and Programmes, Oslo, Norway, 25 May 1994.

11. On use of traditional methods, see McNicoll and Singarimbun, *Fertility Decline in Indonesia: I*; and Jon E. Rohde, "Mother Milk and the Indonesian Economy: A Major National Resource," *Journal of Tropical Pediatrics,* vol. 28 (August 1982).

12. KB, "Antara Fakta dan Hura-Hura," *Tempo,* 14 July 1984, parts of which are translated in "Compulsion Being Used in Indonesia's Family Planning Program," *TAPOL Bulletin,* No. 64 (July 1984).

13. McNicoll and Singarimbun, *Fertility Decline in Indonesia*: II, p. 9; and personal communication with health consultant.

14. Terence H. Hull and Valerie J. Hull, *Health Care and Birth Control in Indonesia: Links through Time,* Research Note No. 53, International Population Dynamics Program (Canberra: The Australian National University, 20 March 1986), p. 5. This article sheds an interesting historical light on the program, and has suggestions on how it could be reformed. Also see Ines Smyth, "The Indonesian Family Planning Programme: A Success Story for Women?" *Development and Change,* Vol. 22, no.4 (1991).

15. Diana Smith, "Indonesia Sets New Targets," *People* (IPPF), vol. 10, no. 4 (1983). For an eye-witness account of a safari, see Jill Tweedie's account in Debbie Taylor, ed., *Women: A World Report* (London: Methuen, 1985.)

16. World Bank, *Staff Appraisal Report,* p. 8.

17. Sheila J. Ward et al., *Service Delivery Systems and Quality of Care in the Implementation of Norplant in Indonesia* (New York: Population Council, February 1990), pp. 50-51. For an interesting case study of Norplant in an Indonesian community, see Jannemieke Hanhart, "Women's Views on Norplant: A Study from Lombok, Indonesia," in *Norplant: Under Her Skin* (Amsterdam: Women's Health Action Foundation and WEMOS, 1993).

18. Ward, *Service Delivery Systems,* p. 45.

19. Ibid.; also see World Bank, *Staff Appraisal Report,* for targeting of these areas.

20. *AID's Role in Indonesian Family Planning,* pp. 33-34.

21. See, for example, Parsons, "What Makes the Indonesian Family Planning Program Tick?"

22. *AID's Role in Indonesian Family Planning,* p. 47.

23. See *Tempo,* 14 July 1984; and *TAPOL Bulletin,* No. 64 (July 1984).

24. Ibid.

25. Terence Hull, "Reports of Coercion in the Indonesian Vasectomy Program: A Report to AIDAB," The Australian National University, Department of Political and Social Change, 21 February 1991, pp. 8, 11.

26. Warda Hafidz, Adrina Taslim, and Sita Aripurnami, "Family Planning Programme in Indonesia: A Plight for Policy Reorientation," presented at the INGI Conference, Washington, D.C., 29 April-2 May 1991.

27. Hanhart, "Women's Views on Norplant."

28. Parsons, "What Makes the Indonesian Family Planning Program Tick?"

29. Ibid.

30. Ibid.

31. Hull and Hull, *Health Care and Birth Control in Indonesia,* p. 10.

32. UNDP, *United Nations Population Fund,* pp. 8-9.

33. Adrina, "Family Planning Programme in Indonesia."

34. Population Education in Asia and the Pacific, "New Project Proposed to Strengthen Youth Participation in Family Planning Education," *Newsletter and Forum,* no. 32 (1990), p. 18.

35. For this view, see Parsons, "What Makes the Indonesian Family Planning Program Tick?"

36. AID, *AID's Role in Indonesian Family Planning,* p. 65.

37. See *Human Development Report 1993,* Table 4.

38. BKBBN, *Basic Information on Population,* p. 68.

39. Letter from Dr. Henry Mosley, 13 August 1984, quoted with his permission.

40. Adrina, "Family Planning Programme in Indonesia."

41. World Bank, *Staff Appraisal Report,* p. 14.

42. World Bank, *Population and the World Bank: Implications from Eight Case Studies* (Washington, D.C.: Operations Evaluation Department, 1991), pp. 29, 31.

43. See World Bank, *Staff Appraisal Report,* and Adrina, "Family Planning Programme in Indonesia."

44. World Bank, *Staff Appraisal Report.*

45. See Parsons, "What Makes the Indonesian Family Planning Program Tick?," for a description of a typical field visit, and the role foreigners play in legitimizing the program.

46. Hafidz et al., "Family Planning Programme in Indonesia," p. 13.

47. Wisner, *Power and Need in Africa,* p. 170. Wisner offers a detailed critique of the Kenyan development model.

48. Bertil Egerö and Edward Mburugu, "Kenya: Reproductive Change Under Strain," in B. Egerö and Mikael Hammarskjöld, *Understanding Reproductive Change: Kenya, Tamil Nadu, Punjab, Costa Rica* (Lund, Sweden: Lund University Press, 1994).

49. Quoted in Sujaya Mishra, "Poignant Problems," *People* (IPPF), vol. 10, no. 4 (1983). Also see Faruquee and Gulhati, *Rapid Population Growth in Sub-Saharan Africa,* on position of women.

50. See Gill Shepherd, *Responding to the Contraceptive Needs of Rural People* (Oxford: OXFAM, 1984). Lack of access to contraception is indicated by the prevalence of illegal abortion. See "Abortion in Kenya Today," *Life and Leisure* (Nairobi), 22 March 1985.

51. Quoted in Warwick, *Bitter Pills,* p. 77. For history of Kenyan program, see Warwick; and Lars Bondestam, "The Foreign Control of the Kenyan Population," in Bondestam and Bergström, *Poverty and Population Control.*

52. World Bank, *Kenya, Population and Development,* A World Bank Country Study (Washington: 1980), p. 174.

53. See Wisner, *Power and Need in Africa,* Chapter 2.

54. World Bank, *Kenya, Population and Development,* p. 176.

55. See ibid.

56. "African men are such animals. When he wants to he does," *People,* vol. 10, no. 4 (1983).

57. *World Development Report 1984,* p. 139.

58. Letter to author, dated 5 October 1983.

59. Margrethe Silberschmidt, *Survey on Research Concerning Users' Perspectives on Contraceptive Services, with Emphasis on Sub-Saharan Africa* (Copenhagen: Center for Alternative Social Analysis, August 1993).

60. Ibid., p. 7.

61. World Bank, *Population and the World Bank: Implications from Eight Case Studies,* p. 54.

62. Ibid., p.52.

63. Egerö and Mburugu, "Kenya."

64. World Bank, *Population and the World Bank,* p. 52.

65. Egerö and Mburugu, "Kenya."

66. Ibid., p. 54.

6. BIRTH OF AN IDEOLOGY

1. See Vivien Walsh, "Contraception: The Growth of a Technology," in the Brighton Women and Science Group, *Alice Through the Microscope* (London: Virago Press, 1980); Peter Fryer, *The Birth Controllers* (London: Secker and Warburg, 1965); Norman E. Himes, *Medical History of Contraception* (New York: Gamut Press, 1963); and Clive Wood and Beryl Suitters, *The Fight for Acceptance, A History of Contraception* (Aylesbury, U.K.: Medical and Technical Publishing Co. Ltd., 1970).

2. See Linda Gordon, *Woman's Body, Woman's Right, A Social History of Birth Control in America* (London and New York: Penguin Books, 1977); and Bonnie Mass, *Population Target: The Political Economy of Population Control in Latin America* (Toronto: Women's Press, 1976).

3. See Wood and Suitters, *The Fight for Acceptance.*

4. Speech by Margaret Sanger at Hartford, Connecticut, 11 February 1923, quoted in Bonnie Mass, *Population Target*, p. 26.

5. Quoted in David Kennedy, *Birth Control in America: The Career of Margaret Sanger* (New Haven: Yale University Press, 1970), p. 94.

6. Linda Gordon, "Birth Control: An Historical Study," *Science for the People*, January-February 1977, p. 16.

7. Quoted in Mass, *Population Target*, p. 21.

8. First quote from Mass, *Population Target*, p. 29; second and third from Linda Gordon, "Birth Control and the Eugenists," *Science for the People*, March-April 1977, p. 11.

9. Quoted in Mass, *Population Target*, p. 29.

10. Quoted in Gordon, "Birth Control and the Eugenists," p. 14.

11. *The Eugenics Review*, April 1936, quoted in Mass, *Population Target*, p. 21.

12. Gordon, *Woman's Body, Woman's Right*, p. 396.

13. Ibid., p. 332.

14. Ibid., p. 326.

15. Quoted in ibid., p. 345.

16. See ibid., Chapter 12.

17. See *Report of the U.S. President's Materials Policy Commission*, quoted in William Barclay, Joseph Enright, and Reid T. Reynolds, "Population Control in the Third World," *NACLA Newsletter*, vol. 4, no. 8, p. 4.

18. See, for example, Steve Weissman, "Why the Population Bomb Is a Rockefeller Baby," *Ramparts*, May 1970, p. 44.

19. *Report of the Population Council, Inc., November 1952-December 1955*, pp. 5-6, quoted in Mass, *Population Target*, p. 37.

20. From John Enson Harr and Peter J. Johnson, *The Rockefeller Conscience* (New York: 1991), page reproduced in Susanne Heim and Ulrike Schaz, *Population Explosion: The Making of a Vision* (Hamburg: FINRRAGE and Frauenanstiftung, December 1993). This booklet has fascinating and horrifying documentation of the views of the early population control establishment.

21. T. O. Greissimer, *The Population Bomb* (New York: The Hugh Moore Fund, 1954), quoted in Mass, *Population Target*, p. 40.

22. Weissman, "Why the Population Bomb is a Rockefeller Baby," p. 44.

23. See Nicholas J. Demerath, *Birth Control and Foreign Policy, The Alternatives to Family Planning* (New York: Harper and Row, 1976), Chapter 2; and on cult of population control, Charles K. Wilber, "Population and Methodological Problems of Development Theory," in Wilber, ed., *The Political Economy of Development and Underdevelopment* (New York: Random House, 1979), pp. 55-56.

24. Paul Demeny, "Social Science and Population Policy," in *Demography in Development: Social Science or Policy Science?*, PROP Publication Series No. 3 (Lund, Sweden: Program on Population and Development in Poor Countries, 1992), p. 29. Demeny's piece is reprinted from *Population and Development Review*, vol. 14, no. 3 (September 1988).

25. Stephen Enke, "Birth Control for Economic Development," *Science*, vol. 164 (16 May 1969); and Stephen Enke and Richard G. Zind, "Effect of Fewer Births on Average Income," *Journal of Biosocial Science*, vol. 1, no. 1 (January 1969), p. 41. For critique of this approach see Amiya Kumar Bagchi, *The Political Economy of Underdevelopment* (Cambridge: Cambridge University Press, 1982), p. 209.

26. Quoted in Mass, *Population Target*, p. 152.

27. Quoted in Phyllis Tilson Piotrow, *World Population Crisis: The United States Response* (New York: Praeger Publishers, 1973), p. 37.

28. Ibid., p. 39.

29. *Report on the U.S. President's Committee to Study the U.S. Military Assistance Program*, vol. 1 (Washington, D.C.: August 1959), pp. 185-87, quoted in Mass, *Population Target*, p. 41.

30. U.S. Congress, House Committee on Agriculture, *The Food for Freedom Act of 1966*, 89th Congr., 2d sess., 1966 HR Rept. 1558, p. 4.

31. Quoted in Barclay, et al., "Population Control in the Third World," pp. 5-10.

32. Paul Wagman, "U.S. Goal: Sterilize Millions of Third World Women," *St. Louis Post-Dispatch*, 22 April 1977.

33. Quoted in Warwick, *Bitter Pills*, p. 49.

34. Ibid., p. 50.

35. Marshall Green, U.S. Department of State, "U.S. Responsibilities in World Population Issues," address to Commonwealth Club of California, San Francisco, 10 September 1976.

36. Quoted in Piotrow, *World Population Crisis*, p. 200.

37. Quoted in Mass, *Population Target*, p. 66.

38. Chinese and Indian statements quoted in William F. Ryan and Peter J. Henriot, "Message from Bucharest for Washington and Rome," *America*, 2 November 1974. See also by the same authors, "Opposing Views on Population," *Worldview*, February 1975.

39. Quoted in Ryan and Henriot, "Message from Bucharest," p. 248.

40. U.N. Department of Economic and Social Affairs, *The Population Debate: Dimensions and Perspectives*, vol. 1, Papers of the World Population Conference, Bucharest, 1974 (New York: 1975).

41. For a discussion of this and other related human rights matters, see Katarina Tomasevski, *Human Rights in Population Policies* (Lund, Sweden: Swedish International Development Authority, 1994).

42. Elizabeth Soto, "Why Washington Cares," *The Progressive*, September 1990, p. 28.

43. Information Project for Africa, *Ambassadors of Colonialism: The International Development Trap*, Working Paper No. 4, IPFA Foreign Policy Series (Washington, D.C.: IPFA, 1993), pp. 26-27.

44. See Wisner, *Power and Need in Africa*, for an analysis of how the basic needs strategy was weakened and a critique of the cost-effective, limited intervention approach of agencies such as UNICEF.

7. THE POPULATION ESTABLISHMENT TODAY

1. Population, Health and Nutrition Department, *Population in Developing Countries: Implications for the World Bank*, Discussion Draft (Washington, D.C.: World Bank, June 1994), pp. 62-63; *Human Development Report 1993*, p. 7.

2. Shanti R. Conly and J. Joseph Speidel, *Global Population Assistance: A Report Card on the Major Donor Countries* (Washington, D.C.: Population Action International, 1993), p. 45.

3. *USAID Strategy Papers*, Draft, LPA Revision 10/5/93 (Washington, D.C.: USAID), 1993, p. 31.

4. Ibid., p. 7.

5. S. Greenhouse, "U.S. to Spend More on Birth Control," *New York Times*, 23 January 1994.

6. *USAID Strategy Papers*, p. 32.

7. Remarks of the Hon. J. Brian Atwood, USAID administrator, to the Central Council of the International Planned Parenthood Federation, Washington, D.C., 22 November 1993, p. 4.

8. Japanese Ministry of Foreign Affairs, "Japan's Global Issues Initiative (GII) on Population and AIDS," n.d.; also personal communications with activists.

9. *Population in Developing Countries: Implications for the World Bank*, pp. 80-82.

10. "Europeans Adopt Population Agenda," *Population* (UNFPA), vol. 18, no. 3, March 1992, p. 1. (Also personal communications.)

11. "MPs Call for Doubling of Aid Budget to Halt World Population Explosion," *Guardian* (London), 8 March 1994, and All Party Parliamentary Group on Population and Development, *NGO Review 1993* (London: House of Commons, March 1994).

12. Budget figures from UNFPA 1991 Report (New York: UNFPA, 1992), pp. 42, 49. Quote from UNFPA, *Women, Population and the Environment* (New York: UNFPA, 1992).

13. Personal interviews, February 1984.

14. *Population in Developing Countries: Implications for the World Bank.*

15. See Fred T. Sai and Lauren Chester, "The Role of the World Bank in Shaping Third World Population Policy," in Geoffrey Roberts, ed., *Population Policy: Contemporary Issues* (New York: Praeger, 1990); Operations Evaluation Department, *Population and the World Bank: Implications from Eight Case Studies* (Washington, D.C.: World Bank, 1992); and the Cairo Group, *Population Control and Coercive Lending: How the U.S. and the International Financial Institutions Impose Policies on Borrowers* (Washington, D.C.: 1993-1994.)

16. Peter Gibbon, "Population and Poverty in the Changing Ideology of the World Bank," in Mikael Hammarskjöld et al., eds., *Population and the Development Crisis in the South:* Proceedings from a conference in Bastad, April 17-18, 1991 (Lund, Sweden: Program on Population and Development in Poor Countries, University of Lund, 1991), p. 135.

17. Ibid., p. 143.

18. *Population in Developing Countries: Implications for the World Bank,* p. i. This document also admits that there is little evidence that population growth directly causes poverty or that reducing birth rates will bring about development; however, it stresses the negative environmental impact of population growth.

19. Ibid., pp. 54, 2.

20. Personal communication with Dr. Thomas Merrick, World Bank senior population adviser, March 1994.

21. *IPPF Annual Report 1993-94,* London.

22. *Population Council Annual Report 1991,* New York.

23. The Ford Foundation, *The Ford Foundation's Work in Population* (New York: 1985). On India, see Demerath, *Birth Control and Foreign Policy.*

24. Quote from Oscar Harkavy, "Foundation Strategy for Population Work," Discussion Paper, Session X, March 1968, p. 3, Ford Foundation Archives no. 009491, reproduced in Heim and Schaz, *Population Explosion: The Making of a Vision.*

25. *Population in Developing Countries: Implications for the World Bank,* p. 81.

26. James C. Knowles, "Tools for Population Policy Development," OP-TIONS for Population Policy Project, n.d., p. 15, cited in Information Project for Africa, *Ambassadors of Colonialism*. See Chapter 7 of this booklet for an extensive critique of OPTIONS, and Appendix 2 for OPTION reports on various countries.

27. Population Crisis Committee, "Private Organizations in the Population Field," *Population*, no. 16 (December 1985).

28. Population Crisis Committee, *Highlights of 1983 Activities*, Summary Report (Washington: 1983), p. 3.

29. The Global Committee of Parliamentarians on Population and Development, "Statement on Population Stabilization by World Leaders," *New York Times*, 20 October 1985.

30. Warwick, *Bitter Pills*, p. 16.

31. Robert S. McNamara, "Time Bomb or Myth: The Population Problem," *Foreign Affairs*, Summer 1984.

32. Ibid., p. 1127.

33. *World Development Report 1984*, pp. 156-61.

34. Ibid., p. 155.

35. Ibid., pp. 160-61.

36. Bernard Berelson and Jonathon Lieberson, "Government Efforts to Influence Fertility: The Ethical Issues," *Population and Development Review*, vol. 5, no. 4 (December 1979), p. 609.

37. Ibid., pp. 596, 603.

38. Personal interview, February 1984.

39. Jyoti Shankar Singh, "Ten Years On..." *Development Forum*, June 1984.

40. Amy Goodman and Krystyna von Henneberg, "Population Conference Ignored Key Issues," *Boston Globe*, 29 August 1984.

41. "U.S. Policy Statement for the International Conference on Population."

42. Personal communication with Ireen Dubel, who attended the conference as an observer.

BOX. MAKING POPULATION POLICY: SOME UNSALUTARY EXAMPLES

1. Sai and Chester, "The Role of the World Bank," pp. 183, 189. On OPTIONS, see Final Report, OPTIONS First Phase, Submitted to U.S. Agency for International Development, 15 May 1992, sections reproduced in Information Project for Africa (IPFA), *Ambassadors of Colonialism*, Appendix Two. Also see chapter on Senegal in World Bank, *Population and the World Bank: Implications from Eight Case Studies*.

2. Sai and Chester, "The Role of the World Bank," p. 184.

3. Cited and analyzed in Dixon-Mueller, *Population Policy and Women's Rights*, pp. 94-95. See also Mere N. Kisekka, ed., *Women's Health Issues in Nigeria* (Zaria: Tamaza Publishing Co., 1992).

4. Nik Ogbulie, "Family Planning Gulps N1.53b," *Guardian*, 25 October 1992.

5. "Nigeria Census: All Present and Accounted For?" *Populi*, vol. 1, no. 1 (1992), and James A. Miller, "Nigeria's Population Bomb Fizzles Out," *Wall Street Journal*, 12 May 1992.

Even in Botswana, which already had a well-established, effective family planning program within the Ministry of Health, the World Bank pressured the government to set up an independent population control unit to pursue demographic targets. Enter OPTIONS as well, to orchestrate a population constituency and identify "awareness raising activities". World Bank, *Botswana: Population Sector Review* (Washington: D.C.: 31 October 1989) and IPFA, *Ambassadors of Colonialism.*

6. World Bank, *Population and the World Bank: Implications from Eight Case Studies*, pp. 4, 61.

8. BUILDING A CONSENSUS FOR CAIRO AND BEYOND

1. On the UNFPA's strategy of building a consensus, see Nafis Sadik, "The Role of the United Nations – From Conflict to Consensus," in Roberts, ed., *Population Policy*. For a critique of consensus ideology, see Cecile Jackson, "Questioning Synergism: Win-Win with Women in Population and Environment Policies," *Journal of International Development*, vol. 5, no. 6 (Nov.-Dec. 1993).

2. U.S. Department of State, "The United States and the International Conference on Population and Development" (Washington, D.C.: June 1994), p. 2.

3. *Population in Developing Countries: Implications for the World Bank*, p. i.

4. There is a need for more research on the internationalization of the anti-abortion movement. Catholics for a Free Choice in Washington, D.C. monitors Catholic groups, but Christian fundamentalist networks have been less studied. On the United States, see Frederick Clarkson and Skipp Porteous, *Challenging the Religious Right: An Activist's Handbook* (New York: Ms. Foundation for Women, 1993.) On Human Life International, see Jodi L. Jacobson, *The Global Politics of Abortion*, Worldwatch Paper no. 97 (Washington, D.C.: July 1990).

5. Margrethe Silberschmidt, *Rethinking Men and Gender Relations: An investigation of men, their changing roles within the household, and the implications for gender relations in Kisii District, Kenya*, CDR Research Report no. 16 (Copenhagen: Center for Development Research, 1991), p. 6. This interesting study adds a new and needed dimension to gender studies.

6. *Population and the World Bank: Implications from Eight Case Studies,* p. 7.

7. UNFPA, *Women, Population and the Environment* (New York, 1992), p. 11.

8. Judith Bruce, "Implementing the User Perspective," *Studies in Family Planning,* vol. 11, no. 1 (January 1980).

9. Anrudh Jain and Judith Bruce, "Quality: The Key to Success," *People,* vol. 16, no. 4, 1989.

10. Adrienne Germain, Sia Nowrojee and Hnin Hnin Pyne, "Setting a New Agenda: Sexual and Reproductive Health and Rights," in Sen at al, eds., *Population Policies Reconsidered.*

11. Anrudh Jain and Judith Bruce, "A Reproductive Health Approach to the Objectives and Assessment of Family Planning Programs," in Sen et al., eds., *Population Policies Reconsidered,* pp. 196-197.

12. *Population in Developing Countries: Implications for the World Bank,* pp. 57-61.

13. See Inter-Church Coalition, *Responding to the Health Crisis in Africa* (Toronto: 1993) for an excellent critique of the World Bank model, and Meredeth Turshen, "The Impact of Economic Reforms on Women's Health and Health Care in Sub-Saharan Africa," in N. Aslanbeigui et al., eds., *The Impact of Economic Reforms on Women* (London: Routledge, 1994).

14. World Bank, *World Development Report 1993.*

15. Meredeth Turshen, "The New World Bank Health Service Delivery Model," *Political Environments,* no. 1, Spring 1994, p. 16.

16. *Population in Developing Countries: Implications for the World Bank,* p. 56.

17. First document: Draft U.N. International Conference on Population and Development *Program of Action,* A/Conf. 171/PC/5, 24 January 1994, p. 72. Second: April 1994 Draft.

18. "USAID Offers Rs 800 Cr to UP," *Times of India,* 15 February 1992.

19. "USAID-Sponsored Population/Environment Activities," 1993.

20. See John McCormick, *Reclaiming Paradise: The Global Environmental Movement* (Bloomington: Indiana University Press, 1989), and Ramachandra Guha, "Radical American Environmentalism and Wildnerness Preservation: A Third World Critique," *Environmental Ethics,* vol. 2, no. 1 (1989).

21. National Audubon Society and Population Crisis Committee, *Why Population Matters: A Handbook for the Environmental Activist* (Washington, D.C.: 1991).

22. Larry Lohmann, "Whose Common Future?" *The Ecologist,* vol. 20, no. 3 (1990). *The Ecologist* is an important source of alternative analysis of global environmental issues and politics.

23. See Brad Erickson, *Call to Action: Handbook for Ecology, Peace and Justice* (San Francisco: Sierra Club Books, 1990); Tom Goodkind et al., eds., Joint Issue on Environmental Activism: Reclaiming the Landscape,

Reshaping a Movement, *Crossroads,* no. 20 and *Forward Motion,* vol. 2, no. 2; Mark Dowie, "American Environmentalism: A Movement Courting Irrelevance," *World Policy Journal,* Winter 1991/92; and Joni Seager, *Earth Follies,* for a feminist critique.

24. National Audubon Society and PCC, *Why Population Matters,* and Laurie Ann Mazur, *Population and the Environment: A Grantmaker's Guide* (New York: Environmental Grantmakers Association, 1992).

25. Cited in Lappé and Collins, *Food First: Beyond the Myth of Scarcity* (New York: Ballantine Books, 1978), p. 6.

26. Maurice King, "Health is a Sustainable State, *Lancet,* vol. 336, no. 8716, pp. 666-667. Editorial is in this same issue.

27. Miss Ann Thropy, Letter to Earth First!, *The Radical Environmental Journal,* 1 May 1987.

28. Guha, "Radical American Environmentalism."

29. Michael Novick, "Was Hitler an Ecologist?," Background Research Report no. 6 (Burbank, CA.: People Against Racist Terror, 1994), and by same author "Sin Fronteras: Anti-Immigrant Hysteria and the Rise of the Racist Right" (PART: 1993).

30. Women's Watch: An Anti-Abortion Monitoring Project, c/o Loretta Ross, Center for Democratic Renewal, Atlanta, Georgia.

31. "Priority Statement on Population," ZPG and the Humane Society, 1991.

32. Mazur, *Population and the Environment,* p. 39.

33. Pat Baldi, "1990 IUCN General Assembly Embraces Population," *Population Program Activity Report* (Washington, D.C.: National Audubon Society, 1-2 February 1991).

34. Peter Adamson, "The Power of Planning Births," *People and the Planet,* vol. 1, no. 1, 1992, pp. 30-31.

35. Raghaven Chakravarthi, "UNCED Debates South Population vs. North Lifestyle as Main Cause of Crisis," *Third World Resurgence,* nos. 14/15, and Jessica Matthews, "Politically Correct Environmentalists," *Washington Post,* 12 April 1992.

36. Women's Environment and Development Organization, *Official Report of the World Women's Congress for a Healthy Planet,* 8-12 November 1991 (New York: 1992), p. 20.

37. Matthews, "Politically Correct Environmentalists."

38. For a copy of the treaty and a report on the Women's Tent proceedings, see Brazilian Women's Coalition, *Planeta Femea* (Rio de Janeiro, October 1993).

39. See Edward S. Herman and Noam Chomsky, *Manufacturing Consent: The Political Economy of the Mass Media* (New York: Pantheon, 1988).

40. See Stephen Greene, "Who's Driving the Environmental Movement?" *Chronicle of Philanthropy,* 25 January 1994. no. 35.

41. Pew Global Stewardship Initiative, *White Paper,* July 1993.

42. *Report of Findings from Focus Groups on Population, Consumption and the Environment,* conducted for the Pew Charitable Trusts Global Stewardship Initiative by R/S/M Mellman Lazarus Lake and Beldon & Russonello, July 1993, pp. 73-74.

43. *Global Stewardship,* vol. 1, no. 2, February 1994.

44. *Global Stewardship,* May/June 1994.

45. Carnegie Endowment for International Peace, National Commission, *Changing Our Ways: America and the New World* (Washington, D.C.: The Brookings Institution, 1992.) A useful bibliographical resource on population and security is Alex de Sherbinin, *Population Issues of Concern to the Foreign Policy Community* (Washington, D.C.: Population Reference Bureau, October 1993).

46. Thomas F. Homer-Dixon, Jeffrey H. Boutwell, and George W. Rathjens, "Environmental Change and Violent Conflict," *Scientific American,* February 1993, and "Sustainable Development Vital to New U.S. Foreign Policy," speech by Under Secretary of State for Global Affairs Timothy Wirth, National Press Club, Washington, D.C., July 12, 1994.

47. Robert Kaplan, "The Coming Anarchy," *Atlantic Monthly,* February 1994. Also see Nalini Visvanathan's critique of the article in *Political Environments,* no. 1, Spring 1994.

48. Remarks by the President to National Academy of Sciences, U.S. Department of State, 29 June 1994 (Washington, DC: White House, Office of the Press Secretary).

49. April 1994 Draft Program of Action, pp. 9, 44, 46, 82, 93, 103-4, and summary of the Cairo Conference and Program of Action in International Institute for Sustainable Development, *Earth Negotiations Bulletin,* vol. 6, no. 39, 14 September 1994.

50. See, for example, John Bongaarts, "Population Policy Options in the Developing World," *Science,* vol. 263, 11 February 1994.

BOX. THE HYDRA AT HOME

1. See Alexander Cockburn, "Welfare, Norplant and the Nazis," *The Nation,* 18 July 1994, and on teen pregnancy, Laura Briggs, "Teen Pregnancy and Welfare Reform: Don't Believe the Hype," *Reproductive Rights Network Newsletter,* Boston R2N2, Summer 1994.

2. Pen Loh, "Border-Patrol Ecology," *San Francisco Bay Guardian,* 1 December 1993.

3. Hannah Creighton, "The Sierra Club Immigration Policy Wars," *Race, Poverty and the Environment,* vol. 4, no. 2, Summer 1993.

4. Ruth Coniff, "The Right Calls the Shots," *The Progressive,* October 1993.

5. R. Estrada, "On the Ethics of Immigration," *CCN Clearinghouse Bulletin,* vol. 4, no. 2, February 1994. Also personal observation of these groups in action.

6. See, for example, Larry Rohter, "Revisiting Immigration and the Open-Door Policy," *New York Times,* September 19, 1993.

7. Ruth Hubbard and Elijah Wald, *Exploding the Gene Myth* (Boston: Beacon Press, 1993).

9. CHINA—"GOLD BABIES" AND DISAPPEARING GIRLS

1. Shanti R. Conly and Sharon L. Camp, *China's Family Planning Program: Challenging the Myths,* Country Studies Series No. 1 (Washington, D.C.: Population Crisis Committee, 1992). On recent decline see Peng Pei-yun, "Accomplishments of China's Family Planning Program: Statement by a Chinese Official," *Population and Development Review,* vol. 19, no. 2 (June 1993).

2. Murdoch, *The Poverty of Nations,* p. 80.

3. William Vogt, quoted in Lappé and Collins, *Food First,* p. 83.

4. See Leo A. Orleans, "China's Experience in Population Control: The Elusive Model," *World Development,* vol. 3, nos. 7 and 8 (July-August 1978).

5. See Kay Ann Johnson, *Women, the Family and Peasant Revolution in China* (Chicago: University of Chicago Press, 1989).

6. On the decline see "Population and Birth Planning in the People's Republic of China," *Population Reports,* Series J, no. 25 (January-February 1982), p. J597.

7. See ibid. for a description of the various stages of the early population program.

8. D. Gale Johnson, "Effects of Institutions and Policies on Rural Population Growth with Application to China," presented at International Conference on China's Rural Reform and Development in the 1990s, Beijing, 3-7 December 1993.

9. Patrick E. Taylor, "Nature and Economic Boom Devouring China's Farmland," *New York Times,* 27 March 1994.

10. Peiyun, "Accomplishments of China's Family Planning Program," p. 401. See Ashwani Saith, "China's New Population Policies," in Keith Griffin, ed., *Institutional Reform and Economic Development in the Chinese Countryside* (London: Macmillan, 1984), for a discussion of population growth and the economy.

11. Quote from WGBH Educational Foundation, "China's Only Child," *Nova,* no. 1103, 1984.

12. Susan Greenhalgh, "Controlling Births and Bodies in Village China," *American Ethnologist,* vol. 21, no. 1 (1994).

13. Conly and Camp, *China's Family Planning Program.*

14. WGBH Educational Foundation, "China's Only Child."

15. Cecilia Milwertz, "Control as Care—Interaction Between Urban Women and Birth Planning Workers," paper presented at "State and Society

in East Asia," Network Conference on Regionalism and Globalism in East Asia, Copenhagen, 12-15 May 1994.

16. Greenhalgh, "Controlling Births and Bodies," p. 13.

17. Ibid. and Nicholas D. Kristof, "China's Crackdown on Births: A Stunning, and Harsh, Success," *New York Times,* 25 April 1993. Also see Susan Greenhalgh and Jiali Li, "Engendering Reproductive Policy and Practice in Peasant China," paper presented at the Annual Meeting of the American Anthropological Association, Washington, D.C., 17-21 November 1993, for a regional example.

18. Sheryl WuDunn, "Births Punished by Fine, Beating, or Ruined Home," *New York Times,* 25 April 1993.

19. See Greenhalgh, "Controlling Births and Bodies"; and Conly and Camp, *China's Family Planning Program.*

20. Conly and Camp, *China's Family Planning Program,* p. 34.

21. Greenhalgh, "Controlling Births and Bodies," pp. 23, 20, 6.

22. Kay Johnson, "Chinese Orphanages: Saving China's Abandoned Girls," *The Australian Journal of Chinese Affairs,* no. 30, July 1993.

23. See Jonathon Mirsky, "The Infanticide Tragedy in China," *The Nation,* 2 July 1983. Also see E. Croll, "China's First-Born Nightmare Returns," *Guardian,* 28 October 1983.

24. Zeng Yi et al., "Causes and Implication of the Recent Increase in the Reported Sex Ratio at Birth in China," *Population and Development Review,* vol. 19, no. 2 (June 1993), and Kristof, "China's Crackdown on Births."

25. Johnson, "Chinese Orphanages," p. 65. Greenhalgh and Li, "Engendering Reproductive Policy," also found ratios to get worse with the crackdown of the late eighties.

26. Johnson, "Chinese Orphanages," p. 70.

27. Ibid., p. 84; and drawing on the analysis of Greenhalgh and Li, "Engendering Reproductive Policy."

28. The hard-line position is typified by Lester Brown of the Worldwatch Institute. See Hobart Rowen, "Overpopulation Means Famine and War," *Honolulu Advertiser,* 17 February 1985.

29. Conly and Camp, *China's Family Planning Program,* pp. 48, 19.

30. John Aird, *Slaughter of the Innocents: Coercive Birth Control in China* (Washington, D.C.: AEI Press, 1990), p. 11. Aird's book is a courageous attempt to break the silence on China.

31. See, as an example, Joan Kaufman, "Fertility and Choice for Women in China," WID Working Paper no. 11 (Cambridge, MA: Women and International Development, Joint Harvard/MIT Group, 1985).

32. Aird, *Slaughter of the Innocents,* p. 6.

33. P. E. Tyler, "China Weighs Using Sterilization and Abortions to Stop 'Abnormal' Births," *New York Times,* 21 December 1993.

34. Personal communication with Dr. Thomas Merrick.

35. Conly and Camp, *China's Family Planning Program.*

36. Conly and Camp discuss the role of social security. Also see D. Gale Johnson, "Effects of Institutions and Policies," for a mapping of alternatives.

37. Holzhausen quote from his letter, dated 18 January 1984, to Dr. Nafis Sadik, assistant executive director, UNFPA, New York, which was leaked to the press. It is reproduced in full in Betsy Hartmann and Hilary Standing, *Food, Saris and Sterilization: Population Control in Bangladesh* (London: Bangladesh International Action Group, 1985), pp. 37-39.

38. Sinding quotes from personal interview, February 1984.

10. SHAPING CONTRACEPTIVE TECHNOLOGY

1. Quoted in P. Vaughan, *The Pill on Trial* (London: Weidenfeld and Nicolson, 1970), in Walsh, "Contraception: The Growth of a Technology," p. 202.

2. Quoted in Barbara Seaman and Gideon Seaman, M.D., *Women and the Crisis in Sex Hormones* (New York: Rawson Associates Publishers, Inc., 1977), p. 62.

3. Frances Gulick, "The Indian Family Planning Program: The Need for New Contraceptives," staff memorandum, AID/India, April 1968, quoted in Piotrow, *World Population Crisis*, p. 174.

4. Linda E. Atkinson, Richard Lincoln, and Jacqueline D. Forrest, "Worldwide Trends in Funding for Contraceptive Research and Evaluation," *Family Planning Perspectives*, vol. 17, no. 5 (September-October 1985), Table 7, p. 204.

5. Drawn from Luigi Mastroianni, Jr., Peter J. Donaldson, and Thomas Kane, eds., *Developing New Contraceptives: Obstacles and Opportunities* (Washington, D.C.: National Academy Press, 1990), Table 5.1, pp. 72-74. This book gives background information on many of these institutions.

6. See ibid., p. 90; Office of Technology Assessment, *World Population and Fertility Planning Technologies, The Next 20 Years* (Washington, D.C.: U.S. Government Printing Office, 1982); and Forrest C. Greenslade and George F. Brown, "Contraception in the Population/Development Equation," background paper to the Presentation by George Zeidenstein, Population Council, New York, 1983.

7. See Constance Holden, "Contraceptive Research Lagging," *Science*, vol. 229, no. 4718 (13 September 1985); Matt Clark, "Contraceptives: On Hold," *Newsweek*, 5 May 1986; and Frank E. James, "With Most Contraceptive Tests on Hold, Couples Face Grim Birth Control Choices," *Wall Street Journal*, 17 April 1986.

8. No exact figures on size of the market are available. Estimates from Cary LaCheen, "Population Control and the Contraceptive Industry," in Kathleen McDonnell, ed., *Adverse Effects. Women and the Pharmaceutical Industry* (Penang, Malaysia: International Organization of Consumers Unions, 1986). On profitability of oral and injectable contraceptives see Marjorie Sun, "Depo-Provera Debate Revs up at FDA," *Science*, vol. 217, no.

4558 (30 July 1982), p. 429; and OTA, *World Population and Fertility Planning Technologies,* p. 116.

9. See Mastroianni et al., eds., *Developing New Contraceptives;* and OTA, *World Population and Fertility Planning Technologies,* for description of how public and private sectors interact. See LaCheen, "Population Control," for examples of how industry officials lobby for more population research.

10. LaCheen, "Population Control."

11. Informational brochure, SOMARC, The Futures Group (Washington, D.C.: n.d.), quoted in LaCheen, "Population Control," p. 114. LaCheen presents an excellent analysis of CSM projects.

12. AID Office of Population, *Users Guide to the Office of Population* (Washington, D.C.: AID, 1990), p. 33; and AID Office of Population, "Family Planning Services Delivery," n.d.

13. LaCheen, "Population Control," p. 116.

14. Ibid.

15. Ibid.

16. See Atkinson et al., "Worldwide Trends in Funding."

17. Personal communication, February 1984.

18. Domination of contraceptive field by men from Judy Norsigian, "Redirecting Contraceptive Research," *Science for the People,* January/February 1979. Quote from Bruce Stokes, *Men and Family Planning,* Worldwatch Paper no. 41 (Washington, D.C.: Worldwatch Institute, December 1980), p. 24.

19. Atkinson et al., "Worldwide Trends in Funding."

20. See Table "Percentage Distribution of Public Sector Expenditures for Development of New Contraceptive Methods, 1978," in OTA, *World Population and Fertility Planning Technologies,* p. 110.

21. Atkinson et al., "Worldwide Trends in Funding," Table 3, p. 198.

22. Ibid.; and OTA, *World Population and Fertility Planning Technologies,* p. 109.

23. Mastroianni et al., *Developing New Contraceptives,* p. 102, and Chapter 7.

24. Information in this paragraph and previous one from Seaman and Seaman, *Women and the Crisis in Sex Hormones,* pp. 73-84.

25. Mastroianni et al., *Developing New Contraceptives,* pp. 2-3, 12-14.

26. Legislative information obtained from Philip Lee.

27. John W. Egan, Harlow N. Higinbotham, and J. Fred Weston, *Economics of the Pharmaceutical Industry* (New York: Praeger Publishers, 1982), p. 105.

28. Atkinson et al., "Worldwide Trends in Funding."

29. See Vimal Balasubrahmanyan, "Drug Trials: Charade of 'Informed Consent,'" *Economic and Political Weekly* (Bombay), vol. 18, no. 25 (18 June 1983).

30. The study is described by Anibal Faundes et al., "Acceptability of the Contraceptive Vaginal Ring by Rural and Urban Population in Two Latin American Countries," *Contraception*, vol. 24, no. 4 (October 1981). On lack of knowledge concerning long-term effects, see "Injectables and Implants: Long-Acting Progestins–Promise and Prospects," *Population Reports*, Series K, no. 2, May 1983, p. K-42.

31. For examples see Barbara Ehrenreich, Mark Dowie, and Stephen Minkin, "The Charge: Gynocide, The Accused: The U.S. Government," *Mother Jones*, November 1979, p. 32; and OTA, Office of Technology Assessment, Drug Labeling in Developing Countries (Washington, D.C.: U.S. Government Printing Office, February 1993), p. 1.

32. T. K. Sundari Ravindran, "Women and the Politics of Population and Development in India," *Reproductive Health Matters,* no. 1, May 1983, p. 30.

33. *Population Reports*, Series J, no. 27 (May-June 1984), p. J658.

34. See Judith Bruce and S. Bruce Schearer, *Contraceptives and Common Sense: Conventional Methods Reconsidered* (New York: Population Council, 1979), p. 51. This earlier work is, sadly, out of print.

35. Judith Bruce and S. Bruce Schearer, "Contraceptives and Developing Countries: The Role of Barrier Methods," paper read at the International Symposium, Research on the Regulation of Human Fertility, Needs of Developing Countries, and Priorities for the Future, Stockholm, February 1983, p. 416. This paper, available from the Population Council, is an informative examination of the present neglect and future potential of barrier methods. Also see Helen B. Holmes, "Reproductive Technologies: The Birth of a Woman Centered Analysis," in H. B. Holmes, B. B. Haskins, and M. Gross, eds., *Birth Control and Controlling Birth: Women-Centered Perspectives* (Clifton, NJ: Humana Press, 1980).

36. Carl Djerassi, "Future Methods of Fertility Regulation in Developing Countries: How to Make the Impossible Possible by December 31, 1999," paper read at the International Symposium, Research on the Regulation of Human Fertility, Needs of Developing Countries, and Priorities for the Future, Stockholm, February, 1983.

11. HORMONAL CONTRACEPTIVES AND THE IUD

1. Quoted in Ehrenreich et al., "The Charge: Gynocide," p. 34.

2. Hale H. Cook, Clarence J. Gamble, and Adaline P. Satterthwaite, "Oral Contraception by Norethynodrel: A 3-Year Field Study," *American Journal of Obstetrics and Gynecology*, vol. 82, 1961, reprinted in Jay Katz, *Experimentation with Human Beings* (New York: Russell Sage Foundation, 1972), pp. 739, 741. See Katz's book for excellent material on the introduction of the pill and the controversies it generated.

3. Gregory Pincus, John Rock, and Celso R. Garcia, "Field Trials with Norethynodrel as an Oral Contraceptive," *Report of the Proceedings of the*

Sixth International Conference on Planned Parenthood (London: IPPF, 1959), reprinted in Katz, *Experimentation with Human Beings*, p. 745.

4. Information on Searle and quote from Seaman and Seaman, *Women and the Crisis in Sex Hormones*, pp. 66-69.

5. FDA Advisory Committee on Obstetrics and Gynecology, *Second Report on the Oral Contraceptives* (Washington, D.C.: 1 August 1969), reprinted in Katz, *Experimentation with Human Beings*, pp. 761-65. Hellman quote from "Testimony of Dr. Louis M. Hellman," 22 January 1970, reprinted in Katz, p. 765.

6. Personal communication with Norma Swenson of the Boston Women's Health Book Collective. Also see Alice Wolfson "The Reselling of the Pill," *CARASA News*, vol. 7, no. 4 (July-August 1983). The pill in fact engendered vociferous debate among the medical profession on the individual woman's right to full disclosure of side effects. At issue was the basic power relationship between doctor and patient. Dr. Alan Guttmacher, former president of Planned Parenthood, expressed the view of many of his colleagues:

> Unfortunately, the physician has to make the decisions for patients... Now, I certainly feel the more we can instruct the American physician about the intricacies of the birth control pill, the wiser the effort. My feeling is that when you attempt to instruct the American womanhood in this, which is a pure medical matter which I am afraid she has not the background to understand, you are creating in her simply a panic reaction without much intellectual background... I think that the dispenser of the therapy is the person who must be educated and not the recipient.

Quotation from "Testimony of Dr. Alan F. Guttmacher," 25 February 1970, reprinted in Katz, *Experimentation with Human Beings,* pp. 774-775.

7. See "Oral Contraceptives in the 1980s," *Population Reports*, Series A, no. 6 (May-June 1982).

8. See "Lower-Dose Pills," *Population Reports*, Series A, no. 7 (November 1988).

9. See, for example, AID, *Indonesia—Oral Contraceptives*, project paper (Washington, D.C.: 13 March 1978), for the demographic aims underlying pill promotion. The possibility of side effects is minimized to such an extent in this document that appended in the back is a telegram from headquarters in Washington asking what provisions exist for treatment of pill acceptors who suffer side effects. In virtually every discussion of the pill by population control agencies, the maternal mortality argument is used as the main defense against those who urge greater caution in its distribution.

10. Westinghouse Health Systems, "Family Planning Program Effectiveness Study," in AID, *Family Planning Program Effectiveness: Report of a Workshop*, AID Program Evaluation Report no. 1 (Washington, D.C.: December 1979), p. 27.

11. Stephen F. Minkin, "Abroad, the U.S. Pushes Contraceptives like Coca-Cola," *Los Angeles Times*, 23 September 1979.

12. Westinghouse Health Systems, "Family Planning Program," p. 40. Sinding quote from personal interview.

13. Marianne C. Burkhart, "Issues in Community-Based Distribution of Contraceptives," *Pathpapers,* no. 8 (Boston: September 1981), p. 30.

14. *Population Reports*, Series J, no. 27, p. J658.

15. See LaCheen, "Population Control."

16. "Contraceptive Social Marketing: Lessons from Experience," *Population Reports,* Series J, no. 30 (July-August 1985), p. J781.

17. Quoted in S. Minkin, "Bangladesh: where there's a Pill there's a way," *New Internationalist*, No. 79 (September 1979).

18. J. Davies, S. N. Mitra, and W. P. Schellstede, "Oral Contraception in Bangladesh: Social Marketing and the Importance of Husbands," *Studies in Family Planning,* vol. 18, no. 3 (May-June 1987), p. 165.

19. Manuel Ylanan and Cecilia C. Verzoza, *Commercial Retail Sales of Contraceptives*, PIACT Paper no. 6, Program for the Introduction and Adaptation of Contraceptive Technology (Seattle: n.d.), p. 12, cited in LaCheen, "Population Control," p. 118.

20. *Population Reports,* Series J, no. 30, p. J794.

21. Stated by Dr. Stephen Sinding in personal interview.

22. Rheumatic heart disease from *Population Reports*, Series A, no. 6. At least one study has suggested that female circulatory mortality rates are actually higher in Third World countries such as the Philippines, Mexico, Venezuela, and Chile than in the United States. See Dexter Tiranti, "The Small Miracle," *New Internationalist*, No. 79 (September 1979).

23. See *Population Reports*, Series A, No. 6.

24. See "Breast-feeding and Fertility Regulation: Current Knowledge and Program Policy Implications," *Bulletin of the World Health Organization*, vol. 63, no. 1 (1983).

25. *Population Reports,* Series A, no. 7, p. 16.

26. *Population Reports*, Series A, No. 6.

27. Minkin, "Abroad, the U.S. Pushes Contraceptives." One AID-funded evaluation of a household distribution scheme in Bangladesh blamed high dropout rates on "a variety of side effects. The mass distribution strategy unfortunately contributed to this problem. The field staff was given only limited training and even less information was transmitted to the recipients." M. Rahman et al., "Contraception Distribution in Bangladesh: some lessons learned," *Studies in Family Planning*, vol. 2, no. 6 (June 1980), cited in Keysers, *Does Family Planning Liberate Women?*, p. 252.

28. See Minkin, "Abroad, the U.S. Pushes Contraceptives"; and Maggie Jones, "The Biggest Contraceptive in the World."

29. *Population Reports,* Series A, no. 7, p. 16.

30. S. Bhatia, S. Becker, and Y. J. Kim, "The Effect on Fecundity of Pill Acceptance During Postpartum Amenhorrhea in Rural Bangladesh," *Studies in Family Planning*, vol. 13, no. 6/7 (June-July 1982).

31. *Population Reports*, Series A, No. 6. Also see Wolfson, "The Reselling of the Pill."

32. "Oral Contraceptives and Cancer," FDA Drug Bulletin, 1984. For more detail on the cancer debate also see *Population Reports*, Series A, No. 7.

33. WHO, *Steroid Contraception and the Risk of Neoplasia*, WHO Technical Report Series No. 619 (Geneva: WHO Scientific Group, 1978).

34. *Population Reports*, Series A, no. 7.

35. See Ehrenreich et al., "The Charge: Gynocide."

36. Pomeroy quote from personal interview, February 1984. "Imperialist arrogance" from discussion with Norma Swenson of the Boston Women's Health Book Collective, who has heard this phrase used by defenders of the pill. (It has been applied to myself as well.)

37. See Wolfson, "The Reselling of the Pill." Also see *Population Reports*, Series A, No. 6. This issue of *Population Reports* begins with the two subtitles, "Beneficial Effects Noted," and "Risks Limited." See p. A-11 for AID statement to an FDA advisory committee.

38. Letter from James Shelton, chief, Research Division, AID Office of Population, and Cynthia Calla, medical officer, Family Planning Services Division, to Carlos Huezo, medical director, IPPF, 21 August 1991.

39. D. F. Hawkins and M. G. Elder, *Human Fertility Control: Theory and Practice* (London: Butterworths, 1979), p. 109.

40. One percent figure from Mahmoud F. Fathalla, "Fertility Control Technology: A Women-Centered Approach to Research," in Gita Sen et al., eds., *Population Policies Reconsidered: Health, Empowerment and Rights* (Cambridge: Harvard University Press, 1994), p. 226. On Kenya, see Egerö and Mburugu, "Kenya: Reproductive Change Under Strain," p. 54.

41. See "Long-Acting Progestins—Promise and Prospects," *Population Reports*, Series K, No. 2 (May 1983).

42. *Population Reports*, Series K, No. 2.

43. See Ana Blanco, *Norethisterone Oenanthate: The Other Injectable Contraceptive*, briefing paper (London: War on Want and the International Contraception, Abortion and Sterilization Campaign, February 1984). Also see Center for Education and Documentation, *Injectables: Immaculate Contraception?* Counterfact No. 3 (Bombay: March 1983). On recent injectables: Marge Berer, "More and More Injectables," Women's Global Network on Reproductive Rights Newsletter (Amsterdam: January-March 1986).

44. Edwin B. McDaniel and Tieng Pardthaisong, "Acceptability of an Injectable Contraceptive in a Rural Population of Thailand," paper presented to the IPPF Southeast Asia and Oceania Congress (n.p.: n.d.). It is interesting to note that the disadvantage of having to remember to take the pill each day was not pointed out by the population community until inject-

ables came on the scene (personal communication with Norma Swenson of the Boston Women's Health Book Collective).

45. UBINIG, *Injectables: Whose Convenience and Safety?* (Dhaka: UBINIG, February 1988.)

46. *Population Reports*, Series K, No. 2.

47. Judith Bruce, "Users' Perspectives on Contraceptive Technology and Delivery Systems: Highlighting Some Feminist Issues," *Technology in Society*, vol. 9, 1987, p. 373.

48. Corea quoted in Quebec Public Interest and Research Group, *Depo-Provera, A Shot in the Dark* (Montreal: 1982), p. 7. For Corea's excellent critique of the drug and drug studies, see "Testimony of Gena Corea" submitted to FDA Public Board of Inquiry on Depo-Provera, January 1983, available from Corea. On Depo Provera as a male contraceptive, see S. Minkin, "Nine Thai Women Had Cancer—None of Them Took Depo-Provera: Therefore Depo-Provera is Safe. This is Science?" *Mother Jones*, November 1981.

49. *Population Reports*, Series K, No. 2, p. K27.

50. For information regarding recent studies on cancer and bone density, see "Is Depo Provera Safe?," *Ms.*, January/February 1993; and "Safety of Depo Provera," *Reproductive Health Matters*, no. 1, May 1993. This latter article dismisses cancer concerns, in my view prematurely. Upjohn quote from Upjohn patient information, reproduced in *Rolling Stone*, Fall 1993 issues.

51. *Population Reports*, Series K, No. 2, p. K30.

52. See Seaman and Seaman, *Women and the Crisis in Sex Hormones*. DES, incidentally, is still used as a contraceptive morning-after pill, despite the warnings of its manufacturer.

53. IPPF, *Statement on Injectable Contraception* (London: October 1982), p. 3.

54. "Facts about Injectable Contraceptives," *Bulletin of the WHO*, vol. 60, no. 2 (1982), p. 206.

55. Marjorie Sun, "Panel Says Depo-Provera Not Proved Safe," *Science*, vol. 226, no. 4677 (23 November 1984). Sybil Shainwald of the National Women's Health Network reported that the Indian Health Service routinely gave the drug.

56. Letter from Dr. Griff T. Ross to Dr. Judith Weisz, 23 July 1984, appended p. 181 of the *Report of the Public Board of Inquiry on Depo-Provera* (Washington, D.C.: 17 October 1984).

57. World Bank, *Population Growth and Policies in Sub-Saharan Africa* (Washington, D.C.: World Bank, 1986), pp. 5, 41-42, 54-55.

58. Personal correspondence, 29 December 1983. W. Silapa-archa also reports that in Bangkok young prostitutes were brought to a clinic where they received the injection without knowing what it was. Later many developed side effects.

59. *Population Reports*, Series K, No. 2, p. K22.

60. Personal communication with Boston Women's Health Book Collective.

61. See Minu Jain, "Hazardous Hormones," *Sunday* (India), 29 May-4 June 1994; "Activists Force DCI to Examine Contraceptive" (article sent by Kalpana Mehta, Saheli, from an Indian newspaper); and "Contraceptives' Lauch Rouses Ire of Women," *The Statesman,* 4 May 1994. On NET-EN, see Vimal Balasubrahmanyan, "Finger in the Dyke: The Fight to Keep Injectables out of India," in McDonnell, ed., *Adverse Effects.*

62. See Barbara Klugman, "Balancing Means and Ends—Population Policy in South Africa," *Reproductive Health Matters,* no. 1, May 1993. Also on coercive use of Depo Provera: "Population Control," *Cultural Survival,* Fall 1981; "Crimes Against Women," *Africa,* no. 170 (October 1985); and Eleanor J. Bador, "Contraception and Control," *Guardian* (New York), Apartheid Supplement, Spring 1986. On Namibia, see Jenny Lindsay, "The Politics of Population Control in Namibia," in Meredeth Turshen, ed., *Women and Health in Africa* (Trenton, N.J.: Africa World Press), 1991.

63. "Depo-Provera: Control of Fertility—Two Feminist Views," *Spare Rib* (London), No. 116 (March 1982).

64. Personal correspondence, 9 February 1984.

65. Personal communication.

66. Population Council, *1983 Annual Report,* p. 4.

67. Greenslade and Brown, "Contraception in the Population/ Development Equation," p. 10.

68. See Anita Hardon, "Norplant: Conflicting Views on its Safety and Acceptability," in B. Mintzes, A. Hardon, and J. Hanhart, eds., *Norplant: Under Her Skin* (Netherlands: Women's Health Action Foundation and WEMOS, 1993). In the U.S. this important book is distributed by the Boston Women's Health Book Collective. See also Health Action International *Update,* vol. 3, no. 1 (November 1993)

69. Paola Marangoni et al., "Norplant Implants and the TCu 200 IUD: A Comparative Study in Ecuador," *Studies in Family Planning,* vol. 14, no. 6-7 (June-July 1983), p. 180.

70. Hardon, "Norplant."

71. Reservations expressed by Stephen L. Isaacs, professor of Clinical Health, Columbia University, in letter to author of study, Dr. Philip Darney, 20 November 1990. (Darney's study is entitled "Acceptance and Perceptions of NORPLANT among Users in San Francisco, USA," *Studies in Family Planning,* May/June 1990.)

72. Eeva Ollila, Kristiina Kajesalo, and Eline Hemminki, "Experience of Norplant by Finnish Family Planning Practitioners," in Mintzes et al., eds., *Norplant.*

73. On infection problems see various studies in *Studies in Family Planning,* vol. 14, no. 6-7 (June-July 1983). In the Ecuadorian study a "certain overconfidence" about the ease of the insertion procedures led to "carelessness" (p. 179).

74. Ward et al., "Service Delivery Systems," p. 69.

75. *Norplant: Guide to Effective Counseling* (New York: Population Council, June 1989), p. 22; and Norplant: One Method of Family Planning, n.d.

76. Irving Sivin et al., "Norplant: Reversible Implant Contraception," *Studies in Family Planning*, vol. 11, nos. 7-8 (July-August, 1980), on removal advice. Indonesian case from Firman Lubis et al., "One-Year Experience with Norplant Implants in Indonesia," *Studies in Family Planning*, vol. 14, nos. 6-7 (June-July 1983). There are also potential problems with screening. Because of the possible risk of birth defects, pregnant women should not be given Norplant. However, even in carefully controlled studies (see above issue of *Studies in Family Planning*) pregnant women have apparently been given the drug by mistake.

77. Giselle Garcia and Solange Dacach, "Norplant—Five Years Later [Brazil]," in Mintzes et al., eds., *Norplant.*

78. The Population Council, *Norplant Worldwide*, no. 4 (New York: April 1986), p. 2.

79. Unclassified State Department Telegram 417045/01, "Population: FDA Approval of Norplant," 11 December 1990.

80. The Population Council, *Norplant Worldwide.*

81. Greenslade and Brown, "Contraception in the Population/ Development Equation," p. 14. Greenslade and Brown suggest Norplant could be used in mobile clinics or contraceptive camps, hardly places where informed consent is likely to be respected.

82. See Sohier A. Morsy, "Bodies of Choice: Norplant Experimental Trials on Egyptian Women," in Mintzes et al., eds., *Norplant.* Bangladesh information from Nasreen Huq of Naripokkho and UBINIG, *Norplant: The Five Year Needle* (Dhaka: February 1988). Activist pressure led AID to recommend against further expansion of Norplant trials in Bangladesh in 1990.

83. Personal communications and information from Indian activists, including Daisy Dhanraj, Malini Karkal, and Kalpana Mehta. The campaign against Norplant has involved women's groups and health activists around the country.

84. Don Kimelman, "Poverty and Norplant: Can Contraception Reduce the Underclass?," *Philadelphia Inquirer,* 12 December 1990, p. A18.

85. See Julia R. Scott, "Norplant: Its Impact on Poor Women and Women of Color," National Black Women's Health Project, Washington, D.C., n.d.; Sally Jacobs, "Norplant Draws Concerns Over Risks, Coercion," *Boston Globe,* 21 December 1992; and K. Ravi Srinivas and K. Kanakamala, "Introducing Norplant: Politics of Coercion," *Economic and Political Weekly* (Bombay), 18 July 1992.

86. See Jacobs, "Norplant Draws Concerns"; and Native American Women's Health Education Resource Center, "Native American Women Uncover Norplant Abuses," *Ms.,* September/October 1993.

87. See Jacobs, "Norplant Draws Concerns."

88. Ibid.

89. Richard Cohen, "Racism Muddies River of Illegitimacy Debate," *Patriot Ledger,* 27-28 November 1993.

90. Sheldon Segal, "Letter to the Editor," *New York Times,* 6 January 1991.

91. Christopher Tietze and Sarah Lewitt, eds., *Intrauterine Contraceptive Devices: Proceedings of the First Conference on the IUCD,* April 30-May 1, 1962 (Amsterdam, London, New York: Excerpta Medica, 1962).

92. *Population Reports,* Series B, no. 4 (July 1982). 1989 figure from Fathalla, "Fertility Control Technology," Table 2, p. 226.

93. Quoted in Jeanie Kasindorf, "The Case Against IUD's: What Your Doctor Never Told You About Infection, Infertility and IUD's," *New West,* 5 May 1980. This is an excellent article for anyone interested in the history of the IUD and its effects.

94. See Jane E. Hutchings, Patti J. Benson, Gordon W. Perkin, and Richard M. Soderstrom, "The IUD After 20 Years: A Review," *Family Planning Perspectives,* vol. 17, no. 6 (November-December 1985). On postpartum use see, for example, "Breast-feeding and Fertility-Regulation," *Bulletin of the World Health Organization,* vol. 63, no. 1, for recommendations against postpartum IUD use. According to Norma Swenson of the Boston Women's Health Book Collective, nursing mothers run an even higher risk of imbedding and perforation, so that contraindication warnings are now being circulated to physicians.

95. On estimates of PID risks see, for example, Ronald T. Burkman, "Intrauterine Device Use and the Risk of Pelvic Inflammatory Disease," *American Journal of Obstetrics and Gynecology,* vol. 138, no. 861 (1980); *Population Reports,* Series L, no. 4 (July 1983); and the results of a study in the United States summarized in "New CDC Data Link Contraceptive Method, PID and Infertility," *Contraceptive Technology Update,* vol. 5, no. 11 (November 1984). This study found that users of IUDs had more history of PID than users of the pill. Jocelyn Knowles points out that often PID risk figures "are little better than guesses," helping to explain the variation.

96. For FDA caution, see Kasindorf, "The Case Against IUD's."

97. Quoted in ibid.

98. Ibid.

99. See Sybil Shainwald, "The History of the Dalkon Shield," in National Women's Health Network, *The Dalkon Shield* (Washington, D.C.: 1985), pp.1-12, for how data was ignored or manipulated. For attorney's testimony, see Barry Siegel, "The 'Yes' that Made Dalkon's Maker Ill," *Boston Globe,* 25 August 1985.

100. Quoted in Ehrenreich et al., "The Charge: Gynocide." Information on AID and the Dalkon Shield from this article.

101. Lord's statement reproduced in the National Women's Health Network, *The Dalkon Shield,* p. 15. Also see Sonja Steptoe, "Women Challenge Right of Robins to Drop Claims," *Wall Street Journal,* 14 February 1986.

102. See, for example, "In Court and 'Out of Control,'" *The Network News* (National Women's Health Network), January-February 1986. For the most recent information on the Dalkon Shield, see Karen Hicks, *Surviving the Dalkon Shield IUD: Women v. the Pharmaceutical Industry* (Vermont: Teachers College Press, 1993).

103. See Kaval Guhati, "Compulsory Sterilization: A New Dimension in India's Population Policy," *Draper World Population Fund Report* No. 3 (Washington, D.C.: Autumn-Winter 1976).

104. Quoted in S. P. Jain, *A Status Study on Population Research in India*, vol. 2 (New Delhi: Family Planning Foundation, 1975), cited in Vimal Balasubrahmanyan, "Women as Targets in India's Family Planning Policy," in Arditti et al., eds., *Test-Tube Women*, p. 154.

105. For examples of Indian abuse, see Vimal Balasubrahmanyan, "Towards a Women's Perspective on Family Planning," *Economic and Political Weekly*, vol. 21, no. 2 (11 January 1986). On Bangladesh see Betsy Hartmann and Hilary Standing, *The Poverty of Population Control: Family Planning and Health Policy in Bangladesh* (London: Bangladesh International Action Group, 1989), Chapter 4.

106. *Population Reports*, Series A, no. 6, p. A-211.

107. A. Kessler and C. C. Standley, "Fertility Regulating Methods," *WHO Chronicle*, vol. 31, no. 5.

108. Results of the study reported in Beverly Winikoff, "Women's Health: An Alternative Perspective for Choosing Interventions," *Studies in Family Planning*, vol. 19, no. 4 (July/August 1988), p. 209. On reproductive tract infections in general, see Ruth Dixon-Mueller and Judith Wasserheit, *The Culture of Silence: Reproductive Tract Infections Among Women in the Third World* (New York: International Women's Health Coalition, 1991); and Jodi L. Jacobson, *Women's Reproductive Health: The Silent Emergency*, Worldwatch Paper 102 (Washington, D.C.: Worldwatch Institute, 1991).

109. Quoted in Eric van Praag, "Mid-term Review of the Third World Bank Co-Financiers Population and Family Health Project, 1986-1991," *Bangladesh: Views of the Netherlands Delegation*, 12-30 March 1988, Amsterdam, 1988, p. 12.

110. See *Population Reports*, Series L, no. 4; and Bruce and Schearer, "Contraceptives and Developing Countries."

111. Hutchings et al., "The IUD After 20 Years: A Review," p. 252. Also see Daniel R. Mishell, Jr., "Current Status of Intrauterine Devices," *The New England Journal of Medicine*, vol. 312, no. 15 (11 April 1985).

BOX. TAKING THE PILL IS GOOD FOR YOUR RELIGION

1. AID, *AID's Role in Indonesian Family Planning: A Case Study with General Lessons for Foreign Assistance*, AID Program Evaluation Report No. 2 (Washington, D.C.: December 1979), pp. 71-72.

12. BANGLADESH—SURVIVAL OF THE RICHEST

This chapter has greatly benefitted from the work of Jane Hughes, with whom I co-authored articles on the Bangladesh sterilization program. Also thanks to Hilary Standing, with whom I worked closely on the issue and co-authored two campaigning documents, *Food, Saris and Sterilization: Population Control in Bangladesh* (London: Bangladesh International Action Group, September 1985), and *The Poverty of Population Control* (London: BIAG, 1989). Katni is a pseudonym.

1. See Farida Akhter, "Depopulating Bangladesh: A Brief History of External Intervention into the Reproductive Behavior of a Society," paper delivered to the Women's International Tribunal on Reproductive Rights, Amsterdam, July 1984.

2. World Bank, *Bangladesh: Staff Appraisal Report,* Third Population Project, p. 22; also Annex 3 of same document.

3. See World Bank, *Bangladesh: The Determinants of Reproductive Change* (Washington, D.C.: World Bank Population and Human Operations Division, 28 December 1992), pp. 56-64. Also see Betsy Hartmann and Jim Boyce, *A Quiet Violence: View from a Bangladesh Village* (London: Zed Books, San Francisco: Food First, 1983), for a description of the dynamics of poverty in a Bangladesh village. Adult literacy rate from *Human Development Report 1993.*

4. See Rehman Sobhan, *The Crisis of External Dependence: The Political Economy of Foreign Aid to Bangladesh* (London: Zed Press, 1983); Stefan de Vylder, *Agriculture in Chains: Bangladesh—A Case Study in Contradictions and Constraints* (London: Zed Press 1982); Francis Rolt and Tom Learmouth, *Underdeveloping Bangladesh* (London: War on Want, 1982); Lawrence Lifschultz, *Bangladesh: The Unfinished Revolution* (London: Zed Press, 1979), on the military; Hartmann and Boyce, *A Quiet Violence*; and North-South Institute, *Rural Poverty in Bangladesh: A Report to the Like-Minded Group* (Ottawa: 1985).

5. Donors' Community in Dhaka, *Position Paper on the Population Control and Family Planning Program in Bangladesh* (draft), (Dhaka: 1 March 1983).

6. Letter dated 30 June 1983.

7. Holzhausen letter, dated 18 January 1984, to Dr. Nafis Sadik, UNFPA, New York.

8. Ershad stated this priority in an interview with Robert Bradnock, "Upazilla Struggle," *Guardian,* 10 May 1985.

9. Information obtained from a field worker for a European voluntary agency.

10. See World Bank, *Bangladesh: Staff Appraisal Report,* Third Population Project, p. 22; also Annex 3 of same document.

11. Information on unofficial disincentives and motivation fees is from Farida Akhter, personal communication.

12. Eighty-five percent figure from World Bank, *Bangladesh: Staff Appraisal Report,* Third Population Project, p. 12. AID also supports the activities of the Bangladesh Association for Voluntary Sterilization, which performs 30 percent of all sterilizations in Bangladesh (ibid, p. 10). Thomas quote obtained by J. Hughes in Dhaka.

13. Information on clothing handed out after the operation obtained from voluntary agency field workers. On the use of the word "incentives," see, for example, letter from Frank Vogl of the World Bank's Information and Public Affairs Department in *The Nation,* 24 November 1984; and PIACT, *Preliminary Report on a Study of the Motivational and Referral Fee System Under the Population Control Program* (draft), (Dhaka: 24 October 1984), p. 1.

14. For example, in October 1983, after the incentive payments were increased, the number of sterilizations more than doubled from the September figure to 62,399, and rose again to 70,612 in November. In December, when the rice harvest began, they fell to 37,099. These figures were acquired by Jane Hughes from AID in Dhaka.

15. See UBINIG, *Preliminary Report of UBINIG's Study on Incentives and Disincentives System in the Population Control Program of Bangladesh* (Dhaka: February 1986); UBINIG, *Faces of Coercion: Population Control Program of Bangladesh* (Dhaka: September 1986); and Subash Chandra Saha and R. W. Timm, *A Survey of 950 Sterilized Persons in Bangladesh* (Dhaka: Commission for Justice and Peace of the Catholic Bishops Conference of Bangladesh, 1986).

16. Bangladesh Sterilization Surveillance Team, "First Four-Partite Review (September 1983).

17. Ibid.

18. Jane Hughes interview in Dhaka.

19. Saha and Timm, *A Survey of 950 Sterilized Persons.*

20. PIACT, *Preliminary Report.*

21. On the military campaign, see: "A Successful Human Rights Action Against Compulsory Sterilization," *Asia Link,* vol. 5, no. 1 (January 1984), published by Center for the Progress of Peoples. Thomas' quotes from Jane Hughes in Dhaka.

22. On food aid abuses: communications with field workers from European voluntary agencies: also UBINIG, *Preliminary Report.* The Catholic Commission for Justice and Peace found that thirteen out of their 950 respondents had also been offered food as an inducement.

23. *Bangladesh Observer,* 14 December 1984.

24. Letter from David A. Oot, chief of AID's Population, Health and Nutrition Division, Bureau for Asia, to author, dated 28 March 1985; letter from John D. North, director of the World Bank's Population, Health and Nutrition Department, to author, dated 18 April 1985; and Bangladesh Government, Ministry of Health and Population Control, "Office Memorandum:

Subject: Grant of Unapproved Inducements for Sterilization Acceptance," 25 March 1985.

25. SIDA, *Incentives and Disincentives in the Bangladesh Population and Family Health Project*, position and discussion paper (Stockholm-Dhaka: January 1985), p. 1. For more on the Population III controversy, see first edition of *Reproductive Rights and Wrongs;* and Hartmann and Standing, *The Poverty of Population Control.*

26. John Cleland and W. Parker Mauldin, *Study of Compensation Payments and Family Planning in Bangladesh* (Dhaka: World Bank and NIPORT, December 1987). For a more detailed critique of the report, see Hartmann and Standing, *The Poverty of Population Control.*

27. World Bank, *The Determinants of Reproductive Change*, p. 49.

28. Cleland and Mauldin, *Study of Compensation Payments*, p. 16.

29. Ibid., p. 16.

30. Ibid., p. 17.

31. Ibid., p. 102.

32. Personal communication.

33. World Bank, Project Completion Report, *Bangladesh: Third Population and Family Health Project* (South Asia Regional Office, Population and Human Resources Operations Division: 14 September 1993.)

34. World Bank, *Bangladesh: Staff Appraisal Report,* Fourth Population and Health Project (Washington, D.C.: Population and Human Resources Division, 20 May 1991), pp. 1-3.

35. World Bank, *Bangladesh: Staff Appraisal Report*, Third Population Project. For a longer discussion of health policy in Bangladesh, see Hartmann, "The Impact of Population Control Policies on Health Policy in Bangladesh," in Meredeth Turshen and Briavel Holcomb, eds., *Women's Lives and Public Policy* (Westport, CT.: Greenwood Press, 1993.)

36. See Akhter, "Depopulating Bangladesh," and Bangladesh Ministry of Health and Population Control, "Population Control Program in Bangladesh," a status paper prepared for the Bangladesh Aid Group Meeting held in Paris in April 1984 (draft), p. 15.

37. World Bank, *Staff Appraisal Report,* Fourth Population Project, pp. 4, 63.

38. Quoted in Farida Akhter, *On Population Control Policies and Practices in Bangladesh* (Dhaka: UBINIG, March 1984), p. 10.

39. Holzhausen letter to Dr. Nafis Sadik.

40. Both quoted in Loes Keysers, *Does Family Planning Liberate Women?,* Master of Development Studies Thesis (The Hague: Institute of Social Studies, 1982), pp. 216-218.

41. D. S. DeGraff et al., "Integrating Health Services into an MCH-FP Program in Matlab, Bangladesh: An Analytical Update," *Studies in Family Planning,* vol. 17, no. 5 (1986), pp. 228-34.

42. Findings of ICDDR,B study reported in James F. Phillips, Ruth Simmons, J. Chakraborty, and A. I. Chowdhury, "Integrating Health Services

into an MCH-FP Program: Lessons from Matlab, Bangladesh," *Studies in Family Planning*, vol. 15, no. 4 (July-August 1984).

43. M. A. Koenig et al., "Trends in Family Size Preference and Contraceptive Use in Matlab, Bangladesh," *Studies in Family Planning*, vol. 18, no. 3 (1987), p. 123.

44. John Bongaarts, "Does Family Planning Reduce Infant Mortality Rates?" *Population and Development Review*, vol. 13, no. 2 (1987), p. 331.

45. M. A. Koenig et al., "Maternal Mortality in Matlab, Bangladesh," *Studies in Family Planning*, vol. 19, no. 2 (1987).

46. Ibid., p. 79.

47. Beverly Winikoff and Maureen Sullivan, "Assessing the Role of Family Planning in Reducing Maternal Mortality," *Studies in Family Planning*, vol. 18, no. 3 (1987), pp. 128-43. Also see Beverly Winikoff, "Women's Health: An Alternative Perspective for Choosing Interventions," *Studies in Family Planning*, vol. 19, no. 4 (1988).

48. World Bank, *Staff Appraisal Report*, Fourth Population Project, pp. 11, 40, 64.

49. See World Bank, *Bangladesh: The Determinants of Reproductive Change*. Observation about women's employment from discussions with Bangladeshi health activists.

13. STERILIZATION AND ABORTION

1. First quote from John P. Robin, "Comment on Agenda Paper for Session II, Population, Nairobi Meeting," Ford Foundation Archives, Nairobi Meeting 6.-8.6.1968, reproduced in Heim and Schaz, *Population Explosion: The Making of a Vision*, p. 73. Second quote from Henry Kamm, "Indian State Is Leader in Forced Sterilization," *New York Times*, 13 August 1976. Dr. Pai is still active in international sterilization circles.

2. See Fathalla, "Fertility Control Technology," p. 226, for percentages; and "Voluntary Female Sterilization: Number One and Growing," *Population Reports*, Series C, no. 10, November 1990; and "Vasectomy: New Opportunities," *Population Reports*, Series D, no. 5, March 1992, for latest figures.

3. Mortality rate from Population Reports, Series C, no. 10. "Band-Aid surgery" from Petchesky, "'Reproductive Choice' in the Contemporary United States." Sterilization may have a long-term effect on menstruation, leading to heavier periods in some women, though the evidence is not conclusive one way or the other. See, for example, Coralie Sunanda Ray, "The Long-Term Menstrual Side Effects Associated with Tubal Sterilization, A Literature Review and Case-Control Study with Special Reference to Women in South Asia," unpublished dissertation, London School of Hygiene and Tropical Medicine, September 1983, and "Menstrual Function Following Tubal Sterilization," *AVS Medical Bulletin*, vol. 2, no. 1 (February 1981).

4. "Vasectomy–Safe and Simple," *Population Reports*, Series D, no. 4 (November-December 1983).

5. Ibid. Also see special issue on vasectomy, *Studies in Family Planning*, vol. 14, no. 3 (March 1983).

6. George Zeidenstein, former president of the Population Council, expressed this view in a letter to the author. Also see Alaka M. Basu, "Family Planning and the Emergency: An Unanticipated Consequence," *Economic and Political Weekly*, vol. 20, no. 10 (9 March 1985).

7. Ravenholt quoted in Paul Wagman, "U.S. Goal: Sterilize Millions of World's Women," *St. Louis Post-Dispatch*, 22 April 1977.

8. Ad Hoc Committee to End the Sterilization Program, "Documentation of the Ejection of the PIEGO Program from Washington University Medical School," n.d. Also personal communications with those involved.

9. Personal interview with Terrence Jezowski, February 1984; and *Quality of Life, Quality of Service*, Association for Voluntary Sterilization *1982 Annual Report* (New York: 1982). I would like to thank Mr. Jezowski for making many materials available to me.

10. See first edition of this book for more details of Sri Lankan case. On Kenya, see *Population Reports,* Series C, no. 10, pp. 12-13. "I would like to spread the gospel of tubal ligation to my friends and others," *Population Reports* quotes a Kenyan woman.

11. See James W. Wessman, "Neo-Malthusian Ideology and Colonial Capitalism: Population Dynamics in Southwestern Puerto Rico," in Michaelson, ed., *And the Poor Get Children*. See also chapter on Puerto Rico in Mass, *Population Target*.

12. Helen Rodriguez-Trias, "The Women's Health Movement: Women Take Power," in Victor W. Sidel and Ruth Sidel, *Reforming Medicine: Lessons of the Last Quarter Century* (New York: Pantheon Books, 1984).

13. J. M. Stycos, "Female Sterilization in Puerto Rico," *Eugenics Quarterly*, vol. 1, no . 1 (1954), p. 3, quoted in Mass, *Population Target*, p. 95. Also see Petchesky, "'Reproductive Choice' in the Contemporary United States," for discussion of the context of sterilization choice in Puerto Rico. On contraceptive options today, see Harriet B. Presser, "Puerto Rico: Recent Trends in Fertility and Sterilization," *Family Planning Perspectives*, vol. 12, no. 2 (March-April 1980). The Puerto Rican sterilization program is the subject of a powerful documentary film, *La Operación*, directed and produced by Ana Maria Garcia. On incidence in the U.S., see Northeast Project on Latina Women and Reproductive Health, *Puertorriqueñas: Sociodemographics, Health and Reproductive Issues Among Puerto Rican Women in the U.S., A Fact Handbook* (Hartford: Hispanic Health Council, n.d.)

14. Helen Rodriguez-Trias, "Puerto Rico, Where Sterilization of Women Became 'La Operación,'" *Political Environments*, no. 1, Spring 1994.

15. Dr. Trias' comments from U.S. Congress, House, *Population and Development in Latin America and the Caribbean*. Hearing before the

Subcommittee on Inter-American Affairs of the Committee on Foreign Affairs, 97th Cong., 2d sess., 8 September 1982, p. 52.

16. Trias quoted in Alan Riding, "Battleground in Colombia: Birth Control," *New York Times*, 5 September 1984.

17. Ruth Holly, "Population Control in Colombia," paper prepared for the International Contraception, Abortion and Sterilization Campaign, London, 1981.

18. *Ob. Gyn. News*, vol. 15, no. 20 (15 October 1984), cited in ibid.

19. Holly, "Population Control in Colombia."

20. Personal interview, February 1984.

21. "Mental Health and Female Sterilization: A Follow-up, Report of a WHO Collaborative Prospective Study," *Journal of Biosocial Science*, vol. 17, no. 1 (January 1985). On Mexico, see Terezita de Barbieri, "Gender and Population Policies: Some Reflections," *Reproductive Health Matters*, no. 1, May 1993.

22. See Thais Corral, "Consequences of Population Control Programmes in Brazil," *Development*, no. 1, 1994. Also see Chapter 4 on the Brazilian women's movement in Dixon-Mueller, *Population Policy and Women's Rights.*

23. See Vicziany, "Coercion in a Soft State," for excellent analysis of the program's assumptions and failures in its early stages. For a more recent overview see T. K. Sundari Ravindran, "Women and the Politics of Population and Development in India."

24. See "Entire Village Sterilized," *India Now*, August 1978.

25. Information on forced sterilization in India from Debabar Banerji, "Political Economy of Population Control in India," in Bondestam and Bergström, *Poverty and Population Control*; Davidson R. Gwatkin, "Political Will and Family Planning: The Implications of India's Emergency Experience," *Population and Development Review*, vol. 5, no. 1 (March 1979); "Delhi to Penalize Couples for Not Limiting Births," *New York Times*, 26 February 1976.

26. McNamara quote from Government of India, Department of Family Planning, *Centre Calling*, Vol. XI (11 November 1976), cited in Banerji, "Political Economy of Population Control in India." Ehrlich quote from 1983 edition of *The Population Bomb*, cited in John Tierney, "Fanisi's Choice," *Science,* vol. 86 (January-February 1986), p. 42. Van Arendonk quote from personal interview, February 1984. An article published by the Population Crisis Committee, instead of condemning the program, states: "For a coercive program to work, a hugely expanded commitment of administrative and financial resources will be necessary. The world will be watching India's policy closely to see if, and how, state governments follow up their new legislation with bigger budgets and more effective action." See Gulhati, "Compulsory Sterilization."

27. John C. Caldwell, P. H. Reddy, and Pat Caldwell, "Demographic Change in Rural South India," *Population and Development Review*, vol. 8, no. 4 (December 1982), p. 712.

28. "In India, Birth Control Focus Shifts to Women," *New York Times*, 7 March 1982.

29. Basu, "Family Planning and the Emergency."

30. Ravindran, "Women and the Politics of Population."

31. "A Family Planning Story," *Economic and Political Weekly*, vol. 20, no. 40 (5 October 1985), p. 1668.

32. Ravindran, "Women and the Politics of Population."

33. Government of India, Planning Commission, *Fifth Five Year Plan, 1992-97*, Volume II, New Delhi, p. 337.

34. For the effect on health services, see Ravindran, "Women and the Politics of Population."

35. *Population Reports,* Series C, no. 10.

36. See Petchesky, "'Reproductive Choice' in the Contemporary United States."

37. Quoted in Anti-Sexism Committee, National Lawyers Guild, *Reproductive Freedom: Speakers' Handbook on Abortion Rights and Sterilization,* reprinted in *Stop Forced Sterilization: A Collection of Reprints about Sterilization and Population Control* (Minneapolis/St. Paul: Twin Cities Reproductive Rights Committee, 1981). Also see ibid. Possible long-term effects of hysterectomy include early menopause, osteoporosis, and greater susceptibility to coronary disease.

38. Quoted in Rosalind P. Petchesky, "Reproduction, Ethics, and Public Policy: The Federal Sterilization Regulations," *Hastings Center Report*, October 1979.

39. Quoted in ibid.

40. Ibid. These regulations, however, have not been strictly enforced, and groups such as the Committee for Abortion Rights and Against Sterilization Abuse (CARASA) and the National Women's Health Network are now working to ensure that they meet with compliance.

41. Association for Voluntary Sterilization *Annual Report*, 1982, p. 6. See Petchesky, "Reproduction, Ethics and Public Policy," for defense of current moratorium on the sterilization of the mentally handicapped.

42. See OTA, *World Population and Fertility Planning Technologies*, p. 89; and Malcolm Potts, Peter Diggory, and John Peel, *Abortion* (Cambridge: Cambridge University Press, 1977), p. 211.

43. On fertility, see Bruce and Schearer, *Contraceptives and Common Sense*; and Lisa Cronin Wohl, "Anti-Abortion Violence on the Rise," *Ms.*, October 1984. On menstrual regulation, see Seaman and Seaman, *Women and the Crisis in Sex Hormones*; Potts et al., *Abortion*; and Boston Women's Health Book Collective, *The New Our Bodies, Ourselves* (New York: Simon and Schuster, 1984, 1992).

44. Seaman and Seaman, *Women and the Crisis in Sex Hormones.*

45. K. Kaufmann, "Abortion, a Woman's Matter: an Explanation of Who Controls Abortion and How and Why They Do It," in Rita Arditti et al., eds., *Test-Tube Women.*

46. For a discussion of the basic values underlying the abortion debate, see Kristin Luker, *Abortion and the Politics of Motherhood* (Berkeley: University of California Press, 1984).

47. *Reproductive Freedom News*, vol. 3, no. 10 (May 27, 1994).

48. Potts et al., *Abortion*, p. 2.

49. Although accurate figures are not available, the abortion rate in the former Soviet Union might have been 115 per 1000 women of reproductive age, compared to 23 in the United States in 1978. See Christopher Tietze, *Induced Abortion: A World Review, 1983* (New York: Population Council, 1983); also OTA, *World Population and Fertility Planning Technologies*, p. 63. On Sweden, see Staffan Bergström, "Critical Remarks on 'Draft Final Document of the Conference' (UNFPA)," Department of Obstetrics and Gynaecology, University of Oslo, Oslo, Norway, 1993.

50. Jodi Jacobson, *The Global Politics of Abortion*, Worldwatch Paper 97 (Washington, D.C.: Worldwatch Institute, July 1990), Table 2. Also see Chapter 7 in Dixon-Mueller, *Population Policy and Women's Rights,* for an in-depth look at abortion policies in the Third World; and *Reproductive Health Matters*, no. 2, November 1993, an issue devoted to the subject of abortion.

51. Dixon-Mueller, *Population Policy and Women's Rights,* p. 163.

52. Potts et al., *Abortion*, pp. 270-71, and Seaman and Seaman, *Women and the Crisis in Sex Hormones*, p. 237.

53. Rodriguez-Trias, "The Women's Health Movement."

54. See Marlene Gerber Fried, "Reproductive Wrongs," *The Women's Review of Books,* vol. 11, nos. 10-11 (July 1994) for information on the latest status of abortion rights in the U.S. Also see the excellent anthology edited by Fried, *From Abortion to Reproductive Freedom: Transforming a Movement* (Boston: South End Press, 1990), for a comprehensive look at the politics of abortion in the U.S.

55. Quoted in Bernard Rosenfeld et al., *A Health Research Study Group on Surgical Sterilization: Present Abuses and Proposed Regulation* (Washington, D.C.: Health Research Group, October 1973), p. 22. Information on England from the London Women's Reproductive Rights Information Center; and Wendy Savage, "Taking Liberties with Women: Abortion, Sterilization and Contraception," *International Journal of Health Services*, vol. 12, no. 2 (1982).

56. General IUD cases in Potts et al., *Abortion*. India case from Balasubrahmanyan, "Towards a Women's Perspective on Family Planning"; Ravindran, "Women and the Politics of Population"; and Malini Karkal, "Abortion Laws and the Abortion Situation in India," *Issues in Reproductive and Genetic Engineering,* vol. 4, no. 3 (1991).

57. Personal communication with Rita Parikh, Interpares.

58. See Dixon-Mueller, *Population Policy and Women's Rights,* Chapter 7.

59. Ravindra Rukmini Pandharinath, "Fighting Female Foeticide: A Long Way to Go," *The Lawyers* (India), August 1991. Also see S. H. Venkatramani, "Born to Die," *India Today*, 15 June 1986; Viola Roggencamp, "Abortion of a Special Kind: Male Sex Selection in India," in Arditti et al., eds., *Test-Tube Women*; and Radhika Balakrishnan, "The Social Context of Sex Selection and the Politics of Abortion in India," in Gita Sen and Rachel C. Snow, eds., *Power and Decision: The Social Control of Reproduction* (Cambridge: Harvard University Press, 1994).

60. Government of India, *Census of India 1991*, New Delhi. On discrimination against girls, see Malini Karkal, "Invisibility of the Girl Child in India," *The Indian Journal of Social Work,* vol. 52, no. 1, January 1991.

61. R. Venkatachalam and Viji Srinivasan, *Female Infanticide* (New Delhi: Har-Anand Publications, 1993), p. 55.

62. 1984 seminar from Balasubrahmanyan, "Towards a Women's Perspective on Family Planning." John F. Burns, "India Fights Abortion of Female Fetuses," *New York Times*, 27 August 1994. See for general overview Helen B. Holmes, "Sex Selection: Eugenics for Everyone?," in James Humber and Robert Almeden, eds., *Biomedical Ethics Reviews, 1985* (Clifton, N.J.: Humana Press, 1986).

63. Marsha Saxton, "Born and Unborn: The Implications of Reproductive Technologies for People with Disabilities," in Arditti et al., eds., *Test-Tube Women*, p. 306. See also Anne Finger, "Claiming All of Our Bodies: Reproductive Rights and Disability," in same volume; Gena Corea, *The Mother Machine* (New York: Harper and Row, 1985); and Barbara Katz Rothman, *The Tentative Pregnancy* (New York: Viking Press, 1986).

BOX. STERILIZATION SIDE EFFECTS: UNANSWERED QUESTIONS

1. Quoted in Joyce Pettigrew, "Problems Concerning Tubectomy Operations in Rural Areas of the Punjab," *Economic and Political Weekly*, vol. 19, no. 26 (30 June 1984). All Pettigrew quotes from this article.

2. John C. Caldwell and Pat Caldwell, "Family Planning in India: A Worm's Eye View from a Rural Area in South India," *South Asia*, vol. 5, no. 1 (June 1982).

3. On Bangladesh, see Chapter 12. On El Salvador, see A. Bronstein, *The Triple Struggle*.

BOX. QUINACRINE: POPULATION CONTROLLER'S DREAM MAY BECOME WOMAN'S NIGHTMARE

1. General information on quinacrine from Fawn Vrazo, "Sterilization Method Raises Hopes, Fears," *Philadelphia Inquirer,* 2 December 1993;

Judy Norsigian of the Boston Women's Health Book Collective; "Controversy Over Quinacrine Sterilization Pellet," *Political Environments,* no. 1, Spring 1994; and AVSC, "AVSC Technical Statement: Quinacrine Pellets for Nonsurgical Female Sterilization" (New York: September 1993).

2. Do Trong Hieu et al., "31,781 Cases of Non-Surgical Female Sterilization with Quinacrine Pellets in Vietnam," *Lancet,* vol. 342, 24 July 1993. AVSC critique referenced above.

3. Cited in reply from Vietnam Insight to Southeast Asia Discussion List, "Women Subjected to Sterilization Against Will," electronic mail, 3 September 1993.

4. AVSC, "AVSC Technical Statement," p. 7.

5. E. Kessel, J. Zipper, D. T. Hieu, B. Mullick, and S. D. Mumford, "Quinacrine Pellet Method of Non-Surgical Female Sterilization," Proceedings of VIIIth World Congress on Human Reproduction and IVth World Congress on Fallopian Tube in Health and Disease, Bali, Indonesia, April 1993, to be published in *Advances in Human Reproduction* (page proofs).

6. "Death of a Study: WHO, What and Why," *Lancet,* vol. 343, no. 8904 (23 April 1994), p. 988. Also see correspondence in the *Lancet* before and after.

BOX. RU486 WILL NOT SOLVE THE ABORTION PROBLEM

1. Katharine Q. Seelye, "Enter RU-486, Exit Hype," *New York Times,* 22 May 1994.

2. Feminist Majority Foundation, "RU486 and Women in Developing Nations" (Boston: 1991).

3. See "RU-486: A Dialogue," *Network News,* September/October 1992 (Washington, D.C.: National Women's Health Network); National Black Women's Health Project, "Facts: RU 486 and African American Women" (Washington, D.C.: NBWHP Public Education/Policy Office, n.d.); Judy Norsigian, "RU-486," in Fried, ed., *From Abortion to Reproductive Freedom;* and, for the most critical account, Janice G. Raymond, Renate Klein, and Lynette J. Dumble, *RU 486: Misconceptions, Myths and Morals* (Amherst, MA: Institute on Women and Technology, 1991).

14. BARRIER METHODS, NATURAL FAMILY PLANNING, AND FUTURE DIRECTIONS

1. Bruce and Schearer, "Contraceptives and Developing Countries," p. 406.

2. Program for Appropriate Technology in Health (PATH), "Vaginal Barrier Methods: Underutilized Options?" *Outlook,* vol. 11, no. 4 (December 1993); and Fathalla, "Fertility Control Technology," Table 2.

3. Malcolm Potts, "The Implementation of Family Planning Programs," in R. V. Short and D. T. Baird, *Contraceptives of the Future* (London: The Royal Society, 1976).

4. Bruce and Schearer, "Contraceptives and Developing Countries," p. 427.

5. See "Condoms—Now More Than Ever," in *Population Reports,* Series H, no. 8 (September 1990), for estimates of condom use.

6. OTA, *World Population and Fertility Planning Technologies*, p. 89. Also see PATH, "Vaginal Barrier Methods."

7. Bruce and Schearer, "Contraceptives and Developing Countries."

8. PATH, "Vaginal Barrier Methods." Also see "FDA Advisory Committee Says No to Warning Label on Spermicides," *Medical World News*, 13 February 1984.

9. *Population Reports*, Series H, no. 7, p. H-157.

10. Bruce and Schearer, "Contraceptives and Developing Countries," p. 412. Also see ibid. for details of a number of different studies.

11. Bruce and Schearer, "Contraceptives and Developing Countries," p. 410.

12. Bruce and Schearer, *Contraceptives and Common Sense*, p. 78.

13. *Population Reports*, Series H, no. 7, p. H-181.

14. On Bombay clinic, see Bruce and Schearer, *Contraceptives and Common Sense.*

15. Brazilian clinic described in PATH, "Vaginal Barrier Methods."

16. *Population Reports*, Series H, no. 7, and Series H, no. 8.

17. *Population Reports,* Series H, no. 7, pp. H182-83. On condoms see *Population Reports,* Series H, no. 8, p. 26.

18. WHO/HRP, *Fertility Regulating Vaccines: Report of a meeting between women's health advocates and scientists to review the current status of the development of fertility regulating vaccines* (Geneva: WHO, 1993), pp. 48-51.

19. Bruce and Schearer, "Contraceptives and Developing Countries," p. 426; and *Contraceptives and Common Sense*. Also information from Judy Norsigian, Boston Women's Health Book Collective.

20. See Dana Gallagher, "Cervical Caps and the Women's Health Movement: Feminists as 'Advocate Researchers,'" in Helen B. Holmes, ed., *Issues in Reproductive Technology* (New York: Garland Publishing, 1992).

21. Even Potts has revised his assessment of barrier methods. Malcolm Potts and Robert Wheeler, "The Quest for a Magic Bullet," *Family Planning Perspectives*, vol. 13, no. 6 (November-December 1981).

22. See "Periodic Abstinence: How Well Do New Approaches Work?" *Population Reports*, Series I, no. 3 (September 1981); also see "Natural Family Planning: Periodic Abstinence as a Method of Fertility Control," *Population*, no. 11 (June 1981).

23. Seven percent user figure from Fathalla, "Fertility Control Technology," p. 226. See *Population Reports*, Series I, no. 3. For a critique of the

Billings method see Katharine Betts, "The Billings Method of Family Planning: An Assessment," *Studies in Family Planning*, vol. 15, no. 6 (November-December 1984).

24. *Population Reports*, Series I, no. 3.

25. Audrey Bronstein, "Notes on Family Planning Training Course in El Salvador," background notes to her book *The Triple Struggle*, made available to author.

26. Quoted in *Population Reports*, Series I, no. 3, p. 154.

27. Ibid.; and Constance Holden, "'Right to Life' Scores New Victory at AID," *Science*, vol. 229, no. 4718 (13 September 1985).

28. *Population*, no. 11 (June 1981), p. 7.

29. Quoted in *Population Reports*, Series I, no. 3, p. I-162. Note this statement by *Population Reports* (I-161): "Teaching and helping couples interested in periodic abstinence to use the method effectively takes time and continued counseling. In fact, in contrast to other family planning methods, which depend on advanced technology and medical skills, periodic abstinence programs have been described as 'educational delivery systems.'" Other family planning methods could well use such "educational delivery," despite their advanced technical nature.

30. Atkinson et al., "Worldwide Trends in Funding," Table 3, p. 198.

31. See *Population Reports*, Series I, no. 3, and on hand temperature changes, Martin Wainwright, "Scientific Significance in the Cool Feminine Touch," *Guardian*, 10 January 1985.

32. Quoted in *Population Reports*, Series I, no. 3, p. I-63.

33. Quoted in "Immunological Contraceptives: Designed for Populations Not People," contraceptive policy report (Amsterdam: Health Action International–Europe and Women's Health Action Foundation, 1994.)

34. I wish to thank Judith Richter and Faye Schrater for keeping me current on vaccine issues, and for their valuable research on the subject. Richter's booklet *Vaccination against Pregnancy: Miracle or Menace?* (Amsterdam: Health Action International; Bielefeld, Germany: BUKO Pharma-Kampagne, 1993) is a comprehensive and critical account of the research. It is also available through the Boston Women's Health Book Collective. Immunologist Faye Schrater has also written extensively on the subject. She feels more positively about the WHO hCG vaccine than Richter, but is concerned about other formulations as well as the potential for abuse. See Faye Schrater, "Contraceptive Vaccines: Promises and Problems," in Holmes, ed., *Issues in Reproductive Technology*. Also see articles by both women in Sen and Snow, eds., *Power and Decision*.

35. "Immunological Contraceptives: Designed for Populations Not People."

36. Quoted in ibid. Also see Richter's booklet for other quotes.

37. See previous references for information on problems and risks. For WHO's assessment, see WHO/HRP, *Fertility Regulating Vaccines*.

38. Quoted in Richter, *Vaccination against Pregnancy*, p. 58. The film is entitled "Antibodies Against Pregnancy," and is available from U. Schaz, Bleicherstr. 2, D2267 Hamburg, Germany.

39. Letter available from Women's Global Network for Reproductive Rights, NZ Voorburgwal 32, 1012 RZ Amsterdam, Netherlands.

40. Quoted in Stokes, *Men and Family Planning*, p. 23.

41. A. Kessler and C. C. Standley, "Fertility-regulating Methods: Recent Progress in the WHO Programme of Research in Human Reproduction," *WHO Chronicle*, vol. 31, no. 5.

42. See Mary-Louise O'Callaghan, "Sterility Fear Fails to Halt Chinese Male Pill Tests," *Guardian*, 17 August 1984.

43. I wish to thank C. Alvin Paulsen for sending me information on current research. See Paulsen, "Androgen-Progestogen Combinations," in G. I. Zatuchni et al., eds., *Male Contraception: Advances and Future Prospects* (Philadelphia: Harper and Row, 1986); Paulsen et al., "Male Contraception: Clinical Trials," in Daniel R. Mishell, Jr., *Advances in Fertility Research* (New York: Raven Press, 1982); and WHO Task Force on Methods for the Regulation of Male Fertility, "Contraceptive Efficacy of Testosterone-Induced Azoospermia in Normal Men," *Lancet,* vol. 336, 20 October 1990. On vas and heat methods, see Elaine A. Lissner, "Frontiers in Nonhormonal Male Contraceptive Research," in Holmes, ed., *Issues in Reproductive Technology.*

44. See Miriam H. Labbock, "The Lactational Amenorrhea Method (LAM): Another Choice for Mothers," *Breastfeeding Abstracts,* vol. 13, no. 1 (August 1993); and Alan Berg and Susan Brems, "A Case for Promoting Breastfeeding in Projects to Limit Fertility," *Technical Paper,* no. 102 (Washington, D.C.: World Bank, 1989).

45. Fathalla, "Fertility Control Technology," p. 226.

46. WHO/HRP and International Women's Health Coalition, *Creating Common Ground: Report of a Meeting between Women's Health Advocates and Scientists* (Geneva: WHO, 1991).

47. Fathalla, "Fertility Control Technology," p. 231.

48. Reported by Judith Richter, "Research on Antifertility Vaccines: Priority or Problem," Women's Global Network for Reproductive Rights Newsletter, no. 39, April-June 1992.

49. WHO/HRP, *Fertility Regulating Vaccines*, p. 20.

50. Personal communication.

51. Personal communication, May 1994.

BOX. BARRIERS TO AIDS

1. Information from Center for Women Policy Studies, "Woman-Controlled Microbicides for Prevention of HIV/STDs" (Washington, D.C.: 1993); and Microbicide Research Advocacy Project, "Questions and Answers about the Need for a Women-Controlled Method of HIV Prevention" (Washington,

D.C.: Center for Women Policy Studies and Reproductive Health Technologies Project, 1993). Both of these publications draw on Christopher L. Elias and Lori Heise, *The Development of Microbicides: A New Method of HIV Prevention for Women* (New York: Population Council, 1993) and Patricia Donovan, *Testing Positive: Sexually Transmitted Disease and the Public Health Response* (New York: Alan Guttmacher Institute, 1993.)

2. See Gena Corea, *The Invisible Epidemic: The Story of Women and AIDS* (New York: HarperCollins, 1992); and Marge Berer, and Sunanda Ray, *Women and HIV/AIDS: An International Resource Book* (London: Pandora Press, 1993).

15. THE LIGHT AT THE END OF THE DEMOGRAPHIC TUNNEL

1. Bryant Robey, Shea O. Rutstein, and Leo Morris, "The Fertility Decline in Developing Countries," *Scientific American*, December 1993, p. 65.

2. See *World Development Report 1984*, Chapter 4. In some European countries, fertility fell while mortality remained high. For a possible explanation, see John Knodel and Etienne van de Walle, "Lessons from the Past: Policy Implications of Historical Fertility Studies," *Population and Development Review*, vol. 5, no. 2 (June 1979).

3. See Caldwell, *Theory of Fertility Decline*.

4. *World Development Report 1984*, p. 63.

5. See Cain, "Risk and Insurance," and "Fertility as an Adjustment to Risk." Cain postulates that there may be two stages in fertility decline. In the first, people adjust their fertility to the decline in mortality, but they still need the same number of surviving children to meet their security goals. In the second stage, they start to need fewer surviving children because they have alternative sources of security. The tendency of fertility decline to level off in a number of Third World countries may be because they are caught between the stages. See also Caldwell, *Theory of Fertility Decline*.

6. *World Development Report 1993*, Table 27. For more on the relationship between income distribution and fertility decline, see William Rich, *Smaller Families Through Social and Economic Progress* (Washington, D.C.: Overseas Development Council, January 1973); Murdoch, *The Poverty of Nations*; Robert Repetto, *Economic Equality and Fertility in Developing Countries* (Baltimore: Johns Hopkins University Press, 1979); Michael P. Todaro, *Economic Development in the Third World*, 2d ed. (New York: Longman, 1981), pp. 166-68.

7. John Ratcliffe, "Toward a Social Justice Theory of Demographic Transition: Lessons from India's Kerala State," *Janasamkhya*, vol. 1 (June 1983).

8. See U.S. Bureau of the Census, *World Population Profile: 1994*, Table 4. Analysis in this section from David Werner, "Health Care in Cuba: A

Model Service or a Means of Social Control-or Both?," in Morley, et al., eds., *Practicing Health for All.*

9. Repetto, *Economic Equality*, p. 69. Land tenure figures from Repetto.

10. Dae Hwan Kim, *Rapid Economic Growth and National Integration in Korea, 1963-78,* Oxford University DPhil Thesis (Economics), 1985, pp. 239-40.

11. Repetto, *Economic Equality.*

12. See Kim, *Rapid Economic Growth.*

13. See Murdoch, *The Poverty of Nations*, pp. 69-75. Recent figures from *World Development Report 1993.*

14. Ratcliffe, "Toward a Social Justice Theory." On Kerala, also see Richard W. Franke and Barbara H. Chasin, "Kerala State, India: Radical Reform as Development," *Monthly Review*, vol. 42, no. 8, (January 1991).

15. Government of India, *Economic Survey 1992-93* (New Delhi, 1993), Table 9.3, p. 198, and Government of India, *Census of India 1991, Provisional Population Totals* (New Delhi), p. 55.

16. K. N. Raj, "Land Reforms and Their Effects on Distribution of Income," *Poverty, Unemployment and Development Policy: A Case Study of Selected Issues with Reference to Kerala*, ST/ESA/29 (New York: United Nations, 1975), quoted in John Ratcliffe, "Social Justice and the Demographic Transition: Lessons from India's Kerala State," in Morley, et al., eds., *Practicing Health for All*, p. 81.

17. Ratcliffe, "Social Justice and the Demographic Transition," p. 71.

18. See, for example, Vicziany, "Coercion in a Soft State," and Vimal Balasubrahmanyan, "A Bizarre Medley of Carrots," *Women's Global Network on Reproductive Rights Newsletter*, January-March 1986. This article is a collection of recent newspaper clips on population control excesses in India.

19. Wim Dierckxsens, "Costa Rica–The Unfinished Demographic Transition," in Bertil Egerö and Mikael Hammarskjöld, eds., *Understanding Reproductive Change* (Lund, Sweden: Lund University Press, 1994), p. 138. This book has interesting case studies of the demographic transition in Kenya, Tamil Nadu, Punjab and Costa Rica.

20. Robey, et al, "The Fertility Decline," p. 60.

21. See Paul Demeny, "Social Science and Population Policy," *Population and Development Review*, vol. 14, no. 3 (September 1988).

22. Lant H. Pritchett, "Desired Fertility and the Impact of Population Policies," *Population and Development Review*, vol. 20, no. 1 (March 1994), pp. 17-18. Also see Amartya Sen, "Population: Delusion and Reality," *The New York Review of Books,* September 22, 1994, for a critique of the "family planning first" approach.

23. Ibid., p. 35.

24. Ibid., p. 38.

16. THE POPULATION FRAMEWORK: INSIDE OR OUTSIDE

1. For an overview of the women's health movement, see Claudia Garcia-Moreno and Amparo Claro, "Challenges from the Women's Health Movement: Women's Rights versus Population Control," in Sen, et al, eds., *Population Policies Reconsidered*. Also see Dixon-Mueller, *Population Policy and Women's Rights*, and chapters 26 and 27 of Boston Women's Health Book Collective, *The New Our Bodies, Ourselves* (New York: Simon and Schuster, 1992).

2. Adrienne Germain and Jane Ordway, *Population Control and Women's Health: Balancing the Scales* (New York: IWHC, June 1989).

3. "Women's Declaration on Population Policies," reproduced in Sen, et al, eds., *Population Policies Reconsidered*, p. 32.

4. Quoted in Susan A. Cohen, "Competition, or Consensus?" *Populi*, vol. 21, no. 7 (July/August 1994), p. 8.

5. Judith Richter and Loes Keysers, "Toward a Common Agenda? Feminists and Population Agencies on the Road to Cairo," *Development*, no. 1, 1994.

6. Declaration of People's Perspectives on "Population" Symposium, 12-15 December 1993, Comilla, Bangladesh.

INDEX

See also Contraceptive technology choices

DES, 204, 346n52

Developed countries: abortion, 54, 55, 261; demographic transitions in, 5, 33-34, 39, 290-91; and environmental degradation, 23; racism in, 55, 131, 142-43, 144-45, 211-12, 254-55; role of children, 7-8, 37, 315-16n6; role in population establishment, 85, 115; women's lack of reproductive control in, 54-55. *See also* North-South relations; United States; U.S. *headings*

Development. *See* Third World economic development

Development Alternatives with Women for a New Era (DAWN), 151

Development Associates, 121

Dhanraj, Dheepa, 254

Diaphragm, 93, 272; neglect of, 38, 180, 275. *See also* Barrier methods

Djerassi, Carl, 186-87

Dowie, Mark, 216

Draper, William H., 105, 122

Draper Committee, 104

Dukes, Graham, 279

Dyson, Tim, 16-17

E

Earth Follies (Seager), 26

Earth Summit. See U.N. Conference on Environment and Development

East Germany, 54

Eastern Europe, 54, 55

Economic development: China, 160-61; and demographic transitions, 39, 291-92. *See also* Eco-

nomic/social reform; Third World economic development

Economic inequalities, xi, 24, 70, 84, 293. *See also* Economic/social reform; Poverty; Power relations

Economic/social reform: Bucharest conference views, 109-11, 128-29; China, 158-59; and demographic transitions, ix, xviii, 294, 295, 297, 298-99, 300; and food production, 20; importance of, ix, xii, xviii, 39-40, 152; neglect of, xvii, 37, 40, 71, 128, 134, 237; and son preference, 169

Egypt, 64, 211

Ehrenreich, Barbara, 216

Ehrlich, Anne, 22, 23, 30

Ehrlich, Paul, 4, 13, 15-16, 21-22, 23, 30, 103, 141, 252

Eisenhower, Dwight D., 105

El Salvador, 29, 30, 277

Elder, M. S., 200

Emory University, 204

Employment/unemployment, 7, 32, 33, 34, 85. *See also* Women's paid employment

English Eugenics Society, 102

Enke, Stephen, 104

Enovid, 190

Enter-Educate program, 62

Environmental degradation: deforestation, 26-30; and food production, 20-21; population growth as cause of, x-xi, 20-23, 26-27, 30, 141, 332n18; and technology, 23, 25-26. *See also* Environmental groups

Environmental Fund, 15

Environmental groups: and fascism, 131, 142-43; and population establishment, 122; and population policy consensus, 140, 141-43,

208; critiques of, 147, 152; and environmental groups, 140, 141-43, 145-48; and fascism, 142-43, 144-45; focus on women, 133-36, 147-48, 151, 153-54, 306; and free market economics, 131-32; and Mexico City conference, 128-30; NGO role, 138, 139-40; public campaigns, 148-51; and quality of care, 136-39; and religious fundamentalism, 132; and voluntarism, 170

Population Reference Bureau, 99

Population Reports, 184, 194, 197, 203, 273

Population Services International, 195

Population Target (Mass), 94

Potts, Malcolm, 178, 189, 193, 270

Poverty, 224-25; and birth rates, 88, 109-10; and circulatory disorders, 196; and incentive/disincentive programs, 66-67, 70, 228, 230-31, 232; and maternal mortality, 185; New Deal views on, 100; population establishment acceptance of, xvii, 117, 118, 134, 237; population growth as cause of, 4, 30-31, 62-63, 94, 332n18; and quality of care, 139; and subordination of women, 48-49. *See also* Economic inequalities; Economic/social reform; Land distribution; Third World economic development

Power relations: and demographic transitions, 299-300; and environmental degradation, 23-24, 30; and incentive/disincentive programs, 71-72; and Third World economic development, 34-35; and Third World family planning programs, 78-80; and women's lack of reproductive control, 55. *See also* Coercion; Economic inequalities; Economic/social reform

Presidential Message on Population (Nixon), 108

Pritchett, Lant, 301-3

Profamilia, 249

Program for Applied Research on Fertility Regulation, 175

Program for Appropriate Technology in Health (PATH), 175

Program for International Education in Gynecology and Obstetrics (PIEGO), 246-47

Program for the Introduction and Adaptation of Contraceptive Technology (PIACT), 175, 229-30

Puerto Rico, 247, 248

Q

Qian Xinzhong, 168

Quality of care: and birth control pill, 184, 194-96, 198, 199-200, 344n27; China, 164-65; and Depo-Provera, 205, 206-7, 346n58; Indonesia, 76, 77-78; and IUD, 216, 217, 218; Kenya, 86-87, 88; and natural family planning, 278, 362n29; and Norplant, 77-78, 136, 209-11, 348n76; and population policy consensus, 136-39; and sterilization, 229, 244, 245, 253-54; and structural adjustment programs, 138-39; and target orientation, 63. *See also* Contraceptive safety and side effects

Quinacrine, 247, 256-58

R

Race Betterment Foundation, 98

About Betsy Hartmann

Betsy Hartmann is the Director of the Population and Development Program at Hampshire College. She has spoken widely on development, reproductive rights, and human rights, and has written for *Ms.*, *The Progressive*, *The Nation*, and scholarly journals. She is the co-author of several books, including *A Quiet Violence: View from a Bangladesh Village.*

About South End Press

South End Press is a nonprofit, collectively run book publisher with over 170 titles in print. Since our founding in 1977, we have tried to meet the needs of readers who are exploring, or are already committed to, the politics of radical social change.

Our goal is to publish books that encourage critical thinking and constructive action on the key political, cultural, social, economic, and ecological issues shaping life in the United States and in the world. In this way, we hope to give expression to a wide diversity of democratic social movements and to provide an alternative to the products of corporate publishing.

Through the Institute for Social and Cultural Change, South End Press works with other political media projects—*Z Magazine;* Speak Out!, a speakers bureau; the New Liberation News Service; and the Publishers Support Project—to expand access to information and critical analysis. If you would like a free catalog of South End Press books, please write to us at: South End Press, 116 Saint Botolph Street, Boston, MA 02115. Also please consider participating in our membership program: your $40 annual fee entitles you to two free books and a 40 percent discount on all purchases within the year.

Other South End Press Titles of Interest:

From Abortion to Reproductive Freedom:
Transforming a Movement
Edited by Marlene Gerber Fried ($14)

Abortion Without Apology:
a Radical History for the 1990s
Ninia Baehr ($6)

Women Under Attack:
Victories, Backlash and the Fight for Reproductive Freedom
Committee for Abortion Rights and Against Sterilization Abuse
Edited by Susan E.Davis ($5)

Women, AIDS, and Activism
ACT UP/New York Women and AIDS Book Group ($9)

Sex and Germs:
The Politics of AIDS
Cindy Patton ($12)

Regulating the Lives of Women:
Social Welfare Policy from Colonial Times to the Present
Mimi Abramovitz ($16)

Women in the Global Factory
Annette Fuentes and Barbara Ehreneich ($16)

Global Visions:
Beyond the New World Order
Edited by Jeremy Brecher, John Brown Childs, and Jill Cutler ($16)

Global Village or Global Pillage:
Economic Reconstruction from the Bottom Up
Jeremy Brecher and Tim Costello ($14)

50 Years is Enough:
The Case Against the World Bank
and the International Monetary Fund
Edited by Kevin Danaher
A Project of Global Exchange ($14)

When ordering by mail, please enclose $3 postage and handling
for the first book and 75 cents for each additional.